READING JOHN

READING THE NEW TESTAMENT SERIES

Reading Corinthians
by Charles H. Talbert

Reading John
by Charles H. Talbert

Reading Luke
by Charles H. Talbert

Charles H. Talbert

READING JOHN

A LITERARY AND THEOLOGICAL COMMENTARY ON THE FOURTH GOSPEL AND THE JOHANNINE EPISTLES

CROSSROAD • NEW YORK

1994

The Crossroad Publishing Company
370 Lexington Avenue, New York, NY 10017

Printed in the United States of America

Library of Congress Cataloging-in-Publication Data

Talbert, Charles H.
  Reading John : a literary and theological commentary on the fourth
Gospel and the Johannine Epistles / Charles H. Talbert.
    p. cm.
  ISBN 0-8245-1179-4; 0-8245-1414-9 (pbk.)
  1. Bible. N.T. John—Commentaries. 2. Bible. N.T. Epistles of
John—Commentaries. I. Title.
BS2615.3.T28 1992
226.5'07—dc20   92-5999
                                                            CIP

To Mabry Lunceford,
who embodies the values of the
Johannine Community

CONTENTS

Acknowledgments ix

Editor's Preface xi

Author's Preface xiii

Abbreviations xv

The Johannine Epistles 1

Introduction 3

Getting Oriented (2, 3 John; 1 John 1:1–5) 9

Walking in the Light (1 John 1:6–2:17; 2:18–28) 18

Discerning the Spirits (1 John 2:29–3:24a; 3:24b–4:6) 28

Perfect Love and Proper Belief (1 John 4:7–12; 4:13–16a; 4:16b–5:4a; 5:4b–12) 37

Bases for Christian Confidence (1 John 5:13, 14–21) 50

The Fourth Gospel 59

Introduction 61

A Revealing, Empowering Presence (John 1:1–18) 66

Creator of a New Community (John 1:19–2:12) 80

Proponent of a New Birth (John 2:13–3:21) 95

The Object of the Baptist's Praise (John 3:22–4:3) 105

The Savior of the World (John 4:4–44, 45–54) 111

Dutiful Apprentice of the Father (John 5:1–47) 121

The Bread of Life (John 6:1–71) 131

Water of Life/Light of the World (John 7:1–9:41) 143

The Door/The Good Shepherd (John 10:1–11:54) 164

The One Whose Hour Has Come (John 11:55–12:50)   179

Washer of the Disciples' Feet (John 13:1–35)   189

The Way, the Truth, and the Life (John 13:31–14:31)   200

The True Vine (John 15:1–16:33)   211

The Intercessor (John 17:1–26)   223

The Enthroned King (John 18–19)   232

The Living Lord (John 20–21)   248

Appendix: Descending-Ascending Redeemer Figures
   in Mediterranean Antiquity   265

ACKNOWLEDGMENTS

Quotations from the Bible are from the Revised Standard Version, second edition, or are by the author unless otherwise specified. Quotations from church fathers are normally taken from *The Ante-Nicene Fathers*. Citations from Greek and Roman authors are usually from the Loeb Classical Library. Quotations from the Pseudepigrapha are normally taken from James Charlesworth, ed., *The Old Testament Pseudepigrapha*, 2 vols. (Garden City, N.Y.: Doubleday, 1983, 1985). Citations from the Nag Hammadi documents are drawn from *The Nag Hammadi Library*, ed. James M. Robinson (New York: Harper & Row, 1977). Material from the Apocryphal New Testament is ordinarily taken from M. R. James, *The Apocryphal New Testament* (Oxford: Clarendon, 1955). Quotations from the Dead Sea Scrolls are taken from *The Dead Sea Scrolls in English*, ed. Geza Vermes (Baltimore: Penguin Books, 1962). Citations from the Mishnah are from *The Mishnah*, trans. Herbert Danby (Oxford: Clarendon, 1933). Material from *The Fathers according to Rabbi Nathan* is taken from the translation by Judah Goldin (New Haven: Yale, 1955). Permission to use material from my article "The Myth of a Descending-Ascending Redeemer in Mediterranean Antiquity," *NTS* 22 (1976): 418–39, has graciously been granted by Cambridge University Press.

EDITOR'S PREFACE

"Reading the New Testament" is a commentary series that aims to present cutting-edge research in popular form that is accessible to upper-level undergraduates, seminarians, seminary educated pastors, and educated laypeople, as well as to graduate students and professors. The volumes in this series do not follow the word-by-word, phrase-by-phrase, verse-by-verse method of traditional commentaries. Rather they are concerned to understand large thought units and their relationship to an author's thought as a whole. The focus is on a close reading of the final form of the text. The aim is to make one feel at home in the biblical text itself. The approach of these volumes involves a concern both for *how* an author communicates and *what* the religious point of the text is. Care is taken to relate both the *how* and the *what* of the text to its milieu: Christian (NT and non-canonical), Jewish (scriptural and post-biblical), and Greco-Roman. This enables both the communication strategies and the religious message of the text to be clarified over against a range of historical and cultural possibilities. Moreover, a section of commentary on a large thought unit will often contain a brief excursus on some topic raised by the material in the unit, sometimes sketching OT, post-biblical Jewish, Greco-Roman, NT, and non-canonical Christian views on the subject. Throughout, the basic concern is to treat the NT texts as religious documents whose religious message needs to be set forth with compelling clarity. All other concerns are subordinated to this. It is the hope of all participants in this project that our efforts at exposition will enable the NT to be understood better and communicated more competently.

Charles H. Talbert, General Editor

AUTHOR'S PREFACE

This volume, written during the school year, 1990–91, owes its appearance to the support given me by numerous persons, of whom four deserve special mention. Frank Oveis and the Crossroad Publishing Company have encouraged me on this as on earlier volumes. Wake Forest University, with a Reynolds Research Fellowship, provided the free time necessary to think of one thing only. My family sacrificially gave up time and energy to see that I was able to do my work. Above all, the Wake Forest students who took my course on the Johannine literature over a twenty-five year period have significantly shaped my understanding of the Fourth Gospel and the Johannine epistles. Their refusal to be impressed by names and fads and their insistence on reading the text to decide issues have kept me from many a pitfall. To these and many more I owe my gratitude. In spite of all their contributions, however, they must not be held responsible for the deficiencies that remain.

It is my hope that this volume, like its predecessors *Reading Luke* and *Reading Corinthians,* will assist in an accurate reading and a trustworthy exposition of the Fourth Gospel and 1, 2, 3 John.

Charles H. Talbert

ABBREVIATIONS

BBC	*Broadman Bible Commentary*. Ed. Clifton Allen. Nashville: Broadman Press, 1969)
BDF	F. Blass, A. Debrunner, R. W. Funk. *A Greek Grammar of the New Testament*. Chicago: University of Chicago Press, 1961.
BJRL	*Bulletin of the John Rylands Library*
BTB	*Biblical Theology Bulletin*
CBQ	*The Catholic Biblical Quarterly*
ETL	*Ephemerides Theologicae Lovanienses*
HibJ	*Hibbert Journal*
HTR	*Harvard Theological Review*
IB	*The Interpreter's Bible*. Ed. George Buttrick. Nashville: Abingdon, 1951.
IDB	*The Interpreter's Dictionary of the Bible*. Ed. George Buttrick. Nashville: Abingdon Press, 1962.
Int	*Interpretation: A Journal of Bible and Theology*
JBL	*The Journal of Biblical Literature*
JTS	*Journal of Theological Studies*
NHL	*The Nag Hammadi Library*. Ed. James M. Robinson. New York: Harper & Row, 1977.
NovT	*Novum Testamentum*
NTS	*New Testament Studies*
RevBib	*Revue Biblique*
RevExp	*The Review and Expositor*
SwJournTheol	*The Southwestern Journal of Theology*
TDNT	*Theological Dictionary of the New Testament*. Ed. G. Kittel; trans. G. W. Bromiley. Grand Rapids: Eerdmans, 1964–76.
ZNW	*Zeitschrift für die Neutestamentliche Wissenschaft*

THE JOHANNINE EPISTLES

INTRODUCTION

A sense of the general audience must be recovered. All literary criticism should be accessible to the literate general reader.... [S]uch a general audience... has been arrogantly blocked out by obscurantist theorists (laughably claiming... populist aims).... Literature and art are never created for scholars but for a universal audience.

Camille Paglia, "Opinion," *The Chronicle of Higher Education,* May 8, 1991, B 1–2.

Like its predecessors, *Reading Luke* (New York: Crossroad, 1982) and *Reading Corinthians* (New York: Crossroad, 1987), this volume does not follow the word-by-word, phrase-by-phrase, verse-by-verse method of traditional commentaries. Rather it is concerned to understand large thought units and their relationship to Johannine thought as a whole. The focus, moreover, is on a close reading of the text. Although the author's dialogue with the Johannine writings is carried on in light of the history of interpretation, the commentary makes little reference to secondary literature. Its aim is not to direct one through the maze of scholarship but to make one feel at home in the biblical text itself. If one wants to use a traditional research commentary alongside this volume, one should consider Raymond E. Brown's *The Gospel according to John,* 2 vols. (Garden City, N.Y.: Doubleday, 1966, 1970), and his *The Epistles of John* (Garden City, N.Y.: Doubleday, 1982). The most productive use of *Reading John* will be facilitated by first reading it straight through, as a monograph, before going back to consult its individual segments, as a reference work.

Because the positions one takes about the Johannine epistles seriously affect the perspective from which one reads the Fourth Gospel, it is necessary that *Reading John* include not only an interpretation of the Gospel of John but also a survey of 1, 2, and 3 John as well. The dominant construct in current research regards the Fourth Gospel as written before the epistles and as dealing with the problems related to Christian exclusion from the synagogues and sees the epistles as written after the Gospel and dealing with a community conflict between orthodox and

3

progressives over the proper interpretation of the Fourth Gospel (e.g., R. E. Brown, *The Community of the Beloved Disciple* [New York: Paulist, 1979]; J. Louis Martyn, *History and Theology in the Fourth Gospel* [rev. ed.; Nashville: Abingdon, 1979]), and "Glimpses into the History of the Johannine Community," *The Gospel of John in Christian History* [New York: Paulist, 1978], 90–121). This volume, however, contends that the Gospel of John was written either after 1, 2, 3 John or at about the same time as they and is dealing with some of the same problems (as e.g., F. F. Segovia, "The Theology and Provenance of John 15:1–17," *JBL* 101 [1982]: 115–28, and Kenneth Grayston, *The Johannine Epistles* [Grand Rapids: Eerdmans, 1984]). Evidence for this assertion will be presented at the end of the upcoming survey of the epistles.

Regarding the order in which the epistles were written, virtually every combination has had its advocates (Birger Olsson, "The History of the Johannine Movement," in *Aspects on the Johannine Literature,* ed. Lars Hartman and Birger Olsson [Uppsala: Uppsala Universitet, 1987], 27–43). The order assumed in this volume is 2, 3, 1 (as I. H. Marshall, *The Epistles of John* [Grand Rapids: Eerdmans, 1978]), with the Fourth Gospel's final form coming either alongside or after 1 John.

External attestation for the three Johannine letters is mixed. (a) Polycarp's words, "For everyone who does not confess that Jesus Christ has come in the flesh is an anti-Christ" (*To the Philippians* 7:1a), echo either 1 John 4:2–3 or 2 John 7 or both; his statement that "everyone whosoever does not confess the testimony of the cross is of the devil" (7:1b) may echo 1 John 5:6–8; and his exhortation to "turn back to the word which was delivered to us in the beginning" (7:2) is similar to the expression found in 1 John 2:24, 3:11, 2 John 5–6 and to the idea in 2 John 9. (b) Moreover, according to Eusebius, *Church History* 3.39.17, Papias used quotations from the former (*proteras*) epistle of John, implying thereby that, for Eusebius and possibly for Papias, there was at least a second. Polycarp and Papias, then, confirm knowledge of 1 and possibly 2 John in the early second century. (c) The Muratorian Canon, near the end, says, "The Epistle of Jude indeed and the two with the superscription, 'Of John,' are accepted." Since earlier, at the end of the discussion of the Fourth Gospel, 1 John is referred to ("What we have seen with our eyes and have heard with our ears and our hands have handled, these things we have written to you"), the later reference is probably to 2 and 3 John. (d) Origen (so Eusebius, *Church History* 6.25.10) speaks explicitly about all three epistles of John. The association of 3 John with the other two letters is, then, established by the early third century.

Although the canonical status of 1 John was achieved by the end of the second century, 2 and 3 John did not attain such status into the fourth century (so Eusebius, *Church History* 3.25.3). After Athanasius's Easter letter of 367 C.E., they rapidly achieved full acceptance.

The early Fathers regarded the author of 1 John and the Fourth Gospel as the same person, John, the Lord's disciple (Irenaeus, *Against Heresies* 3.11.7), the son of Zebedee (Muratorian Fragment; Jerome, *Illustrious Men* 9), the beloved disciple (Origen, so Eusebius, *Church History* 6.25.8–10), but had questions about whether or not the same person also wrote 2 and 3 John (Origen, so Eusebius, *Church History* 6.25.10; Dionysius, so Eusebius 7.25.10; Eusebius 3.25.3), some attributing 2, 3 John to John the elder (Eusebius, *Church History* 3.39.5–7; Jerome, *Illustrious Men* 9). The basis for this judgment was that both Gospel and first epistle seem to make eyewitness claims for their authors, whereas 2, 3 John's author calls himself merely "the Elder" (Papias understood the "elders" to be members of the older generation who were not themselves eyewitnesses but were mediators of the authentic tradition and reliable teachers — so Eusebius, *Church History* 3.39.4–15; so also Irenaeus, *Against Heresies* 5.36.2 — "the elders, the disciples of the apostles").

Modern scholars, however, are not agreed about whether the same person was responsible for 1 John and the Fourth Gospel, although opinion seems to favor different authors for Gospel and first epistle even if from the same Community (against common authorship, cf. C. H. Dodd, "The First Epistle of John and the Fourth Gospel," *BJRL* 21 [1937]: 129–56; for common authorship, cf. W. F. Howard, "The Common Authorship of the Johannine Gospel and Epistles," *JTS* 48 [1947]: 12–25). Nor are modern scholars of one opinion about whether there is one or more authors for the three letters, although the current climate seems to favor a common author for the three letters. There is general reluctance to attribute either the Gospel or 1 John to an eyewitness, although allowance is made for an eyewitness to stand at the origin of the community's tradition.

Although there was in the ancient church a tradition that linked the Johannine writings to Ephesus (e.g., Eusebius, *Church History* 3.39, interprets Papias's statement to mean that there were two men in Asia named John, each with a tomb in Ephesus; Jerome, *Illustrious Men* 9, says Ephesus was the site of the sepulchre of John the Elder who was responsible for 2, 3 John. There was possibly also a second gravestone, that of John the Evangelist.), modern scholars regard the evidence for Ephesus, as well as that for Syria, or Alexandria as falling short of demonstration.

We are dealing, then, with three Johannine writings probably from a common author, dealing with a common problem, not much later than 100 C.E., in an unknown locale, prior to the composition of the final form of the Fourth Gospel. The earliest, 2 John, is a true letter with the expected form:

> SALUTATION (vv. 1–3)
> BODY (vv. 4–11)
> CONCLUSION (vv. 12–13).

It is from the Elder (v. 1), who is based in one community (v. 13), to another congregation (vv. 1, 4–5) and concerns the problems of christology (vv. 7, 9) and ethics (vv. 5–6). The brief note expresses the hope that the Elder can communicate more fully face to face on a future visit. This assumes that the Elder travels among the churches.

3 John, like 2 John, fits the typical letter format:

> SALUTATION (v. 1)
> PRAYER (v. 2)
> BODY (vv. 3–12)
> CONCLUSION (vv. 13–15).

It is from the Elder (v. 1) to an individual (Gaius, v. 1) who had offered hospitality to representatives of the Elder (vv. 5–8) after they, as bearers of a written communication, were not welcomed by Diotrephes (vv. 9–10), commending Gaius and recommending the bearer of this letter (Demetrius, v. 12; cf. Rom 16:1). There is again the expressed desire to communicate more fully in person (vv. 13–14).

The genre of 1 John is problematic because it has neither the expected letter introduction nor the conventional letter conclusion. There were, however, certain Hellenistic letters that had neither the usual opening nor the customary closing conventions (e.g., 1 Macc 8:23–32; 10:25–45; Josephus, *Antiquities* 8.2.6, 7 §50–52, 53–54), so 1 John with neither could conceivably be classed as an ancient epistle. If so, our understanding of the document would not be advanced significantly. Recognition of 1 John as beginning with a quotation of known eyewitness tradition (1:1–5) and as followed by its exposition by one who was not an eyewitness (1:6–5:12) offers the most assistance in understanding the document. Like 2 Peter, which is a farewell speech in letter form, 1 John is an exposition of eyewitness tradition in what is arguably a letter form.

THE PROCLAMATION (1:1–5)
THE EXPOSITION (1:6–5:13)

A   Ethical exposition (1:6–2:17)

   B   Christological exposition (2:18–28)

A′ Ethical exposition (2:29–3:24a)

   B′ Christological exposition (3:24b–4:6)

A″ Ethical exposition (4:7–12)

   B″ Christological exposition (4:13–16a)

A‴ Ethical exposition (4:16b–5:4a)

   B‴ Christological exposition (5:4b–12)

THE STATEMENT OF PURPOSE (5:13)
THE POSTSCRIPT (5:14–21)

Like 1 Peter, 1 John's exposition alternates between two foci of concern (cf. Charles H. Talbert, ed., *Perspectives on First Peter* [Macon, Ga.: Mercer University Press, 1986], 149–51); like the Fourth Gospel, its statement of purpose (5:13; cf. John 20:30–31) is followed by a Postscript (5:14–21; cf. John 21). This document is also probably from the same person who produced 2, 3 John but is written in the name of the eyewitnesses whose tradition is cited at the beginning (1:1–5) and again possibly at two points later on (4:6, 14). It is devoted largely to an exposition of what the eyewitnesses saw (christology) and what they heard (ethics).

GETTING ORIENTED

2, 3 John; 1 John 1:1–5

2 John

Because the false teachers still had access to the church in 2 John but had already seceded from it in 1 John 2:19, 2 John is treated as the earliest of the Johannine letters. As a letter, it opens with the conventional A to B Greeting (vv. 1–3). Its author is "the Elder," who is to be understood not as a ruling official analogous to synagogue elders (e.g., Acts 11:30; 14:23; James 5:14; 1 Peter 5:1) but as a teacher of the type mentioned by Papias (Eusebius, *Church History* 3.39.4), that is, a member of the older generation who was a mediator of the authentic tradition of the eyewitnesses and so regarded as a reliable teacher. Its recipients, "the Elect Lady and her children," are a Johannine church and its members (e.g., in Hermas, *Vision* 2.4.1; 3.1.3, the church is pictured as an old lady who is identified as *kyria*/lady). The greeting is a Christianized form that holds together "God the Father" and "Jesus Christ, the Father's Son," anticipating the christological problem plaguing the community at large.

In the Johannine community, God is pre-eminently "the Father" (of the Son). The root of such language is the Johannine Jesus' address of God as "Father" in prayer (e.g., John 12:27; 17:1), just as the Synoptic Jesus does (Mk 14:36; Lk 11:2). The Father is metaphysically the source of all life (John 5:26; 6:57). He is ontologically distinct from the creation (John 1:1–3; 6:46). As cosmic judge, he holds the creation accountable (John 5:45; 1 John 2:1). He is also creator of Israel (John 8:41) and of the Johannine community (John 17:6; 1 John 3:1–2). He is related to the Son: (a) ontologically (1:1, 18: they both share a *theos*/divine nature), (b) relationally (John 5:17; 10:30; 14:9; 5:19–20, 31, 43; 6:28, 38, 42; 15:15) in that Jesus speaks what he hears from the Father (12:49) and does what he sees the Father doing (5:10–20a), and (c) by delegation (1:4; 5:26; 10:18; 11:41; 14:6: he has given the Son to have life in himself; 5:27, 22: he has committed all judgment to the Son). The one who is

9

qualitatively different from the creation loves the creation and relates to it/us in personal ways.

The Body of the letter begins with the equivalent of a conventional expression of confidence in the addressees: "I rejoiced greatly to find some of your children following the truth [i.e., living in fidelity to God's commands, 2 Kings 20:3; Ps 86:11; 1 QS 8:4], just as we have been commanded by the Father" (v. 4). In antiquity, such expressions function to undergird the requests that follow, creating a sense of obligation through praise (Stanley N. Olson, "Pauline Expressions of Confidence in His Addressees," *CBQ* 47 [1985]: 282–95). True to form, the expression of confidence here is followed by requests in two areas: (1) proper behavior and (2) proper belief.

(1) Regarding proper behavior, the Elder writes: "And now I beg you, lady, . . . love one another, . . . as you have heard from the beginning, . . . follow love" (vv. 5–6). In the Hebrew Old Testament there is a distinction between *'ahabah* (God's election love) and *chesed* (God's covenant love). In the LXX *agapē* is the term used to translate *'ahabah*. In the Johannine literature this distinction does not hold. *Agapē* covers both election love and covenant love. To "follow love" in the sense of John 13:34–35 is to manifest covenant love. So in Johannine circles, the love command means acting with covenant fidelity toward others in the community after the pattern of Jesus. This is the proper behavior requested.

(2) Regarding proper belief, he says: "Many deceivers have gone out into the world, those who will not continually acknowledge [present tense] the ongoing coming [present tense] of Jesus Christ in the flesh; . . . Look to yourselves. . . . Anyone who goes ahead and does not abide in the doctrine of Christ does not have God; the one who abides in the doctrine has both the Father and the Son" (vv. 7–9). The present participles are significant. In contrast to 1 John 5:6 (Jesus Christ *came* in the flesh), 2 John 7 speaks of the *coming* of Christ with a linear tense. It is possible that this is intended to say the Word became flesh and remained flesh even after the resurrection (cf. 1 John 1:1; Ignatius, *Smyrnaeans* 3:1). Since the problem cited in v. 9 is that some "go ahead" / "run ahead" / "progress beyond," leaving the doctrine of Christ behind, the emphasis on "continuing to acknowledge" the coming of Jesus Christ in the flesh is important. The need is for a continuing commitment to a correct christology (cf. John 20:31: "These things are written that you may go on believing that Jesus is the Christ, the Son of God, and that going on believing you may go on having life in his name"; 1 John 5:13: "These things I have written to you who go on believing in the name of the Son of God

that you may know you have eternal life"). Given the context, "doctrine of Christ" refers to teaching about Christ. Those who teach otherwise are not to be welcomed with hospitality (vv. 10–11; cf. Didache 11:1–2; Ignatius, *Smyrnaeans* 4:1; *Ephesians* 7:1; 9:1; Tertullian, *Prescription of Heretics* 37:1–7).

The letter's conclusion includes the Elder's expression of hope for a visit (v. 12) and greetings from the church where the Elder is based (v. 13: "The children of your elect sister greet you"). Already in the first extant written communication from the Johannine circle we learn that the community is divided over the issues of correct christology and proper behavior. Some have progressed beyond the traditional teaching about Christ and no longer acknowledge that the coming of the Christ in the flesh continued through Jesus' death and even after the resurrection (cf. Ignatius, *Smyrnaeans* 2:1: "For he suffered all these things for us that we might attain salvation . . . , not as some unbelievers say, that his Passion was merely in semblance"; 3:1: "For I know and believe that he was in the flesh even after the Resurrection"). Neither do they practice covenant loyalty (follow love) toward the community that continues to abide in the doctrine about Christ (cf. Ignatius, *Smyrnaeans* 6:2: "For love they have no care, none for the widow, none for the orphan, none for the distressed, none for the afflicted, none for the prisoner, or for him released from prison, none for the hungry or thirsty"). The Elder calls for adherence to what the recipients "have had from the beginning" (the command to love one another) and for their abiding in the doctrine about Christ (the coming of Jesus Christ in the flesh). He also calls for withholding of hospitality from those who bring the false teaching (cf. Ignatius, *Smyrnaeans* 4:1: "you must not only not receive, but if it is possible not even meet, but only pray for them, if perchance they may repent"; 7:2: "It is right to refrain from such men and not even to speak about them in private or public"). The problems of the Johannine community reflected in 2 John and the prescribed solutions of the Elder seem remarkably similar to those echoed in Ignatius of Antioch's letter to the church in Smyrna.

3 John

3 John is a letter from the Elder addressed to an individual, Gaius (v. 1). The greeting is omitted but a typical prayer for the recipient's health is included (v. 2). The Body of the letter begins, as did 2 John's, with a lengthy expression of confidence (vv. 3–6a): "I greatly rejoice when brethren re-

peatedly come and bear witness to your truth, even as you are walking in truth. I do not have greater joy than this, that I hear my children [converts, 1 Cor 4:14; Gal 4:19; Phil 2:22] walk in the truth [proper behavior toward fellow Christians, 1 John 1:6; 2:4; 3:18–19; 4:20]. Beloved, it is a faithful thing you are doing when you render service to the brethren, especially to strangers, who have testified to your love before the church." The Elder's expression of confidence in Gaius is followed with the expected request: "You will do well to send them on their journey [assist them, Acts 15:3; 1 Cor 16:6, 11; 2 Cor 1:16; Tit 3:13]. . . . We ought to support such men, that we may be fellow workers in the truth" (vv. 6b–8).

The mobility of the Mediterranean world of this period was accompanied by a system of inns, which did not enjoy a good reputation because of their questionable activities (cf. Petronius, *Satyricon*). Whenever possible, therefore, travellers availed themselves of the hospitality of acquaintances. Christian hospitality was linked to the house churches (e.g., Acts 17:5–9). The recommended bearer of a letter or a travelling missionary would expect to be given hospitality by the church and to be assisted in the further journey. The Johannine circle apparently was composed of multiple congregations guided by the Elder and his associates. His guidance was effective, as was that of Paul at an earlier time, through correspondence and through helpers sent from him to various congregations. The expression of confidence (vv. 3–6a) and the request for hospitality (vv. 6b–8) set up offering hospitality to fellow Christians within the Johannine circle as the right thing to do.

Following the praise of Gaius (vv. 3–8) in the Body of the letter is the censure of Diotrephes (vv. 9–10). "I have written something to the church but their lover of pre-eminence, Diotrephes, does not receive us [the Elder and his representatives] as a guest. Because of this, if I come I will bring up his works which he is doing with evil words, talking nonsense about us; and not content with this, neither is he receiving the brethren [Johannine Christians in general] as guests, and those wishing to do so he puts out of the church." Diotrephes' behavior has two sides to it — he does not accept the letter from the Elder and he does not offer hospitality to the brethren — but it is one policy. The censure of Diotrephes sets up denial of hospitality as the wrong thing to do.

Having clarified the right way and the wrong way to act, the Elder gives his exhortation, "Beloved, do not imitate evil but imitate good" (v. 11a), and its basis, "The one who does good is of God; the one who does evil has not seen God" (v. 11b). The point is: continue to offer hospitality as you have done in the past and do not act like Diotrephes. If Gaius does continue to act the right way, he will accept this letter and its probable bearer (cf. Rom 16:1–2; 1 Cor 16:3; Phil 2:25–30; Col 4:7–9), Demetrius, who has a threefold recommendation (v. 12): (a) from everyone, (b) from the truth itself, and (c) from us ("And we also bear witness, and you know that our testimony is true"), apparently a reference to the Elder and his assistants.

The situation presupposed is far from clear (cf. John B. Polhill, "An Analysis of 2 and 3 John," *RevExp* 67 [1970]: 468–70), but may have been due to the fact that the church in the location addressed was composed of more than one house church group: one in the house of Gaius, the other in the house of Diotrephes (cf. a similar circumstance in Corinth, 1 Cor 14:23, and in Rome, Rom 16:3–5, 23). The leader of one house group, Diotrephes, rejected the Elder's authority; the leader of the other, Gaius, accepted it. With this letter the Elder tries to maintain his link with at least one of the groups.

The letter concludes with an expression of hope for a future visit and expanded communication at that time, as in 2 John 12 (vv. 13–14), with a peace wish (v. 15a), and greetings (v. 15b). In the second extant document from the Johannine community we learn that the normal lines of authority have broken down: the Elder's letter has not been accepted and the recommended brethren have been rejected, which is the equivalent of a rejection of the authority of the recommender, namely, the Elder. The Elder's authority in the Johannine circle is due not to his office but to his links with the tradition of the eyewitnesses. Because of those connections, he is a reliable teacher. Anyone of those mentioned in 2 John who had "progressed beyond" the doctrine about Christ would inevitably progress beyond the need for a teacher whose authority is based on his links with the past and for his associates. If 3 John is read as part of the same series of correspondence as 2 and 1 John, then implicit within the letter are the issues of the other two. 3 John merely gives the reader a glimpse of an institutional side effect of the larger conflict. If, for the Elder, welcoming the progressives is wrong, because "the one who greets them shares their wicked work" (2 John 11), then, for a progressive, welcoming those who contend that ties to the past are necessary is inappropriate and is to be avoided. After all, as Philo said about the Essenes' practice of hospitality: "The door is open to visitors from elsewhere *who share their convictions*" (*Every Good Man* 12 §85). 3 John represents a stage of conflict in between that reflected in 2 John and that manifest in 1 John.

1 John

Since it possesses neither the conventional introduction nor the expected conclusion, 1 John has sometimes been denied the status of a letter. Because there were ancient letters without either the standard introduction or the normal closing (e.g., 1 Macc 8:23–32 has neither but is called a letter in 8:22; Josephus, *Antiquities* 8.2.6, 7 §50–52, 53–54, have neither but are called letters in 8:55), 1 John may indeed be a letter. This does not advance one's understanding of 1 John, however. It is most helpful to see the document as an exposition (1:6–5:12) of a piece of eyewitness proclamation (1:1–5), known to the readers, that is cited by the author (the Elder?) at the start.

1 John 1:1–5 is a thought unit that is dominated by a "we" that makes an eyewitness claim (we saw, touched, and heard him), distinguishing it from the "you" of the readers (vv. 2, 3, 5). It is a different "we" from that of 1:6–2:2, where the "we" means writer and readers together. The "we" of v. 5 is like that of vv. 1–4 and different from that of 1:6–2:2, pointing to the fact that v. 5 belongs with 1:1–4 and not with 1:6–2:2 (Kenneth Grayston, *The Johannine Epistles* [Grand Rapids: Eerdmans, 1984], 33). Moreover, the language of v. 5 links it with what comes before: *akēkoamen* (we have heard), vv. 1 and 5; *apaggellomen humin* (we proclaim to you), vv. 2 and 3, and *hē aggelia* (the message) and *anaggellomen humin* (we proclaim to you), v. 5. If v. 5 is taken together with vv. 1–4, then there is a thought unit that falls into an ABA'B' pattern:

A   That which we have heard and seen is the Word of Life (v. 1)

   B   That which we *saw* we proclaim to you (v. 2)

A'   That which we have seen and heard is the basis of our fellowship and joy (vv. 3–4)

   B'   That which we *heard* we proclaim to you (v. 5).

Of the various options to explain the claim to eyewitness experience ([a] 1 John is written by an eyewitness; [b] the eyewitness claim is a polemical fiction characteristic of a certain period of church history, [c] the eyewitness claim represents the author's identification with the tradition-bearers reaching all the way back to the eyewitnesses, [d] 1 John 1:1–5 is a piece of tradition from eyewitnesses cited by the author who was not, as one basis for his argument from beginnings), the last is to be preferred. We may read vv. 1–5 in these terms, following the ABA'B' pattern.

A (v. 1) speaks about the word of life which was from the beginning which "we" have heard, seen, looked upon, and touched with our hands. Elsewhere "the things we have heard and seen" describes the content of apostolic preaching (Acts 4:20; 22:15). That the word of life was seen and touched guarantees that it is a person. Since the Christian message and the person of Christ are ultimately one (1 Cor 1:23: We preach Christ), the word of life is Christ whom we preach. "From the beginning" here refers to the beginning of the Christian movement, the time of the Incarnation, although elsewhere (2:7; 2:24; 3:11) "from the beginning" refers to the time of the readers' Christian initiation. These two moments of the Christian past form the author's defense against "the progressives." In the Mediterranean world the ancient was what was valued. The most ancient, the beginning, was best. The past fixed the rules. So what happened at the beginning was decisive for the present (e.g., Isocrates, *Nicocles* 35; *To Demonicus* 34; Polybius 1.1.2; Livy 1, Preface 10–11; Plutarch, *Aemilius Paulus* 1:1; Lucian, *Demonax* 2). The noun *archē*, therefore, means not only "beginning" but also "sovereignty." This mind-set was also characteristic of Christian leaders (e.g., Tertullian, *Against Marcion* 4.4: "the authority lies with that which shall be found to be more ancient . . . corruption of doctrine belongs to the side which shall be convicted of comparative lateness in its origin"). The tack taken by the author of 1 John, reflecting this cultural assumption, was an appeal to two beginnings, both the beginning of the Christian movement (the time of the Incarnation) and the beginning of the readers' Christian life (the time of their initiation). If the readers adhered to the content connected to these two beginnings, they would not be led astray by the progressives. The eyewitness tradition cited in 1:1–5 focuses on one beginning, the beginning of the Christian movement.

The one who was the content of the Christian message was one whom the eyewitnesses had heard, had seen with their eyes, had looked upon, and had touched with their hands. The reference to seeing with their eyes and touching with their hands almost certainly refers to a post-resurrection event: e.g., John 20:25, 27 (Thomas); 20:17 (Mary Magdalene); Luke 24:39, which uses the same verb for "touch" and functions to prove to the Eleven that the risen Jesus is still flesh and bones; Ignatius, *Smyrnaeans* 3:1–2, where the intent is to prove "he was in the flesh even after the Resurrection," also uses the same verb when speaking of an appearance to those with Peter in which the risen Lord invites touch. "And they immediately touched him and believed"; Epistle of the Apostles 11–12, where the risen Lord invites Peter and Thomas to touch him and they say, "we touched him that we might learn of a truth whether he were risen in the flesh." As with Luke 24, Ignatius, and the Epistle of the Apostles, the intent of 1 John 1:1 is to establish that he was in the flesh even after the resurrection. (Lucretius, *De Rerum Natura* 1:304, "For nothing can touch or be touched except a bodily substance," was known to Christians like Tertullian, *De Anima* 5; *Against Marcion* 4.8, and was used to argue for the corporeality of Jesus.) The Incarnate One who was "the beginning" of the Christian movement and who is the content of Christian proclamation was in the flesh even after his resurrection (remember 2 John 7; contrast the spiritualizing Coptic Gospel of Thomas 17: "Jesus said: I will give you what eye has not seen and ear has not heard and hand has not touched and which has not come into the heart of man").

B (v. 2) speaks about what the eyewitnesses *saw* as the content of what they proclaim. If A (v. 1) defined the content of what they saw (Christ was in the flesh even after the resurrection), B (v. 2) says what was seen is what the eyewitnesses proclaim. What they saw controls their christological confession.

A′ (vv. 3–4) speaks about the communication of what the eyewitnesses saw and heard as the basis for fellowship both at the human and the divine level. The logic runs: (1) The eyewitnesses are already in fellowship with the Father and with his Son Jesus Christ (v. 3b); (2) The eyewitnesses communicate what they have seen and heard to "you all" in order that "you all" may go on having fellowship with "us" (v. 3a). The Fourth Gospel knows two types of believers: those who have seen and believe (eyewitnesses) and those who have not seen and yet believe (non-eyewitnesses) (20:29–31). It also knows of the latter coming to faith by means of the former. John 17:20–21, 23 reads:

> I do not pray for these [the eyewitnesses] only, but also for those who believe in me through their word, that they may all be one; even as thou, Father, art in me, and I in thee, that they may also be in us. . . . I in them and thou in me, that they may become perfectly one. . . .

Here oneness involves: first, union between Father and Son; second, union between Son and eyewitnesses; and, third, union between eyewitnesses and those who believe because of their word. For the author of the Fourth Gospel and 1 John, the second generation of Christians could not bypass those who had heard, seen, and touched the word of life any more than they could bypass the Son in a relation to the Father. Fellowship with Father and Son is contingent upon fellowship with the eyewitnesses and is grounded in what they saw and heard. If the recipients respond aright and follow the truth, the witnesses' joy will be complete (v. 4; cf. 2 John 4).

V. 3 says "you" are recipients of the eyewitnesses' proclamation "in order that you may go on having [present subjunctive] fellowship with us." This implies several things: (a) the recipients are already Christians, as is confirmed by the rest of the document (e.g., 5:13: "These things I write to you who go on believing in the name of the Son of God that you may know that you do go on having eternal life); (b) they already are in fellowship with the eyewitnesses (if they need to go on having fellowship, then they do in fact have it); (c) their need is to continue in fellowship with the eyewitnesses and not "progress beyond" it (2 John 9); (d) the eyewitness proclamation has the function of confirming in the faith those who have believed and of insuring that they remain in fellowship with the apostolic tradition (cf. Acts 8:4–8, 14–17; 9:27; 11:19–24, etc.). The last implication points to the fact that after the community's formation the eyewitnesses sent them a written communication to confirm them in the faith and in the fellowship. It is a part of this Proclamation that the author of 1 John uses as the basis for his Exposition.

B' (v. 5) speaks about the eyewitnesses' proclamation of what they *heard:* "God is light and in him is no darkness at all." The expression refers not to God's essence but to how God relates to humans, as the later "God is love" does. Light here has an ethical connotation. What the eyewitnesses heard about God's character is the basis for their ethical instruction.

1 John opens with the citation of a tradition from the eyewitnesses that gives what they saw and what they heard as the basis for their christological and ethical message. This Proclamation, from which the community's formation doubtless came, is followed by an Exposition offered by the author (the Elder?) that alternates between christological and ethical foci: 1:6–2:17; 2:29–3:24a; 4:7–12; 4:16b–5:4a giving ethical exposition, and 2:18–28, 3:24b–4:6, 4:13–16a, 5:4b–12 offering christological teaching. Throughout, many of the discrete sections may have had their own distinct histories, some being set pieces that the Elder now pulls together and applies to the situation at hand (J. L. Houlden, *A Commentary on the Johannine Epistles* [San Francisco: Harper & Row, 1973], 25, 31), hoping to show the explicit connections between such teaching and the eyewitness proclamation of 1:1–5. After all, this was the ground of an Elder's authority!

WALKING IN THE LIGHT

1 John 1:6–2:17; 2:18–28

After beginning his communication with a citation from the community's tradition of "The Proclamation of the Eyewitnesses" (1:1–5), the author turns to his own "Exposition of the Eyewitness Tradition" (1:6–5:12), using both set pieces from his past teaching and material newly constructed for this occasion to expound the implications of what the eyewitnesses *saw* (their christological message) and *heard* (their ethical message). The Exposition alternates between ethical (1:6–2:17; 2:29–3:24a; 4:7–12; 4:16b–5:4a) and christological exposition (2:18–28; 3:24b–4:6; 4:13–16a; 5:4b–12). The section 1 John 1:6–2:17 is the first large section of ethical exposition. It is composed of three sub-units — 1:6–2:2; 2:3–11; and 2:12–17 — each of which will be discussed in order.

1 John 1:6–2:17

1 John 1:6–2:2 is a thought unit held together by an inclusion (1:6, we are liars; 1:7, his blood cleanses us from sin // 1:10, we make him a liar; 2:1–2, he is the expiation for our sins). It is connected to the eyewitness testimony of 1:1–5 by certain link words: e.g., fellowship, vv. 3 and 7; light and darkness, vv. 5 and 6–7. It consists of three erroneous boasts and their consequences (1:6, 8, 10) answered by three contrary assertions together with their implications (1:7, 9; 2:1–2; R. E. Brown, *The Epistles of John* [Garden City, N.Y.: Doubleday, 1982], 231, 237)

> *The First Pair* (1:6–7)
>
> > Error (If we say) + consequence (we lie) (v. 6)
> >
> > Positive contrast (If we walk) + consequence (we have) (v. 7)
>
> *The Second Pair* (1:8–9)
>
> > Error (If we say) + consequence (we deceive ourselves) (v. 8)
> >
> > Positive contrast (If we confess) + consequence (he will) (v. 9)

18

The Third Pair (1:10–2:2)

Error (If we say) + consequence (we make him a liar) (1:10)

Positive contrast (If any one does sin) + consequence (he is the expiation) (2:1–2)

The first pair begins: "If we say, *'we have fellowship with him,'* while we walk in darkness, we lie and do not live according to the truth." The problem here is the opponents' belief that it is possible to have fellowship with God while one's life has an unethical orientation. Since God is light (v. 5), however, one cannot dwell with him in light and walk in darkness (cf. 1 QS 3:20–21: "The sons of righteousness walk in the ways of light; the sons of iniquity walk in the ways of darkness"). To claim such is to lie and not "to do the truth" (i.e., live according to God's commandment; 2 Chron 31:20; Tobit 4:6; 13:6; 1 QpHab 7:10–11; T. Benjamin 10:3: "Do the truth, each of you to his neighbor; keep the Law of the Lord and his commandments"; Ignatius, *Ephesians* 6:2).

The positive contrast follows: "if we walk in the light, as He is in the light, we have fellowship with one another, and the blood of Jesus his Son cleanses us from all sin" (v. 7). To live in the light involves two things: (1) having fellowship with one another (i.e., covenant fidelity toward others in the Johannine community, 2 John 4–6; 3 John 3–6), and (2) having the blood of Jesus his Son cleanse one from all sin (i.e., the stain of sin, not just the guilt, is taken away). The point of the first pair is: fellowship with God implies ethical living.

The second pair begins: "If we say, *'we have no sin,'* we deceive ourselves, and the truth is not in us." The problem here is the progressives' claim to sinlessness, accompanying their fellowship with God. How should this be understood? (a) Jewish tradition spoke of sinless patriarchs: e.g., T. Zebulon 1:4–5: "I am not aware, my children, that I have sinned in all my days, except in my mind. Nor do I recall having committed a transgression, except what I did to Joseph in ignorance"; T. Joseph 1:3: "In my life I have seen envy and death. But I have not gone astray: I continued in the truth of the Lord"; Jubilees 35:3–6: Jacob says, "From the day I was born until this day all of my deeds and everything which is in my heart, that I always think of good for everyone. . . . Tell me, Mother, what perversity you have seen against me and I will withdraw from it. . . . " And she said "My son, all my days I have never seen against you anything perverse but only uprightness." It was this mind-set reflected by Paul in Philippians 3:6: "as to righteousness under the law blameless." (b) Jewish tradition also anticipated a sinless Messianic Age: e.g., T. Levi 18:9

speaks of the Messianic times when the priestly Messiah comes as a time when "sin shall cease and lawless men shall rest from their evil deeds"; 1 Enoch 5:8 says that in the ideal future the elect will "not return again to sin"; Psalms of Solomon 17:32 contends that in the days of the kingly Messiah "there will be no unrighteousness among them...for all shall be holy." (c) This was a not uncommon problem in early Christianity: e.g., 1 Cor 6:12–20; 10:23 ("All things are lawful for me"); Justin Martyr, *Trypho* 141:2, contends that Ps 32:2 does not mean that if sinners know God no sin will be imputed to them; Irenaeus, *Against Heresies* 1.6.4, says of the Valentinians, "they highly exalt themselves and claim to be perfect and the elect seed.... On this account they tell us that it is necessary for us whom they call animal men...to practice continence and good works...but that to them who are called 'the spiritual and perfect' such a course of conduct is not at all necessary' "; the Gospel of Philip from Nag Hammadi, 77:15–16, says: "He who has knowledge of the truth is a free man, but the free man does not sin."

The progressives who claim sinless perfection for themselves here do not have their roots in the Jewish tradition about sinless patriarchs because it assumes sinlessness means ethical, law-abiding behavior, something they clearly do not assume. The Johannine progressives have more affinities with the Christian stream that joins claims to perfection with libertine behavior. The unanswered question, at this point, is whether the roots of their position are in an overrealized eschatology due to a misunderstanding of Jewish visions of the endtimes (cf. Jubilees 1:23; T. Benjamin 8:2–3: "He has no pollution in his heart because upon him is resting the spirit of God"; 1 QS 3:6–9: "He shall be cleansed from all his sins by the spirit of holiness uniting him to His truth and his iniquity shall be expiated by the spirit of uprightness and humility"), in a dualistic anthropology as in Gnosticism, or in both as reflected in 1 Corinthians (C. H. Talbert, *Reading Corinthians* [New York: Crossroad, 1987], 36, 38).

The positive contrast runs: "If we regularly confess [present tense] our sins [Prov 28:13], he is faithful and just [Deut 32:4; 1 Clement 27:1; 60:1], and will go on forgiving [present tense] our sins and cleansing us from all unrighteousness" (v. 9). Regular confession yields regular forgiveness of guilt and cleansing from the stain of sin. Given the practices of the milieu, the prescribed confession is probably public (cf. Lev 5:5–6, confession of sin is public and in a Jewish liturgical context; Mk 1:5//Matt 3:6, confession is public and in connection with John's baptism; Acts 19:18, Christian confession is public; James 5:16, confession by Christians is before the church; Didache 4:14 and 14:1, confession is public and within the context of the church's worship). The point of the second pair is: to claim sinlessness is self deception that deprives one of the benefits of forgiveness and cleansing following upon confession.

The third pair begins: "If we say, *'we have not sinned'* [a repetition of the claim in v. 8], we make him a liar, and his word is not in us" (because God's word speaks plainly about the universality of human sin — e.g., 1 Kings 8:46; Ps 14:3; Prov 20:9; Eccl 7:20; Isa 53:6; 64:6). Before the positive contrast the author clarifies his intent: "My little children, I am writing this to you so that you may not sin" (2:1a).

The positive contrast reads: "If any one does sin, we have an advocate [*parakleton*] with the Father, Jesus Christ the righteous; and he is the atoning sacrifice [NIV: *hilasmos*] for our sins, and not for ours only but also for the sins of the whole world." (a) In ancient Jewish thought one sometimes hears of a heavenly intercessor: e.g., T. Levi 5:6: "I am the angel who makes intercession for the nation Israel"; T. Dan 6:2: "Draw near to God and to the angel who intercedes for you, because he is the mediator between God and men for the peace of Israel. He shall stand in opposition to the kingdom of the enemy"; cf. 1 Enoch 89:76; 90:14; Daniel 10:13, 21; 12:1. Early Christians spoke of the risen Christ performing this function: Romans 8:34: "Christ Jesus, who is at the right hand of God, who indeed intercedes for us"; Hebrews 9:24: "For Christ has entered . . . into heaven itself, now to appear in the presence of God on our behalf." (b) Sometimes in Judaism the intercessor's power came from his being blameless: Wisdom of Solomon 18:21 speaks of Aaron's "prayer and propitiation" as the act of a blameless man who "withstood the anger and put an end to the disaster." 1 John 2:1 says the Christians' intercessor/advocate is "Jesus Christ the righteous." (c) In Judaism sometimes an advocate's death functioned as the basis for his intercession: e.g., Isaiah 53:10, 12; 4 Maccabees 6:28–29: Eleazar, dying as a martyr, prays: "You know, O God, that though I could have saved myself I am dying in these fiery torments for the sake of the Law. Be merciful to your people and let our punishment be a satisfaction on their behalf. Make my blood their purification and take my life as a ransom for theirs." This was clearly the case in Hebrews 9:11–26, where Christ's intercession is based upon his sacrifice of himself. So too in 1 John 2:1–2 Jesus Christ is the Christians' advocate with the Father based on his atoning sacrifice.

The Greek term translated "atoning sacrifice" (*hilasmos*), used in 1 John 2:2 and 4:10, is a subject of debate. Should it be rendered "propitiation" (implying that Jesus' death is directed toward the offended person,

God) or "expiation" (implying that his blood is directed toward the sinner and removing the sin)? Both meanings seem possible in the milieu
and in 1 John. The former seems dominant in 2:1–2 because Jesus is here
functioning as advocate or intercessor (as Eleazar in 4 Maccabees?). The
latter may be dominant in 4:10. The translation "atoning sacrifice" (so
NIV) attempts to capture both.

The point of the third pair is: Although the author's hope is that his
readers will not sin, he knows from God's word that they will; he knows
also that when that happens, the Christian's recourse is Jesus Christ, the
heavenly advocate, whose atoning death covers not only the community's
sins but those of the whole world (John 1:29).

In the first subunit of ethical exposition we learn that the author's opponents claim (a) to have fellowship with God even though they live
unethically, (b) to be sinless because they have an alleged relation with
God, and (c) to have no need of the benefits of Jesus' atoning death and
heavenly intercession (anticipating what becomes explicit in 5:6–8). The
author links (a) the necessity of ethical behavior to any relation with God,
(b) the claim of sinlessness to self-deception and denial of God's word,
and (c) the need for forgiveness and cleansing to Jesus' atoning death
and heavenly intercession.

1 John 2:3–11 is the second of three small subunits in the larger ethical
section 1:6–2:17. It is connected with the preceding subunit, 1:6–2:2, by
means of link words: darkness and light, 1:6–7//2:8–11; truth not in us/
him, 1:8; 2:4; liar, 1:10//2:4; his word, 1:10//2:5; I am writing, 2:1//2:7. It
is built around a recurring boast about intimacy with God: "The one who
says," vv. 4, 6, 9. (R. E. Brown, *The Epistles of John*, 277). In each case the
boast is put to the test of ethical behavior.

The First Boast Tested (2:3–5)

> The one who says, "I know him," but disobeys his command-
> ments is a liar. (v. 4)

The Second Boast Tested (2:6–8)

> The one who says he abides in him ought to walk in the same
> way in which he walked. (v. 6)

The Third Boast Tested (2:9–11)

> The one who says he is in the light and hates his brother is in
> the darkness still. (v. 9)

The first boast is tested in 2:3–5. This paragraph is held together by an
inclusion: "By this we may be sure that we know him," v. 3 / "By this we

may be sure that we are in him," v. 5. The boast itself is tested in v. 4: "The one who says, *'I know him,'* but disobeys his commandments is a liar, and the truth is not in him; but whoever keeps his word, in him truly love for God is perfected." The problem reflected here is: the opponents do not think that keeping the commandments is related to the knowledge of God or love for God. Hosea 4:1–2 says there is no knowledge of God in the land because there is swearing, lying, killing, stealing, and committing adultery. That is because in a covenant context "to know God" is to be faithful to the covenant stipulations, which include proper behavior toward others in the community (cf. Jer 31:31–34). The Johannine context reflects two different views of knowing God. One, represented by the progressives, was basically an individualistic mysticism without moral implications (cf. the pagan mystery cults where salvation was dependent upon initiation and had nothing to do with uprightness of conduct, prompting the sneer of Diogenes: "Pataicion the thief will have a better fate when he comes to die than Epaminondas [a virtuous man], because he has been initiated" [Diogenes Laertius, *Lives of Eminent Philosophers* 6.39]). The other, represented by the author (Elder?), was modelled on covenant thinking. In covenant thinking, "those that love me" are "those that keep my commandments" (Exod 20:6). Hence, "whoever keeps his word, in him truly love for God is perfected" (v. 5; cf. John 14:15, 21, 23, 24). In covenant thinking, however, obeying God's commands is not the condition but rather the characteristic of a knowledge of God.

The second test comes in 2:6: "the one who says, *'I abide in him,'* ought to walk in the same way in which he walked." The problem is the recurring one: the progressives claim to possess intimacy with Christ but their lives do not follow his example (John 13:15: "I have given you an example, that you should do as I have done to you"). Such a test is nothing new to the readers. It is the old commandment which they had from the beginning of their lives as Christians (v. 7), which they heard at their Christian initiation (2 John 5: "the one we had from the beginning, that we love one another"). Yet "it is a new commandment" (v. 8). In what sense? The primary image for covenant thinking was the Exodus from Egypt and its accompaniments. In this pattern, a deliverance by God was followed by a song to celebrate it (Exod 15:1–18, 21) and the giving and receiving of commandments (Exod 20). Early Christians followed the pattern: a new covenant (Lk 22:20), a new song to celebrate a new deliverance (Rev 5:9–10), and a new commandment appropriate to the new covenant (John 13:34: "A new commandment I give to you, that you love one another; even as I have loved you, that you also love one another").

The new commandment of the new covenant is the old commandment that the members of the Johannine community heard from the beginning of their incorporation into fellowship with the eyewitnesses and thereby into fellowship with the Father and his Son Jesus Christ.

The third boast is tested in 2:9–11: "The one who says, '*I am in the light,*' and hates his brother is in the darkness still." The thesis sentence is expounded in the two following sentences, one positive ("The one who loves his brother abides in the light," v. 10), one negative ("The one who hates his brother is in the darkness and walks in darkness," v. 11). Here, of course, light and darkness are ethical categories (as in T. Levi 19:1: "Choose for yourselves *light* or *darkness,* the Law of the Lord or the works of Beliar"; T. Naphtali 2:10: "You are unable to perform the works of *light* while you are in *darkness*"). The point of the second subunit of ethical exposition (2:3–11) is that a covenant understanding of "knowing God / abiding in God / being in the light" implies certain behavior toward others as a corollary.

1 John 2:12–17 is the third of three small subunits in the larger ethical section, 1:6–2:17. It is linked to the preceding subunit by certain key words: know him/the Father, 2:3 and 2:13; I am writing to you, 2:7–8 and 2:12–13; from the beginning, 2:7 and 2:13; love for God/the Father, 2:5 and 2:15. It consists of three parts in an ABA' pattern.

A   a word of assurance, which functions as the experiential foundation for the exhortation that follows (2:12–14)

B   a word of exhortation (2:15a)

A'   a word of clarification, which gives the ontological basis for the exhortation that precedes (2:15b–17).

Each will be examined in order.

A, the word of assurance (2:12–14), contains two blocks of three addresses each, all of which lay the experiential foundation for the admonition to follow in v. 15a.

> I am writing, little children, because (v. 12);
> I am writing, fathers, because (v. 13a);
> I am writing, young men, because (v. 13b).
> I write, children, because (v. 13c);
> I write, fathers, because (v. 14a)
> I write, young men, because (v. 14c).

Since elsewhere the author refers to all his readers as little children (*teknion,* 2:1, 12, 28; 3:7, 18; 4:4; 5:21; *paidion,* 2:13, 18) and since elsewhere in the New Testament fathers and young men are designations for the old and the young in the church (1 Tim 5:1; Tit 2:2–6; 1 Pet 5:1–5), there are two groups within the whole singled out. He says: All of you, old and young alike, have certain experiential components in your spiritual status (forgiveness of sins, knowledge of God and Christ, spiritual power that enables you to overcome the evil one). Because you possess this experiential status spiritually, "Do not love the world (i.e., humankind organized in independence of God, under the control of the evil one, and the source of opposition to God) or the things in the world" (=B: v. 15a, the exhortation). It is because they have received the gift experientially that they can follow the guidance given.

A′, vv. 15b–17, the word of clarification, contains three antitheses which provide the ontological foundation for the exhortation to resist the world.

> *First antithesis:* If anyone loves the world, love for the Father is not in him (v. 15b).
>
> *Second antithesis:* All that is in the world is not of the Father but of the world (v. 16).
>
> *Third antithesis:* The world passes away but whoever does the will of God abides forever (v. 17).

There are two possible covenant partners: (1) the world organized in independence of God with its accompanying human values and desires, and (2) the Father. The two covenants are mutually exclusive. Covenant loyalty (love) toward the one partner excludes covenant loyalty toward the other. The one covenant is transient, the other eternal. This is the ontological basis for the exhortation in v. 15a: "Do not love the world or the things in the world."

In 1:6–2:17 three subunits wrestle with problems posed by the progressives. In each case the unity of the vertical and horizontal dimensions of Christian life is affirmed in the face of claims that the vertical can be detached from the horizontal.

1 John 2:18–28

1 John 2:18–28 is a thought unit held together by an inclusion: children + eschatology, vv. 18–19 // children + eschatology, v. 28. It is connected with the preceding unit by link phrases: the world passes away, 2:17 // It is the last hour, 2:18; when he appears, 2:28. The focus of this unit is christological rather than ethical, as was 1:6–2:17. The heart of

the passage, within the inclusion, is organized around three occurrences of *kai humeis* (and you all, vv. 20, 24, 27) that yield an ABA' pattern:

> A   The anointing (the gift of the Holy Spirit), vv. 20–21
>
>> B   What was heard from the beginning (the apostolic tradition), vv. 24–26
>
> A'   The anointing (the gift of the Holy Spirit), v. 27.

One side of the inclusion (vv. 18–19) forms an introduction to the unit: "[a] Children, it is the last hour [1 Tim 4:1; 2 Tim 3:1; James 5:3; 1 Pet 12:5; Jude 18]; [b] and as you have heard that antichrist is coming [2 John 7; 1 John 2:22; 4:3; 2 Thes 2:3–10; Rev 20:10; Didache 16:3–4; cf. Irenaeus, *Against Heresies* 5.25.1; Tertullian, *Resurrection of the Flesh* 24:18–20], [b'] so now many antichrists have come; therefore [a'] we know that it is the last hour." The apocalyptic expectation is applied to the "progressives" who are also "secessionists": "[a] They went out from us, but [b] they were not of us; for [b'] if they had been of us, (a') they would have continued with us." The problem in the Johannine community has now progressed to the point that the two groups are institutionally separate.

A, 2:20–23, speaks about the readers' anointing as the basis for their knowledge: "And you [*kai humeis*] have been anointed by the Holy One [Jesus — John 6:69; Mk 1:24; Acts 3:14], and you all know." If the anointing is *by* Jesus, it is *with* the Spirit (John 14:26: "He will teach you all things"; 16:13: "He will guide you into all truth"; cf. 2 Cor 1:21–22: "God has anointed us ... and given us his Spirit"). Because the readers have been anointed with the Spirit and have spiritual knowledge, they can recognize a lie and liars. "Who is the liar but the one who makes the denial, *'Jesus is not the Christ'* [or better, 'the Christ is not Jesus'? cf. John 1:1b]?" Here the focus is not on "Christ" but on "Jesus." It is a denial of the Incarnation (2 John 7; 1 John 4:2; cf. Ignatius, *Smyrnaeans* 5:2; *Magnesians* 11; *Trallians* 9). At this point one sees that the schism has christological roots, one part of which was a denial of the Incarnation. "No one who denies the Son has the Father. The one who confesses the Son has the Father" (v. 23). Another part of the christological controversy was the progressives' claim that they could relate to the Father apart from the Son. For the author of 1 John, just as one cannot come to the Father and the Son except in fellowship with the eyewitnesses (1:3), so one cannot come to the Father except through the Son. Having experienced an anointing with the Holy Spirit by Jesus, the readers know that the Christ is Jesus and that denial of such is a lie.

B, vv. 24–26, begins with an exhortation: "Let what you heard from the beginning [of your Christian life] abide in you." This refers to instruction given converts at their initiation. An inference follows: "If what you heard from the beginning [in this case, about christology] abides in you, then you [*kai humeis*] will abide in the Son and in the Father." A second line of defense against christological error is the doctrine about Christ (2 John 9), which they received at their initiation and in which they need to abide. If they do, they will receive eternal life (v. 25).

A', vv. 26–27, returns to the matter of the anointing with the Spirit. It is because of deceivers that the author writes (v. 26; cf. 2 John 7): "but the anointing which you received [in a specific experience] from him goes on abiding in you, and you have no need that any one should teach you; as his anointing teaches you about everything" (v. 27). The secessionists claim that the readers need further instruction so they too can progress. The author contends that they need only listen to the teaching of the Spirit (John 14:26: "He will bring to your remembrance all that I have said to you"; 15:26: "He will bear witness to me"; 16:14: "He will glorify me; 16:15: "He will take what is mine and declare it to you"). If they follow the anointing's teaching, they will go on abiding in the Son (v. 27b).

The resources that enable the readers to discriminate between christological truth and error are two: (1) their anointing with the Spirit at the time of their initiation, and (2) the instruction they received when they became Christians. The content is the same: There was a real incarnation in Jesus; one comes to the Father through him. Armed with truth, the readers can continue to abide in the Son. If so, then "we may have confidence and not shrink from him in shame at his coming" (v. 28).

DISCERNING THE SPIRITS

1 John 2:29–3:24a; 3:24b–4:6

1 John 2:29–3:34a

The second section of ethical exposition in 1 John is 2:29–3:24a, which falls into two subunits, 2:29–3:10 and 3:11–24a, each of which may be examined in order.

1 John 2:29–3:10, the first of the two subunits in the larger ethical section, 2:29–3:24a, is held together by an inclusion ("everyone who does right is born of him," 2:29b // "whoever does not do right is not of God," 3:10b). Another sign of the subunit's unity is the recurrence of nine participles preceded by articles ("the one who . . . "), seven of which also have *pas* ("everyone") preceding the article and the participle (2:29, "everyone who" + participle; 3:3, "everyone who" + participle; 3:4, "everyone who" + participle; 3:6a, 6b, "everyone who" + participle; 3:9, "everyone who" + participle; 3:10, "everyone who" + participle). The material begins with a statement of the thesis that uses the first "everyone who" (2:29), followed by three paragraphs (3:1–4; 3:5–8a; 3:8b–10), each of which is organized in a similar way: (1) a christological premise (3:1–2; 3:5; 3:8b), followed by (2) a corollary (3:3–4; 3:6–8a; 3:9–10) in both a positive (using "everyone who" + participle) and a negative (using "everyone who" + participle) form. In outline form it looks like this.

Thesis (2:29): Since he is righteous, everyone who does right is born of him.

Unit One (3:1–4)

    Christological basis (3:1–2)

    Corollary (3:3–4)

    (1) Positive (v. 3): Everyone who hopes in him purifies himself as he is pure.

    (2) Negative (v. 4): Everyone who commits sin is guilty of lawlessness; sin is lawlessness.

28

Unit Two (3:5–8a)

Christological basis (3:5)

Corollary (3:6–8a)

(1) Positive (v. 6a): Everyone who abides in him does not sin.

(2) Negative (v. 6b): Everyone who sins has neither seen him nor known him.

(1) Positive (v. 7): The one who does right is righteous, as he is righteous.

(2) Negative (v. 8a): The one who commits sins is of the devil, for the devil has sinned from the beginning.

Unit Three (3:8b–10)

Christological basis (3:8b)

Corollary (3:9–10)

(1) Positive (v. 9): Everyone who is born of God does not commit sin.

(2) Negative (v. 10): Everyone who does not do right is not of God.

The thesis of the unit is that people's character and behavior are like that of the one who begot them (cf. John 8:44). This subunit is connected with what precedes by means of the link phrase "when he appears" (2:28//3:2).

The thesis of 2:29–3:10 is given in 2:29: Since he is righteous, everyone who does right is born of him. Doing right is a consequence of and, therefore, a sign of one's spiritual birth. Three paragraphs of explanation (3:1–4; 3:5–8a; 3:8b–10) follow, each with a similar arrangement.

Unit One (3:1–4) begins with a christological premise: "we know that when he appears we shall be like him, for we shall see him as he is" (3:2). That believers will be like the glorified Christ at his parousia is common early Christian conviction (e.g., Phil 3:21; Col 3:4). That we shall see him in his glory is the prayer of the Johannine Jesus (John 17:24) and a normal Christian expectation (1 Cor 13:12; Rev 22:4; Pseudo-Clementine, *Homilies* 17.16). That one becomes like a god upon and because of beholding the deity is a widespread Mediterranean assumption (Seneca, *Epistle* 94.42; 1 QH 4:5–6; 3:3; 4:27–29; 1 QSb 4:24–28; 1 QS 2:2–4; 2 Cor 3:18). This hope has its corollaries: positive ("Everyone who thus hopes in him purifies herself as he is pure," v. 3), and negative ("Everyone who continually does sin is doing lawlessness; sin is lawlessness," v. 4). There is a christological basis for Christian purity. Sin is a matter, not just of the spirit, but of behavior. This can only be an exposé of the progressives for whom sin was entirely spiritual and who consequently claimed to be sinless (1:8, 10).

Unit Two (3:5–8a) also begins with a christological premise: "he appeared to take away sins, and in him there is no sin" (3:5). That he appeared to take away sins was a conviction of the Johannine community (e.g., John 1:29, "take away the sins of the world"). That he was sinless was a common early Christian conviction (e.g., 1 John 2:1; 3:3; John 8:46; 2 Cor 5:21; Heb 4:15; 1 Pet 3:18). The sinless one has as his function the abolition of sin. This conviction has two sets of corollaries, positive and negative. The first set is found in v. 6a and v. 6b: positive ("Everyone who continually abides in him does not sin habitually." Cf. TEV, NIV) and negative ("Everyone who sins habitually has neither seen nor known him." Cf. TEV, NIV). The second set is found in v. 7 and v. 8a: positive ("The one who habitually does right is righteous, even as that one is righteous") and negative ("The one who habitually does sin is of the devil, because from the beginning the devil sins continually").

The simplest explanation of the apparent contradiction in 1 John between statements that insist that all Christians sin (1:8, 10; 2:1; 5:16) and those (3:6 and 3:9) that claim that Christians do not sin is linguistic (for a survey of options, cf. Stephen S. Smalley, *Word Biblical Commentary: 1, 2, 3 John* [Waco: Word, 1984], 159). When the author of 1 John says Christians do not sin, he is using a present tense with a continuous sense. The Christian does not sin as a settled habit; she does not keep on sinning. When the author says Christians do sin he is using an aorist tense, suggesting individual and isolated acts of sin (e.g., 2:1). The Christian does sin on occasion.

Reservations about this explanation are based upon two passages, 5:16 and 1:8, which use the present tense in ways that allegedly contradict the general explanation. In 5:16 ("If anyone should see his brother sinning [present tense] a sin not unto death, he should pray and he will give life to him, to those sinning [present participle] not unto death"), the present tense, it is claimed, if interpreted as we propose to do elsewhere, would point to Christians being involved in continuous sinning. This is not necessarily so. The sentence begins, "If anyone should *see*" (aorist tense, implying a moment of observation). One might paraphrase: "If anyone in a given moment should observe a fellow Christian in the process of sinning a sin." If so, then the inference of the habitual nature of the sinner's action is rendered impossible by the aorist, which controls the sentence. This passage cannot legitimately be used against the linguistic argument. In 1:8 ("If we should say, 'We do not ever have [present tense] sin,' we deceive ourselves") the present tense, it is argued, countermands the claims of the linguistic argument elsewhere. This is not so. The progressives are contending that they do not ever sin; hence the present tense. Their claim is reinforced by the use of a perfect tense in 1:10 ("If we say, 'We have not sinned in the past and this continues up to the present,' we make him a liar"). The author contends that Christians do commit occasional acts of sin (2:1). Rather than being evidence against the linguistic argument, 1:8 supports it. Correctly read, then, 1 John supports the view that every Christian sins, but Christians do not sin habitually (cf. Ignatius, *Ephesians* 14:2: "No one professing faith goes on sinning"). Those who sin as a matter of habit are of the devil who from the beginning sins continuously (cf. John 8:44). Again the argument must be directed against the progressives who are perfectionists, claiming sinlessness at the same time that their behavior does not manifest covenant loyalty.

Unit Three (3:8b–10) likewise begins with a christological premise: "The reason the Son of God appeared was to destroy the works of the devil" (v. 8b). That the appearing of the Son of God was for the purpose of destroying the works of the devil was a belief of the Johannine community (John 12:31). The expected corollaries of this christological conviction follow (vv. 9–10): positive ("Everyone who has been begotten of God does not habitually do sin"; cf. TEV, NIV) and negative ("Everyone who does not habitually do right is not of God, even the one not habitually loving his brother"; cf. TEV, NIV). The point of it all is explicit in v. 10a: "By this it may be seen who are the children of God, and who are the children of the devil." It is possible to distinguish who are the children of God and who are children of the devil *by what they do* (Ignatius, *Ephesians* 8:2: "Spiritual people cannot do carnal things"). Behavior is the evidence that "God's seed" (a reference either to the Spirit [John 14:17b: "he will be in you"] or to the Word [Justin Martyr, *1 Apology* 32:8: "Those who believe in him are people in whom there dwells the *sperma* of God, the Word"]) abides in one, that is, that one is born of God (v. 9b). How do people recognize whose spiritual child one is? By one's behavior! People act like their spiritual parent (cf. Matt 7:15–20, 21–23). Progressives take note!

The second subunit in the larger section of ethical exposition, 2:29–3:24a, is 3:11–24a. It is connected with what precedes by link phrases: love one's brother, 3:10b // love one another, 3:11; love the brethren, 3:14; love one another, 3:23. The unit is organized in the pattern

ABA'B'A"B" with the A components (vv. 11–12; 16–17; 23) being injunctions and the B components (vv. 14–15; 18–22; 24) beings signs.

> A   Injunction (vv. 11–13): We should love one another, as the message from the beginning said.
>
> B   Sign (vv. 14–15): Love of the brethren is the sign that we have passed from death to life.
>
> A'   Injunction (vv. 16–17): We ought to lay down our lives for the brethren, as Christ did for us.
>
> B'   Sign (vv. 18–22): Loving in deed and truth is the sign that we are of the truth.
>
> A"   Injunction (v. 23): We should believe in Jesus and love one another, as he commanded.
>
> B"   Sign (v. 24): Keeping the commandments is the sign of intimacy with God.

The thesis is that if one belongs to God one loves the brethren in deed and truth.

The first injunction, A, comes in vv. 11–13: positive ("This is the message which we heard from the beginning [of our Christian lives], that we should love [show covenant fidelity toward] one another," v. 11) and negative ("and not be like Cain who was of the evil one and murdered his brother," v. 12). From v. 11 we have confirmation that the instruction given new converts in the Johannine community included not only christological (2 John 7, 9; 1 John 2:24) but also ethical content (2 John 5–6). The content is traditional (T. Zebulon 8:5: "Whomever you see, do not harbor resentment, my children; love one another, and do not calculate the wrong done by each to his brothers"; T. Joseph: "love one another"; T. Simeon 4:7; T. Gad 6:1; Jubilees 36:8). The use of Cain in v. 12 also takes advantage of a traditional parenetic motif (T. Benjamin 7:5: "those who are like Cain in the envy and hatred of brothers"). V. 13 makes clear the identification of the progressives/perfectionists/lawless ones and the world for our author (remember 2:15a, upon which this identification sheds light).

The first sign, B, comes in vv. 14–15: positive ("We know that we have passed out of death into life, because we love the brethren," v. 14) and negative ("Everyone who hates his brother is a murderer, and you know that no murderer has eternal life abiding in him," v. 15; cf. Rev 21:8). V. 14 confirms that love for one's brother is the *evidence,* not the *basis* (John 5:24), for spiritual life. V. 15 echoes traditional parenesis (e.g., R. Eliezer ben Hyrcannus, a contemporary of the Johannine writers, said: "The one who hates his neighbor is among the shedders of blood," *Derek Eretz Rabba* 11.13 [57b]).

The second injunction, A', is given in vv. 16–17: positive ("He laid down his life for us, and we ought to lay down our lives for the brethren," v. 16) and negative ("But if anyone has the world's goods and sees his brother in need, yet closes his heart against him, how does God's love abide in him?" v. 17). That v. 16 sets Christ up as an example reflects a widespread tendency in early Christianity (e.g., John 13:12–15; 1 Cor 11:1; Rom 15:2–3; 2 Cor 8:9; Phil 2:3–11; 1 Tim 6:12–13; Heb 12:2–3; 1 Pet 2:21). If Christ's example is the way Christians know love, then failure to lay down one's life for a fellow Christian in need is the antithesis of covenant loyalty (love).

The second sign, B', is found in vv. 18–22. V. 19 ("By this we shall know that we are of the truth, and reassure our hearts before him whenever our hearts condemn us") is linked to v. 18 ("Little children, let us not love in word and speech but in deed and in truth"), so that "By this" refers to "loving in deed and truth." Loving in deed and truth is *evidence* that we are of the truth (cf. T. Gad 6:1–2: "Now, my children, each of you love his brother. . . . Love one another in deed and word and inward thoughts"; James 1:22; 2:15–16; Ignatius, *Ephesians* 14:2). If one has this assurance, then one can approach God in prayer with confidence and receive from him (vv. 21–22; cf. John 14:14; 15:16; 16:23).

The third injunction, A'' appears in v. 23: "This is his commandment, that we should believe in the name of his Son Jesus Christ and love one another, just as he commanded us." In the context there is a shifting back and forth between "commandments" (vv. 22, 24) and "commandment" (v. 23). There is either one commandment with two parts (believe; love) or there are two commandments (believe and love). Covenant thinking involves a vertical as well as a horizontal dimension (cf. Exod 20:3–11, vertical; Exod 20:12–17, horizontal).

The third sign, B'', appears in v. 24a: "All who keep his commandments abide in him, and he in them" (John 14:23). Keeping the commandments (believe; love) is the sign of intimacy with God. Again, the argument undercuts the progressives who have "gone ahead and do not abide in the doctrine about Christ" (2 John 9) and who have withdrawn from the Johannine community that is in fellowship with the eyewitnesses (1 John 2:19), violating in the process both the command to believe in Jesus Christ and to love (show covenant fidelity toward) one another.

1 John 3:24b–4:6

The second section of christological exposition comes in 3:24b–4:6. It is composed of an assertion made by the secessionists (3:24b), doubtless misapplying common belief of the community about the Spirit (John 14:17), followed by the Johannine qualification (4:1–6), connecting the misapplied part of the community's belief to the larger christological context (e.g., John 14:26; 15:26; 16:14).

> *The Secessionist Assertion* (3:24b): "By this we know that he abides in us, by the Spirit which he has given us."
>
> *The Johannine Qualification* (4:1–6)
>
> (1) Exhortation and Warning (4:1): "Test the spirits to see whether they are of God; for many false prophets have gone out into the world."
>
> (2) A Two-sided Christological Criterion for Testing Spirits (4:2–6)
>
>   (a) Does a spirit confess Jesus Christ come in the flesh? (4:2–3)
>
>   (b) Does a prophet listen to/remain in fellowship with (1:3) the bearers of the eyewitness tradition? (4:4–6)

The thesis of the thought unit is: the criterion for distinguishing true prophecy from false is christological. This section is connected to what precedes by link words ("believe in the name of his Son Jesus Christ," 3:23 // "confesses that Jesus Christ has come," 4:2).

The unit begins with a quotation of a secessionist assertion: "And by this we know that he is abiding in us, from the Spirit which he gave to us" (3:24b). The point is that inspiration is evidence of intimacy with God. Inspiration in this context refers to inspired prophetic utterance (cf. 4:1–3) such as one hears about elsewhere in early Christianity (e.g., 1 Cor 14:29–32; Acts 11:27–28; 21:10–11; Ignatius, *Philadelphians* 7:1–2). Some Gnostic teachers relied heavily on prophetic inspiration: e.g., Basilides appealed to the authority of the prophets Barcabbas and Barcoph (Eusebius, *Church History* 4.7.7); Isidore, Basilides' son, expounded the prophet Parchor (Clement of Alexandria, *Miscellanies* 6.6.53); and Apelles based his *Phaneroseis* on the revelations of a prophetess named Philoumene (Tertullian, *Prescription of Heretics* 6.6; 30:6; *On the Flesh of Christ* 6.1; Eusebius, *Church History* 5.13.2). In the Johannine letters it is the progressives who base everything on the Spirit (1 John 5:6–8: the water only, not the blood), using inspiration to subvert belief in the Incarnation. The absolute assertion of 3:24b, therefore, should most likely be understood as a statement of their position (cited by the author of 1 John before he presents his refutation, similar to Paul's procedure in 1 Cor 6:12, 13; 7:1b; 8:1b; 10:23).

What follows in 4:1–6 can only be regarded as a qualification of the assertion in 3:24b: "Beloved, do not believe every spirit, but test the spirits to see whether they are of God; for many false prophets have gone out into the world." Inspiration is not the criterion of truth! There are two spirits in the world (T. Judah 20:1–2: "Two spirits concern themselves with human beings: the spirit of truth and the spirit of deceit"; 1 QS 3:17–21: "God has appointed for human beings two spirits in which to walk until the time of his visitation: the spirits of truth and iniquity"; Eph 2:2–3: The prince of the power of the air is "that spirit which is now at work in the sons of disobedience"; 1 Tim 4:1: "In later times some will depart from the faith by giving heed to deceitful spirits and to the teaching of demons"). There is a demonic as well as a divine inspiration (cf. 1 Kings 22:22–24; 1 QH 4:7, 12–13; 1 Cor 12:1–3; 1 Thes 5:20–21; Didache 11–12; Hermas, *Mandate* 11; Pseudo-Clementine, *Homilies* 1.19.8; 2.6–11). It is necessary to test the spirits to see whether they are of God.

A two-sided criterion for testing the spirits is offered in vv. 2–3, 4–6. (a) The first side of the criterion to test the spirits is given in both positive and negative form: positive — "By this you know the Spirit of God: every spirit which confesses 'Jesus Christ having come and remaining in flesh' is of God" (v. 2); negative — "Every spirit which does not go on confessing 'Jesus' is not of God" (v. 3a). The key to understanding the positive form is the author's use of the perfect tense for "come." The Greek perfect indicates a completed action with a resulting state of being. The primary emphasis is on the resulting state of being (Ray Summers, *Essentials of New Testament Greek* [Nashville: Broadman, 1950], 103). Hence the confession about Jesus Christ is that he "has come and remains in the flesh" (remember 2 John 7, 9; 1 John 1:1; 5:6–8; Ignatius, *Smyrnaeans* 3:1: "He was in the flesh even after the resurrection"). The meaning is that Jesus Christ not only became flesh (John 1:14) but also that he continues in the flesh even after his resurrection (cf. John 20:17, 27). The negative form of the test is but an abbreviation of the positive ("Jesus" stands for "Jesus Christ having come and remaining in the flesh"). By this christological content true prophecy can be distinguished from false (cf. John 14:26; 15:26; 16:14).

There is an analogy here to Jewish experience. The fundamental doctrine of Judaism is monotheism. No utterance, however inspired, can contradict this principle and be regarded as true prophecy (Deut 13:1–5). The fundamental doctrine of Christianity is the Incarnation. No utterance, however inspired, that denies that Jesus Christ was in the flesh even after the resurrection can be regarded as true prophecy (C. H. Dodd, *The Johannine Epistles* [New York: Harper & Row, 1946], 102–3).

The other side of the christological criterion comes in vv. 4–6. (a) If one takes the "we" and the "us" of v. 6 to refer to the author and his readers, then this is an ecclesiastical criterion. The test of prophecy is its response to the message of the church. It is a possible reading but is not in line with the thought elsewhere in the letters. (b) If one takes the "we" as a reference either to the author (Elder?) and his associates whose authority derives from his connections with the tradition of the eyewitnesses or to the eyewitnesses themselves who are quoted here in a fragment of tradition from the same source as 1:1–5, then the test of truth or falsity rests on one's response to eyewitness tradition and the bearers of such tradition. Either of these possibilities is more in line with the overall thought of 2 and 1 John than that of (a). The point is: does a prophet listen to/remain in fellowship with (1:3) the bearers/interpreters of the eyewitness tradition (cf. John 15:27: "you also are witnesses because you have been with me from the beginning")? If so, the prophet is true; if not, the prophet is false, speaking out of the spirit of antichrist ("This is the spirit of antichrist, of which you heard that it was coming, and now it is in the world already," v. 3b).

What the eyewitnesses saw (1:1) is here expounded by means of a diatribe form (quotation of opponent's position, followed by the teacher's qualification of it). The content of the exposition dovetails with eyewitness testimony perfectly. Jesus Christ was in the flesh even after the resurrection (remember 1:1: "we touched"). Any prophecy of the progressives to the contrary is false.

PERFECT LOVE
AND
PROPER BELIEF

---

1 John 4:7–12; 4:13–16a;
4:16b–5:4a; 5:4b–12

The author's (Elder's?) exposition (1:6–5:12) of the eyewitnesses' proclamation (1:1–5) alternates between ethical and christological sections. At the beginning of the letter the sections were longer (e.g., 1:6–2:17, 2:29–3:24a – ethical; 2:18–28, 3:24b–4:6 – christological); toward the end they become briefer (e.g., 4:7–12, 4:16b–5:4a – ethical; 4:13–16a, 5:4b–12 – christological). Because of their increasing brevity, it is possible to treat four sections together, two ethical (4:7–12; 4:16b–5:4a) and two christological (4:13–16a; 5:4b–12). They will be taken up in the order they appear in 1 John.

1 John 4:7–12

1 John 4:7–12 is a thought unit focused on ethical exposition. It is connected with what precedes by means of the link phrase *ek tou theou* / "of God" (vv. 4, 6a, 6b // vv. 7a, 7b). The theme is: a criterion to determine whether or not one is born of God/knows God. Its thesis is that the one who loves is born of God and knows God. This section is composed of two paragraphs (4:7–8; 4:9–12), each of which contains two components: (1) an exhortation and (2) a basis in two parts, the first ontological, the second experiential.

Unit One

Exhortation (4:7a): "Let us love one another."

Basis in two parts, a and b (4:7b–8), in chiastic form

a   *for* love is of God (v. 7b)

    b   so the one who loves is born of God and knows God (v. 7c)

    b′   The one who does not love does not know God (v. 8a)

a′   *for* God is love (v. 8b).

Unit Two

Basis (first part, 4:9–10), in parallelism

a   "*In this* the love of God was made manifest, that God sent his only Son into the world, so that we might live through him" (v. 9).

a′   "*In this* is love, not that we loved God but that he loved us and sent his Son to be the expiation for our sins" (v. 10).

Exhortation (4:11)

    "Beloved, if God so loved us, we also ought to love one another."

Basis (second part, 4:12)

    b   "If we love one another, God abides in us."

The unit 4:7–8 begins with the first component, the exhortation (v. 7a): "Beloved, let us love [show covenant fidelity toward] one another" (cf. T. Joseph 17:2: "love one another"). If you think you have heard this before, you are right (remember 2 John 5–6; 1 John 3:11, 14, 23). The ontological basis for the exhortation is given in two parts: positive ("for love is of God, and everyone who loves has been begotten of God and knows God, v. 7b) and negative ("The one who does not love does not know God, because God is love," v. 8). The affirmation "God is love," like that of "God is light" (1:5), refers not to God's essence but to God's relations with humans. All God's activity in relation to us is loving. God is the origin of love. It is out of this ground (God's love) that love arises in and among those begotten by God. Love's presence or absence is indicative of one's knowledge or lack of knowledge of God. Remember, the author is talking about people within the boundaries of alleged Christian profession, and the issue is how to evaluate such profession, discerning which is true and which is false. The author is not dealing with the larger question of why those outside the bounds of Christian profession sometimes manifest love.

The unit 4:9–12 follows an ABA' pattern: A – experiential basis (vv. 9–10), B – exhortation (v. 11), A' – experiential basis (v. 12). We may consider the components in this order. A, vv. 9–10, the first part of the basis, is given in parallelism. (1) "*In this* the love of God was made manifest, that God sent his only Son into the world, so that we might live through him" (v. 9; cf. John 3:16). Here God's love is manifest in the sending of his only (*monogenēs*) Son. (a) That the Son was sent by God is heard again in John 3:17 (cf. Rom 8:3; Gal 4:4–5). The background for the notion is probably Jewish (e.g., Exod 23:20: God sent his angel; Wisdom of Solomon 9:10, 17: God sent his Wisdom/Holy Spirit; Philo, *On Husbandry* 51, and *On the Confusion of Tongues* 145–48: God sent the Logos/the firstborn Son). The emphasis is on God's initiative. (b) In the LXX, the Hebrew term *yahid* (single, only) is sometimes translated by the Greek *agapētos* (beloved, Gen 22:2, 12, 16) and sometimes by the Greek *monogenēs* (Judg 11:34). In the New Testament *monogenēs* is used for only children (Lk 7:12; 8:42; 9:38; Heb 11:17) and for God's Son (John 1:14, 18; 3:16, 18; 1 John 4:9). The emphasis is on the Son's uniqueness, his being the only one of his kind (Dale Moody, "God's Only Son: The Translation of John 3:16 in the Revised Standard Version," *JBL* 72 [1953] 213–19).

(2) *In this* is love, not that we loved God but that he loved us and sent his Son to be the atoning sacrifice for our sins" (v. 10). Here God's love is defined by the death of his Son as an "atoning sacrifice" (*hilasmos* – remember 2:2) for sin. The nature of God's love is seen in the sending of his Son and in his Son's death as an atonement for our sins. That is, God's love is one that takes the initiative in seeking a relation with us even at great cost to himself. That relation is secured only when a price has been paid by the offended one (propitiation) and a change has been effected in the offending one (expiation), that is, when an "atoning sacrifice" has been offered.

B, v. 11, the exhortation, builds on vv. 9–10 and their affirmations about the nature of God's love: "Beloved, if God so loved us, we also ought to love one another." Love is not only a gift; it is also a duty. The love command is not an optional extra (R. E. Brown, *The Epistles of John* [Garden City, N.Y.: Doubleday, 1982], 245).

A', v. 12, offers the second part of the experiential basis for the preceding exhortation: "No one has ever seen God; if we love one another God abides in us and his love is perfected in us." The invisibility of God is rooted in Jewish tradition (Exod 33:2, 23; Deut 4:12; Sirach 43:31; Josephus, *War* 7.8.7 §346) and Johannine conviction (John 1:18; 5:37; 6:46;

1 John 4:20). Certain Jewish (e.g., T. Levi 5:1–2) and early Christian (e.g., Rev 4:2–3; 5:1) circles held the belief that one could be transported up to the heavens and behold God on his throne. It may be that 1 John 4:12a is a defense against such claims by the progressives (cf. John 3:13). Such sight is reserved for the parousia (1 John 3:2); in the meantime, God is seen in the person of his Son (John 1:18; 14:9: "Anyone who has seen me has seen the Father") and his love is made visible in Christians in whom he abides and who love each other (1 John 4:12b). The polemical thrust is against progressives. It is not mystical vision but covenant fidelity that matters.

The twofold exhortation ("Love one another," vv. 7a, 11) is based upon an ontological ("God is love," v. 8b) and an experiential (God sent his Son as an atoning sacrifice for our sins, v. 10; God abides in us, v. 12) ground. Those who manifest love (covenant loyalty) give evidence that they are born of God and know God.

1 John 4:13–16a

1 John 4:13–16a is a small thought unit whose focus is on christology and which parallels 3:24b–4:6 in form and content. Its theme is: the criterion by which to evaluate all claims about the Spirit. It is composed, like 3:24b–4:6, of a secessionist assertion (4:13) followed by a Johannine qualification (4:14–16a) that appeals to eyewitness tradition (v. 14) in support of orthodox christological confession (v. 15).

> *The Secessionist Assertion* (4:13): "By this we know that we abide in him and he in us, because he has given us of his own Spirit."
>
> *The Johannine Qualification* (4:14–16a)
>
> (1) A two-sided christological criterion for testing the spirits (vv. 14–15)
>
>   (a) Does one's position agree with the eyewitness tradition? (v. 14)
>
>   (b) Does one's position agree with the confession, "Jesus is the Son of God"? (v. 15)
>
> (2) A concluding assurance (v. 16a): "So we know and believe the love God has for us."

It is connected with what precedes by means of a link phrase ("God sent his only Son into the world," 4:9;" God sent his Son," 4:10 // "the Father has sent his Son," 4:14).

In 4:13 one meets virtually the same assertion found in 3:24b: "By this we know that we abide in him and he in us, because he has given us of his own Spirit." Again, this is an all encompassing, absolute assertion. The *one* evidence of intimacy with God is possession of the Spirit (of prophecy?). Given the stance of the progressives in the Johannine epistles, this may be taken as a quotation of one of their assertions (cf. 1:6, 8, 10; 2:4, 6, 9, for other quoted assertions of the opponents). The only other viable alternative would be to take this as the author's statement of a general principle that needs the qualification that follows. Either way, what is said here is severely qualified in the verses that follow.

The Johannine qualification follows in vv. 14–16a. It consists of a two-sided christological criterion for testing the spirits (vv. 14–15) and a concluding assurance (v. 16a). The two-sided christological criterion reminds one of 4:2–6. (1) Does one's position agree with the eyewitness tradition? "And we have seen and testify that the Father has sent his Son as Savior of the world" (v. 14)? The language is similar to that of 1:1–5. The "we" refers to the actual eyewitnesses of the life of Jesus on earth (A. E. Brooke, *A Critical and Exegetical Commentary on the Johannine Epistles* [Edinburgh: T. & T. Clark, 1912], 121); so the author must be quoting a fragment of the eyewitness tradition, with which the readers would have been familiar, just as in 1:1–5. This corresponds to the earlier argument in 4:6a. (2) Does one's position agree with the confession, "Jesus is the Son of God"? "Whoever confesses that Jesus is the Son of God, God abides in him, and he in God" (v. 15). Note the direct contrast between v. 15 and v. 13. How do we know that we abide in him and he in us: by the Spirit or by the confession of Christ? This stance corresponds to that found earlier in 4:2. The issue, then, is whether or not a spirit confesses that the Savior is incarnate in an ongoing way in the human Jesus. If it does, then it is the Spirit of God; if not, then it is not of God. A concluding assurance brings the small unit to an end: "And we know and believe the love which God has in us" (v. 16a). Experience testifies that those who make the correct christological confession of the community are the ones who know the love (covenant fidelity) of God.

1 John 4:16b–5:4

1 John 4:16b–5:4a is a thought unit focused on ethical exposition with some similarities to 4:7–12 in its content. Its theme is: the criterion to determine whether one has an intimate relationship with God. Its thesis is that a relation with God yields love of one's brother. The section falls

into an ABA′ B′ pattern, with A and A′ being assertions (4:16b–19; 5:1) and B and B′ being statements about implications (4:20–21; 5:2–4a).

> A   Assertion (4:16b–19)
> God is love, and those who abide in love abide in God, and God abides in them. We love because he first loved us.
>
>> B   Implication (4:20–21) using an adversary statement (cf. 1:6, 8, 10)
>> If anyone says, "I love God," and hates his neighbor, he is a liar; . . . And this commandment we have from him, that he who loves God should love his brother also.
>
> A′   Assertion (5:1) using *pas ho* + participle (cf. 3:3, 4, 6, 9, 10)
> Everyone who loves the parent (God) loves the child (other Christian).
>
>> B′   Implication (5:2–4a)
>> By this (the principle given in 5:1 above), we know that whenever we love God we love the children of God.

This unit is connected with what precedes by means of link phrases ("God abides in him," 4:15//4:16b, "and love God has for us" / "God is love," 4:16a//4:16b).

A, 4:16b–19, is an assertion with familiar content: "God is love [cf. v. 8b], and those who abide in love abide in God, and God abides in them [v. 16b; cf. v. 12b]. . . . We love, because he first loved us [v. 19; cf. v. 10; Odes of Solomon 3:3: "For I should not have known how to love the Lord, if he had not continuously loved me")." The reality to which the assertion points (that we abide in God and God in us) has a corollary: "In this [the reality of mutual indwelling] love is perfected with us, in order that we may have confidence in the day of judgment, because as he is [John 17:21: "thou, Father, art in me, and I in Thee"] so are we in the world ["we abide in God and he in us"]. There is no fear in love, but perfect love casts out fear. For fear has to do with punishment, and the one who fears is not perfected in love" (vv. 17–18). The mutual indwelling of God and believer, like that of the Father and the Son, is the perfection of love. Because of such a relationship, the believer has no fear when contemplating facing God on the day of judgment (cf. Rom 8:31–39). The one who will be our judge is the one who first loved us and who abides in us and we in him.

B, 4:20–21, offers the implication of the preceding assertion about our loving relationship with God, using an adversary statement (cf. 1:6, 8, 10): "If anyone says, 'I love God,' and hates his brother, he is a liar [cf. 2:4]; for he who does not love his brother whom he has seen, cannot love

God whom he has not seen [cf. 4:12a]. And this is the commandment we have from him, that the one who loves God should love his brother also" [cf. 3:23–24; T. Dan 5:3: "Throughout all your life love the Lord, and one another with a true heart"). Although love for God is not the same as love for the brother, love for God (vertical covenant fidelity) cannot be divorced from love of the brother (horizontal covenant fidelity) because the latter is part of the former in covenant thinking (cf. Exod 20 where the second half of the decalogue is a part of Israel's covenant loyalty to Yahweh just as is the first half).

A', 5:1, is another assertion, this time using *pas ho* ("everyone who" + a participle; cf. 3:3, 4, 6, 9, 10): "everyone who loves the parent [God] loves the child [i.e., everyone who believes that Jesus is the Christ]." Here is a proverbial maxim (If you love me you will love my child) interpreted in a Christian vein so that God is the parent and other Christians are the children.

B', 5:2–4a, states the implication of 5:1. "By this" of v. 2 points back to v. 1 (so Dodd, *Johannine Epistles* 125; Marshall, *Epistles of John*, 227) rather than forward to what follows (as Stephen S. Smalley, *Word Biblical Commentary: 1, 2, 3 John* [Waco: Word, 1984], 268): "by this" refers to the maxim of v. 1 (If you love the parent, you will love the child). "By this [the principle given in v. 1] we know that we love the children of God whenever we love God and keep his commandments." If "by this" is taken to refer to what follows, it yields a meaning out of step with Johannine thought: namely, the evidence of our love for other Christians is the fact of our love for God and the keeping of his commandments. If "by this" is taken to refer back to the maxim of v. 1, then the thought is in line with Johannine theology: namely, our love for fellow Christians is evidence of our love for God (as in 3:17–19). To love God is to keep his commandments. "For this is the love that has God as its object, that we keep his commandments" (v. 3a; Exod 20:6b: "those who love me and keep my commandments"), that is, believe on Jesus and love one another (3:23; 4:21). "And his commandments are not burdensome" (v. 3b; cf. Matt 11:28–30; contrast Matt 23:4; Philo, *On the Special Laws* 1.55 § 299: "God asks nothing from you that is burdensome or complicated or difficult, but only something quite simple and easy"). The unit concludes with a summary statement: "For whatever is born of God overcomes the world" (v. 4a). Since the author identifies the progressives who are lawless with the world (3:13), to assume that the readers keep the commandments (v. 3) is equivalent to saying that they have overcome the world and its lawlessness because they have been born of God (3:9). Throughout the entire thought unit (4:16b–5:4a), our author has pursued the thesis: a relation with God yields love of one's fellow Christian.

1 John 5:4b–12

1 John 5:4b–12 is a thought unit with a christological focus. Its theme is the christological faith of the Johannine community that enables victory over the world. This section falls into two units (5:4b–8 and 5:9–12), each of which is built around a thesis (vv. 4b–5; v. 9a) and an explanation (vv. 6–8; vv. 9b–12).

> *Unit One* (5:4b–8)
>
> Thesis (vv. 4b–5): The christological faith of the Johannine community enables the victory over the world.
>
> Explanation (vv. 6–8)
> (1) This is he who came by water and blood, Jesus Christ; not with the water only but with the water and the blood (v. 6).
>
> (2) The Spirit is the one who bears witness. There are three witnesses, the Spirit, the water, and the blood; and these three agree (vv. 7–8).
>
> *Unit Two* (5:9–12)
>
> Thesis (v. 9a): The testimony of God is greater than that of humans.
>
> Explanation (vv. 9b–12):
> (1) This is the testimony of God that ... (vv. 9b–10)
>   The one who believes ...
>   The one who does not believe ...
>
> (2) This is the testimony that God ... (vv. 11–12)
>   The one who has the Son ...
>   The one who has not the Son ...

This section is connected with what precedes by means of a link phrase ("overcomes the world," 5:4a//5:4b, 5).

The first unit, 5:4b–8, begins with a thesis. The christological faith of the Johannine community enables the victory over the world ("And this is the victory that overcomes the world, our faith. Who is it that overcomes the world but the one who goes on believing that Jesus is the Son of God"). Christians overcome the world because of their faith in the one who himself overcame the world (John 16:33; Rev 5:5).

An explanation follows in vv. 6–8 to make explicit what is involved in confessing Jesus as Son of God. There are two parts to the explanation. (1) "This is he who came by water and blood Jesus Christ; not with the water only but with the water and the blood" (v. 6). The sentence implies that the author's opponents believe that he came "by water only" but that the proper community confession holds that he came "by water and blood." The focus here is upon the historical reality of the Son of God, not his continuing presence in the church. The reference, therefore, is not to the sacraments but to the water of John's baptism at which time the Spirit descended and remained upon Jesus (John 1:33–34; cf. T. Levi 18:7: "The Spirit will rest upon him in the water") and to the blood of Jesus' death (John 19:34). The progressives focus exclusively on the water, the author insists on both water and blood (M. C. de Boer, "Jesus the Baptizer: 1 John 5:5–8 and the Gospel of John," *JBL* 107 [1988]: 87–106).

The closest parallels to what is described here are found among those Gnostics who contend that at his baptism the heavenly Christ descended upon the human Jesus but that the Christ departed from the human Jesus before the crucifixion. (1) Irenaeus, *Against Heresies* 1.26.1, describes the christology of Cerinthus in this way:

> Moreover, after his baptism, Christ descended upon him in the form of a dove from the Supreme Ruler, and that he proclaimed the unknown Father, and performed miracles. But at the last Christ departed from Jesus, and that Jesus suffered and rose again, while Christ remained impassible, inasmuch as he was a spiritual being.

Here the death of a divine being is believed to be impossible.

The Mediterranean world had long held that gods cannot suffer. Aristophanes' play *The Frogs* (632ff.) involves a dispute over which of two travellers is a god and which is his slave. It is decided to settle the matter by finding out which one can feel pain.

> You should flog him well,
> For if he is a god he won't feel it.
> Whichever of us two you first behold
> Flinching or crying out — he's not the god.

It is no surprise, then, to find a late first-century Jewish Christian Gnostic like Cerinthus saying that although the spiritual Christ descended upon Jesus at his baptism, before Jesus suffered and died at the end of his career the spiritual Christ withdrew and ascended back into heaven. For the Hellenistic world, a god could not suffer pain and could not die. Such was impossible.

(2) Irenaeus, *Against Heresies* 1.30.12–13, gives the christological views of the Sethian-Ophites as follows:

Christ united with Sophia descended into him, and thus Jesus Christ was produced. . . .

When he was led away to death, they say that the Christ himself, along with Sophia, departed from him into the state of an incorruptible Aeon, while Jesus was crucified.

(3) Irenaeus, *Against Heresies* 3.11.1, speaks about Gnostics who claimed that "the Christ from above . . . who also continued impassible, descend(ed) upon Jesus . . . and flew back again into his Pleroma."

(4) The *Second Treatise of Seth* from Nag Hammadi reflects a similar christology:

I visited a bodily dwelling. I cast out the one who was in it first, and I went in. . . . He was an earthly man, but I, I am from above the heavens. (7.51.20–7.52.3)

They struck me with the reed; it was another, Simon, who bore the cross on his shoulder. (7.56.8–11)

(5) The *Testimony of Truth* from Nag Hammadi also has this view of Jesus' baptism:

But the Son of Man came forth from Imperishability, being alien to defilement. He came to the world by the Jordan river. . . . And John bore witness to the descent of Jesus. For he was the one who saw the power which came down upon the Jordan river. (9.30.19–29)

(6) Irenaeus, *Against Heresies* 1.24.3–6, describes the christological positions of Basilides, including his contention that Christ did not suffer because he assumed the form of Simon of Cyrene, causing Simon to be crucified in his place. Basilides' conclusion is relevant:

Those, then, who know these things have been freed from the principalities who formed the world; so that it is not incumbent on us to confess him who was crucified, but him who came in the form of a man, and was thought to be crucified. . . . If anyone, therefore, he [Basilides] declares, confesses the crucified, that man is still a slave, and under the power of those who formed our bodies; but he who denies him has been freed from these beings, and is acquainted with the dispensation of the unborn father.

Here death implies bondage to Fate and so a Savior could save only if he did not die. For a Savior, death was impossible.

Although one cannot say that the progressives of the Johannine epistles are to be identified with any one of these individuals or groups, the positions these Gnostics espouse are similar to that implied in 1 John

5:6. If so, then it is clear why the author of 2 and 1 John emphasizes that Jesus Christ was in the flesh even after the resurrection (2 John 7; 1 John 1:1; 4:2). The position of the progressives robbed the death of Jesus of its soteriological power. At most, for them Jesus was a prototype of their experience with the Spirit. They likely understood Jesus' experience of the Spirit in connection with the water of John's baptism as did the author of the Odes of Solomon 36:6. There Christ speaks of God's acts toward him through the Spirit: "He anointed me with his perfection; and I became one of those who are near him." When the progressives, like Christ, had experienced the Spirit, they had no further use for him. Their knowledge of God was then direct, as his had been. They had no need for a mediator or an intercessor.

In the second-century *Apocryphon of James* from Nag Hammadi 11 there is a dialogue between two disciples and the resurrected Christ that parallels what may have been the claim of the progressives to direct knowledge of God. Jesus says to his disciples, James and Peter, "I will intercede on your behalf with the Father, and he will forgive you much." The disciples become glad. Jesus, however, tells them that the true Gnostic does not need an intercessor but can speak to God freely without a mediator. "Blessed will they be who have spoken out and obtained grace for themselves. . . . Do you perhaps think that the Father . . . grants remission to one on another's behalf?" (remember 2:1–2).

For our author, however, only if the Son of God died for our sins is there an atoning sacrifice from which we benefit and a basis for Jesus Christ's heavenly intercession on our behalf. Hence the emphasis on both the water and the blood. The first part of the explanation maintains that our christological faith includes not only that the Spirit descended and remained on Jesus in connection with the water of John's baptism (John 1:33–34), but also that Jesus Christ died (John 19:34).

(2) The second part of the explanation of the thesis of vv. 4b–5 comes in vv. 7–8. The KJV of 1 John 7–8 reads:

> For there are three that bear record [in heaven, the Father, the Word, and the Holy Ghost: and these three are one. And there are three that bear witness in earth], the spirit, and the water, and the blood: and these three agree in one.

The words enclosed in brackets are omitted from the RSV and other reliable translations. They occur in only two late Greek manuscripts, and in each case the absence of articles betrays the Latin origin of the text. They were absent from the Old Latin text used by Tertullian, Cyprian, and Augustine, and also from Jerome's Vulgate. They were first quoted as part of 1 John by the Spanish heretic Priscillian (d. 385). At a later date they were accepted into the Vulgate and then into the Complutensian Polyglot of 1514. Although Erasmus excluded them from his Greek New Testament of 1516, he promised to include them if one Greek manuscript could be found with them. When the late Codex Britannicus was produced, he reluctantly made the disputed words part of his edition of 1522. The questionable words were accepted by Stephanus and thereby found their way into the Textus Receptus and the KJV (G. B. Caird, *IDB*, 2:952). The correct text of vv. 7–8 is reflected in the RSV, NIV, TEV, NEB, JB, and NAB.

In the correct text there are two components (v. 7; v. 8). The first, v. 7, is an absolute claim related to the Spirit: "And the Spirit is the witness, because the Spirit is the truth" (cf. 3:24b; 4:13). The second, v. 8, functions as a qualification of v. 7: "There are three witnesses, the Spirit, the water, and the blood; and these three agree." Either one may take v. 7 as an assertion of the progressives, following up on "by water only," which must be qualified in v. 8, or v. 7 is a general proposition of the community that must be clarified in v. 8. Either way, v. 8 offers the specifics of how the Spirit is a witness to an Incarnation that continues on through Jesus' death. Whereas the progressives claimed that their experience of the Spirit, following the prototypical experience of Jesus connected with the water of John's baptism, validated their emphasis on "water only," the author of 1 John contends that the three witnesses — water, blood, and Spirit — agree in a way that buttresses his inclusion of blood along with water in a proper understanding of the Incarnation. Why is this so?

It was in connection with the water of John's baptism that the Spirit descended and remained on Jesus so that he is the one who baptizes with the Holy Spirit, the Son of God (John 1:33–34). But it is only after the glorification of Jesus (which includes his death) that he gives the Spirit (John 7:39; 16:7; 20:22). The Spirit is a witness to the fact that Jesus is the baptizer with the Holy Spirit; the Spirit is also a witness to the salvific effects of Jesus' death because the Spirit was not given until after Jesus was glorified. The experience of the Spirit agrees with the facts of the tradition. Spirit, water, and blood agree as witnesses to christological reality.

Unit two, vv. 9–12, begins with a thesis (v. 9a): "If we receive human testimony, the testimony of God is greater." Here is a fourth witness added to the three of vv. 7–8. The testimony of God is the Christian's experienced eternal life, referred to in v. 11 (R. E. Brown, *The Epistles of John*, 587). An

explanation of the thesis comes in two parts with similar arrangements
(vv. 9b–10; vv. 11–12). (1) The first part, vv. 9b–10, runs:

> This is the testimony of God that he has borne and continues to bear
> [perfect tense]) witness to his Son.
> Those who believe in the Son of God *have the testimony in them-
> selves.*
> Those who do not believe God have made him a liar (1:10), because
> they have not believed in the testimony that God has borne to his
> Son.

(2) The second part, vv. 11–12, reads:

> This is the testimony, that *God gave us eternal life,* and this life is in
> his Son.
> Those who have the Son have life.
> Those who do not have the Son do not have life.

Who is it that overcomes the world? It is the one who believes that Jesus
is the Son of God. This means belief in an Incarnation that continues
through Jesus' death. This belief is supported both by tradition (water
and blood) and by experience (Spirit and experienced eternal life). For
the author of the Johannine epistles, the faith that overcomes the world
is one that includes christological content as well as commitment.

BASES FOR CHRISTIAN
CONFIDENCE

1 John 5:13, 14–21

1 John 5:13

1 John 5:13 is a statement of the document's purpose (cf. John 20:30–31). It is connected with the preceding section by means of a link word: to have "life," 5:12//5:13. Just as is the case with the Fourth Gospel, the statement of purpose is followed by a postscript (John 20:30–31 + chapter 21; 1 John 5:13 + 5:14–21). The statement of purpose (5:13) is connected with the postscript that follows (5:14–21) by means of a link word: "know," v. 13//vv. 15, 18, 19, 20.

What is the purpose of 1 John? "I write these things to you who continue to believe [present participle] in the name of the Son of God in order that you may know that you continue to have [present tense] eternal life." (a) The "name of the Son of God" is Jesus (1:7; 4:15; 5:5; cf. 2:22; 5:1) or Jesus Christ (1:3; 3:23; 5:20). (b) To believe in the name of the Son of God (3:23) = to confess that Jesus is the Son of God (4:15) = to believe that Jesus is the Son of God (5:5) = to believe that Jesus is the Christ (5:1) = to confess that Jesus Christ has come and remains in the flesh (4:2; cf. 2 John 7) = to believe that Jesus Christ came with the water and the blood (5:6) = to continue to believe that Jesus Christ was in the flesh even after the resurrection. 1 John is written to Christians who continue to believe that Jesus Christ was in the flesh through his passion. The document, then, is not written to persuade unbelievers. (c) "In order that you [the believers] may know" points to the intention of reassuring believers. (d) "That you continue to have eternal life" implies some uncertainty on the part of the readers about the matter. The progressives who have "gone ahead" and "no longer abide in the doctrine about Christ" (2 John 9) apparently claimed to possess "knowledge" (1 John 2:4) needed by their non-progressive counterparts (2:20). The author counters such claims by saying not only that all Johannine Christians have been anointed by the Spirit and, consequently, all know (2:20), but also that only the Spirit that confesses Jesus Christ having come and remaining in the flesh is of God (4:2). The bottom line for the author is that only a faith that is correct christologically gives life (R. E. Brown, *The Epistles of John* [Garden City, N.Y.: Doubleday, 1982], 632). Since the Johannine Christians continue to believe in the one who came and remains in the flesh, they can be sure that they continue to have eternal life. Like the Fourth Gospel (20:30–31: "these are written so that you may go on believing that Jesus is the Christ, the Son of God, and that going on believing you may go on having life in his name"), 1 John is written to confirm Christians in the apostolic faith. Coming at the end of the controversy, when the progressives had already become secessionists, the author is not trying to persuade them. Instead, he attempts to keep in the fold the Johannine Christians who still remain in fellowship with the eyewitnesses and their tradition (Judith M. Lieu, "Authority to Become Children of God: A Study of 1 John," *NovT* 23 [1981]: 210–28).

1 John 5:14–21 is a thought unit held together by an inclusion (eternal life, v. 13 and v. 20) and by the repetition of four "we know" statements (vv. 15, 18, 19, 20). The first and fourth "we know" statements have an exhortation or its equivalent attached (vv. 16–17 and v. 21), yielding an ABB′A′ pattern based on formal considerations.

A   First "we know" (vv. 14–15) + exhortation equivalent
     (vv. 16–17)

>   (1) We know that God hears us when we ask according to his
>   will and grants our requests.

>   (2) So pray for a brother who has committed other than a sin
>   unto death and God will give him life.

B   Second "we know" (v. 18)
     Anyone born of God does not habitually sin but is kept by
     God from the evil one.

B′ Third "we know" (v. 19)
     We are "of God" but the world is "of the evil one."

A′ Fourth "we know" (v. 20) + exhortation (v. 21)

>   (1) We know we know God and are in his Son.

>   (2) Keep yourselves from idols.

The postscript gives certain basic assurances of the Johannine community and offers two suggestions about consequent behavior.

A (vv. 14–17) consists of the first "we know" (vv. 14–15) and an equivalent to an exhortation (vv. 16–17). (1) "And this is the confidence [3:21;
4:17] which we have in him, that if we ask anything according to his will
he hears us. And if *we know* that he hears us in whatever we ask, *we
know* that we have obtained the requests made of him" (vv. 14–15). Here
common Christian conviction yields confidence in prayer. The conviction
is that, given certain conditions, the Christian receives a favorable hearing (to hear = to hear favorably; cf. John 9:31; 11:41–42) by God and is
granted the requests made. There are often preconditions for answered
prayer specified in the Johannine writings: (a) "If you ask anything in
my name, I will do it," John 14:14; "whatever you ask the Father in my
name, he may give it to you," 15:16; "if you ask anything of the Father,
he will give it to you in my name," 16:23; (b) "If you abide in me, and
my words abide in you, ask whatever you will, and it shall be done for
you," 15:7; (c) "We receive from him whatever we ask, because we keep
his commandments and do what pleases him," 1 John 3:22; (d) "If we
ask anything according to his will he hears us," 1 John 5:14. These various conditions are virtual synonyms. Since, according to early Christian
parenesis, one can be sure that it is God's will that Christians pray for
one another and attempt to bring erring brethren back from the error of
their ways when they stray (James 5:16, 19–20; 1 Clement 56:1; 59:2), the
Johannine community can have confidence to pray for fellow Christians
when they sin.

(2) "If at a given moment anyone should see his brother sinning a sin
not unto death, let him ask [future tense functioning as an imperative]),
and God will give life to him, that is, to those not sinning unto death.
There is sin unto death; I am not saying that one is to pray for that. All
wrongdoing is sin, but there is sin which is not unto death" (vv. 16–17).
(a) Intercession (one person's praying for another) has deep roots in the
Jewish and Christian tradition (e.g., Gen 18:27–33; 20:7; Exod 32:11–14,
31–32; 34:8–9; Num 14:13–19; 2 Kings 19:4; Jer 37:3; 42:2; Amos 7:1–6;
2 Macc 7:37–38; 15:14; 4 Macc 6:28–29; 17:21–22; 2 Esdras 7:102–15;
T. Reuben 1:7; T. Judah 19:2; T. Benjamin 3:6–7: "Joseph also urged our
father to pray for his brothers that the Lord would not hold them accountable for their sin which they so wickedly committed against him";
10:1; T. Gad 5:9; 2 Enoch 64:4; Assumption of Moses 1:17; 12:6; Lk 22:23;
John 17; Phil 1:19; 2 Thes 3:1; 1 Tim 2:1–2). Based on the confidence that
intercession for an erring Christian is according to God's will, the readers are asked to pray for the member of the community who, at a given
moment, is seen sinning.

(b) There is an exception. The author does not command the community to intercede for "sin unto death" (John 17:9; 1 John 4:5). In spite of Origen's pessimism (*Homilies on Exodus* 10.3: "What kinds of sins . . . are sins unto death . . . cannot, I think, easily be determined by any man"), understanding of this difficult text is possible. The notion of a mortal sin or sin unto death is found in post-biblical Judaism in documents that otherwise often have parallels with the Johannine epistles. In T. Issachar 7:1, the patriarch says: "I am one hundred twenty two years old, and I am not aware of having committed a sin unto death." From the context we learn what he did not do and what he did do: he did not commit adultery (7:2–3a), covet (7:3b), bear false witness (7:4), or steal (7:5c), but rather he loved the Lord (7:6b) and loved every human being (7:6c). In Jubilees one hears that in some cases sinners act so outrageously that they are cut off and left without pardon: e.g., as in 15:34 when some will not circumcise their sons.

> And great wrath from the Lord will be upon the sons of Israel because they have *left his covenant* and have turned aside from his words. And they have . . . *made themselves like the gentiles* to be removed and uprooted from the land. And there is therefore for them *no forgiveness or pardon* so that they might be pardoned and forgiven from all of the sins of this eternal error.

Such sin usually combines both a particular *content* and a *habit*. Its content is a violation of covenant stipulations (e.g., sabbath violation, killing, stealing, adultery, bearing false witness, coveting, incest) or is a rejection of the sign of the covenant (circumcision). It usually, although not always, involves repeated violations. Such behavior amounts to a forsaking of the covenant, to becoming like the gentiles (those outside the covenant), that is, to apostasy. The author of 1 John also speaks of a sin unto death. Likely this is the Christian equivalent to the repudiation of circumcision in a Jewish context or to the explicit and habitual violation of covenant fidelity in one's relations with other members of the community. It is the Christian equivalent to the apostasy from Judaism described by the Testaments of the Twelve Patriarchs and the Book of Jubilees. Of course, in the context of the Johannine epistles this would amount to progressing beyond christological orthodoxy (cf. John 8:24: "you will die in your sins unless you believe that I am he") and seceding from the community in fellowship with the eyewitnesses and their tradition (cf. 1 John 3:23). For the author of 1 John, to be a progressive and a secessionist is as surely a repudiation of the new covenant as was refusal to circumcise one's sons or deliberate and habitual violation of the decalogue apostasy from Judaism.

B (v. 18) is the second "we know": "We know that everyone one who has been begotten by God [perfect tense] does not make a habit of sinning [present tense], but the one begotten [aorist tense] by God keeps him, and the evil one does not touch him." (a) The use of the present tense to emphasize that a Christian does not continually sin (cf. TEV, NIV) recalls the argument in 3:6, 9. Unlike the progressives who claim perfection but live in darkness, the Johannine community knows that although Christians are not sinless they will not sin habitually. (b) The second part of the sentence is unclear on several counts. First, is "the one begotten by God" Christ or the Christian? In favor of Christ is the fact that John 17:12 says Jesus keeps his disciples (cf. Rev 3:10; but John 17:12 says the Father keeps the disciples safe from the evil one). Against Christ is the fact that nowhere in the Johannine epistles or in the Fourth Gospel is Jesus described as begotten of God. No Greek manuscript supports the third person singular variant reading in John 1:13, which would make Jesus the one begotten by God. In the Johannine literature it is Christians who are begotten by God (John 1:13; 3:5; 1 John 3:9; 5:18a). Moreover, it is Christians who overcome the evil one (1 John 2:13, 14). On balance, Christian should be preferred (R. E. Brown, *The Epistles of John*, 622).

Second, does the Christian who is begotten of God keep "him" (another Christian who has strayed, cf. v. 16) or "himself" (cf. 2:13, 14)? One textual tradition reads "himself" (*heauton;* so Sinaiticus, the corrector of Alexandrinus, the Byzantine tradition, the Peshitta, Sahidic, Armenian, by Origen and other fathers), another has "him" (*auton;* so the original hand of Alexandrinus, Vaticanus, the Vulgate, Harclean Syriac, Boharic Coptic, by Jerome, and others). United Bible Societies ranks its preference for "him" (*auton*) as having only [C] probability. It may be that "himself" is a scribal explanation of "him" because "him" (*auton*) was often used as a reflexive (BDF, 283). The idea of self-protection against the evil one is stated explicitly in 2:13, 14. If the second half of the verse is referring to Christians' guarding themselves, then vv. 16, 18b match early Christian parenesis known elsewhere (e.g., Gal 6:1–2, 3–5) that balances the community's care for its straying members with each member's duty to take responsibility for herself. So tentatively we paraphrase: "Christians who are born of God guard themselves, and the evil one does not touch them" (cf. T. Benjamin 3:4).

B′ (v. 19) is the third "we know": "We know that we are of God (cf. 4:4, 6), and the whole world is in the power of the evil one." Humankind is divided into two camps, and we belong to God. Why do we belong to

God? It is because we are in fellowship with the eyewitnesses who are in fellowship with the Son and the Father (1:3).

A′ (vv. 20–21) offers the fourth "we know" and an exhortation: (1) "We know that the Son of God has come [2 John 7; 1 John 4:2; 5:6], and has given understanding to us [2:20] in order that we may know the true one [God]; and we are in the true one [2:5, 24], in his Son Jesus Christ [2:23–24]. This one [Jesus Christ] is the true God [John 1:1; 1:18, textual variant; 20:28] and eternal life." John 17:3 functions as a starting point for our understanding: "And this is eternal life, that they know thee the only true God, and Jesus Christ whom thou hast sent." Eternal life is linked with a knowledge of the true God and Jesus Christ whom he sent. 1 John 2:23 takes one a step further: "No one who denies the Son has the Father. The one who confesses the Son has the Father also." 1 John 1:3 caps the line of thought: "our fellowship is with the Father and with his Son Jesus Christ." In Johannine thought one knows the Father through the Son (John 14:9); one comes to the Father through the Son (John 14:6); one abides in the Father as one abides in the Son (1 John 2:24); one receives what is promised for such knowledge, coming, and abiding: eternal life (1 John 2:25).

The climactic statement of the last "we know" functions as the transition to the exhortation: "This one is the true God and eternal life." Just as in John 1:1, 1:18's textual variant, and 20:28, so here the Son is called God (*theos*). Just as in John 1:4, 14:6, so here the Son is identified with life. If the Christ of the Johannine community is the true God, then the exhortation is appropriate to the situation: "Children, guard yourselves from idols." This was a traditional warning (1 Cor 10:14; cf. Wisdom of Solomon 14). It is applied here to reinforce the community's adherence to an orthodox christology in the face of progressives who have "gone ahead and are not abiding in the doctrine about Christ" (2 John 9).

At the heart of the crisis reflected in 1, 2, 3 John is a christological problem. The secessionists deny the coming of Jesus Christ in the flesh (2 John 7; 1 John 4:2–3). What this means in context may best be discerned from 1 John 5:6–8, where one learns that the errorists believed Jesus Christ came by water only and that the Spirit is the witness. This probably means that in the water of John's baptism the Spirit descended and remained on Jesus, making him the one who baptizes with the Holy Spirit (John 1:31–33), as one's own experience of the Spirit demonstrates.

This central christological conviction has its corollaries, two positive and two negative. On the positive side, the secessionists believed that if

one possesses the Spirit one (1) knows God (1 John 2:4) / has fellowship with God (1:6) / abides in God (2:6) / is in the light (2:9) / loves
God (4:20), and (2) does not sin (1:8, 10). On the negative side, they believed that (1) neither the death of Jesus (1:7; 2:2; 5:6) nor his heavenly
intercession (2:1) is soteriologically significant, and (2) the communal
character of the Christian life, both historical continuity with the community of the past (2 John 9; 1 John 1:3) and horizontal *koinōnia*
(fellowship) with the community of the present that is in historical
continuity with the community of the past (2:19), is soteriologically
irrelevant.

Over against the progressives/secessionists the author of the Johannine
epistles constructs a defense that focuses on two matters (christology and
ethics) and appeals to the past in two forms (the beginning of the Christian movement and the beginning of the readers' Christian lives). It is
the author's conviction that if his readers' remember that what the eyewitnesses had seen and heard is identical both with what they had been
taught at their Christian initiation and with the author's current composition, they will be confirmed in their christological faith and community
life.

If the Fourth Gospel was written alongside or after the period of
the epistles' composition, then it may be expected to have been produced, at least in part, with an eye to the controversy reflected in 1,
2, and 3 John. Is this the case? It is important in any answer attempted
to distinguish between common themes that might be expected to occur in a Gospel and epistles emanating from a common community
(such as are collected by Stephen S. Smalley, *Word Biblical Commentary: 1, 2, 3 John* [Waco: Word, 1984], p. xxx) and issues involved in
the controversy reflected in the epistles. It is the latter that are crucial.
Related to the matter of christology, one should consider the following: (a) the true humanity of God's Son from the water through the
blood (John 1:14; 4:6, 7–9; 11:33, 35, 38; 13:21; 19:30, 34; 20:17, 27)
(b) the subordination of the Spirit to christology (John 1:33; 4:10; 7:39;
14:16, 26; 15:26; 16:13–15; 20:22); (c) the need of Christians for post-
baptismal cleansing from sin (John 13:8–10) and for Jesus' intercession
on their behalf (John 17:20–24); and (d) the original disciples as eyewitnesses of the Incarnation, especially of "the blood" (John 13:23;
15:27; 18:16; 19:26, 35; 20:2–8; 21:24). Related to the matter of ethics,
consider the following: (a) love one another (John 13:34; 15:12, 17);
and (b) that they may all be one (John 10:16; 11:52; 17:21, 23). It
seems that most of the controversial issues of the epistles are echoed

in the Fourth Gospel at one place or another, although the Gospel's scope is not reduced to the matters of the controversy of the epistles. This would seem to imply that the Gospel of John was written either alongside or after the epistles. For this reason, in this volume the commentary on the Fourth Gospel follows the survey of 1, 2, and 3 John.

THE FOURTH GOSPEL

INTRODUCTION

The date of composition and the time of acceptance of the Fourth Gospel by the church can be established with reasonable ease. (1) On the one hand, the Gospel of John cannot be dated much later than 100 C.E. John Rylands papyrus 457 (P52), a small fragment of a codex of the Fourth Gospel containing parts of John 18:31–33 on one side and pieces of 18:37–38 on the other, can be dated to the early second century (125 C.E.?). Basilides, about 130 C.E., appealed to the Fourth Gospel (John 1:9) in support of his particular Gnostic system (Hippolytus, *Refutation* 7.10). On the other hand, if, as most scholars assume, John does not use the Synoptics, there is little way of knowing just how early it could have been written. (2) By the end of the second century, the Fourth Gospel was accepted, along with the three Synoptics, as canonical in Gaul (Irenaeus, *Against Heresies* 3.1.1–2), in Egypt (Clement of Alexandria, so Eusebius, *Church History* 6.14.5), in North Africa (Tertullian, *Against Marcion* 4.2), and in Rome (Muratorian fragment).

Its authorship and locale are uncertain. Irenaeus, *Against Heresies* 3.1.1, says: "John the disciple of the Lord, who also leaned upon his breast, did himself publish a Gospel during his residence at Ephesus in Asia. Ephrem the Syrian, in an appendix to his commentary on the *Diatessaron* (cf. *ZNW* 3 [1902]: 193), writes: "John wrote that Gospel in Greek at Antioch, for he remained in the country until the time of Trajan." (1) There is agreement in the ancient church about authorship: John the Son of Zebedee, an apostle, the disciple whom Jesus loved. There is disagreement about locale: Ephesus or Antioch. Modern scholars are virtually unanimous in rejecting Christian antiquity's claim about authorship for at least three reasons. (a) The silence of Ignatius of Antioch regarding John's presence in Ephesus and his alleged authorship of the Fourth Gospel is telling. (b) The picture of John, the son of Zebedee, which is found in the Synoptics, Acts, and Paul does not match that of the Fourth Evangelist. (c) Based on the internal evidence of the Fourth Gospel, Lazarus has a better claim to be the beloved disciple whom John 21:24 claims as author or sponsor (cf. John 11:3, 5, 36). Modern scholars are willing, however, to talk about an eyewitness at the root of the tradition that developed over a long period into the Gospel of John (Robert Kysar, *The Fourth Evangelist and His Gospel* [Minneapolis: Augsburg, 1975], 38–66, 267–69). (2) From among the various locales proposed by ancients and moderns (e.g., Ephesus, Antioch of Syria, Alexandria, Palestine, Transjordan), it is impossible to make a satisfactory and compelling case for any one. It is indeed possible that there were several locales of the Johannine community at different stages of the formation of the Gospel tradition (e.g., from Palestine to Syria to Asia?).

The purpose of the Gospel of John is widely regarded as that of confirming Christians in their faith. According to the dominant current construct, the occasion that created the need for such confirmation was the exclusion of Johannine Christians from the synagogue (John 9:34; 12:42; 16:2). This exclusion was, for a time, thought to be connected with the *Birkat ha-minim* (a prayer of cursing against heretics) supplied by R. Samuel the Small at some time between 85 and 95 C.E., in response to the request of R. Gamaliel II who was vexed by the increase of heresy in the Jewish community, and added to the *Shemoneh Esreh* / Eighteen Benedictions (b. Berakoth 28b–29a; so J. Louis Martyn, *History and Theology in the Fourth Gospel* [Nashville: Abingdon, 1968]; the parallel account in j. Berakoth 5:4 does not refer to Gamaliel). Since, however, the Fourth Gospel nowhere mentions exclusion from the synagogue in connection with prayers of cursing, it is now thought that there was no one thing at any one time that precipitated the Johannine Christians' exclusion. If such exclusion created the occasion, however, the dialogue in the Fourth Gospel is almost exclusively with the synagogue. Such a narrow focus for one's reading of John is possible only because the current consensus has relegated the Johannine epistles to a period after that of the Fourth Gospel (so R. E. Brown, *The Community of the Beloved Disciple* [New York: Paulist, 1979]). Whereas the Gospel of John deals with the problem of the community's relations to Judaism, the epistles reflect a later struggle within the community over orthodox christology and correct behavior. If, as has been argued in this volume, however, the epistles are to be regarded as prior to or alongside of the composition of the Gospel in its final form, an entirely different way of reading opens up. Then one might expect to encounter in the Gospel of John, on occasion at least, problems similar to those found in the three letters.

The genre of the Gospel of John is probably that of ancient biography (C. H. Talbert, "Once Again: Gospel Genre," *Semeia* 43 [1988]: 53–73). It focuses on the individual, Jesus Christ, and attempts to lay bare his uniqueness. This ancient biography, moreover, is the foundation document of a community, incorporating the community's tradition from a long and complex history. How should it be understood? Modern study of the Gospels takes a significant clue from the study of Paul's letters. Just as a Pauline letter can be properly understood only if one can specify the particular problem(s) in the church that evoked its writing, so, it is alleged, grasping a Gospel's meaning is contingent upon one's being able to determine the specific problem(s) in the community from which it comes and to which its story is a response. The tendency of a Gospel, it is assumed, makes sense only if it is linked to an immediate occasion. The Gospels, therefore, like the Pauline letters, are best interpreted as arguments addressed to specific pressing problems at the moment of writing.

Is it proper to think of a Gospel as analogous to a Pauline letter? Are foundation documents for religious communities analogous to the type of occasional literature Paul's letters are? Are not such foundation documents rather more analogous to a systematic theology, albeit in a narrative form? That is, a theology attempts to set forth the Christian position not only in light of problems real and pressing but also in light of problems real but past or real but potential. Such a narrative theology would tell the story of the community's founder in a way that expresses the values of the group in a balanced way, not just in response to one or more immediate issues that clamor for attention in the moment. If this way of reading a Gospel is followed, then the theological tendencies of the material need not be linked exclusively with specific, immediate problems in the community but may represent part of the balanced way one stream of early Christianity understands and expresses its faith.

To read the Fourth Gospel as narrative theology has certain corollaries. (a) It is inappropriate to take the occasional Pauline letters as a model for interpreting a Gospel. (b) It is inappropriate to focus on one life situation as *the* occasion. Multiple life situations, past and present, likely have their echoes in the text (e.g., rivalry with the Baptist's disciples; exclusion from the synagogue; christological problems; divisions within the community, etc.), just as issues of potential, rather than either past or present, significance may be reflected. (c) It is inappropriate to focus on only one background for understanding the narrative (e.g., Qumran, rabbinic Judaism, mystical Judaism, Hellenistic Judaism, Greco-Roman philosophy, Hermetica, Gnosticism, etc.) since it will likely take knowledge of most or all to comprehend a tradition that developed not only through time but also moved geographically. (d) It is inappropriate to focus on anything other than the final form of the text of John. It is this form of the Gospel that is canonical and is, therefore, to be interpreted. Rearrangements are not to be attempted. Chapter 21 is to be considered an integral part of the final text, as are the other passages believed by Bultmann to have been editorial additions to an earlier version of John (e.g., 3:5, "and water"; 5:28–29; 6:51c–58; 19:34b–35).

Prior to proposing an outline for the Fourth Gospel, one should consider certain comments of Aristotle in his *Poetics* about the way the composition of a story would be done in antiquity. "The stories . . . should first be sketched in outline and then expanded by putting in episodes" (17.6). For example, the plot/story of the *Odyssey* is quite short:

> A man is for many years away from home and his footsteps are dogged by Poseidon and he is all alone. Moreover, affairs at home are in such a state that his estate is being wasted by suitors and a plot laid against his son, but after being storm-tossed he arrives himself, reveals who he is, and attacks them, with the result that he is saved and destroys his enemies. (17.10–11)

This plot is the essence of the *Odyssey,* says Aristotle; the rest is episodes.

Viewed from this angle, what is the plot/story of the Fourth Gospel? John tells of

> one who came as revealing, empowering presence; who picked/produced a new community and provided them and others during his public ministry with warrants for a different kind of worship; who privately predicted what their future would be like, offering promise, parenesis, and prayer for that time; and who ultimately made provision for their future community life, worship, and ministry before he returned to whence he had come.

This is the plot/story of the life of a holy man, the founder of a religious community. This plot/story is expanded by putting in episodes. These episodes are essentially the large thought units of the Fourth Gospel.

An outline that reflects this plot is as follows:

Prologue, 1:1–18

Picking/producing the new community, 1:19–2:11

Providing warrants for a different kind of worship, 2:12–12:50

Prediction, promise, parenesis, prayer for the future, 12:1–17:26

Provision for future community life, worship, and ministry before return to prior glory, 18:1–20:29

Purpose of the Gospel, 20:30–31

Postscript, 21:1–25.

For a convenient survey of Johannine scholarship since 1945, see D. Moody Smith, "Johannine Studies," in *The New Testament and Its Modern Interpreters,* ed. Eldon Jay Epp and George W. MacRae (Atlanta: Scholars Press, 1989), 271–96; for the last twenty years, see Gerhard S. Sloyan, *What Are They Saying about John?* (New York: Paulist, 1991).

A REVEALING, EMPOWERING PRESENCE

John 1:1–18

John 1:1–18 is a thought unit held together by an inclusion (*theos*/ God, vv. 1, 18). This assumes that in v. 18 the textual variant, *theos*/ God, attested by P66, Sinaiticus, Vaticanus, and others is to be preferred to *huios*/son, attested by Alexandrinus and others. V. 19, moreover, clearly begins a new section of the Gospel. In order to trace the train of thought in this unit, it is necessary to distinguish between the narrative order or surface structure of 1:1–18 on the one hand and the story order or sequence of events narrated therein on the other.

There is widespread recognition that John 1:1–18's surface structure is concentric or chiastic (cf. R. A. Culpepper, "The Pivot of John's Prologue," *NTS* 27 [1980]: 1–31). One possible way to lay it out is:

A   (vv. 1–5): The relation of the Logos/Word to God
                                      to creation
                                      to humans

    B   (vv. 6–8): The witness of John the Baptist

        C   (vv. 9–11): The coming of the Light/Logos and his rejection

            D   (vv. 12–13): The benefits of belief in the Logos/Word

        C′   (v. 14): The coming of the Logos and his reception

    B′   (v. 15): The witness of John the Baptist

   A′   (vv. 16–18): The relation of the Logos/Word to humans
                                        to re-creation
                                        to God.

A first reading ought to take account of this controlling pattern. A (vv. 1–5) begins in eternity ("In beginning was the Word") with the divine Word ("and the Word was with God, and the Word was God"), who is the instrument of creation ("all things were made through him, and without him was not anything made that was made") and the source of life ("In him was life") and light ("and the life was the light of men"). The light either is not understood or is not overcome by darkness (*katelaben* can mean either).

B (vv. 6–8) focuses on the identity of the man, John the Baptist. He was not the light but rather a witness to the light. Should the reader assume that with vv. 6–8 there has been a movement from eternity to history so that what will follow will deal with the Jesus of history?

C (vv. 9–11) does in fact focus on history. If vv. 9–10 do ("The true light which enlightens every man was continually coming [present tense] into the world. He was in the world, and the world was made through him, yet the world knew him not"), v. 11 does so even more ("He came [aorist tense] to his own home, and his own people received him not"). But is the historical focus here on the earthly Jesus or on some other coming(s) in history?

D (vv. 12–13) speaks about the benefits of faith in the name of the one who comes into the world ("But to all who received him, who believed in his name, he gave power to become children of God"). If vv. 9–11 are taken to refer to the earthly Jesus, then vv. 12–13 seem to be in sequence.

C' (v. 14) is a clear statement about the Incarnation ("And the Word became flesh and dwelt among us, full of grace and truth"). Whereas failure to recognize (v. 10) or receive (v. 11) the Word was previously noted, here a community ("we") has beheld his glory and has been formed as a result of their faith. If vv. 9–11 refer to the Incarnate One, then v. 14 seems out of sequence. When v. 14 speaks about the event of the Incarnation, it has already happened in vv. 9–11. There is a problem with the proposed solution.

B' (v. 15) returns to John the Baptist and gives the content of his witness ("This was he of whom I said, 'He who comes after me ranks before me, for he was before me' "). John's witness seems out of sequence as well. If vv. 9–11 speak about the coming in the Incarnation, then v. 15 ought to be adjacent to vv. 6–8 or after vv. 9–11. Even if v. 14 is the first reference to the Incarnation, v. 15 comes after the formation of a believing community. John, as a result, bears witness after the disciples believe. The problem of sequence becomes more complex.

A' (vv. 16–18) deals with salvation in relation to the new community ("we" all received, grace upon grace), in relation to the new covenant ("law was given through Moses, grace and truth came through Jesus Christ"), and in relation to God ("the only Son/God who is in the bosom of the Father, he has made him known"). There is no problem with the sequence of this segment of the text.

It ought to be obvious from this initial reading that the narrative order does not necessarily reflect the story order or sequence of events. The central issue to be resolved is: at what point does the passage cease to talk about the pre-existent Logos and begin to speak about the incarnate Word?

The key to any determination of the story order of 1:1–18 is the history of religions parallels. There is widespread agreement that the background against which the prologue should be read is the Wisdom myth of ancient Judaism (cf. Appendix). A list of specific parallels is instructive.

(1) Pre-existence is common to both the Johannine Logos and Jewish Wisdom (John 1:1: "In beginning was the Word" // Proverbs 8:22:; "The Lord created me at the beginning of his work, the first of his acts of old"; Sirach 1:4: "Wisdom was created before all things"; 24:9: "From eternity, in the beginning, he created me").

(2) Both are said to be "with God" (John 1:1: "and the Word was with God" // Proverbs 8:30: "then I was beside him, like a master workman"; Wisdom of Solomon 9:4: "the wisdom that sits by thy throne").

(3) Both are said to be divine (John 1:1: "and the Word was God" // Wisdom of Solomon 7:25–26: "For she is a breath of the power of God, and a pure emanation of the glory of the Almighty; . . . she is a reflection of eternal light, . . . and an image of his goodness").

(4) Both are described as the instrument of creation (John 1:3: "All things were made through him, and without him was not anything made that was made" // Proverbs 8:30: "I was beside him like a master workman"; 3:19: "The Lord by wisdom founded the earth"; Wisdom of Solomon 7:22: "wisdom, the fashioner of all things"; 9:1–2: "who hast made all things by thy word, and by thy wisdom hast formed man").

(5) Both are called the source of life (John 1:4: "In him was life" // Prov 8:35: "he who finds me finds life"; Baruch 4:1b: "All who hold her fast will live") and light (John 1:4: "and the life was the light of men" // Wisdom of Solomon 7:26: "she is a reflection of eternal light"; Sirach 24:27: "It makes instruction shine forth like light"; Baruch 4:2: "walk toward the shining of her light").

(6) Neither can be overcome by darkness/evil (John 1:5: "And the light shines in the darkness, and the darkness cannot overcome it" // Wisdom of Solomon 7:29–30: "Compared with the light she is found to be superior, for it is succeeded by the night, but against wisdom evil does not prevail"). The parallels settle the translation problem of 1:5. In this context *katelaben* means "overcome," not "comprehend."

(7) Both continually come into the world (John 1:9: "The true light

which enlightens every person was continually coming [present tense, periphrastic participle] into the world" // Wisdom of Solomon 6:13, 16: "She hastens to make herself known...she goes about seeking those worthy of her"; 7:27: "in every generation she passes into holy souls and makes them friends of God"; Sirach 24:6–7: "in the whole earth, and in every people and nation, I have gotten a possession. Among all these I sought a resting place; I sought in whose territory I might lodge"; 1 Enoch 42:1: "Then Wisdom went out to dwell with the children of the people") and are in the world (John 1:10: "He was in the world" // Wisdom of Solomon 8:1: "She reaches mightily from one end of the earth to the other"). The parallels, together with the present tense (continually coming) in 1:9, point to a general revelation to all people. This idea would be compatible with other early Christians from Paul (Rom 1:19–20) to Justin (*1 Apology* 5).

(8) Both are rejected by humans generally (John 1:10b: "He was in the world, and the world was made through him, yet the world knew him not"; 1:11b: "and his own people received him not" // 1 Enoch 42:2: "but she found no dwelling place. So Wisdom returned to her place and she settled permanently among the angels"; Baruch 3:20–21: "they have not understood her paths, nor laid hold of her. Their children have strayed far from her way").

(9) Both create a relation with God among those who are receptive (John 1:12–13: "But to all who received him, who believed in his name, he gave power to become children of God; who were born not of blood nor of the will of the flesh nor of the will of man, but of God" // Wisdom of Solomon 7:27: "she renews all things; in every generation she passes into holy souls and makes them friends of God, and prophets, for God loves nothing so much as the man who lives with wisdom"; "because of her I shall have immortality"), saving humans (Wisdom of Solomon 9:18: "and were saved by wisdom").

(10) Both appeared on earth and lived among humans, tabernacling among them (John 1:14a: "The Word became flesh and tabernacled among us" // Baruch 3:37: "she appeared upon earth and lived among humans"; Sirach 24:8, 11–12: "Then the Creator of all things gave me a commandment, and the one who created me assigned a place for my tent. And he said, 'Make your dwelling in Jacob'... in the beloved city he gave me a resting place. So I took root in an honored people").

(11) Both possess glory as *monogenēs*/unique (John 1:14, 18: "we have beheld his glory, glory as of the only son [*monogenēs*] from the Father... the only [*monogenēs*] Son/God who is in the bosom of the Fa-

ther, he has made him known" // Wisdom of Solomon 7:22, 25: Wisdom, the fashioner of all things, taught me. For in her there is a spirit that is . . . unique [*monogenēs*]. . . . For she is . . . a pure emanation of the glory of the Almighty").

(12) Both know God and make him known (John 1:18: "No one has ever seen God; the only Son/God who is in the bosom of the Father, he has made him known" // Wisdom of Solomon 8:4: "For she is an initiate in the knowledge of God"; 9:9–10: "With thee is wisdom, who knows thy works and was present when thou didst make the world, and who understands what is pleasing in thy sight and what is right according to thy commandments. Send her forth . . . that she may be with me . . . and that I may learn what is pleasing to thee").

The similarities are remarkable. The question remains: why does John call the figure Logos/Word when the Jewish sources employ the name Wisdom? In Mediterranean antiquity one divine reality could be called by many names. (a) Cleanthes' *Hymn to Zeus* begins: "Thou, O Zeus, are praised above all gods: many are they names and thine is all power for ever." (b) Tacitus, *History* 4.84, says the god Serapis was identified by some as Asclepios, by others as Osiris, by still others as Jupiter, but by most as Pluto. (c) No passage is clearer than that in Apuleius' *Metamorphoses* 11, where Lucius cries out to Isis:

> O blessed queen of heaven, whether thou be the Dame Ceres . . . or the celestial Venus . . . or . . . the sister of the god Phoebus . . . or . . . Proserpine . . . by whatsoever name or fashion or shape it is lawful to call upon Thee, I pray Thee. . . .

Lucius' cry to the goddess is heard. Isis replies:

> For the Phrygians . . . call me the Mother of the gods at Pessinus; the Athenians . . . Cecropian Minerva; the Cyprians . . . Papian Venus; the Cretans . . . Dietynnian Diana; the Sicilians . . . infernal Proserpine; the Eleusinians . . . Ceres; some Juno, others Bellona, others Hecate, others Rhamnusia . . . and the Egyptians . . . do call me by my true name, Queen Isis.

In ancient Judaism, Wisdom and Word of God are sometimes used interchangeably for the same reality: e.g., (1) Wisdom of Solomon 9:1–2: "O God of my fathers and Lord of mercy, who hast made all things by thy *word* and by thy *wisdom* hast formed man"; (2) Sirach 24:3: Wisdom says, "I came forth from the mouth of the Most High"; (3) Philo, *Allegorical Interpretation* 1.65: "now wisdom is the word of God"; cf. *On Dreams* 2.242–45; *Who Is the Heir?* 191. Indeed, Philo's *logos* has many of the attributes of the Word in the Johannine prologue: e.g., (a) the *logos* is *theos*/divine (*On Dreams* 1.228–30); (b) the *logos* is the instrument of creation (*On the Cherubim* 125–27; cf. 1 Cor 8:6; Heb 1:2); (c) the *logos* is associated with light (*On the Creation* 31) and life (*On the Creation* 24, 30); (d) the *logos* makes God known (*On Dreams* 1.68–69; *Allegorical Interpretation* 3.169–78); (e) the *logos* enables humans to become sons of God (*Confusion of Languages* 1.146–47; Thomas H. Tobin, "The Prologue of John and Hellenistic Jewish Speculation," *CBQ* 52 [1990]: 252–69).

The Fourth Gospel's prologue happens to use Logos/Word instead of Sophia/Wisdom, perhaps because both it and the LXX of Genesis 1 begin alike (*en archē*/in beginning), perhaps because a masculine term (*logos*) seemed more appropriate for the man Jesus than the feminine wisdom (*sophia*). This interchangeably of names is in line with other early Christian usage: e.g., cf. Odes of Solomon 41:9, 15's use of "wisdom" with 41:11, 14's use of "word" and 41:12 where wisdom becomes word.

If John 1:1–18 is a Christianized form of the Jewish wisdom myth of late antiquity, then the parallels ought to be able to assist the reader in determining where the prologue speaks of the pre-existence of the Word and where, when it moves to history, it focuses on the earthly Jesus. The following parts of the prologue seem to belong to the period of the pre-existence of the Word: (a) in beginning with God (v. 1), (b) the instrument of creation (v. 3), (c) the source of life and light (v. 4), (d) light that is not overcome by darkness (v. 5), (e) the light that is continually coming into the world as general revelation (v. 9), and (f) the one who came to his own people, Israel, only to meet rejection (v. 11). To the period of the earthly Jesus the following parts belong: (a) became flesh and tabernacled among us (v. 14), (b) giving grace (v. 16), truth (v. 17), and knowledge of God (v. 18), and (c) to those who received him, he gave power to become children of God (v. 12) through a new birth (v. 13). The two sections dealing with John the Baptist (vv. 6–8, 15) also would be connected to the period of the Incarnation. The story order/sequence of events is different from the narrative order/surface structure. The latter is recognized by noting the repetitions in the text; the former is discerned by means of the parallels between John 1:1–18 and the wisdom myth of Jewish antiquity.

With the aid of such guidance, another reading may be attempted designed to trace the train of thought. A (vv. 1–5) and A' (vv. 16–18) should be read together. The pre-existent divine one who was the instrument of creation and the source of life and light (vv. 1–5) is also the revealer (the unique son, the divine one, the one who is in the bosom of the Father; D. A. Fennema, "John 1:18: 'God the Only Son,' " *NTS* 31 [1985]: 124–35), the source of grace and truth from whom the Johannine community has received in abundance (vv. 16–18). For the prologue, the one who made you is the one who saves you. The Creator and the Redeemer are the same God.

B (vv. 6–8) and B' (v. 15) may also be read together. John the Baptist is not the light but is a witness to the light (vv. 6–8). His testimony is to the superiority of the Son, based upon the pre-existence of the Son (v. 15).

C (vv. 9–11) and C' (v. 14) also need to be read together. Prior to the Incarnation, the Word was active in the world both in general revelation to all people (vv. 9–10; cf. Justin, *1 Apology* 46; *2 Apology* 10) and in special revelation to Israel (v. 11; cf. Justin, *Dialogue with Trypho* 126–28). In neither case did he find acceptance (vv. 10b, 11b). When the Word became flesh and tabernacled among humans, however, he found a positive response among a community that beheld his glory (v. 14; cf. 2:11; Justin, *2 Apology* 13), "glory as of a *monogenēs*/only Son from the Father." For the prologue, revelation is general (to all people) and particular (to Israel before Jesus and in Jesus).

D (vv. 12–13) is the centerpiece of the prologue: "But to all who received him, who believed in his name, he gave power to become children of God." Are we to think of "receiving him" as encompassing all three forms of revelation (to all prior to the Incarnation; to Israel prior to the Incarnation; through Jesus in the Incarnation), or only a positive response to the Incarnation? In the Johannine literature, "believing in his name" is an activity of positive response to the Incarnate Word (John 3:18; 1 John 3:23; 5:13). This response results in a new birth from God (v. 13).

There were three different versions of the wisdom myth in ancient Judaism: (1) Wisdom finds her resting place in Israel as the Law (so Sirach 24:2–22; Baruch 3:28–4:4); (2) Wisdom finds her dwelling place in the souls of righteous individuals in every generation (Wisdom of Solomon 6:12–9:18); and (3) Wisdom finds a resting place nowhere on earth and so returns to heaven (1 Enoch 42:1–2). The prologue to the Fourth Gospel wants to make the point that the divine Wisdom/Word of God incarnate in Jesus, not the Law, has found a dwelling place and acceptance among certain disciples of Jesus ("we," v. 14; John 17:24 prevents limiting the "we" to eyewitnesses, but 2:11 shows it can include the eyewitnesses).

How does the prologue (vv. 1–18) function literarily and theologically in the Fourth Gospel? At the literary level, it functions like an overture, introducing themes that will reappear later: e.g., (1) the Word was in the beginning (vv. 1–2; cf. 8:58); (2) in him was life (v. 4a; cf. 5:26); (3) the light of men (v. 4b; cf. 8:12 and chapter 9); (4) John the Baptist (vv. 6–8, 15; cf. 1:19–34; 3:27–30); (5) the new birth (vv. 12–13; cf. 3:3, 5); (6) disciples behold his glory (v. 14b; cf. 2:11; 17:24); (7) only the Son who is divine has seen God and can make him known (v. 18; cf. 3:16; 6:46; 20:28).

At the theological level it sets the framework within which the rest of the Gospel story is told. Four fenceposts mark the boundaries. (1) The Creator and the Redeemer are the same God. This would have answered at least a potential problem near the time when John was put in its final form. Irenaeus, *Against Heresies* 1.26.1, says: "A certain Cerinthus in Asia taught that the world was made not by the first God but by a certain power clearly separate and distinct from the Power above all, and ignorant of the God above all." Moreover, Irenaeus, *Against Heresies* 3.11.1, understood this feature of the prologue to be a defense against Cerinthus. He says:

> John . . . seeks . . . to remove that error which by Cerinthus had been disseminated among men . . . that he might confound them, and persuade them that there is but one God, who made all things by his Word; and not as they allege, that the Creator was one, but the Father . . . another.

One cannot say what the Evangelist's intent was; one can, however, say this is likely how it would have been heard in a context where teaching such as that of Cerinthus was known. John's story of Jesus is told within the framework of the conviction that the one who saves is also the one who creates.

(2) The divine agent of creation, who has continually been attempting to communicate with creatures by means of general and special revelation but with little success, became flesh (*sarks egeneto*). Two questions arise: (a) What does this mean in a Johannine context, and (b) when was it believed to have taken place?

(a) In the Johannine epistles there was a recurring attempt to insure belief that Jesus Christ continued in the flesh even after the resurrection: e.g., 2 John 7 (the use of a present participle for "coming" in the flesh to imply continuation through time); 1 John 1:1 (the appeal to post-resurrection sight and touch to guarantee that the risen one was still flesh); 4:2 (the use of a perfect participle, "having come and remaining" in flesh); and 5:6–8 (the emphasis on water and blood as opposed to water only to insure that Jesus Christ's coming extended through his death). In three of four cases, the attempt to guarantee that the Savior's coming in flesh extended through his passion and beyond is expressed by the use of the verb "come" in a variety of ways (2 John 7: present tense; 1 John 4:2: perfect tense; 5:6–8: by water and blood). In all cases, the intent is to protect the permanent union of Jesus Christ against the progressives' attempt to separate the divine Son of God from the human Jesus as quickly as possible and certainly before the passion. What better way to speak about a permanent union than by shifting from "come in the flesh" to "became flesh"? Irenaeus, *Against Heresies* 3.11.1, understood it this way. He says:

> John...seeks...to remove that error which by Cerinthus had been disseminated among men...that the Son of the Creator was...one, but the Christ from above another, who also continued impassible, descending upon Jesus, the Son of the Creator, and flew back again into his Pleroma.

In 3.11.3, after discussing other Gnostics who took the same stance as Cerinthus, he says: "according to the opinion of no one of the heretics was the Word made flesh." It seems that the expression, "the Word became flesh," functions to insure the permanent union of the pre-existent Word and the human Jesus after a given point in time. It would have been heard as a defense against the type of error espoused by the progressives of the epistles and exemplified by Cerinthus.

(b) When did this permanent union, the Incarnation, occur? The possibilities are three: (1) at Jesus' conception by the Spirit (so the textual variant at 1:13: "the one not born of blood nor of the will of the flesh nor of the will of man, but of God"; so also the Epistle of the Apostles, Coptic Version, 7:10: "I entered into her womb: I became flesh"; also 3: "We believe that the Word, which became flesh through the virgin Mary, was born not by the lust of the flesh but by the will of God"; so Aristides, *Apology* 15:1: "Now the Christians trace their origin from the Lord Jesus Christ. And he is acknowledged by the Holy Spirit to be the Son of the most high God, who came down from heaven for the salvation of men. And being born of a pure virgin..., he assumed flesh"; Justin, *1 Apology* 21: "we say also that the Word, who is the firstborn of God, was produced without sexual union"; 33: "It is wrong, therefore, to understand the Spirit and the power of God as anything else than the Word, who is also the firstborn of God...; and it was this, when it came upon the virgin and overshadowed her, caused her to conceive; *Dialogue* 63; Melito of Sardis, *Discourse on Faith* 4; Tertullian, *On the Flesh of Christ* 19, 24; Irenaeus, *Against Heresies* 3.16.1; 3.19.2; so probably Ignatius, *Smyrnaeans* 1:1: "God's Son by the will and power of God, truly born of a virgin"; cf. also *Ephesians* 18; *Trallians* 9); (2) in connection with Jesus' baptism by John (E. C. Colwell and E. L. Titus, *The Gospel of the Spirit* [New York: Harper & Row, 1953], chap. 5); (3) after Jesus' glorification when his abiding presence indwells the community of his disciples (P. S. Minear, " 'We Don't Know Where . . . ' John 20:2," *Int* 30 [1976]: 125–39; "The Idea of Incarnation in First John," *Int* 24 [1970]: 291–302).

In terms of canonical criticism, the first option is clearly the correct reading. Within the canon, John is to be read in light of the Synoptic Gospels with birth narratives, as the early church did. In terms of the Johannine literature detached from its canonical context, the second reading is compelling for several reasons.

(1) 1 John 5:6–8 combats the progressives' understanding of Jesus Christ in terms of an exclusive focus on the water by an appeal to the water and the blood. The dominant reading of such an argument is that the progressives focused on the descent of the Spirit on Jesus at his baptism while the author of the letter wanted to insure that the coming of the Son of God continued through Jesus' death. If so, then the author of 1 John agreed in his assumptions with the progressives about the water; his disagreement was about the blood. Both orthodox and progressive Johannine Christians alike assumed that the coming of the Son of God was in the water, i.e., in connection with the water of John's baptism (M. C. de Boer, "Jesus the Baptizer: 1 John 5:5–8 and the Gospel of John," *JBL* 107 [1988]: 87–106).

(2) In a milieu where one divine reality could be called by many names, the Hellenistic Jewish context of the Fourth Gospel used Wisdom, Word, and Holy Spirit interchangeably (cf. Wisdom of Solomon 9:1–2, 10, 17–18: "who hast made all things by thy *word,* and by thy *wisdom* hast formed man"; "Send her [wisdom] forth from the holy heavens"; "Who hast learned thy counsel, unless thou hast given *wisdom* and sent thy *Holy Spirit* from on high? And thus were the paths of those on earth set right . . . and were saved by *wisdom*"). For such a person, 1:14 and 1:33 would sound like synonymous expressions of the same event: the Word became flesh = the Spirit descended and remained on him. There were also Greek-speaking Jewish Christian circles where the Holy Spirit and the Son of God were interchangeably terms (e.g., Hermas, "Parable," 9.1: the angel tells Hermas that "the Holy Spirit . . . is the Son of God"). For such circles, the Johannine claim that the Son of God came by water (1 John 5:5–6) would signify the same thing as the contention that the Spirit descended and remained on Jesus in the water (John 1:33).

(3) Four passages from later in the Gospel offer supporting evidence

for a reader's impression that the Word's becoming flesh and the Spirit's descending and remaining on Jesus are variant expressions of the same event. The first three form a group. (a) John 1:45 has Philip describe him as "Jesus of Nazareth, the son of Joseph." (b) John 6:42 has the Jews in the synagogue at Capernaum say: "Is this not Jesus, the son of Joseph, whose father and mother we know?" (c) John 7:41–42 has some say, "This is the Christ," and others respond, "Is the Christ to come from Galilee? Has not the scripture said that the Christ is descended from David, and comes from Bethlehem, the village where David was?" In 7:50–52 a similar exchange takes place. Nicodemus asks, "Does our law judge a man without first giving him a hearing and learning what he does?" The other Pharisees reply, "Are you too from Galilee? Search and you will see that the prophet is not to rise from Galilee." In all three of these texts, the public perception of Jesus is that he is from Galilee and is the son of Joseph. This raises the question of whether or not the Johannine community even knew the facts about the Davidic lineage of Jesus and the birth in Bethlehem. Or did the Evangelist assume his readers knew the tradition of Jesus' Davidic descent but without any connection to a supernatural conception (as in the tradition cited in Rom 1:3–4; 2 Tim 2:8; Mk 10:47–48; 12:35–37; Rev 3:7; 5:5; 12:5; 22:16)? Either way, there would seem to be nothing in these texts that might change a reader's mind about impressions gained from 1:14 and 1:33.

The fourth passage, John 8:41, has the Jews say to Jesus, "We were not born of fornication; we have one Father, even God." Although this has sometimes been taken to be a reference to irregularities surrounding Jesus' birth, as in Matthew 1:18–25, and therefore an indication that John assumed a miraculous conception (so Origen, *Against Celsus* 1.28; the Acts of Pilate 2:3–4), the context argues otherwise. The context is focused not on Jesus' person but on the issue of Jewish faithfulness/faithlessness. The Jews are saying, "We are not like the Israelites of Hosea's time, unfaithful to God, children of fornication" (LXX Hos 1:2; 2:4; Rudolf Schnackenburg, *The Gospel according to St. John* [New York: Seabury, 1980], 2:207). If 8:41 is read as a part of a controversy over Jewish faithfulness/faithlessness instead of a debate over christology, then there is nothing here or elsewhere in the Gospel that would lead a hearer to infer that the Incarnation took place in connection with a miraculous conception as opposed to a moment in connection with the water of John's baptism.

If this is a correct reading of the Johannine community's view of the time of the Incarnation, it should be clear that this reading is not adoptionism. Adoptionism, in later Christianity, held that Jesus became Christ/ Son of God at either baptism or resurrection because of his virtue. Implicit in adoptionism is "works righteousness." If Jesus became God's Son because of his righteousness, then so do Christians. The Johannine stance, however, has no notion of merit. That the Word becomes flesh, at whatever time, is an act of pure grace. Both the potential for exploitation and its actuality, nevertheless, pushed the church to a position that defended against merit, both in Jesus and in the lives of Christians. The tradition of Jesus' miraculous conception functioned for this end.

Logically, if not chronologically, Matthew and Luke represent a development beyond the Fourth Gospel in this matter. The development found in the two Gospels with birth narratives became the controlling context for reading John (also Mark) in the New Testament canon. Read in a canonical context, as opposed to being read in isolation from the other Gospels, the Fourth Gospel's emphasis on Incarnation (the descent of the divine into human life that continued through passion, resurrection, and ascension) became dominant, but its assumptions about the time of the event were subordinated to the miraculous conception tradition of Matthew and Luke. The result: the Incarnation is understood to have taken place at the miraculous conception. By early in the second century, this had already become a widespread reading of John 1:14, a reading that ultimately was to win out in mainline Christian circles.

(3) The Word become flesh offers a new birth to those who believe in his name. He gives his creatures power to become children of God. To hear this as it would have been heard in Mediterranean antiquity requires attention to a common Greco-Roman epistemological conviction: "like is known by like" (Plato, *Protagoras* 337C–338A; *Timaeus* 45C; Philo, *On the Change of Names* 6; Plotinus, *Enneads* 4.5.7, 23–62; 1.6.9, 30–45). There are two implications of this assumption. (a) Clement of Alexandria (*Miscellanies* 6:15) verbalizes one:

> If, then, according to Plato, it is only possible to learn the truth either from God or from the progeny of God, with reason we . . . boast of learning the truth by the Son of God.

Only God can reveal God. (b) Philo give expression to the second (*Questions on Exodus,* fragment): "To see God man must first become God." Only God can know God.

The prologue of John speaks to both implications. (a) On the one hand, because the revealer is *theos*/divine (vv. 1, 18), he can make the Father known (v. 18). (b) On the other hand, he gives the power/new birth from

God that enables creatures to have the capacity to know God. The Incarnation of the Word and the resulting new birth of humans solve the epistemological difficulty and make salvation possible.

(4) There is a community of belief that confesses their christological faith ("we," vv. 14, 16). They are who they are because they have beheld his glory, received of his grace, believed in his name, and have been given power by him to become God's children by virtue of a new birth. In Johannine thought, the Incarnate Word enables the eyewitnesses to believe (15:16); through their word, others believe (17:20). Those who have not seen the Incarnate One and still believe (20:29) do so by accepting the proclamation of the eyewitnesses and by coming into fellowship with them and thereby into fellowship with the Father and the Son (1 John 1:3).

It is critical orthodoxy to call this Johannine community "an introversionist sect" (using the categories of Brian Wilson, "An Analysis of Sect Development," in *Patterns of Sectarianism: Ideology in Social and Religious Movements* [London: Heinemann, 1967], 22–45), that is, a group that rejects the world's values and replaces them with other higher values.

It is sometimes claimed that the christology of a descending-ascending redeemer in John functions in the interests of this sectarian alienation from the world. The Word become flesh is alien from all people in the world; the community that is aligned with him is also alien from the world. His unearthly strangeness creates a church that is an unearthly community with him (Wayne Meeks, "The Man From Heaven in Johannine Sectarianism," *JBL* 91 [1972]: 44–72). The christology thereby provides a reinforcement for the community's social identity as an inward-looking body isolated over against the world. There is implicit in this description of Johannine christology, just as in the characterization of the community as sectarian, a denigration of Johannine Christianity.

Is there any form of Christianity reflected in the New Testament that was not sectarian? Probably not. Is the myth of a descending-ascending redeemer necessarily connected with sectarian forms of Christianity? Obviously not. Is the sectarian character of early Christianity an inherent flaw? Hardly. Recent research has pointed rather to the virtues of Johannine sectarianism.

> The meaning of John's sectarianism is that *because it was sectarian* it challenged the world on the basis of the love of God and the word of God. No religion that sees itself as the backbone of society, as the glue that holds a society together, can easily lay down a challenge to that society's wrongs. A cultural religion is all too readily told to

mind its own business, because it *has* a business, a well-known role in maintaining society's fabric unmolested. It is the sect, which has no business in the world, that is able to present a fundamental challenge to the world's oppressive orders. Precisely because it sees itself alienated from the world, its commitment to the world's orders is attenuated. . . . (David Rensberger, *Johannine Faith and Liberating Community* [Philadelphia: Westminster, 1988], 142)

Most criticism of Christian sectarianism is based on the unexamined assumption that the mission of the church is primarily to reform the world by direct assault on its structures (H. Richard Niebuhr's "Christ transforming culture"), rather than to be the church and thereby subvert the world's structures by offering the witness of a counterculture. Rensberger grasps the genius of Johannine Christianity: the mission of the church is first of all to be the church! The Johannine community recognized that the basis of that mission is christology and that the only christology that is effective is one that put humans into living contact with God.

These four fenceposts form the framework within which the Gospel story will be told: (1) The creator and the redeemer are the same God; (2) the Incarnation implies a permanent union of pre-existent Word and the human Jesus (that took place probably in connection with the water of John's baptism); (3) since like is known only by like, the divine Revealer is able to make God known to creatures whom he has given the power to become children of God; (4) the sectarian character of the Johannine community is its strength, not its denigration.

CREATOR OF A NEW COMMUNITY

John 1:19–2:12

"We have before us a consciously created composition" (E. Haenchen, *A Commentary on the Gospel of John* [Philadelphia: Fortress, 1980], 1:168). John 1:19–2:11 is a thought unit organized into a scheme of seven or eight days (1:19–27; 1:29–34; 1:35–39; 1:40–42; 1:43–51; 2:1–11), paralleling a similar scheme at the end of the Gospel (cf. 12:1, 12, etc.). It focuses on the creation of discipleship, the picking/production of a new community. Even a cursory reading lays bare the care with which each component of the section has been crafted.

Day One (1:19–27) is composed of two units (vv. 19–23 and vv. 24–27) that are loosely parallel to one another in normal order.

Unit One (vv. 19–23)

1. Jews sent . . . from Jerusalem to ask him . . . (v. 19)

   2. I am not the Christ (Lk 3:15), nor Elijah, nor the prophet (vv. 20–21)

      3. He said, "I am. . . ." (v. 23)

Unit Two (vv. 24–27)

1. They had been sent from the Pharisees. They asked him. . . . (vv. 24–25a)

   2. If you are neither the Christ, nor Elijah, nor the prophet (v. 25b)

      3. John answered them, "I baptize with water; but . . . he who comes after me. . . ." (vv. 26–27)

John is here center stage and intent on clarifying his role: what he is not (the Christ: 7:41–42; Elijah: Mal 4:5–6; the prophet: 6:14, 7:52, cf. 1 QS 9:11; 4QTest 5–8), and what he is (the voice of one crying in the wilderness). The focus is on the question: why is John baptizing? The Jewish interrogators (sent by the Jews, v. 19 = sent by the Pharisees, v. 24, i.e., the ever-watchful and suspicious religious leaders who keep the people under surveillance: 4:1; 7:32, 47; 9:13, 18, 22; 11:46; 12:19, 42) assume he baptizes because he is an eschatological figure, either the Messiah or a preparer for the Messiah. John says he is indeed a preparer figure, but the one mentioned in Isaiah 40:3 (cf. 1:6–8; 5:35).

Day Two ("the next day," vv. 29–34) is composed of two units that are loosely parallel to one another in inverse order.

Unit One (vv. 29–32)

1. Two confessions of John:

   (a) Behold the Lamb of God who takes away the sin of the world (v. 29)

   (b) This is the one who comes after me but ranks before me (v. 30; cf. 1:15).

2. "I myself did not know him";
   "for this I came baptizing with water" (v. 31);
   "I saw the Spirit descend and remain on him" (v. 32).

Unit Two (vv. 33–34)

2. "I myself did not know him";
   "he who sent me to baptize with water";
   "He on whom you see the Spirit descend and remain" (v. 33).

1. Two confessions of John:

   (a) I have seen him who baptizes with the Holy Spirit;

   (b) This is the Son of God (v. 34).

Day Two (vv. 29–34) is linked to Day One (vv. 19–27) not only by the seven- or eight-day scheme but also by link phrases: "the one who comes after me," v. 27//v. 30; "I baptize," v. 26//vv. 31, 33. On Day Two, John the Baptist points to Jesus. A variety of titles and functions are attributed to Jesus in this brief section, some clear and some problematic. "Son of God" is familiar from the epistles (cf. 1 John 5:5, 12, 13, 20). "Lamb of God who takes away the sin of the world" is problematic. If "takes away the sin of the world" were absent, then the background would surely be Exodus 12:1–11, the paschal lamb. If one understands "takes away the sin of the world" as in the sin offering (cf. 1 John 2:2; 4:10), then the servant of Isaiah 53:7–12, who is like a lamb, who makes himself an offering for sin, and who makes many to be accounted righteous is a likely possibility. If one reads "takes away sin" as synonymous with "destroy the works of the devil" (1 John 3:5, 8), then the apocalyptic lamb who is raised up by God to destroy evil in the world (T. Joseph 19:8; 1 Enoch 90:38; Rev 7:17; 17:14; 5:9) is a credible candidate. That Jesus is "the one who baptizes with the Holy Spirit" precludes any attempt to understand him solely as a prototype of the experience of the Spirit whose function is finished after he has served as a model for others' experience. For the Johannine community, if one experiences the Spirit, it is because Jesus has performed the baptism.

Day Two answers the question of Day One (Why does John baptize?): John baptizes with water so that the Baptizer with the Spirit may be revealed to Israel (vv. 31, 33). There is some evidence that in Jewish circles there existed a belief that the Messiah was hidden and that his identity had to be revealed before he could become known (1 Enoch 62:7; 2 Esdras 12:32; 2 Baruch 29:3; 39:7; Justin, *Dialogue with Trypho* 8:3; 49:1; 110:1). In the Fourth Gospel the baptismal activity of John is the means by which the Baptist comes to a recognition of Jesus.

Day Three ("the next day," 1:35–39) is composed of an exchange of disciples from John to Jesus (cf. 3:30: "He must increase, but I must decrease").

> John's words of testimony, "Behold the Lamb of God" (vv. 35–36).
>
> The disciples' response: they followed Jesus (v. 37).
>
> Jesus' question, "What do you seek?" (v. 38a).
>
> The disciples' response, "Where are you staying/abiding?" (v. 38b)
>
> Jesus' invitation, "Come and see" (v. 39a).
>
> The disciples' response: they abode with him that day (v. 39b).

Day Three is linked to Day Two not only by the seven or eight day scheme but also by the link phrase, Lamb of God (vv. 29, 36). John, who has been center stage on Days One and Two, now passes offstage and is replaced by Jesus, who attracts disciples to himself (cf. 1:6–8).

Day Four ("they stayed with him that day," v. 39, signals the close of the previous day, making the textual variant in v. 41, "early in the morning," found in the Old Latin and Old Syriac, unnecessary, 1:40–42) consists of one disciple's bringing another to Jesus. One who followed him was Andrew (v. 40):

> He found his brother Simon and said to him, "We have found the Messiah" (v. 41).
>
> He brought him to Jesus (v. 42a).
>
> > Jesus looked and said: a prophecy related to a disciple (v. 42b; cf. Matt 16:17–18; Mk 3:16).

Day Four is related to Day Three not only by the seven- or eight-day scheme but also by the link word "followed" (vv. 37, 40). Jesus here is center stage, drawing disciples to himself and giving them a new identity (v. 42b: a change of name signals a new identity; cf. Gen 32:27–28). This is facilitated by the fact that a newly acquired disciple, for his part, finds another follower, normally among his circle of intimates.

Day Five ("the next day," 1:43–51) is, like Day Four, a unit consisting of one disciple's bringing another to Jesus. It is unique in the seven- or eight-day scheme in that only here does Jesus, on one occasion, take the initiative and summon someone to discipleship.

> "Follow me," Jesus said to Philip (v. 43).
>
>> Philip found Nathanael and said to him, "We have found him of whom Moses and the prophets wrote" (v. 45).
>>
>>> Nathanael's incredulous query: "Can anything good come out of Nazareth?" (v. 46a)
>>
>> Philip said to him, "Come and see" (v. 46; cf. v. 39a).

Jesus saw him and said: a prophecy related to the disciple, revealing who he is (vv. 47–48), followed by one offered to the disciples as a whole, promising knowledge of the heavenly world (v. 51).

Day Five is related to Day Four not only by the seven- or eight-day scheme but also by the link word "found" (vv. 41, 45) and the use of prophecy related to new disciples (vv. 42b, 47, 51). It manifests two patterns of gaining disciples: the dominant pattern of drawing by means of another's witness and Jesus' magnetism (vv. 36–39, 40–42, 45–49) and the exceptional one of Jesus' summoning a potential disciple to follow him (v. 43b). These two patterns reflect the ideas and practices of the culture.

The first pattern, that of summons and response, has deep roots in Greek culture. (a) Plato, *Apology* 19E, speaks of the sophists' habit of seeking out young men to join up with them. (b) Aristophanes' *The Clouds* pictures Socrates as a sophist who commands a prospective disciple to "follow me . . . come." (c) Diogenes Laertius, *Lives of Eminent Philosophers* 2.48, tells of Socrates' call of Xenophon:

> The story goes that Socrates met him in a narrow passage, and that he stretched out his stick to bar the way, while he inquired where every kind of food was sold. Upon receiving a reply, he put another question. "And where do men become good and honorable?" Xenophon was fairly puzzled; "Then follow me," said Socrates, "and learn." From that time onward he was a pupil of Socrates.

This summons-response pattern is, of course, that found in the Synoptics (e.g., Mk 1:16–20; 2:14; Lk 5:1–11; 19:5; cf. Vernon K. Robbins, *Jesus the Teacher* [Philadelphia: Fortress, 1984], chap. 4.)

The second pattern, that of attraction of individuals by the teacher's magnetism, is also part of the Greco-Roman world. Its rationale is expressed by Epictetus:

> Does a philosopher invite people to a lecture? — Is it not rather the case that, as the sun draws its own sustenance to itself, so he also draws to himself those to whom he is to do good? What physician ever invites a patient to come and be healed by him? (3.23.27)

In the Fourth Gospel the new community is formed following both patterns. The exceptional pattern is summons-response (Jesus sovereignly picks the members of his community); the dominant pattern is witness-attraction (Jesus produces the community by his magnetism after attention is called to him by a witness). Doubtless, the Johannine community's experience resonated with both. It is the witness-attraction pattern, however, that is reflected in 1 John 1:3 (the eyewitnesses bear testimony and those who hear are drawn into fellowship with them and thereby into fellowship with the Son and the Father) and John 17.

Day Five also has Jesus make a prophecy about himself to the disciples as a group (v. 51) that will be fulfilled in 2:1–11. "You [plural] will see the heaven standing open [cf. Acts 10:11; Rev 4:1; 19:11] and the angels of God ascending and descending upon the Son of Man." This is almost certainly an echo of Genesis 28:12. The prepositional phrase *bo* in Hebrew can mean either "upon it" (the ladder) or "upon him" (Jacob), since both nouns are masculine in Hebrew. The LXX favors "upon the ladder" and translates *ep' autē* (upon it). *Genesis Rabba* 68:12:6, records a debate between R. Hiyya the Elder and R. Yannai (third century C.E.): One of them said, "They were ascending and descending on the ladder"; the other one said, "They were ascending and descending on Jacob." If such exegesis existed in the time of the Fourth Gospel it would make sense of John 1:51. Instead of "upon Jacob," the Evangelist substitutes "upon the Son of Man." The meaning is that Jesus is the locus of revelation, the place where the vision of God is given. If Nathanael confesses faith in Jesus ("Rabbi, you are the Son of God," v. 49; cf. 1 Sam 26:17, 21, 25; 2 Sam 7:14; 4QFlorilegium 1:6–7; 1 QSa 2:11ff; 1 Enoch 105:2; 2 Esdras 7:28–29; 13:52; 14:9) on the basis of Jesus' knowledge of him, how much more will they all believe on the basis of their knowledge of God through Jesus.

Day Seven ("on the third day," 2:1–12) is composed of a miracle story expanded so as to teach key Johannine themes: (a) Jesus' actions are not directed by human influence (v. 4; cf.7:8; 11:6); (b) the wine (spiritual reality) that Jesus gives is better than that which preceded him (v. 10); (c) the disciples are those who have beheld Jesus' glory (v. 11; cf. 1:14, 16). The unit is held together by an inclusion: vv. 1–2 (Jesus' mother, Jesus, Jesus' disciples go to Cana) and v. 12 (Jesus, his mother and brothers, Jesus' disciples go to Capernaum). The miracle story consists of the customary three parts.

(1) The problem (when the wine failed, v. 3). This component of the miracle story is expanded by an exchange between Mary and Jesus and by a word from Mary to the servants (vv. 3–5). Mary's expression of concern about the wine's running out is based on the expectation that guests at such a marriage feast would assist with supplies. Her word with Jesus is based on the assumption that, in the absence of her husband, the woman would depend upon the resources of her eldest son. Jesus' reply shifts the story from one level to another, from helping out at a marriage feast where supplies have run out to providing the wine of the new age/eternal life to those in need. His reply ("What have you to do with me?" = Why this interference?; cf. 2 Sam 16:10; 19:22; Plautus, *Menaechmi*, line 323) indicates that his action to do the latter is not dictated by human initiative, even by those closest to him, but by God's timing ("My hour has not yet come," v. 4b; cf. 7:8; 12:23; 13:1; cf. 1:13). Mary's word to the servants brings the story back to the earthly level ("Do whatever he tells you"); she is confident her son will do what is right.

(2) The miracle (the water now become wine, v. 9). This component is expanded by the symbolic actions of Jesus (vv. 6–8). The two commands of Jesus take the story back to a religious level. (a) Fill the six stone jars (stone because stone vessels did not contract uncleanness, Lev 21:29–30), used for Jewish rites of purification, with water drawn from the cistern or well. (b) Draw some more out of the well (*antlein*, 4:7, 15 = to draw from a well) and take it to the steward of the feast. The Jewish rites of purification (incomplete even when fully implemented) are superseded when the servants draw yet again and take it to the steward.

(3) The reaction to the miracle (the steward's word, vv. 9–10; the disciples' response, v. 11). When the steward of the feast tasted the water now become wine, he called the bridegroom and said, "Everyone serves the good wine first; and when people have drunk freely, then the poor wine; but you have kept the good wine until now." The steward's words of ad-

monishment about a breech in social propriety function in addition at the level of religious meaning. The good wine that Jesus supplies surpasses the benefits promised and provided by the Jewish purification rites. The wine (religious reality) made available by the events of Jesus' hour supersedes Jewish purificatory ritual. This miracle of water into wine is called a sign (v. 11). It is an act that points beyond itself to spiritual reality. It manifests Jesus' glory (that which makes him impressive to others, here, God's power). The disciples, unlike the steward of the feast, see his glory and believe in him (v. 11b; cf. 1:14). The miracle story of 2:1–11 functions as the fulfillment of the prophecy of 1:51 (cf. 2:11). A reading of 1:19–2:11 reveals that the whole is tied together with the same care with which the individual units are composed.

The large thought unit 1:19–2:11 functions in a number of ways in the Gospel: (1) it shows the proper role of the Baptist (cf. 3:30: "He must increase, I must decrease"); (2) it presents the witnesses to Christ (John: 1:29, 34, 36; the Father: 1:33; the Scriptures: 1:45; the works of Jesus: 2:11; cf. 5:31–47); (3) it establishes the presence of witnesses from the beginning (cf. 15:27: "you also are witnesses, because you have been with me from the beginning"); (4) it foreshadows the passion week at the end of the Gospel (cf. 12:1, 12, etc.); (5) it depicts Jesus as the many-named one (Lamb of God: 1:29, 36; the one who baptizes with the Holy Spirit: 1:33; Son of God: 1:34; Rabbi: 1:38; Messiah: 1:41; the one of whom Moses wrote: 1:45; the King of Israel: 1:49; Son of Man: 1:51; Philo, *On the Change of Names* 125, says: "The chief prophet turns out to be many-named"). Its primary function within the plot/story of the Fourth Gospel is to describe the picking/production of a new community. It focuses on discipleship. There are, in fact, two sections of the Fourth Gospel that consider discipleship in a special way: 1:19–2:11, which professes to discuss discipleship before Easter, and chapters 12, 13–17, and 20–21, which paint a picture of discipleship after Easter.

Discipleship before Easter, as it is portrayed in 1:19–2:11, involves at least three components: (1) how one comes to Jesus (usually by attraction/drawing after one's attention has been called to him by a witness, e.g., 1:36–37); (2) what a relationship with Jesus involves (abiding with him; cf. 1:38, "Where are you abiding?"; 1:39, "They came and saw where he was abiding, and they abode with him"); (3) what effects discipleship has on one: (a) public confession of faith (e.g., 1:41: "We have found the Messiah"; 1:45: "We have found him of whom Moses in the law and also the prophets spoke"; 1:49: "You are the Son of God. You are the King of Israel"), and (b) bringing others to Jesus (e.g., 1:42: "and he brought him to Jesus"; 1:45, 46: "Philip found Nathanael...and said to him, 'Come and see' ").

Discipleship after Easter, as portrayed in the prophecy of 12, the farewell speech of 13–17, and the post-resurrection narratives of 20–21, involves at least the same three components that were present in 1:19–2:11: (1) how one comes to Jesus (again primarily by attraction/drawing; 12:32: "And I, when I am lifted up from the earth, will draw all people unto me"); (2) what a relationship with Jesus involves (abiding/acquaintance; cf. 15:4: "Abide in me and I in you"; 15:5: "the one who abides in me and I in him"; 14:23: "we will come to him and make our abiding place with him"; 14:25–26: the Holy Spirit will "bring to your remembrance all that I have said to you"; 15:26: the Holy Spirit will "bear witness to me"; 16:13–15: the Spirit will "take what is mine and declare it to you"); (3) what effects discipleship has on one: (a) confession of faith in Jesus (e.g., 21:24 implies that the Gospel of John is such a post-resurrection confession); (b) mission to the world (e.g., 17:18: "As thou didst send me into the world, so I have sent them into the world"; 20:21b: "As the Father has sent me, even so I send you"); (c) love of one another (e.g., 13:34; 15:12; 15:17: "This I command you, to love one another") and Christian unity (e.g., 17:21–23: "that they may all be one"). From the vantage point of the Gospel of John, discipleship before and after Easter involves most of the same components.

It is significant that the episode 1:19–2:11, which focuses on Jesus' picking/production of a new community, ends the way it does. It ends with the fulfillment of Jesus' prophecy that the disciples will see the traffic between heaven and earth localized in his person (1:51). The fulfillment comes in a miracle story that has been shaped so as to speak about spiritual reality (the wine) that will be made available by Jesus' glorification. The spiritual reality that will be dispensed is contrasted with the purification rites of the Jews. Jesus' wine is given at the end of the fulfillment of such rituals and supersedes them. If the episode as a whole is about gathering disciples into a new community, the conclusion is about what Jesus offers them: a religious reality that supersedes traditional Jewish worship. Discipleship leads to a revaluation of Jewish worship in light of what Jesus offers. This thesis, that the worship Jesus offers supersedes traditional Jewish worship, is pursued at length in the episodes that follow in John 2:13–12:50.

To grasp the significance of what follows in John's plot, it is necessary to be sensitized to the varying views about worship in Mediterranean antiquity. How does one gain access to God? How does one properly honor God? In other words, what constitutes appropriate worship of God? These basic questions were answered in various ways in the ancient world. A spectrum of opinion follows.

The traditional answer to such questions is that one honors a deity by building a temple and by offering sacrifices; one gains access to a deity by means of what goes on in such sacred space, that is, the temple cultus. This was true for both pagan and Jewish cultures. (1) That pagan popular religion of this type was still a reality well into our era is indicated by the fact that it is satirized by Lucian in the third century (*On Sacrifices* 1 and 9). (2) Jewish evidence for such traditional worship is abundant. Josephus says that whoever had control of the fortified places at the Temple mount had the Jewish nation in its power,

> for sacrifices could not be made without (controlling) these places, and it was impossible for any of the Jews to forego offering these, for they would rather give up their lives than the worship which they are accustomed to offer God. (*Antiquities* 15.7.8 §248)

Indeed, 1 Maccabees 1:41–50 and 4:47–53 regard the Temple and its cultus as at the core of Jewish religion and identity. It is no wonder, then, that as R. Johanan ben Zakkai came from Jerusalem one day with his disciple, R. Joshua, the disciple, upon seeing the Temple in ruins, cried out: "Woe unto us, for the place where the iniquities of Israel were atoned is destroyed" (*The Fathers according to Rabbi Nathan* 6). In both pagan and Jewish contexts near the beginning of our era, the sacred space of a temple and its cultus were both a proper way to honor a deity and the sufficient means to gain access to him/her, that is, appropriate worship.

There was, of course, a long history of prophetic/philosophical critique of such cultic worship. (1) The philosophical critique had its roots in Socrates. On the one hand, Socrates followed the Delphic Oracle's advice, "Follow the custom of the State. That is the way to act piously." He therefore offered sacrifices. On the other hand, his sacrifices were humble:

> He thought himself not a whit inferior to those who made frequent and magnificent sacrifices out of great possessions. The gods (he said) could not well delight more in great offerings than in small — for in that case must the gifts of the wicked often have found more favor in their sight than the gifts of the upright.... No, the greater the piety of the giver, the greater (he thought) was the delight of the gods in the gift. (Xenophon, *Memorabilia* 1.3.1–3; for similar perspectives, cf. Isocrates, *Oration* 2; Pseudo-Plato, "Alcibiades," 2.149E; Persius, *Satires* 2.69–75; Seneca, *On Benefits* 1.6.3)

(2) A similar critique is found in Judaism. The pre-exilic prophets speak eloquently about the need for morality to accompany one's participation in the cult:

> I hate, I despise your feasts, and I take no delight in your solemn assemblies. Even though you offer me your burnt offerings and cereal offerings, I will not accept them, and the peace offerings of your fatted beasts I will not look upon. Take away from me the noise of your songs; to the melody of your harps I will not listen. But let justice roll down like waters, and righteousness like an ever-flowing stream. (Amos 5:21–24; cf. Isaiah 1:12–17; Hosea 6:6; 8:11–13; for a later time, cf. Aristeas 234)

Here the temple cultus is not rejected as such. It is the cultus without morality and without covenant faithfulness that is critiqued.

Alongside the traditional veneration of sacred space and sacrifice there developed a conviction that appropriate worship of deity was of a different nature. Sacred space was reconceptualized. The universe is the temple and the holy of holies is the inner self. Knowledge of God and ethical behavior are the true cultic activities. (1) Seneca, "On Superstition," is critical of external cult with its images and temple ritual. He advocates instead a rational mysticism, the piety of which consists in the consciousness of the deity present in each individual, which issues in lofty morality. In Epistle 41 ("On the God Within Us") he writes:

> We do not need . . . to beg the keeper of a temple to let us approach his idol's ear, as if in this way our prayers were more likely to be heard. God is near you, he is with you, he is within you. That is what I mean, Lucilius: a holy spirit indwells within us, one who marks our good and bad deeds, and is our guardian. As we treat this spirit, so are we treated by it. (For similar views, cf. Apollonius of Tyana, "On Sacrifices" [so Eusebius, *Preparation for the Gospel* 4.12–13]; Epistle 26; *Poimandres* 31; Porphyry, "On Abstinence" [so Eusebius, *Preparation* 4.11])

(2) Jewish evidence is supplied by Philo (*Every Good Man Is Free* 75). He tells us that Essenes showed themselves devoted servants of God, "not by offering animal sacrifices but by resolving to sanctify their minds." Whether this described all Essenes is to be doubted, but it seems to capture at least some Jewish appropriation of the same type of spiritualization of the cult that is observed among pagans.

At the same time, there were both pagans and Jews who believed that appropriate worship of deity is spiritual but who nevertheless retained some participation in traditional worship. (1) Oxyrhynchus Papyrus 215 is a fragment of Epicurean literature from the Augustan period. It says that the essence of piety is not external worship (1.4–11) but rather the proper conception of God which is to be honored (1.16–23). This honor may involve some participation in conventional cultic activity (2:1–6) but it should not involve any fear or any supposition that the gods derive any benefit from human acts of worship (2.8–11). In other words, one could be involved in traditional worship so long as it did not subvert true and appropriate worship. (2) This seems to be the personal position of Philo:

> A man may submit to sprinklings with holy water and to purifica-
> tions . . . he may . . . found a temple, providing all its furniture . . . he
> may never cease sacrificing bullocks; he may adorn the sacred build-
> ing with costly votive offerings . . . yet . . . not be inscribed on the roll
> of the pious. No, for this man . . . has gone astray . . . deeming it to
> be ritual instead of holiness, and offering gifts to Him who can-
> not be bribed . . . and flattering Him who cannot be flattered, who
> welcomes genuine worship of every kind, but abhors all counter-
> feit approaches. Genuine worship is that of a soul bringing simple
> reality as its only sacrifice; all that is mere display, fed by lavish ex-
> penditure on externals, is counterfeit. (*That the Worse Is Wont to
> Attack the Better* 20–21; cf. *Special Laws* 1.290; 1.269–72; *On the
> Unchangeableness of God* 7–9)

At the same time, Philo defends the animal sacrifices and festivals of the Temple against those whose allegorizing had caused them to ne-glect the literal meaning of the Law. He advocates both literal observance and spiritual worship (*The Migration of Abraham* 89–93; *Special Laws* 1.67–68).

Alongside traditional sacrificial worship in temples there stood an alter-nate tradition of spiritual worship consisting of an individual's "inquiring into and imitating God's nature" so as to "make life itself a prayer to Him" (so Porphyry, according to Augustine, *City of God* 19.23). Sometimes ad-vocates of this position continued to participate in the traditional cult, but without allowing such practice to undermine their understanding of true worship. Sometimes practitioners of spiritual worship rejected material temples and external rituals altogether. Either way, they rep-resent an alternative answer to the question of appropriate worship in antiquity.

There was yet a third position regarding worship in the Mediterranean world. Peter Brown offers a general perspective that is helpful:

> Previously, the classical world had tended to think of its religion in
> terms of *things*. Ancient religion had revolved around great temples
> . . . ; the gods had spoken impersonally at their oracle-sites; their cer-
> emonies assumed a life in which the community, the city, dwarfed the
> individual. In the fourth and fifth centuries, however, the individual,

as a "man of power," came to dwarf the traditional communities. . . . In the popular imagination, the emergence of the holy man at the expense of the temple marks the end of the classical world. (*The World of Late Antiquity*: A.D. *150–750* [New York: Harcourt Brace Javonovich, 1971], 102–3)

Simeon the Stylite, gloriously conspicuous on his column, sifting lawsuits, prophesying, healing, rebuking, and advising the governing classes, along with monks like Anthony and Pachomius, epitomize the holy man.

Jonathan Smith, building on Brown's insight, contends that the holy man was already a reality in the Mediterranean world as early as the second century B.C.E. His evidence is a second-century B.C.E. biography of Thessalos the Magician. The mood of the culture, he argues, was the denigration of sacred space. People, in their search for salvation, began to turn from temples and the cultus of the temple and look to savior figures and communities revolving around such figures as havens of salvation. Rather than a sacred place, the new center and chief means of access to the deity came to be a divine man who functioned without a fixed locale. Rather than celebration, purification, and pilgrimage, the new rituals came to be conversion, identification with the divine man, and initiation into the holy man's group. As part of this fundamental shift, the traditional language and ideology of the cult are reinterpreted. Only those parts that contribute to the new, anthropological, and highly mobile understanding of religion are retained (*Map Is Not Territory* [Leiden: Brill, 1978], 186–89).

In this understanding of worship, the material temple and cult of a specific location are replaced, not by a spiritualized holy of holies in the human soul and spiritualized sacrifices of contemplation and moral living, but by a holy man and his group. The mobile holy man is the locus of the divine presence. Honor bestowed on him is the way to honor the deity. His person and words are a revelation from the god. In this system, attachment to a holy man and participation in his community are both the means of access to and a way of honoring deity.

In heterodox Jewish circles there may have been analogies. In the *Clementine Homilies* 2.22–25, there is an account of the competition between Simon and Dositheus for leadership of the Baptist sect that seems akin to what has been suggested by Thessalos the Magician. A group has a holy man who mediates knowledge of God and to whom allegiance is demanded from the group. It is a religious group apparently quite independent of the Temple and any Jewish sacrificial cultus. If so, then the phenomenon noticed by Brown in the fourth century and recognized by

Smith in the second century B.C.E. in certain pagan circles is also present in heterodox Jewish circles at the beginning of our era.

What constitutes proper worship of God? So far we have attempted to describe three answers offered in Mediterranean antiquity. (1) Proper worship is in sacred space (a temple), using sacred means (a sacrificial cultus), at sacred times (e.g., festivals), and is presided over by sacred persons (priests). This was traditional worship. (2) Proper worship is spiritual. Instead of a material temple, the individual soul was the place of meeting with deity. Instead of a sacrificial cult, contemplation of God's nature and the practice of a lofty morality constituted true sacrifice. One's daily life thereby becomes a festival of worship. (3) The presence of the divine is localized, neither in a temple of stone nor in the individual soul, but in a holy man. Honor is shown to the deity through reverence for and attachment to him. These three positions existed side by side in the Mediterranean world at the beginning of our era.

It was possible, moreover, for the second and third streams to flow together on occasion. The Epicurean School may serve as an example. During Epicurus' lifetime, he was regarded as the locus of divine reality and treated as an object of worship (Cicero, *Tusculan Disputations* 1.21.48; Plutarch, *Reply to Colotes* 1117 B, C; i.e., position 3). After his death, the School continued to reverence him. Cicero speaks of an ongoing banquet (a sacred meal) to honor the founder of the School (*On the Ends of Good and Evil* 2.31.101). After Epicurus' death, however, the community's focus was on spiritualized worship, even if it did on occasion permit participation in traditional cult (position 2).

These Mediterranean views of what constitutes appropriate worship serve as lenses through which one may look at the Fourth Gospel. Read in this way, the Gospel of John seems to be saying that the entire system of traditional Jewish worship has been superseded by Jesus and what he made available. John's depiction of the supersession of Jewish worship by Jesus assumes two time periods: (a) the period prior to Jesus' glorification, and (b) the period after Jesus' glorification.

When the Evangelist focuses on Jesus' earthly life, it is in terms of that view of antiquity which sees the material temple and cult replaced by a mobile holy man in whom the presence of God is localized so that conversion/attachment to him constitutes one's cultic obligation (position 3). This explains why the Jesus of the Fourth Gospel reveals that he is the Revealer. Within position 3, John belongs to the option that is hostile to and exclusive of traditional cult. According to the Fourth Gospel, the earthly Jesus advocates the supersession of the entire system of traditional Jewish worship. The Evangelist tries to ground the Christian practice of worship after Jesus' glorification in something Jesus did or said prior to his glorification.

When the Gospel focuses on the period after Jesus' glorification, it continues to reverence Jesus (and more!) but also spiritualizes worship. Worship is through the Spirit given by Jesus, which points to Jesus. In a way similar to, but not exactly like, the Epicurean School before and after the founder's death, the Fourth Evangelist blends two streams of ancient thinking about appropriate worship (positions 2 and 3). Traditional worship is superseded in the Christian community. That is why the Evangelist can speak of the Passover of the Jews (2:13); a feast of the Jews (5:1), the Passover, the feast of the Jews (6:4), the Jews' feast of Tabernacles (7:2), the Passover of the Jews (11:55), and the Jewish day of Preparation (19:42).

Is the Johannine view of worship merely a common Christian conviction, or does it represent a Johannine alternative to other early Christian options? In a sense, all four Gospels see Jesus, prior to his death and resurrection, as a holy man in whom the divine presence is manifest, by whom one gains access to God, and through attachment to whom one honors God (position 3). The emphasis is only heightened in John. They differ, however, in their attitude toward the traditional cult. The Fourth Gospel begins Jesus' public ministry with his actions that effectively suspend Temple sacrifices (2:13–22). Thereafter Jesus participates in Jewish worship only in order to show he fulfills and supersedes it. In Matthew and Mark, the rejection of the traditional cult comes only at the end of Jesus' career (Matt 21:12–13; Mk 11:15–18). In Luke 19:45–46, the so-called cleansing pericope, which comes at the end of Jesus' ministry, is so brief as to have minimal impact. The Temple itself is not rejected. Rather it functions in what follows as a place of teaching for the people (19:47–21:38) and in Acts as a place of prayer (3:1) and sacrifice (21:26). Among early Christian portrayals of Jesus as a holy man, the Gospel of John has him manifest the greatest degree of hostility to traditional worship.

In early Christianity generally, after Jesus' resurrection he continues to be reverenced, and worship is spiritualized. The church (sometimes the individual, 1 Cor 6:19) is the Temple (1 Cor 3:16–17; 2 Cor 6:16; Eph 2:21–22) or God's house (1 Pet 2:5; Heb 3:6). The sacrifices of Christians are "living" (Rom 12:1) or "spiritual" (1 Pet 2:5) sacrifices. They include praise (Heb 13:15), good deeds (Phil 4:18; Heb 13:16), and martyrdom (Phil 2:17). Christians, however, differ in their attitudes toward traditional worship. Most Christians who spiritualize worship do so to the exclusion of traditional cult. John stands with Paul, Matthew/Mark, and Hebrews in this regard. Only Acts, among the New Testament authors, seems willing to allow traditional worship for Jews who had become Christians (3:1; 21:23–24; 22:17; 24:18) for as long as the Temple was standing. In his spiritualizing of worship after Jesus' glorification, in his continued reverence for the holy man Jesus, and in his disdain for traditional worship, the Fourth Evangelist stands with the Christian majority in the New Testament.

From the extraordinary amount of space given to the matter of worship in the Gospel of John, it is clear that the community from which the Gospel comes understands itself as first and foremost a worshipping community. Its worship, moreover, had warrants in the deeds and words of the earthly Jesus. It was the earthly Jesus who had acted and spoken repeatedly in ways that indicated he superseded Jewish worship in all its forms. Indeed, in the section of the Gospel that follows, 2:13–12:50, there are seven episodes that make essentially the same point: Jesus supersedes traditional Jewish worship. They are: (1) 2:13–3:21; (2) 3:22–4:3; (3) 4:4–54; (4) chapter 5; (5) chapter 6; (6) chapters 7–9; (7) chapters 10–11. Chapter 12 functions as a conclusion to what precedes and as an introduction to what follows.

In its use of Jesus' public career to illustrate the principle of Christian worship's supersession of Jewish traditional worship, the Fourth Gospel fits into the ancient world's normal treatment of characters. In ancient narrative's treatment of characters,

> we are not called upon to understand their motivation as if they were whole human beings but to understand the principles they illustrate through their actions in a narrative framework. (R. Scholes and R. Kellog, *The Nature of Narrative* [London: Oxford University Press, 1966], 88)

In the Fourth Gospel's "revelation to the world" (chaps. 2–12), the story of Jesus functions to illustrate and to give warrant for the supersession of traditional worship in the Johannine community.

PROPONENT
OF A NEW BIRTH

John 2:13–3:21

The one who came as revealing, empowering presence (1:1–18) has picked/produced a new community and has shown them that what he offers as the result of his hour supersedes Jewish purification ritual (1:19–2:12). In John 2:13–3:21 the reader is offered the first of seven episodes that present the earthly Jesus as giving warrants for the supersession of Jewish worship in that of the Johannine community. This section (2:13–3:21) is composed of two units, 2:13–22 and 2:23–3:21. These are linked *formally* by the references to Jerusalem and the Passover (2:13; 2:23) and by the Johannine custom of associating Jesus' symbolic acts with his discourses (e.g., acts followed by discourses: chap. 5; chap. 6; discourses followed by acts: chaps. 7–9; chaps. 10–11). They are related *thematically* by the issue of legitimation: what is it that legitimates Jesus? In 2:18 the Jews ask for a sign to legitimate Jesus' actions; 2:23 implies Jesus' miracles legitimate him with many (cf. 9:16); 3:2 indicates Nicodemus was one of the many who regarded Jesus' signs as his legitimation. That Jesus cuts Nicodemus off and changes direction in 3:3 indicates that he is presenting a different ground for legitimation (e.g., the new birth by the Spirit enabled by Jesus' glorification) that is basically the same as that offered in 2:19 (his resurrection). Since only like can know like, for one to see/enter the sphere of God's reign, one must be born of the Spirit, for God is Spirit (4:24). For these reasons, 2:13–3:21, which is made up of diverse pre-existing traditions, will be treated as one large thought unit of the Evangelist. Tracing the train of thought offers further support for such a reading.

Unit One (2:13–22), after an introduction (v. 13), falls into two parts, 2:14–17 and 2:18–22, each climaxed by a reference to Jesus' disciples remembering. The first (vv. 14–17; cf. Mk 11:15–18)) focuses on what Jesus does:

> The circumstances: sellers of animals and money changers are in the Temple (v. 14).

>> Jesus' response in deed ("and making a whip of cords, he drove them all out of the Temple, both the sheep and the oxen, and he poured out the coins of the moneychangers and overturned their tables," v. 15) and word ("And he told those who sold the pigeons, 'Take these things away; you shall not make my Father's house a house of trade,'" v. 16, cf. Zech 14:21b).

>> The disciples remembered the Scripture: "Zeal for thy house will consume me" (v. 17, cf. Ps 69:9).

What Jesus does is to render Temple sacrifices impossible. M. Shekalim 1.3 says that money-changers serve to change coinage into the shekel required for the Temple. T. Shekalim 1.6 says money-changers in the Temple "exact pledges from those who had not yet paid" so public offerings might be made that atone for Israel's sins — after analogy with practice in the wilderness (Exod 30:16). So money-changers were essential to the system of atonement for sin. They were not blemishes on the cult but part of its perfection. Jesus' action called into question the very system. The overturning of the money-changers' tables represents an act of the rejection of the most important rite of the Israelite cult, the daily whole offering (J. Neusner, "Money-Changers in the Temple: The Mishnah's Explanation," *NTS* 35 [1989]: 287–90). "The purging of the temple . . . signifies the destruction and replacement of the system of religious observance of which the temple was the centre" (C. H. Dodd, *The Interpretation of the Fourth Gospel* [Cambridge: Cambridge University Press, 1958], 301).

The second part of Unit One (vv. 18–22) is concerned with Jesus' authority for acting in a way that rendered Temple sacrifices impossible (i.e., his resurrection).

> The challenge: "The Jews then said to him, 'What sign have you to show us for doing this?'" (v. 18; cf. Mk 11:27–28).

>> Jesus' response: "Destroy this temple and in three days I will raise it up" (v. 19; cf. Mk 14:58; 15:29; 13:2; Acts 6:14).

>>> Jewish misunderstanding: "It has taken forty-six years to build this Temple, and will you raise it in three days?" (v. 20; cf. 3:3–4; 4:13–15; 4:31–34; 6:41–42; 6:52; 7:33–36; 8:31–33; 8:56–57; 11:11–14; 12:32–34, for a misunderstanding motif in John; cf. Hermetica 4:6; 10:6–7; 12:15–16; 13:1, for such a technique outside John).

>>> Clarification by the narrator: "But he spoke of the temple of his body" (v. 21; cf. 1:38; 1:41; 1:42; 4:2, for other explanatory comments).

> The disciples remember: "When he was raised from the dead. his disciples remembered that he had said this; and they believed the Scripture and the word which Jesus had spoken" (v. 22).

When the Jews demand to know his authority for rendering Temple sacrifices impossible, Jesus appeals to his future resurrection. How can his resurrection legitimate non-involvement in Jewish Temple worship? The answer comes in the Nicodemus episode that follows.

Unit Two (2:23–3:21) is a framed dialogue in three parts that shifts the question of legitimation from Jesus' signs to the new birth by the Spirit that comes as a result of Jesus' descent-ascent. Its pattern is clear.

2:23–3:2: (a) many believed in his name (2:23)

(b) Nicodemus comes to Jesus by night (3:1–2a)

(c) You are come from God (3:2b)

(1) 3:2–3: Nicodemus said (v. 2)
Jesus answered: Truly, truly, I say (v. 3)

(2) 3:4–8: Nicodemus said (v. 4)
Jesus answered: Truly, truly, I say (v. 5–8)

(3) 3:9–12: Nicodemus said (v. 9)
Jesus answered: Truly, truly, I say (v. 11–12)

3:13–21: (c) Jesus has come from God (3:13–17)

(a) believe in his name (3:16, 18)

(b) people love darkness; the one who does what is true comes to the light (3:19–21)

A reading needs to take account both of the pattern of 2:23–3:21 and its connections with 2:13–22.

The Jews had demanded a sign to legitimate Jesus (2:18). Now there is the note that "many believed in his name when they saw the signs which he did" (v. 23). Jesus here (vv. 24–25) is no more positively disposed toward miracle as a legitimating device than in v. 18. He knew what was in their hearts (*Mekhilta*, Exodus 15:32: "Seven things are hidden from man — the day of death, the day of consolation, the depths of judgment, one's reward, the time of the restoration of the kingdom of David, the time when the guilty kingdom will be destroyed, and *what is within another*"). If Jesus knows what these people really are, what will it take for humans to know who he really is? When Nicodemus says he believes Jesus is from God because "no one can do these signs that you do, unless God is with him" (3:2), he is an example of those who believed because of signs. The Jews (2:18), the many (2:23), and Nicodemus (3:2) all assume the marvelous as such can legitimate Jesus' spiritual authority. There is no recognition of the ambiguity of the marvelous such as one finds, for example, in the Revelation to John 13:11–14 (where the second beast makes the inhabitants of the earth worship the first beast, deceiving people by means of working great signs) or the Pseudo-Clementine, *Recognitions* 3.51–60 (where, in 52, Niceta asks Peter how Simon who is the enemy of God is able to do great miracles and, in 57, how the Egyptian magicians were able to do many of the same marvels as Moses).

To the Jews, Jesus offered his resurrection as legitimation; from the many, Jesus merely held back; for Nicodemus, Jesus presents a new birth as the necessity for seeing God and entering his realm (i.e., as necessary for recognizing God in Jesus). He says: "Truly, truly, I say to you, unless one is born *anōthen* [either "again" or "from above"], one cannot see the kingdom of God" (v. 3; cf. Justin, *1 Apology* 61:4; Pseudo-Clementine, *Homilies* 11.26; *Recognitions* 6.9, for mention of a similar saying; cf. 1 John 2:29; 3:9; 4:7; 5:1, 4, 18; Titus 3:5; 1 Pet 1:3, 23, for new birth). The argument hinges on the common Greco-Roman epistemological conviction: like is known by like (Plato, *Protagoras* 337C–338A; *Timaeus* 45C; Philo, *On the Change of Names* 6; Plotinus, *Enneads* 4.5.7, 23–62; 1.6.9, 30–45).

A parallel to what is going on in John 3 may be found in the *Corpus Hermeticum*, tractate 13, a dialogue where Hermes Trismegistos tells his disciple Tat the prerequisite for a revelation concerning divinity. Such a revelation is not possible prior to regeneration or new birth, something that must be experienced. So Hermes summons the divine, heavenly powers to enter into Tat. The result is Tat's deification. Now Tat can see and understand in ways that were impossible for him before. Having become divine, Tat can know god and understand divinity. This was the objective of his regeneration. Like can be known only by like. "Unless you are born from above you cannot see the kingdom of God" (John 3:3; W. C. Greese, "Unless One Is Born Again: The Use of a Heavenly Journey in John 3," *JBL* 107 [1988]: 677–93).

The ambiguity of *anōthen* enables earthbound Nicodemus to misunderstand. He takes the temporal meaning ("again") and says: "How can people be born when they are old? Can they enter a second time into their mothers' wombs and be born?" (v. 4). Jesus' second response is a variation on his first: "Truly, truly, I say to you, unless one is born of water and the Spirit, one cannot enter the kingdom of God" (v. 5). Of the options ([a] physical birth; cf. Pirke Aboth 3:1; 3 Enoch 6:2; [b] John the Baptist's baptism; cf. 1:33; 3:23; [c] Christian baptism; cf. Justin, *1 Apology* 61; Hermas, "Parable," 9.16.2; [d] the cleansing power of the word; cf. 15:3; 6:63; [e] water = Spirit; cf. 4:7–12; 7:37–39), it the last that captures John's meaning.

The expression "of water and Spirit" is best paraphrased as "of water which is Spirit." Two arguments support this reading. (1) The construction in Greek is that of two terms joined by "and" (*kai*) and governed by one preposition. This Greek construction normally points to one act: e.g., Titus 3:5 ("by the washing of regeneration and renewal in the Holy Spirit" = "by the cleansing renewal which the Holy Spirit works in regeneration"). If two acts were involved, normally two prepositions would occur (R. Summers, "Born of Water and Spirit," in *The Teacher's Yoke: Studies in Memory of Henry Trantham* [Waco: Baylor University Press, 1964], 117–28; X. Leon-Dufour, "Towards a Symbolic Reading of the Fourth Gospel," *NTS* 27 [1981]: 439–56). (2) In John there are two types of references to water: those using water to refer to the lower world (e.g., John's baptism, 1:33; 3:22; Jewish purifications, 2:6–7; water from the Samaritan well, 4:6–7; troubled water in pool of Bethesda, 5:7), and those using water to point to the upper world (e.g., 4:14; 7:37–39). In John 3:5, "born of water" is contrasted to physical birth (v. 4, 6) and linked with spiritual birth (v. 5); hence, in 3:5 water points away from the lower and to the heavenly world. "Unless one is born of water which is Spirit, one cannot enter into the kingdom of God."

Cyprian, *Epistle* 1:3–4 (To Donatus), captures the essence of John 3:3, 5 in an account of his own conversion:

> While I was still lying in darkness... remote from truth and light, I used to regard it as a difficult matter... that a man should be capable of being born again... and... be able to put off what he had previously been.... (3)

> But after..., by the agency of the Spirit breathed from heaven, a second birth had restored me to a new man; — then, in a wondrous manner, doubtful things at once began to assure themselves to me, hidden things to be revealed, dark things to be enlightened, what before had seemed difficult began to suggest a means of accomplishment, what had been thought impossible, to be capable of being achieved; so that I was enabled to acknowledge that what previously, being born of the flesh, had been living in the practice of sins, was of the earth earthly, now had now begun to be of God, and was animated by the Spirit of holiness. (5)

Once Jesus has clarified the new birth as "from above" (of water which is Spirit) and not merely "again," Nicodemus asks: "How can this be?"

(v. 9). Just as Jesus' response in the first two parts of the dialogue pointed to the impossibility of one's understanding without a new birth (vv. 3, 5), so here in the third part of the dialogue Jesus verbalizes the impossibility of someone who does not participate in the heavenly world ever to understand. "How can you believe if I tell you heavenly things?" (v. 12). There has been a threefold pattern of failure to understand: the Jews (2:18), the many (2:23), and Nicodemus, three times (3:1–12). Each has assumed that the marvelous is the means by which one recognizes God and, therefore, the way to gauge the legitimacy of Jesus' actions. Over against the threefold failure, Jesus has claimed the authority for his actions rests on his resurrection and on others' new birth. The progression of thought has come to the point where an answer must be furnished to the question about the new birth: "How can this be?"

At 3:12 the dialogue between Jesus and Nicodemus comes to an end; at 3:13 the theological reflections of the Evangelist begin (cf. 3:31–36, where a similar shift takes place). V. 13 states the thesis. The new birth is not brought about by means of human ascent into heaven but by means of the descent-ascent of the Son of Man. There are negative and positive sides to this thesis. V. 13 emphasizes the negative: "No one has ascended into heaven except the one who descended from heaven, the Son of Man." The background for such a statement is both Jewish and Christian (Peder Borgen, "The Son of Man Saying in John 3:13–14," in *Philo, John and Paul* [Atlanta: Scholars, 1987], 103–20).

On the one hand, there is a Hellenistic Jewish tradition about Moses' ascent into heaven at Mount Sinai that was a second birth for him, a birth from above in contrast to the first from earth. Philo says that Moses

> was named God [*theos*] and king of the whole nation, and entered we are told, into the darkness where God was, that is into the unseen, invisible, incorporeal and archetypal essence of existing things. Thus he beheld what is hidden from the sight of mortal nature, and, in himself and his life displayed for all to see, he has set before us, like some well-wrought picture, a piece of work beautiful and godlike, a model for those who are willing to copy it. Happy are they who imprint, or strive to imprint, that image in their souls. (*Moses* 1.158–59)

Here Moses is set forth as a godlike model to copy because he has ascended into heaven (i.e., a mystic vision that is identified allegorically with his ascent of Mount Sinai).

Elsewhere Philo refers to Moses' ascent into Mount Sinai and says, "the calling above of the prophet is a *second birth* better than the first... the calling above or, as we have said, the *divine birth*" (*Questions and An-*

swers on Exodus 2.46). Here Philo contrasts the first birth from the earth with the second birth from above.

On the other hand, there is a similar Christian tradition that thinks in terms of an individual's mystical ascent into heaven where he sees God and returns to earth with revelation for others. The Martyrdom and Ascension of Isaiah, a composite work, contains a Jewish martyrdom of Isaiah (1:1–3:12; 5:1–16) that has been supplemented by Christian additions (3:13–4:22 = a vision that Isaiah experienced before his arrest by Manasseh; and chaps. 6–11 = Isaiah's ascent into heaven where he sees God and joins in the heavenly worship before being given a revelation of what is to take place). Here is a Christian text, not far from the time of John, that speaks of an individual's ascent into heaven where he sees God and receives revelation of spiritual matters.

John 3:13, "No one has ascended into heaven, except the one who descended from heaven," defends against such claims, be they Jewish or Christian. A similar rabbinic defense, which also includes a polemic against Christian claims of Incarnation, is found in a midrash on the words, "And the Lord came down upon Mount Sinai."

> R. Jose says: Behold it says: "The heavens are the heavens of the Lord, but the earth hath he given to the children of men (Ps 115:16). Neither Moses nor Elijah ever went up to heaven, nor did the Glory ever come down to earth." (*Mekilta de Rabbi Ishmael*, trans. J. Z. Lauterbach [Philadelphia: Jewish Publication Society of America, 1976], 2:224)

The Johannine community, as it is known from the epistles, is experiencing conflict with progressives who base their new position on direct revelation of the Spirit severed from ongoing connections with Jesus. In 3:13a there is a defense against such a posture. One is not born from above by the Spirit by one's own mystical ascent.

The positive part of v. 13 consists of the affirmation that the Son of Man has descended from and ascended into heaven and that this descent-ascent answers the question of how the new birth is possible. What follows in vv. 14–21 is commentary on the descent–ascent schema. Vv. 14–15 are commentary on the ascent, vv. 16–21 on the descent. (1) Vv. 14–15 reflect the author's acquaintance with the typological interpretation that the Christian tradition had given Numbers 21:8–9 (cf. Barnabas 12:5–7; Justin, *Dialogue* 91, 94, 112; *1 Apology* 60). "And as Moses lifted up the serpent in the wilderness, so must the Son of Man be lifted up [8:28; 12:32, 34], that whoever believes in him may have eternal life." The ascent of the Son of Man is a saving event for those who believe in him. (2) Vv. 16–21 focus on various dimensions of the descent. (a) The descent is a saving event (v. 16). A woodenly literal translation of v. 16 helps with the problem of overfamiliarity: "For in this manner God loved the world [humanity mobilized in defiance of the divine purpose: 7:7; 8:23; 12:31; 14:17–18; 15:18–19; 16:8, 11; 16:20, 33; 17:9, 25], with the result that he gave his only Son [*monogenē*] with the purpose that everyone who goes on believing [present tense] in him may not perish but may go on having eternal life" (i.e., knowledge of God and Christ, 17:3). When it is said that God "gave" his Son, the reference is to the Incarnation as a whole, including the water and the blood (cf. 1 John 5:6–8). The emphasis on continuing belief in the Son is characteristically Johannine (1 John 5:13; John 20:30–31; cf. 2 John 9). (b) The intent of the descent is beneficent (v. 17): "For God sent the Son into the world, not to condemn the world, but that the world might be saved through him." Since "the one sent by a man is as the man himself" (m. Berakoth 5.5), the Son represents God's intent: not to condemn but to save. (c) Yet the result of the Son's coming is often judgment. "Those who do not believe in him are condemned already, because they have not believed in the name of the only Son of God" (v. 18). If the divine intent is to save, why then does judgment result from the Son's coming? Judgment (separation) is the result of human decision reflecting human nature. "For those who do evil hate the light, and do not come to the light, lest their deeds should be exposed. But those who do what is true come to the light, that it may be clearly seen that their deeds have been wrought in God" (vv. 20–21).

How can people be born from above so that they can see the kingdom of God (v. 9)? The answer is: not by individual mystical ascent into heaven (v. 13a) but by virtue of the descending-ascending Son of Man (vv. 13b–21). How does the descent-ascent of the Son of Man enable it? This text does not explicitly say how, but later in the Gospel the reader is told. It is by the Spirit that is given after Jesus' glorification (7:37–39; 20:22) and made possible by it (16:7: "it is to your advantage that I go away, for if I do not go away, the Counselor will not come to you; but if I go, I will send him to you").

By what authority can the earthly Jesus suspend Temple sacrifices (2:18)? The answer of this thought unit is: Jesus' resurrection (2:19–21). How can the resurrection of Jesus (part of his ascent) legitimate Christian non-involvement in Temple sacrifices? This text does not say explicitly, but later in the Gospel the reader is told. It is after his resurrection that Jesus gives the Spirit (20:22) and true worship is in Spirit (4:24). Implicit in the train of thought of 2:13–3:21 is the conviction that Jesus' resurrection/ascent enables a new birth by the Spirit and thereby makes possible true worship in Spirit. It is in this sense that Jesus' resurrection legitimates non-involvement in Temple sacrifices. John 2:13–3:21 is the first of seven episodes making the point that Christian worship that supersedes Jewish worship has a warrant in something the earthly Jesus did and said.

The lack of explicitness in 2:13–3:21 should not be surprising on at least two counts. (1) There are gaps in all artful narratives. Gaps, deliberate ambiguity, and reticence assist the narrative to avoid being boring by serving as invitations for readers or hearers to fill in the narrative according to their expectations as fostered by literary conventions or community convictions. The ancient rhetorician, Demetrius, puts it thusly:

> Not everything should be given lengthy treatment with full details but some points should be left for our hearer to grasp and infer for himself. If he infers what you have omitted, he no longer just listens to you but acts as your witness, one too who is predisposed in your favor since he feels he has been intelligent and you are the person who has given him this opportunity to exercise his intelligence. In fact, to tell your reader everything as if he were a fool is to reveal that you think him one. (*On Style* 222)

(2) A foundation document of a group that embodies the corporate traditions and that has evolved over a lengthy period of time within the community would be telling a story that is already known to its hearers. It is not as though the readers know nothing except what has come before in the Gospel's narrative. They know the story from beginning to end and so can enjoy, as only insiders can, the stupidity of the Jews and the denseness of Nicodemus, knowing for themselves the answers to every question that arises in the story.

Since the modern reader does not know the story from the inside out as did the members of the Johannine community, it may be a help if something is said here about the overall attitude toward miracles in the Fourth Gospel. In John's Christian context there was a diversity of belief about the miracles of Jesus. In Luke-Acts, for example, Jesus' miracles are catalysts for faith (e.g., Lk 4:31–5:11) and the disciples' miracles herald the expansion of the faith (Acts 3:1–4:4; 5:12–14; 8:6–8; 13:4–12). This is a positive view of miracle. In Mark, however, one hears that not everyone believes in Jesus because of his mighty works (e.g., Mk 3:22, 30; 6:1–6) and that to confess Jesus as Christ on the basis of his power is partial vision that must be supplemented by the vision of his cross (cf. Mk 8:14–21, 22–26, 27–31). This is a more negative view of miracle. The Fourth Gospel's position is complex. (1) Jesus' signs sometimes provoke faith (4:53; 10:41–42; 11:45, 47–48; 14:11). (2) However, not everyone believes in him as a result of his signs. Signs are ambiguous (10:25–26; 11:45–48). (a) Some are interested in the signs only for the physical benefits (6:26). (b) Others reject them as a threat to the nation's security (11:46–48). (c) Still others reject them as not from God because Jesus' behavior otherwise seems out of bounds (9:16, 30, 34). Such rejection is a fulfillment of Scripture (12:37–40). (3) In order for people to see through the miracle to the sign (i.e., Jesus' identity) some preliminary faith is sometimes present (e.g., 2:11; 4:46–54; 20:30–31; 21:6–7), but at other times it is not present (2:23; 3:2; chap. 9; 11:45). (4) When faith is already there, the miracle deepens it (2:11; 4:46–54; 20:30–31). When the signs evoke faith or openness to faith, a further development is necessary if Jesus is to be understood properly (e.g., chaps. 3 and 9). This is a nuanced view of Jesus' signs.

Regarding Jesus' disciples, there is general agreement in early Christianity that they share in his miracle-working activity: e.g., Romans 15:18–19; 1 Corinthians 2:4; 12:10, 28; 2 Corinthians 12:12; Mark 3:15; 6:7, 12; Matthew 10:1; Acts 3:1–10; 9:32–35; 9:36–42. John 14:12–14 ("Truly, truly, I say to you, those who believe in me will also do the works that I do; and greater works than these will they do, because I go to my Father") locates the Fourth Gospel within the common consensus. The Johannine community believed that Jesus' miracle working activity continued in their church. From John 2:13–3:21, however, one learns that miracle is not by itself (i.e., without the new birth enabled by the Spirit as a result of Jesus' resurrection) a legitimation of Jesus' actions.

THE OBJECT
OF THE BAPTIST'S PRAISE

John 3:22–4:3

John 3:22–4:3 is a large thought unit held together by an inclusion: 3:22–26 ([a] Jesus comes into Judea, 3:22a; [b] Jesus is baptizing, 3:22b; [c] John's disciples feel competition with Jesus, 3:26) and 4:1–3 ([c] Pharisees hear about competition over baptism, 4:1; [b] Jesus himself does not baptize, but only his disciples, 4:2; [a] Jesus leaves Judea, 4:3). It functions in the Fourth Gospel as the second of seven episodes that illustrate the thesis: Jesus supersedes traditional Jewish worship. In it Jesus is shown to be making and baptizing more disciples than John the Baptist, whose baptism is depicted as part of the Jewish purification system (3:25). It is composed of two parts, 3:22–30 and 3:31–36. The first (vv. 22–30) gives John the Baptist's interpretation of the fact of Jesus' success. The second (vv. 31–36) offers the Evangelist's reasons for the superiority of Jesus.

Unit One (3:22–30) is a composite paragraph that, in its final form, is very much like a Synoptic pronouncement story (cf. Mk 2:15–17; 2:18–20; 2:23–28; 12:13–17). It begins with a narrative setting (vv. 22–26) that serves as a springboard for the authoritative words of John the Baptist (vv. 27–30). The narrative foundation (vv. 22–26) tells of a baptizing ministry of both Jesus (v. 22: Christian baptism, so incorrectly Augustine, *Epistle* 44:10; 265:5; not Christian baptism, so correctly Tertullian, *On Baptism* 11:4) and John the Baptist (v. 23) in Judea, not Transjordan (v. 26), before John was arrested (v. 24; cf. Mk 1:14, where Jesus' ministry in Galilee begins after John is arrested). The ministry of the Baptist at this point involves his disciples in two issues. (1) There is first a controversy over purifying between John's disciples and "a Jew" (so P75, Vaticanus, and others) or "Jews" (so P66, Sinaiticus, and others). The conjectures that "Jesus" should be the reading are unfounded and unnecessary. The purpose of v. 25, with its reference to a debate between the Baptist's disciples and a Jew or Jews over purifying, is to locate John's baptism in the context of other Jewish purification practices. In ancient Jewish thought, ritual purifications were sometimes given a metaphorical meaning, symbolizing the eschatological cleansing of God's people with the sprinkling of water, often described as the Spirit (Ezk 36:25–27; 1 QS 3:1–2: "He will cleanse him of all wicked deeds with the spirit of holiness; like purifying waters He will shed upon him the spirit of truth to cleanse him of all abominations of falsehood"; 4:21). When the Jews ask the Baptist if he is the Christ, Elijah, or the prophet (1:21, 25), what they want to know is if he is claiming his baptism belongs to the eschatological cleansing of Jewish expectation. John's denial that he is such an eschatological figure has the effect of relegating his baptism to the same level as other Jewish purification rites (1:26, 33). That is also the function of 3:25.

(2) The second issue in which John's disciples find themselves involved is the greater success of Jesus. "And they came to John, and said to him, 'Rabbi, he who was with you beyond the Jordan, to whom you bore witness [cf. 1:29, 34, 36], here he is, baptizing, and all are going to him'" (v. 26). It is this second issue that prompts the Baptist's pronouncement.

John's words (vv. 27–30) involve four components. (1) The cause of Jesus' success is first stated as a general principle: "No one can receive anything except what is given him from heaven" (v. 27). If there is greater success on Jesus' part, it is God's doing. Each person, whether Jesus or John, plays the part God gives (cf. 1 Cor 3:5–10; 4:7). Two contrasts make this clear. (2) "You yourselves bear me witness, that I said, I am not the Christ [1:20], but I have been sent before him" (v. 28; cf. 1:15; 1:27; 1:30). In this first contrast, Jesus' part assigned by God is that of the Christ; John's part is that of going before him. (3) "He who has the bride is the bridegroom; the friend of the bridegroom, who stands and hears him, rejoices greatly at the bridegroom's voice; therefore this joy of mine is now full" (v. 29). In this second contrast, Jesus' role is that of bridegroom; John's that of the friend of the bridegroom. In Jewish wedding practice, the friend brought the bride to the groom and then stood guard over the nuptial chamber. Although he could hear the bridegroom's voice exclaiming in joy over the consummation of the union, he would never consider interfering. Indeed, ancient Near Eastern law forbade the giving of the bride to the best man (cf. the violation in Judg 14:20). John, then, would not improperly interfere in the union of bride (Israel: Hos 2:21; Jer 2:2; Isa 62:4–5; Ezk 16:8; Church: 2 Cor 11:2; Eph 5:25–27; Rev 21:2) and bridegroom (Jesus). His joy is full because he has played his part in facilitating the union. (4) The conclusion of the matter comes in v. 30: "He [Jesus] must increase, but I [John] must decrease." The fact that has sparked the controversy is Jesus' greater success in attracting and baptizing disciples. John's interpretation of this success is that it is as it ought to be. It is God's doing and accords with the assigned roles of each in the divine plan ("must" = necessary according to the divine plan).

Unit Two (vv. 31–36), like 3:13–21 of the preceding thought unit, shifts from the speech of the historical actors in the drama to reflections by the Evangelist on the matters under discussion. Here the Evangelist gives his interpretation of the superiority of Jesus' baptism. There are three components in his reasoning (W. E. Hull, "John," *BBC* 9, 247–48).

(1) Jesus' heavenly origins are one base upon which his success is built.

> The one coming from above [Jesus] is above all;
>
> The one from the earth [John] is from the earth and speaks from the earth.
>
> The one coming from heaven [Jesus] is above all;
>
> What he has seen and heard, this he witnesses to, and his witness no one receives. (vv. 31–32; cf. 3:11; 1:18; 5:19)

This is the point of John's witness in 1:15: "He who comes after me [in time] is before me [in status], because he was before me [in eternity]."

(2) Jesus' permanent endowment with the Spirit is a second base upon which his success is founded.

> The one [John] receiving his [God's] witness [1:33] sets his seal [cf. 6:27, a seal that authenticates] that God is true [1:34; 1 John 5:10],
>
> For the one whom God has sent [Jesus] continuously speaks the words of God [6:68],
>
> For God does not give the Spirit to him [Jesus] by measure. [vv. 33–34; cf. 1:33].

To John, as to the prophets, God gave his Spirit by measure, that is, at the time that they spoke (e.g., Num 11:25; 1 Sam 10:5–13; Jer 1:4–10; *Leviticus Rabbah* 15:2 quotes R. Aha as saying that the Holy Spirit who rests on the prophets, rests on them only by measure, for one writes only one book, another writes more). To Jesus, God has given his Spirit not by measure but permanently. He does not, therefore, utter God's words occasionally but continuously.

(3) Jesus' decisive role in judgment is the third base upon which his superiority to John rests.

The Father loves the Son and has given all things into his hand [cf. 5:22, 27].

Those who go on believing in the Son have eternal life [20:30–31; 1 John 5:13].

Those who habitually disobey the Son will not see life but the wrath of God abides upon them. [vv. 35–36; cf. 3:18; 1 John 3:6, 9; 5:18]

Whereas John could do nothing but prepare for the judgment, Jesus himself is both the basis on which judgment is carried out (v. 36) and the agent of judgment (5:22: "the Father . . . has given all judgment to the Son"; 5:27: "the Father . . . has given him authority to execute judgment").

"Now when 'the Lord' [so P66, P75, Vaticanus, and others; or less likely, 'Jesus,' so Sinaiticus, Bezae, and others] knew that the Pharisees had heard that Jesus was making and baptizing more disciples than John . . . he left Judea and departed again to Galilee" (4:1, 3). That Jesus made and baptized more disciples than John was not due to Jesus' personal aggressiveness. He withdrew when the issue of competition arose (cf. Gen 13:2–13). If his success exceeded that of John, it was due only to God (3:27). A note of clarification is given at 4:2 by the final editor: "although Jesus himself was not baptizing but his disciples" (cf. 1 Cor 1:14–17, where Paul distinguishes between the ministries of preaching and baptizing).

In 3:22–4:3, tradition that was originally evangelistic (John's disciples need to affiliate with Jesus) and/or etiological (this is how it came about that some disciples of John followed Jesus) is used to pursue the Gospel's plot at this point: the one who came as revealing, empowering presence, and who picked/produced a new community, provided them with warrants for a new form of worship that supersedes the traditional worship of Judaism of whatever variety. John's baptism, which is but one more form of Jewish purification ritual, is superseded by the worship of the Johannine community. A historical warrant for this is the fact that, already in the earthly life of Jesus and John, Jesus (and/or his disciples) made and baptized more disciples than John, a fact acknowledged and approved by the Baptist himself.

What is the picture of John the Baptist in the Fourth Gospel taken as a whole? John is mentioned in five places in the Gospel (1:1–18; 1:19–2:11; 3:22–4:3; 5:31–47; 10:40–42). (1) 1:6–8, 15 function to define a qualitative difference between the Word and John. The Word is divine (v. 1), is with God (v. 2), is the true light (vv. 5, 9), is the object of belief (v. 12); John is a man (v. 6), is from God (v. 6), is a witness to the light (vv. 7–8, 15), is the means by which people come to believe in the Word (v. 7). Here the focus is on John the Baptist as a witness to Jesus. (2) 1:19–2:11 has as its title, "This is the witness of John." John is not Elijah (in contrast to Mk 1:2, 6; 9:11–13); he is only the voice crying in the wilderness of Isaiah 40:3 (cf. Mk 1:3). Nothing is said about his baptism being "for the forgiveness of sins" (in contrast to Matt 3:6; Mk 1:4; Lk 3:3); it is that Jesus' identity may be revealed to John. So the revelation at the baptism is directed not to Jesus (as in Mk 1:11) but to the Baptist. John's witness facilitates a transfer of disciples from himself to Jesus (1:35–39), one of whom was Andrew (1:40), Simon Peter's brother (contrast Mk 1:16–18). So some of the first disciples of Jesus were former disciples of John. Again the focus is on John as witness. (3) 3:22–4:3 repeats two notes struck earlier. John denies being the Christ. The Baptist is of the earth. He is a self–effacing witness to the bridegroom. (4) 5:31–47 again depicts John as a witness (v. 33). His human witness is not as significant, however, as the divine witness that is also borne to Jesus. (5) 10:40–42, the final reference to John, makes two points. First, John did no sign. Second, everything he said about Jesus is true. The dominant description of the Baptist from start to finish is: John is the ideal witness to Jesus, Christ's best man, friend of the bridegroom (Walter Wink, *John the Baptist in the Gospel Tradition* [Cambridge: Cambridge University Press, 1968], 90–106).

It is clear that a Baptist movement continued both alongside of Jesus' ministry and after Jesus' lifetime. (a) Mark 2:18 indicates that a group of John's disciples existed alongside of Jesus and his group (cf. Lk 11:1). (b) John 3:28 ("You yourselves bear me witness that I said ... ") implies that a community of John's disciples existed alongside Jesus and his disciples. (c) Acts 19:1–7 speaks about a group of the Baptist's disciples at Ephesus in Paul's time. Interestingly, they are mentioned because they became realigned with the Christian movement. (d) The Pseudo-Clementines mention a Baptist movement in several places. In the *Recognitions* 1.54, we hear:

> Yea, some even of the disciples of John, who seemed to be great ones, have separated themselves from the people, and proclaimed their own master as Christ.

The *Recognitions* 1.60 say:

> And, behold, one of the disciples of John asserted that John was the Christ, and not Jesus, inasmuch as Jesus himself declared that John was greater than all men and all prophets. "If then," said he, "he be greater than all, he must be held to be greater than Moses, and than

> Jesus himself. But if he be the greatest of all, then must he be the Christ."

In the *Homilies* 2.23–24 (cf. *Recognitions* 2.8) reference is made to a Johannine sect that continued after John's death that was connected to the Gnostics, Dositheus and Simon Magus.

The Fourth Gospel emphatically notes the subordinate position of John to Jesus. At no point, however, is John ever pictured as an enemy. Indeed, he is the facilitator of a transfer of his disciples to Jesus. Some of Jesus' first disciples came from the Baptist's disciples (1:35–40). The church is, in part at least, regarded as a direct outgrowth of the Baptist movement. All of this argues for the hypothesis that the Fourth Gospel reflects, in these passages about John the Baptist, something of its past. There is no polemic; there is no pressing problem with a Baptist community in the present; the Baptist's disciples have followed the witness of their original leader and have found the light.

THE SAVIOR OF THE WORLD

John 4:4–44, 45–54

This is a large thought unit with two parts: the major part, 4:4–44, which ends with the confession that Jesus is Savior of the world (v. 42), to which is attached 4:45–54, a summary statement (v. 45) and a miracle story (vv. 46–54), illustrating the confession of v. 42. The major section, 4:4–44, is held together by an inclusion: vv. 3–4 and v. 43 (he departed into Galilee). It falls into two scenes: vv. 7–26 and vv. 27–38. The action takes place at two points on the stage: front stage and back stage. The dialogue takes place at two levels: that of Jesus and that of his dialogue partners. Again, as in 3:22–4:3, tradition that formerly functioned evangelistically (other Samaritans need to follow the lead of the woman and other converts and align themselves with Jesus) and/or etiologically (this is how some Samaritans came to be a part of the Johannine community) now is utilized as part of the overall pattern of 2:13–chapter 11: Jesus supersedes traditional Jewish worship in whatever form. John 4:4–54 is the third of seven episodes that make this point. As in the other episodes, so here the supersession of Jewish traditional worship in that of the Johannine community is grounded in a warrant provided by the earthly Jesus' deeds or words. Unlike Matthew 10:5 and Luke 9:52–53, John 4 speaks of a mission in Samaria in which Jesus is involved.

John 4:4–44's introduction (vv. 4–7a) sets the scene. Jesus has withdrawn from Judea because of sensed competition between his ministry and that of the Baptist (vv. 1–3). On his way to Galilee he passes through Samaria (vv. 4, 5), stopping at Jacob's well at noontime, weary and thirsty (v. 6, 7).

In Scene One (vv. 7–26) the woman comes to the well (front stage); the disciples go to the city (back stage); Jesus converses with the woman (front stage). The material falls into two parts built around two imperatives ("Give me," vv. 7b–15; "Go, call, come," vv. 16–26), each of which contains three exchanges between Jesus and the woman. In the first part Jesus is the giver of God's gift; in the second he is the revealer of God's will.

111

The first part (vv. 7b–15) of Scene One (vv. 7–26) is introduced by an imperative. When a woman of Samaria comes, in the heat of the day, to draw water, Jesus says to her: "Give me a drink" (v. 7). This leads to a discussion of the gift of God, the living water that Jesus gives (v. 10). In this conversation there are three exchanges: vv. 7–9, vv. 10–12, vv. 13–15.

> (1) Jesus said, "Give me a drink." (v. 7)
> The woman said, "How is it that you, a Jew, ask a drink of me, a woman of Samaria?" (v. 9)

That Jesus is weary (v. 6) and thirsty (v. 7) confirms the humanity of the one who will, in this conversation, eventually claim divinity (v. 26). The "becoming flesh" (1:14) involves a union that continues beyond John's baptism (remember the problem in 2 John 7, 9; 1 John 1:1; 4:2; 5:6–8). That he speaks to the Samaritan woman as he does is startling to her on at least two counts: (a) he is a man, she is a woman, and (b) he is a Jew, she is a Samaritan.

(a) Certain Jewish literature of antiquity advises against public conversation of a man with a woman. Consider:

> Jose b. Johanan of Jerusalem warned: "Talk not much with womankind." They say this of a man's wife; how much more of his fellow's wife. Hence the Sages have said: "He that talks much with womankind brings evil upon himself." (m. Pirke Aboth 1:5)

Also:

> It is forbidden to give a woman any greeting. (b. Kiddushim 70a)

Given such mores, the woman is surprised at Jesus' request. Indeed, the disciples marvel that he talks with a woman (v. 27).

(b) Jewish literature not only expresses divine displeasure with Samaritans but also warns against Jewish contact with Samaritans. Consider:

> With two nations my soul is vexed, and the third is no nation: Those who live on Mount Seir, and the Philistines, and the foolish people that dwell in Shechem. (Sirach 50:25–26)

> R. Eliezer said: "He that eats the bread of the Samaritans is like to one who eats the flesh of swine." (m. Shebiith 8:10)

> The daughters of Samaria are deemed unclean as menstruants from their cradle. (m. Niddah 4:1)

If a Samaritan woman is considered unclean, then her uncleanness would be conveyed by any vessel she touched (m. Kelim 1:1). Given such assumptions, the Samaritan woman's surprise at Jesus' request is justified. The Evangelist's comment is to the point: "Jews have no dealings with Samaritans," i.e., "Jews do not use dishes Samaritans have used" (v. 9b, so Augustine, *In Johan. Tract.* 15.11, and NIV, fn.; cf. 8:48, where being a Samaritan is the equivalent to having a demon).

> (2) Jesus answered: "If you knew the gift of God, and who it is that is saying to you. 'Give me a drink,' you would have asked him, and he would have given you living water." (v. 10)
>
> The woman said: "Sir, you have nothing to draw with, and the well is deep; where do you get that living water?" (v. 11)

Once again (cf. abiding, 1:39; born anew, 3:3), the Gospel uses an expression with a double meaning: living water. It usually carries the meaning "running fresh spring water" (cf. Gen 26:19; Lev 14:5, 6, 50, 51, 52; Josephus, *Antiquities* 1.16.2 §246; 1.16.3 §254), sometimes with the overtone of "life-giving water" (cf. Ezk 47:1–12). This is how the woman understands it, Jesus' remark being perceived by her as a Jewish boast to be able to supply better water than Jacob (v. 12). Jesus, of course, refers to the water of the Holy Spirit that he will give after his glorification (7:37–39; 20:22), fulfilling Jewish hopes (*Genesis Rabbah* 70.8 in speaking about Jacob's well gives multiple interpretations of the rabbis. An anonymous teacher of unknown date takes "for out of that well they watered the flocks" [Gen 29:1–2] to mean: "they imbibed the Divine Spirit"; cf. Tg. Isaiah 44:3: "As water is given to dry land . . . , so will I give my Holy Spirit to your sons and my blessings to your children's children"). In the third exchange he tries to lift the woman to the level from which he speaks:

> (3) Jesus said: "Everyone who drinks of this water will thirst again, but whoever drinks of the water that I will give will never thirst; the water that I will give will become in her a spring of water welling up to eternal life." (vv. 13–14; cf. *Odes of Solomon* 30:1–3, 7)
>
> The woman said: "Sir, give me this water, that I may not thirst, nor come here to draw." (v. 15)

Jesus tries but to no avail. The woman remains earthbound in her understanding. She does not yet grasp the fact that Jesus is the giver of God's gift (cf. 1:33; 2:8–10).

The second part (vv. 16–26) of Scene One (vv. 7–26) is also introduced by an imperative, "Go, call, come," which leads to a discussion of true worship and to the identity of the true prophet who is expected to instruct about matters of true worship. There are again three exchanges between the woman and Jesus: vv. 16–17a, vv. 17b–20, and vv. 21–25.

> (1) Jesus said: "Go, call your husband, and come here." (v. 16)
>
> The woman answered: "I have no husband." (v. 17a)
>
> (2) Jesus said: "You are right in saying, 'I have no husband,' for you have had five husbands, and he whom you now have is not your husband; this you said truly." (vv. 17b–18)
>
> The woman said: "Sir, I perceive you are a prophet." (v. 19)

Just as in the case with Nathanael (1:47–48) so here; Jesus' knowledge of what is in a person (cf. 2:25; 6:15, 61, 64, 70; 13:27; cf. 1 Cor 12:8: word of knowledge; 14:24–25; Lk 7:39–47) is the basis for the person's first recognition of who Jesus is. Since he has prophetic knowledge, so the woman reasons, let him resolve a thorny issue between Jews and Samaritans, the place where people ought to worship (v. 20).

> (3) Jesus said: "Woman, believe me, the hour is coming when neither on this mountain nor in Jerusalem will you worship the Father. . . . But the hour is coming (and now is) when the true worshippers will worship the Father in Spirit and in truth. . . . God is Spirit, and those who worship him must worship in Spirit and truth." (vv. 21–24)
>
> The woman said: "I know that Messiah is coming; when he comes, he will show us all things." (v. 25)

Jesus speaks about the supersession of traditional worship with its Temple cultus at an appointed hour that is coming (cf. Rev 21:22). The Evangelist adds a parenthetical comment from his vantage point after Easter, "and now is" (so James Garrison; cf. 1:38, 41, 42, 2:9b, 4:2, for similar comments). At that time Temple worship will be replaced by worship "in Spirit and truth" (v. 24). The reason for the new worship is the nature of God's relating to humans (cf. God is love, 1 John 4:16 = God relates to humans lovingly; God is light, 1 John 1:5 = God relates to humans as light). "God is Spirit (= God relates to humans as Spirit), and those who worship him must worship in Spirit and truth" (v. 24). Is this a reference to where or to how worship should be offered?

(a) The context's focus is on where (neither on this mountain nor in Jerusalem). The locus of the divine Spirit is not either of the Temples. It is in the Word become flesh (1:14; 1:33; 3:34) prior to Easter and in the community of Jesus after Easter (20:22; 7:39). The point also comes up yet again: like is known by like (remember 1:18; 3:3, 5). If God belongs to the realm of Spirit, only those who have experienced a birth from above can participate in heavenly reality. The Godlike person alone can have fellowship with God (3:3, 5; 1:12–13); the Godlike person alone can offer true worship to God. Where does true worship take place? It occurs neither in a Temple of stone nor in the holy of holies of the human spirit, but in the realm of Spirit (= Holy Spirit), accessible only to those who have been reborn from above. True worship is possible only for those who know where the locus of the Spirit is and who have been made capable of it by God's grace.

(b) If the focus in the context is on where (neither on this mountain nor in Jerusalem), there is also implicit a how (in a Temple cultus?). The true worship is "in Spirit and truth." The expression is a hendiadys (a figure of speech in which a complex idea is expressed by two words connected by a conjunction, as in "to pour from cups and gold," instead of "from golden cups"). If so, "Spirit and truth" would be paraphrased either "Spirit of truth" (cf. 14:16–17: "I will pray the Father, and he will give you . . . the Spirit of truth"; 15:26: "When the Paraclete comes, whom I shall send to you from the Father, even the Spirit of truth"), or "Spirit which is truth" (cf. 3:5: water which is Spirit; 1 QS 4:20–21:"Then God will purify the deeds of man by his *truth* and he will cleanse the frame of man. He will eradicate the perverse spirit from within his flesh, and cleanse him by the *Holy Spirit* from all his wicked deeds"). The reference either way is to the Holy Spirit that is given by Jesus after his glorification. How is true worship offered to the Father? Jesus' answer is "in the Spirit of truth" / "the Spirit which is truth."

The woman's response is typically Samaritan: "When Messiah comes, he will show us all things [about true worship]." The Samaritan Messiah was to restore true worship. It is not surprising, then, that a messianic pretender who came forward under Pontius Pilate promised to show the Samaritans where Moses had buried the sacred vessels on Mount Gerazim (Josephus, *Antiquities* 18.4.1 §85–87).

The climax of the entire exchange of vv. 16–26 comes in v. 26. Jesus said: "I who speak to you am he." This is the authoritative basis for the instruction on true worship that has just been given. Jesus claims to fulfill the woman's hopes for a Messiah who will show her all things (about true worship).

In Scene Two (vv. 27–44) the disciples come back to the well (front stage); the woman goes to the city (back stage); Jesus converses with the disciples (front stage); the Samaritans come to the well (front stage); and

Jesus stays with the Samaritans two days before departing. The material falls into an ABA' pattern:

A   The woman goes from the well and bears witness to the Samaritans: Can this be the Christ? (vv. 28–30)

B   Jesus instructs the disciples about missions (vv. 31–38)

A'   The Samaritans come to the well and bear witness to the woman: This is indeed the Savior of the world (vv. 39–42).

In A, vv. 28–30, the woman leaves her water jar (she now has water to drink of which others do not know) and goes away into the city to bear witness to what she has personally experienced (vv. 17–18; vv. 25–26). "Come see a man who told me all that I ever did. Can this be the Christ?" Her intent is to bring the people to Jesus (v. 39; cf. 1:40–42; 1:43–46: "Come and see").

In the meantime, while the Samaritans are in the process of coming to the well to see Jesus, Jesus instructs his disciples about missions (B, vv. 31–38: cf. Mk 6:7–13, 30, for the use of a similar interlude). The disciples who had gone into the city to get food (v. 8) have now returned and want Jesus to eat: "Rabbi, eat" (v. 31; cf. 2:3). His response is at another level: "I have food to eat of which you do not know" (v. 32; cf. Deut 8:3: "one does not live on bread alone but by every word that comes from the mouth of the Lord"). The disciples miss the spiritual import and take it to mean that someone else, perhaps the woman, has already supplied his needs (v. 33). Jesus must explain: "My food is to do the will of him who sent me, and to complete [*teleiōsō*] his work" (v. 34). The thing that keeps Jesus going is completing the work of the Father (cf. 17:4: "I glorified you upon the earth, having completed [*teleiōsas*] the work which you gave me to do"; 19:30: "When Jesus had received the vinegar, he said, 'It is finished [*tetelestai*]'; and he bowed his head and gave up his spirit"). The work of the Father that Jesus aims to complete is the work of salvation.

The disciples' work is the focus of vv. 35–38. V. 35a gives a saying of the disciples themselves ("There are yet four months, then comes the harvest"); v. 35b is its correction by Jesus ("Lift up your eyes, and see how the fields are already white for harvest"). The similarity of v. 35 to a traditional Jewish saying makes one wonder whether the disciples' statement indicates laziness on their part, and the word of correction implies divine impatience (R. Tarphon said about the study of Torah: "The day is short, the work is great, the workers are lazy. The reward is great, and the master of the house is pressing" [m. Pirke Aboth 2:15]). Does Jesus gesture toward the approaching Samaritans, with their white robes flowing, as he says this? Even if so, the perspective is still applicable to the post-Easter period (cf. 21:2–14). Vv. 36–38 distinguish between two roles: sowing and reaping. The sowers in the Johannine context are the Father (v. 34; cf. 5:17: "My Father is working"; 6:44, 65) and the Son (5:17; 17:4, 22). Their work is one (14:10–11: "I am in the Father and the Father in me ... the Father who dwells in me does his works"; 10:32). The reapers are the disciples: "I sent you to reap that for which you did not labor" (v. 38). When the reapers harvest the crop, however, sower and reaper rejoice together (v. 36).

The background for this section is the overall Johannine understanding of mission. (a) Jesus is God's envoy. This may be expressed as the Father sends Jesus (5:37; 7:33; 12:44, 45; 13:20; 15:21; 16:5) or as Jesus is sent by the Father (3:34; 5:38; 6:29; 17:3). As God's envoy, Jesus does the Father's work (4:34; 17:4), does the Father's will (5:30; 6:38), witnesses to what he has seen and heard from the Father (3:11, 32; 5:19; 8:26, 28, 38, 40), reveals the Father (1:18; 14:9). This means he comes to save the world (3:17), not to judge it (8:15; 12:47), to give eternal life (3:16; 4:10; 10:10; 17:2; 20:30–31). (b) Jesus' mission is constitutive of the mission of the disciples: 4:38: "I sent you"; 17:18: "As you sent me into the world, so have I sent them into the world"; 20:21: "As the Father has sent me, even so I send you." (c) The disciples, however, do not stand on a par with Jesus in their mission. They bear witness to Jesus and attempt to lead others to Jesus, but it is Jesus who is ultimately the Evangelizer (1:40–42; 1:43–49; 4:29–30, 39–42; 17:20). "In the Johannine conception, every missionary endeavor of every age means essentially and fundamentally a harvesting, a reaping of the fruit of the work of salvation accomplished definitively by Jesus and the Father" (Teresa Okure, *The Johannine Approach to Mission: A Contextual Study of John 4:1–42* [Tübingen: Mohr-Siebeck, 1988], 164).

The instruction of the disciples about mission ends just as the Samaritans from the city arrive. A′ (vv. 39–44) has these Samaritans invite Jesus to stay with them: "and he stayed there two days" (v. 40). This brief note is significant in several ways. (a) Jesus continues to show his unconcern about contracting ritual uncleanness (remember v. 9). (b) Two days is the traditional length of time for a genuine missionary/prophet to stay in one place (Didache 11:5). (c) Staying with a convert offers evidence of the missionary's conviction that the conversion is genuine (Acts 16:15).

Vv. 39–42 is cast in the mold of the typical witness borne to Jesus (cf. 1:35–39). (a) Someone bears witness to Jesus (4:39//1:35–36). (b) People come to/follow Jesus (4:40//1:37, 39a). (c) They want to abide with Jesus and they do (4:40//1:39b). (d) As a result, they make their confession about Jesus (4:42//1:41). Here the confession is that Jesus is "Savior of the world" (v. 42). It is based no longer on the woman's words but on Jesus' word. The Johannine pattern is: a witness points/brings someone to Jesus; Jesus then validates himself with that one; a confession of faith grows out of one's own personal involvement with Jesus himself.

The Samaritans' actions are also similar to those accorded visiting rulers in Roman antiquity: (a) they go out to meet Jesus (v. 40a); (b) they invite him into their town (v. 40b); and (c) they call him Savior (v. 42b). Josephus offers several examples of the practice: (1) during the Jewish revolt when Vespasian arrived at the city of Tiberius, "the population (b) opened their gates to him and (a) went out to meet him, (c) hailing him as Savior and Benefactor" (*War* 3.9.8 §459); (2) when Vespasian returned to Rome as emperor, the populus (a) went to the roadsides outside the city (b) to receive him, (c) "hailing him as Benefactor and Savior" (*War,* 7.4.1 §70–71). For similar situations involving Titus, see Josephus, *War* 4.2.5 §112–13, and *War* 7.5.2–3 §100–103, 119. In so doing the Samaritans associated Jesus not with parochial expectations (a Samaritan or Jewish messianic figure) but with one who exercised worldwide dominion (Savior of the world, v. 42; cf. John 3:17; 12:47). By using the definite article (*the* Savior of the world), they seem to exclude others from the function of savior. It is possible that the Fourth Gospel's audience would have taken it to exclude Caesar (Sebaste, the dominant city in Samaria, contained a large temple in honor of Caesar Augustus, for whom the title Savior was used; Josephus, *War* 1.21.1 §403; Craig R. Koester, "The Savior of the World [John 4:42]," *JBL* 109 [1990]: 665–80).

The episode closes with Jesus' departure from Samaria to Galilee (v. 43). "For Jesus himself testified that a prophet has no honor in his own country" (v. 44; cf. Mk 6:4; Matt 13:57; Lk 4:24; Coptic Gospel of Thomas 31). Whereas the Synoptic tradition understands Jesus' homeland to be Galilee, in John Galilee is the opposite of his country, whatever his country is (Judea, Jerusalem, the country of the Jews).

The second part of John 4:4–54 is 4:45–54. This part is composed of (a) a summary statement (v. 45), and (b) a miracle story (vv. 46–54). The summary statement ("So when he came to Galilee, the Galileans welcomed him, having seen all that he had done in Jerusalem at the feast") is linked to v. 42 as an illustration of that verse's confession: "This is indeed the Savior of the world." Jesus is welcomed by Galileans. The very name Galilee is the abbreviation of a Hebrew phrase (*galil ha goyim*) meaning the "cir-

cle (i.e., the region or district) of the Gentiles (i.e., pagans or foreigners)."
In returning to this culture with its concentration of non-Jews, Jesus pursues the role assigned him by the Samaritans. In receiving a welcome from Jews who live among such people, Jesus fulfills it. He is Savior of the world (cf. 1:29b).

The miracle story (vv. 46–54) has since Irenaeus' time (*Against Heresies* 2.22.3) often been regarded as a variant form of the incident narrated by Matthew 8:5–13 and Luke 7:1–10. The point of the Synoptic story and that in John is quite different, however. In the Synoptics the punch line is: "I tell you, I have not found such faith even in Israel." The faith of a Gentile exceeds that of Jews. In John, the emphasis is different. The Galilean Jews welcome Jesus because they had seen all that he had done in Jerusalem at the feast (v. 45). When the Gentile official at Capernaum hears the reports, he asks for Jesus' assistance for his son who is ill. What follows is analogous to the miracle story associated with a Gentile in Mark 7:24–30. (a) Jesus replies: "Unless you see signs and wonders you will not believe" (v. 48). How is this to be taken? Jesus' words serve an analogous function to those addressed to a Gentile in Mark 7:27 ("Let the children first be fed"). It represents an initial put-off that allows the faith of the person to be revealed. (b) The official responds: "Sir, come down before my child dies" (v. 49). This is analogous to the woman's response in Mark 7:28 ("Yes, Lord; yet even the dogs . . . eat the children's crumbs"). There is persistence on the part of the Gentile. (c) Jesus said: "Go; your son will live" (v. 50). This is analogous to Mark 7:29 ("You may go your way; the demon has left your daughter"). Jesus promises healing for the child. (d) The official goes his way and is met by servants who tell him the child is living (v. 50b–51). This is parallel to Mark 7:30 ("And she went home, and found the child lying in bed, and the demon gone"). The Gentile receives evidence of the dependability of Jesus' word. The major difference between these two stories of Jesus' healing of a child of a Gentile is that the one in the Fourth Gospel emphasizes Jesus' knowledge of exactly what the Father is doing and when (cf. 5:20; 11:42). The healing happens at exactly the hour Jesus speaks (cf. b. Berakoth 34b, a miracle story in which R. Hanina b. Dosa prays for the sick son of R. Gamaliel and knows exactly when the fever has left the lad, a fact confirmed by the disciples of Gamaliel).

In this story Jesus is Savior of the world (v. 42), who possesses perfect knowledge of what the Father is doing (5:20), and whose word is absolutely trustworthy (cf. v. 41). The Gentile official is an example of those who have not seen and yet believe (20:29), just as the Galileans who have been to the feast are representatives of those who have seen and believe (20:29). The function of miracle in this passage is twofold. On the one hand, reports of miracles done by Jesus (the witness of the Galilean Jews) draw the official to Jesus and to a first level of faith (v. 47, 50; cf. 5:36; 10:38). On the other hand, the experience of miracle confirms the official's initial faith and raises it to a new level (v. 53). Faith is here portrayed as a process, with miracle functioning in different ways within it: both as a catalyst for faith and as a confirmation of it.

If one reads 4:4–54 in terms of the organization proposed here, the third exchange (vv. 21–25) of the second imperative (vv. 16–26) and its climax (v. 26) function as the high point of the thought unit. Everything moves up to this point; everything derives from this point. There is, moreover, another surface structure besides the one utilized so far (ancient literature sometimes was written in terms of multiple patterns) that reinforces this conclusion. A loose concentric pattern controls much of the material, showing where the Evangelist's focus is.

A Jesus goes to Galilee (4:3)

   B Jesus needs a drink (4:7)

      C Jesus' witness to the woman based on her experience (4:16–18)

         D True worship explained by the Messiah (4:20–26)

      C′ The woman's witness to Jesus based on her experience (4:28–29)

   B′ Jesus needs to eat (4:31)

A′ Jesus goes to Galilee (4:43).

The centerpiece of such a pattern is where the author's focus is. Whatever the original functions of the material in John 4:4–54, in the final form of the Gospel it functions to allow the earthly Jesus to give a warrant for the supersession of Temple worship, whether on Gerazim or in Jerusalem.

DUTIFUL APPRENTICE
OF THE FATHER

John 5:1–47

John 5 is a large thought unit whose beginning is signaled by 5:1 ("After this . . . Jesus went up") and whose ending is indicated by 6:1 ("After this Jesus went away"). Its organization is similar to that already seen in John 2:13–3:21 (symbolic act of Jesus, followed by dialogue, followed by monologue). Its thesis is that contrary to the impotence of the water rituals of ancient Judaism, Jesus' potent word gives life. That Jesus' word imparts health to a paralytic is a sign that his word gives life both to the spiritually dead and to the physically dead. Such works are, moreover, but one of four witnesses to Jesus.

V. 1, the introduction to the episode, gives the setting in time and space in general terms. "After this there was a feast of the Jews ["a feast," so P66, P75, Vaticanus, and others; "the feast," so Sinaiticus and others; "of Passover," so ∧; "of Tabernacles," so 131], and Jesus went up to Jerusalem."

There follows a miracle story (vv. 2ff) with the customary three parts (the problem, the miracle, the reaction to the cure), two of which are expanded by dialogue. (1) The problem is stated in vv. 2–7. V. 2 gives a specific locale: "Now there is in Jerusalem by the Sheep Gate a pool [so RSV, NIV, NAB, cf. Neh 3:1, 32; 12:39; "by the Sheep pool," so NEB], in Hebrew called Bethesda [so C, A, and others; now supported by the corresponding Hebrew word in the Copper Scroll from Qumran; NIV, NAB; "Bethzatha," so Sinaiticus, and others; RSV; "Bethsaida," so P75, Vaticanus, and others; "Bedsaida," so P66; "Belzetha," so D and others], which has five porticoes." In this century the pool has been discovered and excavated. It measures 165–220 feet wide by 315 feet long. It consists of a twin basin (one side for men, one for women) to which Herod had added five elaborate porticoes surrounding the four sides and dividing the two basins across the middle. Stairways in the corners permitted descent into the pool. The pool was perhaps used by Temple pilgrims for ritual lus-

121

trations. Because the waters were famous for their curative powers, the pool attracted a multitude of the sick. "In these [the five porticoes] lay a multitude of invalids, blind, lame, paralyzed" (v. 3a). Vv. 3b–4 ("waiting for the moving of the water; for an angel of the Lord went down at certain seasons into the pool, and troubled the water; whoever stepped in first after the troubling of the water was healed of whatever disease he had") are missing from P66, P75, Vaticanus, Sinaiticus, and others and do not belong in the text of the story.

Among the afflicted at the pool there is one man who has been ill for thirty-eight years (v. 5). This statement of the problem is expanded in vv. 6–7 by dialogue between Jesus and the man. Knowing that the man had been lying there a long time,

> Jesus said: "Do you want to be healed?"
>
> The sick man answered: "Sir, I have no one to put me into the pool when the water is troubled, and while I am going another steps down before me."

Self-pity, as well as paralysis, afflicts this individual.

(2) The cure comes in vv. 8–9a. "Jesus said to him, 'Rise [cf. vv. 28–29], take up your pallet, and walk.' And at once the man was healed, and he took up his pallet and walked" (cf. Mk 2:1–12; Lucian, *Philopseudes* 11). "Just as the thirty-eight years prove the gravity of the disease, so the carrying of the bed and the walking prove the completeness of the cure" (C. K. Barrett, *The Gospel according to St. John* [London: SPCK, 1958], 212).

(3) The reaction to the cure (vv. 9ff) is also expanded by dialogue, first between the Jews and the healed man (vv. 9b–15) and then between the Jews and Jesus (vv. 16–47). The occasion for the first dialogue is given in v. 9b: "Now that day was the sabbath" (cf. Lk 6:6–11; 13:10–17; 14:1–6, for this type of Gospel scene).

> The Jews said: "It is the sabbath, it is not lawful for you to carry your pallet." (v. 10)
>
> The man answered: "The man who healed me said to me, 'Take up your pallet, and walk.'" (v. 11)
>
> The Jews asked: "Who is the man who said [this]?" (v. 12)
>
> When the man found out, he told that it was Jesus. (vv. 13–15)

The Hebrew word *shabbath* means a cessation of activity or abstinence from labor. Exodus 20:8–11 prohibits work on the sabbath (//Deut 5:12–15). Jeremiah 17:19–27 treats carrying burdens on the sabbath as contrary to the divine will. The Mishnah prohibits thirty-nine classes of work on the sabbath, the last of which is "taking out aught from one domain to another" (m. Shabbath 7:2; exceptions were made, of course, e.g., m. Shabbath 18:3). In terms of their tradition, the Jews correctly say: "It is the sabbath, it is not lawful for you to carry your pallet."

The man's appeal to the words of his healer is predictable. In Jewish circles in antiquity, miracle often legitimates the authority of the one who does it. Sifre Deuteronomy 18:19 states that if a prophet who starts to prophesy gives evidence by signs and miracles, he is to be heeded; if not, he is not to be followed. This anonymous saying is early because a discussion between Jose ha-Gelili and Akiba presupposes the existence of such a statement (b. Sanh 90a; Sifre Deut 13:3). Josephus, *Antiquities* 2.12.3 §280, reports that God gave Moses three signs (the rod became a serpent, the leprous hand, the water turned to blood) and said: "Make use of these signs, in order to obtain belief among all men, that you are sent by me and do all things according to my commands." The man responds in these terms, claiming the healer's authority for his carrying a pallet on the sabbath.

The attempt to discover the identity of the one whose command resulted in the violation of the sabbath bears fruit. Now they know. Jesus is the culprit. At v. 16 the dialogue between the Jews and Jesus begins. V. 16 gives the first reason for the Jewish persecution of Jesus: "he did this on the sabbath." Jesus' response comes in a saying in v. 17: "My Father is working still, and I am working."

There is in antiquity widespread Jewish discussion about the continuing activity of God in the world. (a) *Genesis Rabbah* 11:10 has R. Phinehas quote R. Hoshaiah (early third century) as saying: "When you say that God rested on this day from all his works, it means that he rested from work on his world, but he did not rest from work on the unrighteous and on the righteous." *Exodus Rabbah* 30:6 has an earlier discussion of the issue that likely is to be dated to the end of the first century. An early rabbinic tradition, therefore, has God at work on the sabbath in the sphere of the moral governance of the universe. (b) Philo argues that God could actually labor while at rest since his work did not make him weary (*On the Cherubim* 86–90). He also holds that having finished the creation of mortal things, God began on the seventh day to shape things more divine (*Allegorical Interpretation* 1.5–6). The assumption is that God is in fact at work even on the sabbath in matters divine. (c) In the Epistle of Aristeas 210, the king poses the question: "What is the essence of godliness?" The answer of his Jewish guest that is given is: "The realization that

God is continually at work in everything and is omniscient, and that man cannot hide from him an unjust deed or an evil action. For, as God does good to the whole world, so you by imitating him would be without offense." Again the activity of God in the moral governance of the universe is viewed as continual. The duty of humans is to imitate it. It is against the backdrop of such thinking among ancient Jews that Jesus' words must be understood: "My Father is working still." It is implied in this statement (v. 17) in this context (v. 9b–10) that God is working on the sabbath. "And I am working" (v. 17: on the sabbath) has Jesus claim that he is exercising the same constant activity as the Father *on the sabbath, in the sphere of doing good*. Jesus links his own activity as continuous with that of God.

This claim gives the Jews a second reason to seek to kill him: "he not only broke the sabbath [the first reason] but also called God his Father, making himself equal with God" (v. 18 = the second reason). The language "making himself equal with God" echoes Jewish belief that a son who rejects paternal authority is one who makes himself equal with his father (cf. Phil 2:6–8). The Jews, then, take Jesus' claim to unity of function with the Father to mean equality of status, that is, independence from the Father's authority (equality = independence).

Jesus' monologue in vv. 19–30 argues to the contrary (cf. 14:28b). This subunit falls into a concentric pattern:

A   v. 19: Subordination of the Son to the Father

   B   v. 20: We will marvel at the greater works of the Son

      C   vv. 21–23: Just as the Father, so the Son (life and judgment)

         D   v. 24: Truly, truly, I say to you (has life)

         D'   v. 25: Truly, truly, I say to you (now is — will live)

      C'   vv. 26–27: Just as the Father, so the Son (life and judgment)

   B'   vv. 28–29: Do not marvel at this, for the greater works of future resurrection and judgment are yet to come.

A'   v. 30: Subordination of the Son to the One who sent him

In such an introverted parallelism without a center point (= an *epanodos*), the prominence is given to what comes first and last, here vv. 19–20a and 30. A (vv. 19–20a) uses a parable of the apprentice son. The father, a skilled artisan, works at his craft while the apprentice son first watches and then repeats his actions:

> The Son can do nothing of his own accord, but only what he sees the Father doing; for whatever he does, that the Son does likewise. For the Father loves the Son and shows him all that he himself is doing.

Just as the relationship of a human son learning the family trade involves his complete dependence on his father, so also does the relationship between the Father and his Son, Jesus. A′ (v. 30) makes the same point:

> I can do nothing on my own authority; as I hear, I judge; and my judgment is just, because I seek not my own will but the will of him who sent me.

The point of A and A′ is that Jesus does not make himself independent of God but is totally dependent on him.

B (v. 20b) and C (vv. 21–23) indicate that the two areas in which the Son acts as he sees (v. 21) and hears (v. 30) the Father are (a) giving life (v. 21: "as the Father raises the dead and gives them life [cf. 2 Kings 5:7; 2 Baruch 48:8], so also the Son gives life to whom he will"), and (b) judging (vv. 22: "The Father judges no one but has given all judgment to the Son" [cf. 1 John 2:28; 2 Cor 5:10; Acts 17:31; Matt 25:31–33]). The same point is made in B′ (vv. 28–29) and C′ (vv. 26–27): "as the Father has life in himself, so has he granted the Son also to have life in himself, and has given him authority to execute judgment" (cf. 1 Enoch 49:4; 61:9; 62:2–3; 63:11; 69:27). Throughout the Fourth Gospel the Son is portrayed as dependent on the Father: for the gift of the Holy Spirit (3:34), for testimony (5:37), for disciples (6:37), for his message (7:16), for his mission (7:28), for knowledge (8:16), for guidance (11:9), for instructions (14:31), for authority (17:2), and for glory (17:24). Any language about the unity of Father and Son (5:17–18; 10:30: "I and the Father are one") is conditioned by the persistent motif of the Son's subordination to the Father.

The motive behind such a transfer of authority from the Father to the Son is that "the Father loves the Son" (v. 20a: *philei*; cf. 3:35: *agapa*; 15:10; 17:26). The aim of the transfer of authority is "that all may honor the Son, even as they honor the Father. The one who does not honor the Son does not honor the Father who sent him" (v. 23). The term "honor" is theologically significant. Josephus, *Antiquities* 1.7.1 §156, uses it of cultic honor shown to God ("to whom we ought justly to offer our honor and thanksgiving"); also *Antiquities* 6.2.1 §21 ("by your worship supplicate the Divine Majesty with all your hearts and persevere in the honor you pay him"). Early Christian usage is similar: e.g., 1 Timothy 1:17 ("To the King of Ages, immortal, invisible, the only God, be honor and glory for ever and ever. Amen"); 1 Timothy 6:16 ("To him be honor and eternal dominion"); Revelation 4:9 ("And whenever the living creatures give glory and honor and thanks to him who is seated on the throne"); 4:11 ("Worthy art thou, our Lord and God, to receive glory and honor and power"); 5:12 ("Worthy is the Lamb who was slain, to receive power and wealth and wisdom and might and honor and glory and blessing"); Mark 7:6 ("This people honors me with their lips"). In John, Jesus honors the Father (8:49). From the vantage point of the Gospel, as the holy man in whom the divine presence dwells (cf. 1:14; 1:33; 3:34), Jesus is the designated object of honor. One who does not honor him does not honor the Father who sent him. One does not show honor to God by building a Temple or participating in the sacrificial cult of a Temple, but by showing honor to the holy man in whom the divine presence dwells. If his effective word supersedes the purification/healing rituals of the Jews, his person supplies the worshipper an immediate object for worship/honor.

D (v. 24: "He who hears my word and believes him who sent me has [present tense] eternal life; he does not come into judgment, but has passed [perfect tense] from death to life") and D' (v. 25: "the hour is coming [and now is] when the dead will hear the voice of the Son of God, and those who hear will live") juxtapose two affirmations of present eschatology. One has life through an appropriate response to Jesus' voice/words. If D (v. 24) and D' (v. 25) focus on present eschatology, vv. 28–29 establish beyond any doubt that the monologue also is referring to a future, cosmic eschatology ("the hour is coming when all who are in the tombs will hear his voice and come forth, those who have done good to the resurrection of life, and those who have done evil to the resurrection of judgment"). The Fourth Gospel has a strong emphasis on the present possession of eternal life (e.g., 3:14, 16; 3:36; 5:24; 6:54; 11:26; 20:30–31; cf. 1 John 5:12, 13). It also has a future eschatology (e.g., 3:5; 5:28–29; 6:39, 40, 44, 54; 10:9; 11:24, 25; 12:25, 32, 48; 14:3; 17:24; 21:22; cf. 1 John 2:28; 3:2; 4:17). If the Gospel is read as a literary unity, it will not do to contend that the references to future eschatology are editorial additions by a later editor or reflect pre-Johannine tradition different in perspective from the Evangelist. Both present and future eschatology are part of the total Johannine theological perspective. It is true that the Fourth Evangelist emphasizes the present possession of eternal life. It is also clear that he never makes the claim that the present possession of eternal life exhausts what God has to offer. Possession of eternal life in the present is not the resurrection from the dead (as some heretics in 2 Tim 2:18 claimed; also 2 Thes 2:2; cf.

Irenaeus, *Against Heresies* 1.23.5: Menander claimed his disciples are able to receive resurrection through their baptism into him; "they can no longer die but remain ageless and immortal"). Possession of eternal life in the present represents only the beginning of the Christian life. As one goes on believing (remember 1 John 5:13; cf. John 20:30–31), one goes on having eternal life. The present possession of eternal life in the process of faith, however, does not prevent physical death (cf. 21:23; cf. Rom 6:3–5). The ultimate victory over death comes at the resurrection on the last day (5:28–29). It takes both the present and the future eschatology of the Fourth Gospel to yield a theologically coherent scheme (John T. Carroll, "Present and Future in Fourth Gospel 'Eschatology,'" *BTB* 19 [1989]: 63–68).

Jesus' response to the Jewish charge that by claiming his actions mirror those of the Father (v. 17) he makes himself equal to (= independent of) God (v. 18) has employed a patterned discourse (vv. 19–30) that emphasizes the Son's dependence upon the Father. This lengthy discourse aims to establish that Jesus' action in healing a lame man on the sabbath and in commanding him to take his pallet and walk on the sabbath reflects the activity of the Father to whom Jesus is subordinate. This is Jesus' claim. This defense raises yet another problem. In vv. 19–30, the Jews say, Jesus is bearing witness to himself.

Jewish tradition held that it takes more than one witness to establish the truth (Josephus, *Antiquities* 4.8.15 §219: "But let not a single witness be credited; but three, or two at the least, and those such whose testimony is confirmed by their good lives"; cf. Deut 19:15; m. Rosh ha-Shanah 3:1). This is especially true when one vouches for himself (m. Ketuboth 2:9: "none may be believed when he testifies of himself"). Jesus' words reflect the tradition: "If I bear witness to myself, my testimony is not true; there is another [no specific other here, just the required other] who bears witness to me, and I know the testimony which he bears to me is true" (vv. 31–32).

There follows a section (vv. 33–47) in which Jesus appeals to four witnesses in the face of Jewish unbelief. This material may very well have functioned, prior to its incorporation in the Gospel, as missionary apologetics in the Johannine community's dialogue with the synagogue. It has something of that function here. (1) John the Baptist is the first witness (vv. 33–35):

> He has borne witness to the truth [cf. 1:34; 3:27–30]. . . . He was a burning and shining lamp, and you were willing to rejoice for a while in his light.

The description of John as a lamp in whose light the Jews rejoiced for a time, while awkward after the denial of 1:8 ("he was not the light"), fits Jewish idiom (Sirach 48:1 says, "Then the prophet Elijah arose like a fire, and his word burned like a torch"; *Midrash on the Psalms* 36.6 says many men from Moses down to the sons of the Hasmoneans were as lamps which had been extinguished again) and the fact of his positive reception by the Jews for a while (Josephus, *Antiquities* 18.5.2 §118: "many...came in crowds about him, for they were greatly moved by hearing his words").

(2) "But the testimony which I have is greater than that of John; for the works which the Father has granted me to accomplish [*teleiōsō*], these very works which I am doing, bear me witness that the Father has sent me." Jesus' signs, one of which has just been narrated (vv. 2–9a), are the second witness (v. 36). The Fourth Gospel knows and reflects in its narrative the Jewish mind-set that viewed miracles as legitimating signs (e.g., 2:18; 6:30). A series of messianic pretenders mentioned by Josephus all attempted to authenticate their status by miracles (the Samaritan imposter under Pilate, so *Antiquities* 18.4.1 §85–87; Theudas under the procurator Fadus, so *Antiquities* 20.5.1 §97; certain imposters in Jerusalem under Felix, so *Antiquities* 20.9.6 §167–168; the Egyptian under Felix, so *Antiquities* 20.9.6 §169–172). In b. Sanhedrin 98a, R. Jose ben Qisma (about 110 C.E.) prophesies that when Messiah comes he will authenticate his words with a sign (the water of the caves of Paneas will change to blood). Although this was not the view of all or even a majority of Jews, in certain circles miracles functioned as a testimony to one's religious authority. To such testimony the Johannine Jesus appeals in 5:36 as his second witness.

(3) The third witness to Jesus mentioned in this section is the Father.

> And the Father who sent me has himself borne witness to me. His voice you have never heard, his form you have never seen; and you do not have his word abiding in you, for you do not believe him whom he has sent. (vv. 37–38)

These words involve a denial of three matters of Jewish pride: having seen God (Exod 19:11; Deut 5:4; Sirach 17:13), having heard God (Exod 19:9; Deut 4:12, 15, 33, 36; Neh 9:3; Sirach 17:13), and having been taught by God (Deut 6:6; 30:14; Sirach 17:13–14; 24:11–12; Baruch 3:37–4:4), that is, revelation. The reason they do not have the Father's word abiding in them is that they have not believed in the one sent from the Father. This denial and its reason offer a clue to the correct way to read the Father's witness. The Father's witness is something that comes when one believes in Jesus whom he sent. This echoes 1 John 5:10–11:

> The one who believes in the Son of God has the testimony in himself. The one who does not believe God has made him a liar, because he has not believed in the testimony that God has borne to his Son. And this is the testimony, that God gave us eternal life, and this life is in his Son.

The passage in 1 John 5:10–11 says that God's testimony to his Son is the possession of eternal life, which believers in Jesus have. If John bore an external witness to Jesus, the Father bears an inner testimony, the witness of eternal life possessed by one who believes in Jesus.

(4) The fourth and final witness to Jesus referred to in this section is that of the Scriptures/Moses (vv. 39–47):

> You search the Scriptures... and it is they that bear witness to me. ...(v. 39)

> Do not think that I will accuse you to the Father; it is Moses who accuses you, on whom you set your hope. If you believed Moses, you would believe me, for he wrote of me. But if you do not believe his writings, how will you believe my words? (vv. 45–47)

In contrast to a rabbi like Hillel who said that the more study of the law, the more life (m. Pirke Aboth 2:7), the Johannine Jesus "insists that there is nothing intrinsically life-giving about studying the Scriptures, if one fails to discern their true content and purpose" (D. A. Carson, *The Gospel according to John* [Grand Rapids: Eerdmans, 1991], 263). What is needed is a "comprehensive hermeneutical key," namely, Scripture points to Christ. Without it, the central meaning of Scripture is perverted.

Jewish tradition portrayed Moses as Israel's great defender. Josephus, *Antiquities* 4.8.3 §194, speaks of Israel's fear that God would take less care of them after Moses was gone because while he was alive he interceded for them. The Testament of Moses 11:17 speaks of the reaction of the enemies of Israel when they hear of Moses' death:

> Let us go up against them [Israel]... for there is now no advocate for them who will bear messages to the Lord on their behalf in the way that Moses was the great messenger. He, in every hour both day and night, had his knees fixed to the earth, praying and looking steadfastly toward him who governs the whole earth with mercy and justice, reminding the Lord of his ancestral covenant and the resolute oath.

Jubilees 1:20–21 depicts Moses as the intercessor on behalf of God's people and Beliar as their accuser before God. John 5:45 stands this tra-

ditional Jewish conviction on its head. Moses is no longer the defender
(advocate) of the Jews but their accuser (prosecuting attorney), because
he wrote of Jesus (v. 46: God had shown Moses the secrets of the endtimes, e.g., 2 Esdras 14:5) and they do not receive him (v. 42). Scripture,
like the Baptist, Jesus' works, and the Father, bears witness to Jesus. Jesus'
testimony to himself (vv. 19–30) does not stand alone but is corroborated
by multiple reliable and trustworthy witnesses.

This large thought unit reflects an apologetic *Sitz im Leben* in the life of
the Johannine community. In it one hears the church's past controversy
with the synagogue. When the pre-existing material is taken up into the
Fourth Gospel, however, it functions to affirm Jesus as the holy man to
whom honor is owed and to allow him to give a warrant for the supersession of Jewish water rituals by something he has done or said in the
period before his glorification. The one who came as revealing, empowering presence, and who has picked/produced a new community, now
is involved in providing warrants for his community for a type of worship that supersedes that of traditional Judaism of whatever variety. John
5:1–47 is episode four in a series of seven making that point.

THE BREAD OF LIFE

John 6:1–71

This large thought unit is marked at its beginning and its end by the repetition of the phrase "after this" Jesus went away/went about (6:1; 7:1). It is organized very much like chapter 5: a sign is followed by a four-stage dialogue that attempts to explain it. It falls into three parts: (1) vv. 1–26, held together by an inclusion (the other side of the sea, vv. 1, 25); (2) vv. 27–59, held together by an inclusion (Capernaum, vv. 24, 59); and (3) vv. 60–71. The action takes place at Passover time (v. 4; cf. 2:13) during a day (vv. 1–15), a night (vv. 16–21), and the following day (vv. 22–71). The location is in Galilee: first in the hills (v. 3) on the other side of the Sea of Galilee (v. 1), then back in Capernaum (vv. 24, 59). The theme of replacement runs through the entire chapter. Jesus supersedes the Jewish Passover. John 6 is the fifth episode illustrating the thesis that the holy man Jesus supersedes traditional Jewish worship and allowing Jesus, in his earthly career, to give a warrant for such supersession by something he does or says.

Part One (vv. 1–26) consists of a miracle story expanded in the area of the reactions to the miracle. It includes a sign followed by misunderstanding. In this unit, Jesus is portrayed as the one who nourishes the multitudes. Vv. 1–4 provide the introductory setting: "After this, Jesus went to the other side of the Sea of Galilee, the Sea of Tiberias" (so P66, P75, Sinaiticus, Vaticanus, and others; D and others have Sea of Galilee in the region of Tiberias; V and a few others have Sea of Galilee and Tiberias; certain minuscules have Sea of Tiberias). A multitude "followed him because they saw the signs which he did on those who were diseased" (5:36; 4:45, 53; 2:23; 2:11). Jesus went into the hills and "there sat down with his disciples." He is portrayed as a Jewish rabbi ready to teach his disciples. "Now the Passover, the feast of the Jews, was at hand" (v. 4). It is at this time (Passover) when the holy man, Jesus, is with his disciples and is ready to teach that a "multitude was coming to him" (v. 5a). Already a historical warrant is beginning to be forged: the multitude, by coming

131

to Jesus instead of going to Jerusalem, finds in him the true meaning of Passover.

(1) The first component of the miracle story is a statement of the problem (vv. 5–9). A multitude is coming to Jesus in the hills (v. 5a). Jesus tests Philip: "How are we to buy bread, so that these people may eat?" (v. 5b–6). Philip recognizes the financial impossibility: "Two hundred days' wages would not buy enough bread for each of them to get a little" (v. 7). Andrew accents the meagerness of their resources: "There is a lad here who has five loaves and two fish; but what are they among so many?" (v. 9). The disciples recognize that their resources are not equal to the need of the multitude. Herein lies the problem.

(2) The second component is a description of the miracle itself (vv. 10–13). The actual miracle is narrated in v. 11: "Jesus . . . took the loaves, and when he had given thanks, he distributed them to those who were seated; so also the fish, as much as they wanted." In Luke 9:16 Jesus gives the bread and fish to the disciples to set before the crowd; in Mark 6:41 Jesus gives the loaves to the disciples to set before the people, while he divides the two fish among them all; in John 6:11 Jesus distributes both the bread and the fish to the multitude (cf. v. 27). In the Fourth Gospel, Jesus himself is the one who nourishes the people (cf. 4:14; 5:21). The disciples' role is twofold: they make the people sit down (v. 10: i.e., they help prepare the people to receive from Jesus), and they gather up the remains (vv. 12–13: i.e., they provide compelling testimony of the superabundance of Jesus' provision for people). Here, as elsewhere, the narrative makes a qualitative distinction between the role of Jesus and the roles of disciples (4:42; 3:29; 3:13; 1:15).

(3) The two reactions to the miracle, together with Jesus' responses, come in vv. 14–26. (a) The first reaction is given in vv. 14–15a. When the people saw the sign of feeding, they said, "This is indeed the prophet who is to come into the world," and they tried to make him king by force. One memory ingrained in Jewish consciousness is that of the manna from heaven by which the people were fed in the wilderness (Exod 16:1–36; Num 11:4–9; 21:5; Deut 8:3, 16; Josh 5:12; Neh 9:15, 20; Ps 78:23–25; 105:40; Wisdom of Solomon 16:20–21: "thou didst give thy people the food of angels, and without their toil thou didst supply them from heaven with bread ready to eat"). Part of the eschatological hope in Jewish antiquity is the expectation of the renewal of the manna from heaven. As 2 Baruch 29:3, 8, puts it:

And it shall come to pass when all is accomplished . . . that the Messiah shall then begin to be revealed. And it shall come to pass at that self-same time that the treasury of manna shall again descend from on high, and they will eat of it in those years, because these are they who have come to the consummation of time.

Later rabbinic tradition expresses it in terms of "as the former redeemer caused manna to fall, so the latter redeemer will cause manna to descend" (*Ecclesiastes Rabbah* 1:9; cf. *Mekilta* on Exod 16:25). This form of the hope was associated with "the Prophet" (1:21, 25; cf. Deut 18:15–19 for the origins of the expectation of a prophet like Moses; Acts 3:22–23 for Christian appropriation of it for Jesus; 1 Cor 10:3 for Christian parallelism of feeding by Moses and that by Jesus; Sibylline Oracles 7:149). In Jewish tradition, Moses is regarded as both prophet (Wisdom of Solomon 11:1; Aristobulus, in Eusebius, *Preparation for the Gospel* 8.10.4; Philo, *Biblical Antiquities* 35:6) and king (Ezekiel, in Eusebius, *Preparation for the Gospel* 9.29); in the Johannine narrative, Christ = Messiah = King (1:41, 49), and Christ and Prophet are closely associated (1:20–21, 25); in John 6:14–15, therefore, that the people confess Jesus as the prophet and attempt to make him king is to be taken as a unified act.

Jesus' response to this reaction to his feeding is twofold. He withdraws again to the hills by himself (v. 15b). He then goes to the other side of the sea (vv. 16–21). The Fourth Evangelist uses the story of the storm at sea not to narrate a sea rescue but to explain a sea crossing (C. H. Giblin, "The Miraculous Crossing of the Sea [John 6:16–21]," *NTS* 29 [1983]: 96–103). Although Mark 6:45–54, and especially Matthew 14:22–33, treat the event as a miraculous occurrence, John does not. The key lies in the use of the Greek preposition *epi* in vv. 16, 19, 21. Its use in vv. 16 and 21 controls the way it is understood in v. 19. In v. 16, "when evening came, his disciples went down *to* [*epi*] the sea"; in v. 21, "they were glad to take him into the boat, and immediately the boat was *at* [*epi*] the land to which they were going"; in v. 19, "they saw Jesus walking *beside* [*epi*] the sea [cf. 21:1 where *epi* = beside the sea] and drawing near to the boat." On this rendering, the narrative implies that while the disciples toiled at their oars through the storm, Jesus made his way up the coast toward Capernaum where they sighted him walking along the shore. The story in John 6 functions to explain how Jesus got across the lake (cf. vv. 22–25; W. E. Hull, *BBC* 9:271) Having misunderstood the sign of the feeding, the crowd responds inappropriately and Jesus withdraws first into the hills and then to the other side of the Sea of Galilee.

(b) The second response of the people to the feeding comes in vv. 22–25. When they cannot find Jesus, even though they do not know how he might have left, they get into the boats that have come from Tiberias and go to Capernaum, "seeking Jesus." When they "found him" (cf. 1:41: "we have found the Messiah"; 1:45: "we have found him of whom Moses wrote") on the other side of the sea, they said to him, "Rabbi, when did you come here?" Jesus' reaction is similar to that in 2:23–25. He knows their motives and so says: "Truly, truly, I say to you, you seek me, not because you saw signs [pointers to spiritual reality], but because you ate your fill of the loaves" (v. 26). There are two kinds of "finding" (1:41, authentic; 6:25, inauthentic) just as there are two types of believing (2:23, inauthentic; 4:53, authentic) and following (1:40, 43, authentic; 6:2, inauthentic). That Jesus is the one who feeds the multitudes may be taken on more than one level. To this point in the narrative, Jesus' sign is misunderstood. What follows is a lengthy dialogue that aims at clarification.

Part Two (vv. 27–59) falls into four subunits: vv. 27–31, vv. 32–34, vv. 35–48, and vv. 49–58. Units One and Two specify the identity of the giver of the bread, Unit Three offers the identity of the bread given, and Unit Four deals with the ingestion of the bread given. Unit One (vv. 27–31) is held together by the key word "work." It consists of a dialogue between Jesus and the people:

> Jesus: "Do not work for the food which perishes, but for the food which endures to eternal life, which the Son of Man will give to you" (v. 27; cf. 4:13–14).
>
> The people: "What must we do, to be doing the works of God?" (v. 28).
>
> Jesus: "This is the work of God, that you believe in him whom he has sent."
>
> The people: "Then what sign do you do, that we may see, and believe you? What work do you perform?"

The imperative is: work for the nourishment that yields eternal life. The question is: what are these works that have a divine character to them? The *Damascus Rule* 2:14–15 clarifies "works of God" ("I will open your eyes so that you may see and understand the works of God, and choose what pleases him and reject what he hates"). They are what pleases God. What pleases God in the Fourth Gospel is to believe in him whom he has sent (3:17, 34). The people reflect the popular belief that a true prophet will legitimate himself and his message with a miracle (e.g., Josephus, *Antiquities* 2.12.3 §280, says God gave Moses three signs with instructions to use them "in order to obtain belief among all men that you are sent by me and do all things according to my commands"). "What sign do you do that we may believe you?" Then they specify the sign desired: "Our fathers ate the manna in the wilderness: as it is written, 'He gave them bread from heaven'" (v. 31). They want the return of the manna. These are the folk who shared in the bounty of the multiplication of the loaves the previous day (vv. 22, 24, 25), but who do not see the sign value of it (v. 26). They are earth bound.

Unit Two (vv. 32–34) is held together by the terms "give-gave." Here again there is a dialogue between Jesus and the people. This unit's argument develops out of the text quoted in v. 31 of the preceding unit: "He gave them bread from heaven to eat" (Ps 78:24; cf. Exod 16:4–5; Neh 9:15; Wisdom of Solomon 16:20). Jesus uses the text but challenges their assumed interpretation at two points.

> Truly, truly, I say to you, it was not Moses who gave you the bread from heaven; my Father gives you the true bread from heaven. (v. 32)

(a) "He" is not a reference to Moses but rather to God, as the Old Testament context (e.g., Exod 16:15) makes clear. Only someone in heaven gives heavenly bread. (b) The verb "to give" is not a past tense (gave) but a present tense (gives). Jesus' interpretation runs: it does not say "Moses gave," but "my Father gives." Like the Samaritan woman (4:15), the people ask out of ignorance: "Lord, give us this bread always" (v. 34). Their request sets the stage for what follows.

Unit Three (vv. 35–48) which contains yet another exchange between Jesus and the people, is held together by the phrase "bread from heaven" and falls into a concentric pattern:

A v. 35a: I am the bread of life

    B v. 35b: The one who believes in me shall not hunger

        C v. 36: You have seen me

            D v. 37: The Father gives me/comes to me

                E v. 38: Come down from heaven

                    F v 39: This is the will of him who sent me/raise at the last day

F′ v. 40: This is the will of my Father/raise at the last day

E′ vv. 41–42 (43): Come down from heaven

D′ vv. 44–45: Comes to me/the Father draws them

C′ v. 46: Seen the Father

B′ v. 47: The one who believes in me has eternal life

A′ v. 48: I am the bread of life.

Here the identity of the bread is given. If Units One and Two indicated the identity of the giver of the bread (my Father, v. 32; the Son of Man, sealed by the Father, v. 27), Unit Three specifies the identity of the bread given (I am the bread of life). In a concentric pattern without a clearly defined center, the focus of emphasis is on the two outside components, A and A′, here, "I am the bread of life" (vv. 35a, 48). The expression "bread of life" is known from *Joseph and Aseneth* (8: a God-fearing man eats the "blessed bread of life"; 15: this bread is promised to Aseneth; 16: "See, now you have eaten the bread of life") and means "bread which yields eternal life" (cf. v. 49). In its Johannine context, the bread of life is not only given by Jesus (vv. 11, 27) but also is Jesus (vv. 35, 48). This would not have been alien to Jewish thought processes. Targum *Neofiti* on Exodus 16:15 identifies the heavenly bread and Moses. The children of Israel saw and said to one another, "Who/what is he?" for they did not know Moses. And Moses said, "He is the bread which the Lord has given you to eat." The marginal variant reads: "He is the bread given to you by the word of the Lord for food." Here Moses the Lawgiver identifies himself, in circumlocutional speech, as the heavenly bread itself, a personification of the divine nourishment allotted by God to Israel (Geza Vermes, "He is the Bread: Targum Neofiti Exodus 16:15," in *Neotestamentica et Semitica,* ed. E. E. Ellis and M. Wilcox [Edinburgh: T. & T. Clark, 1969], 256–63). That the giver and the gift are identical means that one does not receive something from Jesus without receiving Jesus himself.

B (v. 35b) and B′ (v. 47) clarify the meaning of terms: "Come to me" = "believe in me" (i.e., not a chore but a companionship); "shall not hunger" = "shall never thirst" = "have eternal life."

C (v. 36) and C′ (v. 46) say that only Jesus has seen the Father (cf. 1:18). The people, however, have seen Jesus but do not believe. Humans are responsible for their unbelief. Certain passages in the chapter presuppose an act of will for which one is responsible either to believe or not believe in Jesus (e.g., 6:29, 35, 36, 37b, 40, 45, 66–67).

D (v. 37) and D' (vv. 44-45) tell us that people cannot come to Jesus unless the Father draws them. A response of faith to Jesus presupposes God's work in making such an act possible. Certain other passages in the chapter suggest that a divine act alone is responsible for faith (e.g., 6:37, 39, 44, 65). Moreover, those whom the Father has given Jesus will not be rejected but will be raised up at the last day.

E (v. 38) and E' (vv. 41-43) indicate that the Jews have difficulty with Jesus' statement, "I have come down from heaven . . . to do the will of him who sent me," because they know his father (Joseph) and his mother (unnamed). Jesus speaks on one level, they understand on another.

F (v. 39) and F' (v. 40) focus on exactly what the Father's will is: that those who believe in the Son should have eternal life, that they should not be lost to the ruler of this world (17:12), but should be raised up at the last day. If D and D' emphasized prevenient grace, F and F' put their emphasis on divine preservation of believers who have been drawn to Jesus. Just as the emphasis on prevenient grace does not eliminate that of individual responsibility, so the stress on the divine preservation of believers does not, for John, exclude the possibility of one's being lost (6:70; 13:21, 30; 17:12).

Unit Three has had a clear christological focus. The point of focus for the section is the twofold "I am the bread of Life" (vv. 35, 48). This is the first of seven "I am + predicate" sayings in the Fourth Gospel (cf. "I am the light of the world," 8:12; "I am the door of the sheep," 10:7, 9; "I am the good shepherd," 10:11, 14; "I am the resurrection and the life," 11:25; "I am the way, the truth, and the life," 14:6; "I am the true vine," 15:1). These sayings do not function to reveal Jesus' essence but rather to reflect his dealings with humans. In each of these seven sayings what Christ does for human beings is identified with a metaphor. If Jesus is the bread of life, then what he does is to nourish us with himself.

Unit Four (vv. 49-59) consists of yet another exchange between Jesus and the people. It is held together by the terms "eat-ate" and falls into a concentric pattern:

A   vv. 49-50: Ate . . . died/eat . . . not die

   B   v. 51: My flesh/eat . . . live

      C   v. 52: How . . . eat

      C'   vv. 53-54: Unless . . . eat

   B'   vv. 55-57: My flesh/eat . . . live

A'   v. 58: Ate . . . died/eat . . . live.

This unit focuses on the ingestion of the bread given. People must take into themselves the heavenly bread in order to know its benefits.

The emphasis in a concentric pattern without a centerpoint is on the two outer components, A and A'. Here A, vv. 49–50, and A', v. 58, concentrate on the contrast between two kinds of bread: the manna that one could eat and still die, and the bread "which comes down from heaven, that one may eat of it and not die." Both may come down from heaven but only one yields life.

B, v. 51, begins to clarify what is the heavenly bread that gives life. In Unit Four, taken as a whole, the bread has a twofold form: christological and eucharistic. V. 51 is christological: v. 51a clearly so, v. 51b perhaps pointing to the Eucharist:

> I am the living bread which came down from heaven; if people eat of this bread, they will live forever; and the bread which I shall give for the life of the world is my flesh.

Its language is understandable in light of a saying of R. Hillel, son of Gamaliel III: "There shall be no Messiah for Israel, because they have already eaten him in the days of Hezekiah" (b. Sanhedrin 99a). Just as one may devour books, drink in a lecture, swallow a story, stomach a lie, and eat one's own words, so one may eat the living bread, Jesus, the incarnate Word.

C, v. 52, gives expression to the incomprehension of the Jews. "How can this man give us his flesh to eat?" The question of "how" is the springboard into what follows. C', vv. 53–54, moves the discussion to the level of the Eucharist:

> Truly, truly, I say to you, unless you eat the flesh of the Son of Man and drink his blood, you have no life in you; those who eat my flesh and drink my blood have eternal life, and I will raise them up at the last day.

The language is not literal. In Judaism and early Christianity literal drinking of blood is prohibited (Gen 9:4; Lev 17:10, 12, 14; cf. Acts 15:29). The combination "eating Jesus' flesh and drinking his blood" is used by Christians near the time of the Fourth Gospel for participation in the Eucharist. Ignatius of Antioch offers clear evidence:

> I have no pleasure in the food of corruption or in the delights of this life. I desire the "bread of God," which is the flesh of Jesus Christ, who was "of the seed of David," and for drink I desire his blood, which is incorruptible love. (*Romans* 7:3)

Be careful therefore to use one Eucharist (for there is one flesh of our Lord Jesus Christ, and one cup for union with his blood....) (*Philadelphians* 4:1)

They [docetists] abstain from Eucharist and prayer, because they do not confess that the Eucharist is the flesh of our Savior Jesus Christ who suffered for our sins.... (*Smyrnaeans* 7:1)

From a slightly later time, Justin's use of language is similar. He says:

For not as common bread and common drink do we receive these; but in like manner as Jesus Christ our Savior, having been made flesh by the Word of God, had both flesh and blood for our salvation, so likewise... the food which is blessed by the prayer of his word... is the flesh and blood of that Jesus who was made flesh. (*1 Apology* 66)

The progression of thought has moved from christology to the Eucharist. The eucharistic bread and wine are, for the Fourth Gospel, a cultic extension of the Incarnation in the Johannine community.

B', vv. 55–57, gives the basis for the assertion in C' (vv. 53–54):

For my flesh is food indeed, and my blood is drink indeed. Those who eat my flesh and drink my blood abide in me, and I in them. As the living Father sent me, and I live because of the Father, so those who eat me will live because of me.

To say that Christians abide in Jesus and Jesus abides in them (cf. 15:4, 5) is to use the language of intermingling. It is a substantival image to communicate what relationally one would call personal intimacy. These verses claim that eucharistic participation is conducive to personal intimacy with Jesus. Intimacy with Jesus results in life for the believer because the Son has life in himself (1:4: "in him was life"; 5:26: "the Son also to have life in himself") that he has been granted by the Father who has life in himself (5:26: "as the Father has life in himself"). So the line runs from the Father who has life in himself, to the Son who has been granted to have life in himself, to believers who have personal intimacy with the Son by means of his eucharistic flesh and blood and who will live as a result of this personal intimacy.

In the narrative of the Last Supper in John 13–17, there is no account of the institution of the Lord's Supper as in the Synoptics (Matt 26:26–29; Mk 14:22–25; Lk 22:14–20) and in 1 Corinthians 11:23–25. The eucharistic language in the Fourth Gospel appears in John 6:53–58, in Galilee not Jerusalem, in the middle of Jesus' public ministry not during the last week of his life. In John 6, vv. 53–58 are located in a context that is strongly christological (vv. 35–48, 49–51). What is the significance of locating the eucharistic passage in John 6 and of placing it after an incarnational one? The answer to these questions gives one the Johannine understanding of the Lord's Supper.

In the New Testament there are at least three views of the Supper: (a) a memorial of Jesus' death as a covenant sacrifice (1 Cor 11:23–25; Mk 14:22–25; Lk 22:14–20, in the long text; Matt 26:26–29, at least in part, in v. 28a); (b) a continuation of the mealtimes with Jesus during his lifetime and after his resurrection, which anticipates the messianic banquet (Luke-Acts); and (c) a cultic extension of the Incarnation in which the bread and wine function dramatically as the incarnate body and blood of Jesus. The Fourth Gospel belongs to the third type. If one's understanding of the Supper is that of a memorial of Jesus' death, what better place to locate the words of institution than in the last week of Jesus' life? If one's concept of the Supper is that of mealtime with the risen Lord, what better place to locate a breaking of bread than in a resurrection appearance, as in Luke 24:13–35? If one's conception of the Supper is that of a cultic extension of the Incarnation, what better context for the eucharistic words than in the middle of Jesus' public ministry immediately after a lengthy treatment of the nourishing dimensions of christology? For John, Jesus' death makes the cultic extension of the Incarnation possible. The cultic meal, however, is not a memorial of his death any more than an anticipation of his second coming, but rather an ingesting of his incarnate life (D. Mollat, "The Sixth Chapter of Saint John," in *The Eucharist in the New Testament* [Baltimore: Helicon, 1964], esp. 146–47, 152).

Jesus' christological and eucharistic words spoken in the synagogue at Capernaum (v. 59) become the source of division among his disciples. The third part of John 6 is vv. 60–71, which focus on this division. This part is composed of two parallel units, vv. 60–65 and vv. 66–71, both concerned with the effects of Jesus' words. The pattern looks like this.

A   v. 60: Many of Jesus' disciples react negatively

   B   vv. 61–63: The words of life

      C   vv. 64–65: Betrayal

A'   v. 66: Many of his disciples react by desertion

   B'   vv. 67–69: The words of life

      C'   vv. 70–71: Betrayal

That it is the incarnate Jesus (vv. 35–48, 49–51) and the eucharistic extension of the Incarnation (vv. 53–58) that offer nourishment leading to life is a scandal to "many of his disciples." They say, "This is a hard saying; who can listen to it?" (v. 60). Their offense at his words is known to Jesus (v. 61), another example of his prophetic knowledge (1:48; 2:25; 4:29; 5:6; 6:64; 11:4, 11; 13:1, 3, 11, 18; 16:19, 30; 18:4; 19:28). His response comes in vv. 62–63:

> Then what if you were to see the Son of Man ascending where he was before? It is the Spirit that gives life, the flesh is of no avail; the words that I have spoken to you are Spirit and life.

The words spoken to them (vv. 35–48, 49–58) are Spirit and life in the sense that the Incarnation and Eucharist are of the realm of Spirit and therefore give life, that is, they put one in touch with the Spirit. They can do so because the Son of Man has ascended and has given the Spirit (7:37–39; 20:22). In contrast, things like the manna in the time of Moses belong to the realm of the flesh and are ineffectual. "But there are some of you who do not believe" (v. 64a). This, of course, has been known to Jesus from the start, as has the identity of his betrayer (v. 64b). His comment on the matter is: "This is why I told you that no one can come to me unless it is granted by my Father" (v. 65; cf. Paul for whom also the faith that saves is a gift, Phil 1:29).

In v. 66 it is stated that "after this many of his disciples drew back and no longer went about with him." Jesus then asks the Twelve: "Will you also go away?" (v. 67). Will the desertion of disciples over difficulties with Incarnation and Eucharist be total? Peter makes clear that it will not. "Lord, to whom shall we go? You have the words of eternal life; and we have believed and come to know, that you are the Holy One of God" (vv. 68–69; cf. Mk 8:29). He assures Jesus that the Twelve will remain faithful. Jesus knows better. "Did I not choose you, the Twelve, and one of you is a devil?" (v. 70). He speaks, of course, of Judas, who is to betray him (cf. 13:11, 18, 26; 18:2).

The chapter that has focused on Jesus as the nourisher of the multitude by means of Incarnation and Eucharist ends with a division among his disciples. Some draw back because of the difficulties associated with Incarnation and Eucharist. They are, as Jesus knows, not really believers, not having been drawn by the Father. This language sounds similar to that in 1 John 2:19 ("They went out from us, but they were not of us; for if they had been of us, they would have continued with us; but they went out, that it might be plain that they are not of us"). It may well be that in John 6 one hears echoes of the community's recent past. Secessionists have drawn back from following Jesus because of difficulties with Incarnation (remember 2 John 7; 1 John 4:2; 5:6–8) and its cultic extension, the Eucharist (cf. Ignatius, *Smyrnaeans* 7:1: "They abstain from Eucharist . . . because they do not confess that the Eucharist is the flesh of our Savior Jesus Christ who suffered for our sins"). If so, then certain segments of the section have anti-docetic overtones as well as an emphasis on Jesus' warrants for the supersession of Jewish traditional worship (i.e., Jesus supersedes the Passover).

WATER OF LIFE/
LIGHT OF THE WORLD

John 7:1–9:41

John 7–9 is a large thought unit composed of discourse material in
dialogue form (chaps. 7–8) linked with a sign (chap. 9), just as chapters 5 and 6 are. Unlike chapters 5 and 6, but like chapters 10–11,
John 7–9 gives the discourse material first and the sign last. The unit
begins, like 5:1 and 6:1, with the phrase "after this" (7:1). Temporally,
the events of these chapters are located at the Feast of Tabernacles
(7:2: "Now the Jews' Feast of Tabernacles was at hand"; 7:14: "About
the middle of the feast"; 7:37: "On the last day of the feast, the great
day"); geographically, they are located first in Galilee (7:1–9), then in
Jerusalem (7:10) in or near the Temple (7:14: "Jesus went up into the
Temple and taught"; 7:28: "as he taught in the Temple"; 8:20: "These
words he spoke in the treasury, as he taught in the Temple"; 8:59:
"Jesus...went out of the Temple"). The large thought unit consists of
an introduction (7:1–14), followed by two major sections of discourse/
dialogue (7:14–52 and 8:12–59), and is concluded by a sign (9:1–41)
that is linked to Jesus' words in 8:12. The material echoes various dimensions of the christological controversies between the synagogue and
the Johannine community during its history, all of which center around
the question of whether Jesus is a true or a false prophet, is or is not
the Messiah. In their present form, however, these chapters function to
depict Jesus as the fulfillment of the Feast of Tabernacles (on Tabernacles, see Exod 23:16; Lev 23:33–36, 39–43; Deut 16:13–15; Josephus,
Antiquities 8.4.1 §100; m. Sukkah). In his fulfilling the water and the
light ceremonies of Tabernacles in himself, the earthly Jesus gives a warrant for the supersession of Jewish worship in that of the Christian
community. As such, John 7–9 functions as the sixth of seven episodes
that portray Jesus as superseding a variety of forms of traditional Jewish
worship.

The introduction, 7:1–14, consists of two paragraphs, vv. 1–9 and

vv. 10–14, held together by the link phrase "in secret" (vv. 4, 10). Vv. 1–9 fall into a concentric pattern:

> A   v. 1: Jesus went about in Galilee, because the Jews sought to kill him
>
>> B   vv. 2–4: His brothers say to Jesus: Go to Judea, because no one works in secret if he seeks to be known
>>
>> B′   vv. 6–8a: Jesus says to his brothers: Go yourselves, because although my time has not come, your time is always here
>
> A′   vv. 8b–9: Because his time had not fully come, Jesus remained in Galilee.

Since Jesus' life is in danger in his home country, Judea (4:44), Jesus stays in Galilee. His unbelieving brothers (cf. Mk 3:21, 31–35) urge him to perform his works publicly in Judea at the Feast of Tabernacles. That Jesus declines serves two Johannine motifs. (a) He uses language with a double meaning (remember 3:5, "born anew"; 4:10, "living water"): "I am not going up (*anabainō*) to/at this feast." For Jesus to go up could mean either to go up geographically to Jerusalem or to go up to the Father (his glorification). At this point, Jesus says that his glorification will not be at the Feast of Tabernacles. His time has not fully come (2:4; 3:14; 7:30, 44; 8:20, 28; 10:17–18, 39; 12:23, 27, 31–36; 13:1, 31). Jesus' prophecy here (I am not going up at this feast) is fulfilled in chapters 7 and 8 (7:30, 44, 45–46; 8:20, 59), linking the introduction to what follows. (b) Jesus refuses to have his salvific timetable determined by human pressures, even from those closest to him (mother, 2:3–5; brothers, 7:3, 10; beloved friends, 11:3–6). If he acts (10:17–18), it will be when he sees what the Father is doing or hears what the Father is saying (5:19; 15:15b; 17:8). So while the brothers go up to the feast, Jesus stays in Galilee.

Vv. 10–14 fall into a chiastic pattern:

> A   v. 10: Jesus went up (*anebēsan*), not publicly but privately
>
>> (a)   The Jews were looking for him at the feast (v. 11)
>>
>> B   vv. 11–13: (b) People mutter, "He is a good man," or "He is leading the people astray" (v. 12)
>>
>> (a′) For fear of the Jews (9:22; 12:42; 19:12–13, 38; 20:19) no one spoke openly of him (v. 13)
>
> A′   v. 14: Jesus went up (*anebē*), publicly.

Although he does not follow human direction, Jesus does eventually go up to the feast in Jerusalem and begins to teach in the Temple. The emphasis in this paragraph is on the centerpiece, especially v. 12. The question is: Is Jesus a good man or is he leading the people astray? Clarification of the question comes from two sources: (1) in the Babylonian Talmud (b. Sanhedrin 43a), one reads: "On the eve of Passover they hanged Jesus, and the herald went before him for forty days, saying, 'Jesus is going to be stoned because he has practiced sorcery and beguiled and led Israel astray'"; (2) in Justin, *Trypho* 69, we hear: "They dared to call him a magician, and a deceiver of the people." The background is in Deuteronomy 13:1–5's discussion of the false prophet (cf. m. Sanhedrin 11:5; CD 5.17b–6.2a; Sibylline Oracles 3.63–70). The issue is whether or not Jesus is a false prophet.

The discourse material that follows is held together by an inclusion (7:14: "into the Temple"; 8:59: "out of the Temple"). It breaks into two self-contained sections of dialogue, 7:14–52 and 8:12–59, focused on the question of whether or not Jesus is the Christ. The first, 7:14–52, falls into two subunits that loosely correspond to one another: vv. 14–36 and vv. 37–52 (B. Lindars, *The Gospel of John* [Greenwood, S.C.: Attic Press, 1972], 286).

A vv. 14–24: Jesus teaches in the Temple in the middle of the feast

   B vv. 25–29, 31: Speculation among the people — Can this be the Christ?

      C vv. 30, 32–36: Abortive attempt to arrest Jesus

A′ vv. 37–39: Jesus' teaching in the Temple on the last day of the feast

   B′ vv. 40–43: Speculation among the people — Is this the prophet/Christ?

      C′ vv. 44–52: Attempt to arrest Jesus aborted.

A (vv. 14–24) begins with Jesus' public teaching in the Temple evoking a query: "How is it that this man has learning when he has never studied [i.e., with a rabbinic teacher]?" One who studies the Bible and Mishnah but has not studied with a rabbi is described as one of the people of the land, as a Samaritan, or as a magician by the Talmud (b. Sota 22a). Three arguments follow to authenticate Jesus' teaching even though he has never studied with an accredited teacher. (a) Since Jesus' teaching is that of the One who sent him (cf. m. Sanhedrin 11:5: "The false prophet — he that prophesies what he has not heard and what has not been told him"; Philo, *Special Laws* 1.15, gives a picture of the true prophet who does not speak on his own behalf), if his hearers desire to do God's will, they will have an inner certainty that his teaching is from God (vv. 16–17). (b) The absence of self-seeking on Jesus' part points to the authenticity of his teaching (v. 18). (c) That Jesus' ministry fulfills the intention of Scripture points to its legitimacy (vv. 19–24).

A reference back to the healing on the sabbath in chapter 5 is the springboard for what follows in vv. 22–23:

> Moses gave you circumcision [Exod 12:44–48] (not that it was from Moses, but from the fathers [Gen 17:10–14]), and you circumcise a man on the sabbath. If on the sabbath a man receives circumcision, so that the law of Moses may not be broken, are you angry with me because on the sabbath I made a whole man healthy?

In Judaism circumcision did indeed supersede the sabbath law (Lev 12:3: since circumcision is always to be administered on the eighth day, babies born on the sabbath would be circumcised on the sabbath; m. Shabbath 19:2: "One can do anything that is necessary for circumcision on the sabbath"). If so, then, certain rabbis argued, by inference the sabbath law could be violated in the interests of saving human life (t. Shabbath 15.16; R. Eliezer [c. 90 C.E.] says that not to perform circumcision on the sabbath would incur the judgment of God. "And does this not justify a conclusion from the less to the greater? If one supersedes the sabbath on account of one of his members, should he not supersede the sabbath for his whole body if in danger of death?"; b. Yoma 85b; R. Eliezer b. Azariah [c. 100 C.E.] says: "If circumcision, which affects one of a man's two hundred forty-eight members, supersedes the sabbath, how much more must his whole body if his life is in danger of death supersede the sabbath?"). Jesus just takes the argument one step further. He does not abide by the limitation, "if someone is in danger of death." In this fulfillment of the intent of Scripture Jesus' ministry is authenticated. Is Jesus a false prophet? The answer of this segment is NO.

B (vv. 25–29, 31) records speculation among the people, both negative and positive. (a) The negative side: "Can it be that the authorities really know that this is the Christ? Yet we know that when the Christ appears, no one will know where he comes from" (vv. 26–27; cf. Matt 24:23–24//Mk 13:21–22, which assume belief in an unknown messiah; cf. Justin. *Trypho* 8 says: "Christ . . . is unknown"). Since in ancient Jewish culture a person is usually identified by where he comes from (place and/or parentage — e.g., Jesus of Nazareth, the son of Joseph — 1:45), the people at the feast assume they know Jesus' identity because they know where he comes from (cf. 6:42: "whose father and mother we know"). His response is ironic: "Do you know me, and do you know where I come from? . . . I come from [God]" (vv. 28–29). The inference is: you do not know me because you do not know where I come from. (b) The positive side: "When the Christ appears, will he do more signs than this man has done?" (v. 31) Mark 13:22//Matt 24:24 reflect the assumption that the Christ/prophet will perform signs and wonders. Signs have their attraction among Jesus' contemporaries (2:23–25; 3:2; 5:36; 6:2, 14–15). The speculation continues. Is Jesus the Christ?

C (vv. 30, 32–36) tells of an abortive attempt to arrest Jesus. He responds: "I shall be with you a little longer, and then I go to him who sent me; you will seek me and you will not find me; where I am you cannot come" (vv. 33–34). The hearers are earthbound and do not understand. They say to one another: "Where does this man intend to go . . . ? Does he intend to go to the Dispersion . . . ? What does he mean?" (vv. 35–36). Whereas Jesus speaks about his glorification, his hearers infer that because he has already been exposed as a false prophet within Israel, he must be going to the Greeks to see if he can find a following there. Ironically, when Jesus does go to the Father, he will indeed go to the Greeks (cf. 11:49–52; 12:20–23).

A' (vv. 37–39) shifts to the last day of the feast, the great day (whether the seventh or eighth day is not clear). There is a saying of Jesus (vv. 37–38) followed by the Evangelist's interpretation of it (v. 39). Jesus' words are capable of two very different interpretations, depending on how the text is punctuated. Either Jesus is the source of the living water in the quotation from Scripture in v. 38 or the believer is the source. RSV, TEV, NIV, and NAB prefer a punctuation that understands the water as flowing from the believer:

> If anyone thirsts, let him come to me [Jesus] and drink;
> The one who believes in me, as Scripture said, "Rivers of living water shall flow out of his [the believer's] heart."

JB and NEB utilize a punctuation that assumes the water flows from Jesus:

> If anyone thirsts, let him come to me [Jesus];
> And let him drink who believes in me [Jesus];
> As Scripture said, "Rivers of living water shall flow out of his [Jesus'] heart."

The source of the quotation from Scripture is uncertain. If the first alternative is preferred, then the source of the quotation could be Proverbs

18:4, Isaiah 58:11, or Sirach 24:30–34, all of which contain the idea of Wisdom as a fountain or river within an individual. If the second option is taken, then the source of the quotation could be Isaiah 43:19–20 or 44:3, which promise water-like rivers, the latter actually equating the water with the Spirit. In none of these, however, is there anything corresponding to "out of his heart." The actual source of the scriptural reference, therefore, remains an insoluble problem.

The disagreement over which reading is to be preferred goes back to the early church, the majority of the Greek Fathers taking the view that the water flows out of the believer, some Western Fathers preferring the understanding that the water flows from Jesus. Regardless of which choice is made about the source of the water in the quotation of v. 38, whether believer or Jesus, v. 37 clearly portrays Jesus as the source of the water ("If anyone thirst, let him come to me"). This is in line with the Gospel elsewhere (4:10, 14a; 7:39; 20:22; 19:34?; cf. Rev 22:1). If v. 37 is taken as a single unit ("If anyone thirst, let him come to me and drink"), Jesus is still the source of the water. All that is at issue is whether or not this text (vv. 37–38) aims to make the additional point that the water Jesus supplies has an element of permanence to it for the believer as in 4:13–14 ("the water that I shall give her will become in her a spring of water welling up to eternal life"). Given the nearly exact parallel of 4:13–14, where Jesus gives the water that then becomes a spring within the believer, preference is given here to the reading of the RSV, NIV, NAB, and TEV. Jesus gives the water which then becomes a river flowing from the believer.

The interpretation of the water offered by the Evangelist comes in v. 39:

> Now this he said about the Spirit, which those who believed in him were to receive; for as yet the Spirit had not been given, because Jesus was not yet glorified.

The water given by Jesus which becomes a permanent feature of the believer's life is the Holy Spirit (cf. Odes of Solomon 6). Just as the Spirit descended and remained on Jesus (1:33; 3:34), so the Spirit, when received, remains with believers. Believers, however, receive the Spirit from Jesus and as a result of his glorification (15:26; 16:7; 20:22). Jesus is more than a prototype of Christians' experience of the Spirit (i.e., we have an experience analogous to his); he is the baptizer with the Holy Spirit (1:33), the one who sends the Spirit (15:26; 16:7), the one who breathes the Spirit on them (20:22), i.e., he is the source of the Spirit and the means by which believers experience the Spirit. Remember the problems of 1 John, of which we may here be hearing echoes (cf. Acts 2:33).

These words of Jesus about the living water almost certainly echo the water ceremony carried out at the feast of Tabernacles. Water drawn from the pool of Siloam was daily poured at the altar into a silver bowl (m. Sukkah 4:9). This symbolic act points backward and forward. On the one hand, it recalls the events of the wilderness years (Lev 23:42–43). It would be difficult for those who witnessed the water ceremony to avoid thinking of the waters in the desert. In the Tosefta (t.Sukkah 3.3, 11, 13), it is asked why the Water Gate is so named:

> It is so called because through it they take the flask of water used for the libation at the Feast.

> R. Eliezer b. Jacob says of it: "The waters are dripping (Ezk 47:2)," intimating that water *oozing out and rising, as if from this flask,* will in the future days come forth from under the threshold of the temple. (3.3)

> So the well, which was with Israel in the wilderness, was like a rock of the size of a k'bara (a large round vessel), and was *oozing out and rising as from the mouth of this flask,* travelling with them up the mountains and going down with them to the valleys. Wherever Israel encamped, it encamped opposite them before the door of the Tabernacle. (3.11)

The water ceremony looked back to the water from the well in the wilderness. On the other hand, it also pointed forward to the Messianic era when there would be an abundance of water (Ezk 47:1–12; Joel 3:18; Zech 14:8: "On that day living waters shall flow out from Jerusalem"). The expectation of living water is sometimes connected with the gift of the Spirit (Isa 44:3; Joel 2:28). Indeed the Jerusalem Talmud (j. Sukkah 5:1) connects the water libation of Tabernacles with the gift of the Spirit: "Why is the name of it called, The drawing out of water? Because of the pouring out of the Holy Spirit, according to what is said: 'With joy shall you draw water out of the wells of salvation.'" When Jesus says on the last day of the feast of Tabernacles, "If anyone thirst, let him come to me and drink," he is claiming to fulfill the hopes of Tabernacles. In so doing, he gives a warrant for its supersession in the worship of the Johannine community to whom has been given the gift of the Spirit by the glorified Jesus.

The background for the Evangelist's interpretation seems to be the belief of some Jews that the efficacy of the Spirit had ceased with the cessation of Old Testament prophecy. (a) 1 Maccabees 9:27 speaks about distress "such as had not been since the time the prophets ceased to appear among them." (b) The Tosefta (t. Sotah 13:2) says: "Since the death of the last prophets, Haggai, Zechariah, and Malachi, the Holy Spirit ceased from Israel, but they received messages by means of a heavenly voice." The Fourth Gospel assumes that the Spirit, given to Jesus as a permanent endowment from the time of the waters of John's baptism (1:33; 3:34), will be given to others after Jesus' glorification (7:39; 20:22).

B' (vv. 40–43) presents the speculation among the people: Is this the prophet/the Christ? After Jesus' words in vv. 37–38, some of the people said, "This is really the prophet" (v. 40; 1:21). Others said, "This is the Christ" (v. 41; 1:20). Objections are offered to such claims:

> Is the Christ to come from Galilee? Has not the Scripture said that the Christ is descended from David, and comes from Bethlehem, the village where David was? (vv. 41b–42)

That the Messiah is to be a descendent of David is deeply rooted in Jewish (2 Sam 7:12–16; Ps 18:50; Isa 11:1, 10; Jer 23:5) and early Christian (Rom 1:3–4; 2 Tim 2:8) tradition. That he comes from Bethlehem also has Jewish (Mic 5:1–2; Tg. Micah 5:1) and Christian (Matt 2:1–6; Lk 2:1–7) roots. These conventional beliefs are reflected by the people who are speculating about Jesus' identity. In John, nothing is said explicitly about Jesus' Davidic lineage or birth at Bethlehem. He is called "Jesus of Nazareth, the son of Joseph" (1:45); his Galilean family ties are assumed (2:1; 6:42). John 4:44, however, seems to imply that Galilee is not his home country, but that Judea, where the Jews seek to kill him (7:1, 19; 8:59; 10:31; 11:8, 16), is. The reader is left with a puzzle. Does the Evangelist assume the readers of the Gospel know the facts about the Davidic lineage (as in the tradition of Rom 1:3–4 and 2 Tim 2:8), and the birth at Bethlehem, or is the Johannine community one in which this was not assumed information? How one answers this question determines how one reads this segment of the text. That no explicit answer is given to this objection would seem to imply that the hearers of the Gospel are expected to know the truth. They would hear the objection with insiders' information and smile at the stupidity of the people who raise the objection. In any case, the Evangelist interprets the situation: "So there was a division among the people over him" (v. 43).

C' (vv. 44–52) returns to the aborted attempt to arrest Jesus. When the Pharisees and chief priests ask why the officers have not brought Jesus, they say: "No man ever spoke like this man" (v. 46). This prompts the Pharisees' retort: "Are you led astray, you also? Have any of the authorities or of the Pharisees (3:2?) believed in him? But this crowd, who do not know the law, are accursed" (vv. 48–49; cf. Deut 27:14–26). This attitude toward the unlearned people (i.e., those not instructed by an accredited teacher) is similar to that of Hillel: "An uneducated man dreads not to sin, and an *'am ha-aretz* [person of the land/one who does not know the Law] cannot be saintly" (m. Pirke Aboth, 2:6). Just as one cannot trust a teacher who has not studied (7:15), so one does not rely on the judgment of an unlearned crowd.

An exchange between Nicodemus and the other Pharisees follows. He asks: "Does our law judge a man without first giving him a hearing and learning what he does?" (v. 51). Deuteronomy 1:16–17 requires that the defendant be heard; 17:2–5 and 19:15–19 state that at least two witnesses be heard before a judgment is made. The rabbis followed this precedent (m. Sanhedrin 5:4: more than one witness is heard and "if the accused said, 'I have somewhat to argue in favor of my acquittal,' they listen to him, provided there is anything of substance in his words"; *Exodus Rabbah* 21:3: "Men pass judgment on a man if they hear his words; if they do not hear his words they cannot establish judgment on him"). Nicodemus had himself followed this rule when he went to Jesus by night to give him a hearing. Now he asks his fellow Pharisees to do the same.

They reply: "Are you from Galilee too? Search and you will see that the prophet [so P66 and possibly P75] / a prophet [so most other witnesses] is not to arise out of Galilee" (v. 52). The indecision about the textual variants, "the prophet" or "a prophet," has to do with how the exchange is to be taken: seriously or ironically. If the text reads "no prophet is to arise out of Galilee," it overlooks the fact that Jonah came from Gath-Hepher (2 Kings 14:25), only three miles north of Nazareth, and it contradicts rabbinic teaching (b. Sukkah 27b: "Thou hast no single tribe in Israel from which a prophet has not come forth"; *Seder Olam Rabbah* 21: "Thou hast no city in the land of Israel in which there has not been a prophet"). If the text reads "the prophet is not to arise out of Galilee," then this problem is avoided. If the text is read seriously, then "the prophet" is to be preferred. If, however, the Evangelist portrays the people and the Jews throughout the chapter as obtuse and even in violation of their own law, then this may be yet another example (cf. vv. 27–28, where the people obviously do not know where Jesus comes from; vv. 35–36, where the Jews do not understand what Jesus means about going away; vv. 41–42, where it is at least conceivable that the comments about the Messiah coming from Bethlehem reflect the people's ignorance of Jesus' true geographical origins; v. 51, where the Pharisees are depicted as violating their own law).

In this case, "no prophet is to arise from Galilee" is a perfectly appropriate part of the scheme of the entire chapter. It is yet another incidence of stupidity (3:10) or culpability (3:11–12). In either case, the attempt to arrest Jesus is aborted and the division among the people and their leaders persists.

John 7:53–8:11 is not an integral part of the Fourth Gospel. (a) It is absent from most ancient manuscripts (e.g., P66, P75, Sinaiticus, Vaticanus, and many others of the Alexandrian family). It is inserted after John 7:52 by Codex Bezae and others reflecting the Western text. It is placed after John 7:36 by 225; after John 21:24 by Family 1 and a few others; and after Luke 21:38 by the Ferrar group. (b) The vocabulary is Synoptic rather than Johannine, bearing closest resemblance to Luke (e.g., "Mount of Olives" is mentioned nowhere else in John but is in the Synoptics nine times; "*parageneto* / he came" is used by Luke twenty-seven times, but only once in John; "*pas ho laos* / all the people" is used seven times by Luke but never in John; "*katekrinen* / condemned" and "*apo tou nun* / again" also are used by the Synoptics but not by John). (c) The paragraph breaks the unity of John's narrative.

The story itself is of great antiquity. In the first half of the second century, Papias (so Eusebius, *Church History* 3:39) refers to an episode of a woman accused of many sins before the Lord. He says it existed in the Gospel of the Hebrews. It gained widespread acceptance when Jerome accepted it into the Vulgate as a part of John, at a time when attitudes toward adultery had become more lenient in the church (cf. *Apostolic Constitutions* 2:24). Because it is not an integral part of John, however, it will not be discussed in this commentary.

The second block of dialogue set at Tabernacles comes in 8:12–59. This section falls into five smaller thought units with similar patterns: there is a provocative statement by Jesus, followed by a Jewish response, to which Jesus gives a retort: sometimes monologue, sometimes involving dialogue (vv. 12–20; vv. 21–30; vv. 31–40; vv. 41–50; vv. 51–59).

Unit One (vv. 12–20) begins with a provocation by Jesus in v. 12: "I am the light of the world (cf. Isa 42:6; 49:6; 51:4; 1 Enoch 48:4); those who follow me will not walk in darkness but will have the light of life (cf. 1:4; Ps 56:13; Job 33:30)." Here is another "I am + predicate" saying (remember "I am the bread of life," 6:35, 48). Here, as there, the statement is not primarily ontological (about Jesus' nature) but soteriological (about his function in salvation). This assertion almost certainly reflects another part of the ritual of Tabernacles, the candlestick ceremony. During the nightly celebration, the court of women was illuminated by golden candlesticks reaching over the height of the walls, crowned by four golden lamps, each of which was reached by a ladder. At the bottom of every ladder stood a son of the priests who held permanent office in the Temple with a pitcher of oil from which he fed the lamp in his charge. The wicks of the lamps were provided from the worn-out breeches and girdles of the common priests, which were torn up into strips, plaited into wicks, and placed in the bowls that served as lamps. According to the Mishnah (m. Sukkah 5:3), there was not a courtyard in Jerusalem that did not reflect the light. At a festival that looked backward to the time of wandering in the wilderness, the light ceremony could not have avoided associations with the pillar of fire (Exod 13:21; 14:24; 40:38) that went before the people. Since the pillar of fire and cloud was expected to return in the endtime (Isa 4:5; Baruch 5:8–9; *Song of Songs Rabbah* 1:8 [R. Akiba]), it is difficult to believe that the light ceremony would not have evoked this eschatological hope. In saying, "I am the light of the world," in this context, Jesus claims to be the fulfillment of the hopes for light associated with Tabernacles. In so doing he gives a warrant by his own words for the supersession of Tabernacles in the worship of the Johannine community centered around him. This indeed would be provocative.

The Pharisees charge: "You are bearing witness to yourself; your testimony is not true" (v. 13; cf. 5:31). This, of course, reflects Jewish tradition (m. Ketuboth 2:9: "none may be believed when he testifies of himself").

Jesus' retort is in two parts (vv. 14–15 and vv. 16–19), each of which has two similar components: (a) Jesus' witness is true because, and (b) the Jews do not know. In the first part, vv. 14–15, (a) Jesus' witness is true because he knows where he has come from and where he is going, i.e., he knows whose agent he is (7:29, 33; cf. 3:13), but (b) the Pharisees do not know this because they judge according to the flesh, i.e., they do not know whose agent Jesus is. In the second part, vv. 16–19, (a) Jesus' witness is true because the Father bears witness (cf. 5:37; 1 John 5:9–12), yielding two witnesses, as the Law demands (Deut 17:6; 19:15), but (b) the Pharisees do not know either Jesus or the Father. Unit One is closed with the Evangelist's note: "These words he spoke in the treasury, as he taught in the temple; but no one arrested him, because his hour had not yet come" (v. 20).

Unit Two (vv. 21–30) also begins with a provocative statement of Jesus comprised of three components, each of which is picked up in what follows: "[1] I go away, and [2] you will seek me and die in your sin; [3] where I am going you cannot come" (v. 21). The question of the Jews in v. 22 picks up the third component. They ask: "Will he kill himself, since he says, 'Where I am going, you cannot come'?" Being earthbound, they think Jesus speaks of committing suicide and going to darkest Hades (cf. Josephus, *War* 3.8.5 §375: "The souls of those whose hands have done violence to their own lives go to darkest Hades"). Jesus' retort is in two parts: vv. 23–27, which picks up the second component of v. 21 ("You will die in your sin"), and vv. 28–30, which picks up the first component of v. 21 ("I go away"). Each part has three ingredients.

Vv. 23–27, the first part, echoes "you will die in your sin" of v. 21. (a) You will die in your sins unless you believe that "I am he." (b) I declare what I have heard from the one who sent me (i.e., I am a faithful agent). (c) The Evangelist comments: "They did not understand that he spoke to them of the Father."

Vv. 28–30, the second part, picks up "I go away" of v. 21a. (a) When you have lifted up the Son of Man, you will know that "I am he." (b) I speak as the Father taught me. (c) The Evangelist comments: "As he spoke thus, many believed in him."

In Unit Two (vv. 21–30) there is another type of "I am" statement. It does not have a predicate (as in "I am the bread of life" or "I am the light of the world") but reads merely *egō eimi* / I am. It can be translated "I am he" as in 4:26 or "It is I" as in 6:20. Here in 8:24, 28 it is translated "I am he" by the RSV. Who is "he"? The context points to "he" being the one who comes from above (v. 23) as an emissary of the Father (vv. 26–27), and who does nothing on his own authority (v. 28). It is a claim to be the revealer.

Unit Three (vv. 31–40) begins with a provocative statement by Jesus in two parts that springs from v. 30. To those who believed in him, he says: "[1] If you continue in my word, you are truly my disciples, and you will know the truth, and [2] the truth will make you free" (vv. 31–32). The question of the believing Jews is: "We are descendants of Abraham, and have never been in bondage to anyone. How is it that you say, 'You will be made free [v. 33]?'" The spirit of what is said is similar to that of R. Akiba: "Even the poorest in Israel are looked upon as freedmen who have lost their possessions" (m. Baba Kamma 8:6). Jesus' retort is in two parts: the first (vv. 34–36) picking up on v. 33b, the second (vv. 37–40) answering to v. 33a.

Vv. 34–36, the first part of the retort, answers to v. 33b ("How is it that you said, 'You will be made free?'"). "Truly, truly, I say to you, every one who commits sin is a slave to sin.... So if the Son makes you free, you will be free indeed." Since evil is submission to a personal tyrant (v. 44), everyone who commits sin is a slave to sin (cf. Rom 6:12–18; Gal 4:3, 8–9; 5:1). The freedom offered by Jesus is from sin.

In the Fourth Gospel sin is both an orientation (5:14; 8:21, 46; 9:34) that is characteristic of the world (1:29; 16:8) and an act or actions (3:19–20; 4:16–18; 8:24; 9:2–3) that lead to dire consequences (e.g., physical illness, 5:14; guilt, 9:41; 15:22, 24; bondage, 8:34; death, 8:24). Some actions have a greater degree of seriousness than others (19:11). The orientation needs to be taken away (1:29) by belief in Jesus (8:24); the actions need forgiving (20:23) and their consequences relieved (5:1–14). (a) Because sin is in its essence a way of life in opposition to God and Christ, it is not dealt with by the concept of forgiveness. From the human side, belief in Jesus destroys the orientation that is in opposition to God. From the divine side, the new birth from above deals with it. The positive aspect of such belief/new birth is eternal life, its negative corollary is the elimination of sin as an orientation in opposition to God (1 John 5:11, 12). Since the orientation of sin is such a complex reality, it cannot be dealt with by any decree of forgiveness. It can be dealt with only by a new way of life that has its origin, not in the devil, but in God. Jesus, in John, destroys sin by healing the whole person, not by mere absolution from guilt. (b) Sinful acts arise out of the sinful orientation. When the sinful orientation is corrected, sinful acts will be affected (8:24). But even believers sin, although not habitually. This post-baptismal sin must be dealt with by forgiveness achieved by Jesus (13:6–10; 20:23; cf. 1 John 1:8–10; 2:1–2; 5:16–17). Whereas the Gospel focuses on breaking the sinful orientation of unbelievers (but cf. 13:8–10), 1 John's emphasis is on the issue of the post-baptismal sins of believers (J. T. Forestell, *The Word of the Cross: Salvation as Revelation in the Fourth Gospel* [Rome: Biblical Institute Press, 1974], chap. 4).

Vv. 37–40, the second part of the retort, answers to v. 33a (you will know the truth). It consists of two parallel units, vv. 37–38 and vv. 39–40, each with four components:

I know you are descendants of Abraham (biologically).	1. If you were Abraham's children, you would act like him.
You seek to kill me.	2. You seek to kill me.
I speak what I have seen with my Father.	3. (I) told you the truth which is from God.
You do what your father says.	4. This is not what Abraham did....

The Jews are not Abraham's spiritual descendants because they do not act like him (e.g., Gen 18 says Abraham received God's messengers; cf. m. Aboth 5:19, for a rabbinic distinction between the children of Abraham who act like him and the children of another who act like another). Jesus acts like his Father; they act like their father (as yet unspecified, but the devil, so v. 44).

Unit Four (vv. 41–50) begins with Jesus' provocative statement: "You do what your father did" (v. 41a). The Jews' first response is: "We were not born of fornication; we have one Father, even God" (v. 41b; cf. Exod 4:22; Jer 31:9). The initial part of the response was taken as an attack on Jesus by Origen (*Against Celsus* 1.28) and the Acts of Pilate (2.3–4). By implication, Jesus was born of fornication. The context here, however, is focused not on Jesus' person but on the issue of Jewish faithfulness/unfaithfulness to God. For that reason, this may be a Jewish claim of faithfulness to God instead of an attack on Jesus (LXX Hos 1:2: "children of fornication"; 2:4: "children of fornication"; 4:15; cf. *Numbers Rabbah* 2: "In the days of Hosea [the Israelites] angered God. They began to horrify God 'for they were children of whores' "). We are not, they are saying, like the Israelites of Hosea's time, unfaithful/children of fornication. Jesus' retort is in two parts, vv. 42–43 and vv. 44–47, each with the same four components.

If God were your Father	1. You are of your father, the devil.
you would love me.	2. Because I tell you the truth, you do not believe me.
Why do you not understand what I say?	3. Why do you not believe me?
Because you cannot bear to hear my word.	4. Because you are not of God.

People act like their parent. The Jews are of their father, the devil, who is a liar and the father of lies (Gen 2–3; 1 Enoch 104:9–10), as well as a murderer (1 John 3:12). This is evidenced by the fact that they seek to kill Jesus and they do not recognize the truth he gives them.

This evokes a second response from the Jews: "Are we not right in saying that you are a Samaritan and have a demon?" (v. 48). In antiquity, to be charged with demon possession is to be discredited. Such a one is not to be taken seriously or followed either because he is deranged (cf. 7:20; 10:20) or because he is a magician/deceiver (cf. Acts 13:8–11; Justin, *1 Apology* 26: Menander, a Samaritan, inspired by devils, deceived many). In this context, for Jesus to have a demon means he is a magician who seeks to lead people astray. Jews associated Samaritans with magic as well as deception (b. Sota 22a: "as a Samaritan or as a magician"). Jesus' second retort is one of denial: "I have not a demon; but I honor my Father, and you dishonor me (5:23). Yet I do not seek my own glory (as a magician does); there is One who seeks it and he will be the judge" (vv. 49–50; cf. 17:1, 5).

Unit Five (vv. 51–59) begins also with a provocative statement by Jesus: "Truly, truly, I say to you, if any one keeps my word, he will never see death" (v. 51; cf. Justin, *1 Apology* 26: Menander persuaded those who adhered to him that they should never die, "and even now there are some living who hold this opinion of his"). The Jews' first response to Jesus is as one today might respond to Menander: "Now we know that you have a demon. Abraham died, as did the prophets; and you say, 'If anyone keeps my word, he will never taste death.' Are you greater than our father Abraham, who died? And the prophets died! Who do you claim to be?" (vv. 52–53). Jesus speaks on one level (realized eschatology, cf. 3:15, 16, 36; 5:24; 11:26), the Jews hear on another (cf. 3:4; 6:42). Jesus' first retort comes in vv. 54–55. The Father, whom Jesus knows, is glorifying him.

Unit Five has a second provocative statement: "Your father Abraham rejoiced that he was to see my day [the day of the Messiah's appearance; cf. 1 Enoch 61:5; 2 Esdras 13:52]; he saw it and was glad" (v. 56). Jewish and Christian tradition reflect the belief that God showed Abraham the endtimes: e.g., (a) 2 Esdras 3:14: "and thou didst love him [Abraham], and to him only didst thou reveal the end of times, secretly by night." (b) *Genesis Rabbah* 44:22: Regarding the meaning of Genesis 15:18, Johanan b. Zakkai and Akiba disagree. The former maintains that God revealed this world but not the next to Abraham; the latter contends that God revealed to him both this world and the next. (c) Cf. 2 Baruch 4:4; Apocalypse of Abraham 9–32, especially 31; Hebrews 11:13: "These [including Abraham, v. 8] all died in faith, not having received what was promised, but having seen it and greeted it from afar." Moreover, T. Levi 18:14 mentions Abraham's rejoicing over the endtimes ("Then [in the days of the new priest] shall Abraham, Isaac, and Jacob exult"). Jesus' words, then, are a claim to be the Messiah of the endtimes. The Jewish response is earthbound, as usual: "You are not yet fifty years old, and have you seen Abraham?" (v. 57).

Jesus' second retort (v. 58) is astonishing: "Truly, truly, I say to you, before Abraham was, I am [*egō eimi*]." Two claims are made in this statement: (a) There is obviously a claim to pre-existence (cf. 1:1–3, 15; 17:5,

24; Ps 90:2). (b) The other claim is connected to the use of an "I am" statement without a predicate. In this place, "*egō eimi* / I am" makes no sense if translated either "It is I" or "I am he." What does make sense, in this Johannine context, is a reading of *egō eimi* as the equivalent of the divine self-predication in Deutero-Isaiah and Deuteronomy 32:39 (*'ani hu* in Hebrew, *egō eimi* in Greek). In the LXX of Isaiah 41:4; 43:10, 25; 46:4; 51:12, for example, God speaks of himself as *egō eimi*. "I am" there functions as the divine name of the one God besides whom there is no other. John 17:6, 26 state that Jesus manifested the name of God during his earthly career. In John 8:58, for Jesus to say, "*egō eimi* / I am," is for him to manifest the divine name. The pre-existent one is God (1:1–2) who, therefore, can reveal God (1:18; Philip B. Harner, *The "I Am" of the Fourth Gospel* [Philadelphia: Fortress, 1970]). The response of the Jews is recorded by the Evangelist in v. 59: "they took up stones to throw at him." The Jews interpret Jesus' claim as blasphemy and attempt to stone him (cf. Lev 24:16; m. Sanhedrin 7:4). But since his hour had not fully come, "Jesus hid himself, and went out of the temple." His prophecy of 7:8 ("I am not going up at this feast, because my time has not fully come") has been fulfilled.

In John 7–9 the discourse material comes first (7–8), the sign comes last (9). John 9:1–41 is a commentary on the claim of Jesus in 8:12 ("I am the light of the world"). In this chapter, the man born blind sees with increasing clarity; the ones who claim sight, however, plunge into progressively deepening darkness. Like all miracle stories, this one has three components, expanded by dialogue, especially in the third component, the reaction to the miracle.

(1) The first component is the statement of the problem: "As he passed by, he [Jesus] saw a man blind from his birth" (v. 1). This statement is expanded by dialogue between the disciples and Jesus. The disciples ask: "Rabbi, who sinned, this man or his parents, that he was born blind?" If sin causes suffering, as the Deuteronomic theology claims, then what sin caused a man to be born blind? Either the iniquity of the fathers was being visited upon the children to the third and fourth generations (Exod 20:5// Deut 5:9; 2 Kings 5:27; Jerusalem Tg. Deut 21:20) or a prenatal sin had been committed by the fetus (*Genesis Rabbah* 63). Which is the case here? Jesus' answer is different, depending upon the punctuation preferred.

> (a) It was neither this man nor his parents who sinned, but that the works of God might be manifested in him. It is necessary for us to work the works of the one who sent me while it is day. Night is coming when no one is able to work.

Here the blindness is not due to human sin, but it exists to heighten the glory of God's acts (e.g., Exod 7:3–5; John 11:4). Given this purpose, Jesus needs to do the works of God.

> (b) It was neither this man nor his parents who sinned. But in order that the works of God might be made manifest in him, it is necessary for us to work the works of the one who sent me while it is day. Night is coming when no one is able to work.

Here blindness is not due to human sin, but no other explanation for it is given. Since the problem exists (for whatever reason), there is a divine necessity for Jesus to do God's work so that it may be manifest in the man.

Either way, the text does not function as Jesus' exclusion of sin as a cause of suffering in all cases (remember 5:14; C. H. Talbert, *Learning through Suffering: The Educational Value of Suffering in the New Testament and in Its Milieu* [Collegeville, Minn.: Liturgical Press, 1991]). Only in this particular case is sin as a cause excluded. The major difference is that the first option gives an alternate explanation for the cause of the blindness, the second does not. Jesus' response to the disciples' question concludes with a near repetition of 8:12: "As long as I am in the world, I am the light of the world" (v. 5). This ties chapters 8 and 9 together.

(2) The cure is described in vv. 6–7. First Jesus acts. "He spat on the ground and made clay of the spittle and anointed the man's eyes with the clay, saying to him, 'Go wash in the pool of Siloam (which means Sent).'" Then the man acts in response to Jesus' action. "So he went and washed and came back seeing."

(3) The reaction to the cure (vv. 8–41) is expanded by dialogue in four parts (vv. 9–12; vv. 13–34; vv. 35–38; vv. 39–41). The first dialogue (vv. 8–12) is between the healed man and his neighbors. The question is: how did this happen? The neighbors and those who had seen him as a beggar are not sure whether or not he who now sees is the same man who used to sit and beg. He tells them, "I am the man." They ask: "Then how were your eyes opened?" He answered: "The man called Jesus made clay and anointed my eyes and said to me, 'Go to Siloam and wash'; so I went and washed and received my sight." Here the man whose sight has been restored speaks of "the man called Jesus" (v. 11).

The second dialogue (vv. 13–34) is between the Pharisees and the man and his parents. There is a first examination of the man (vv. 15–17), an examination of the man's parents (vv. 18–23), and a second examination of the man (vv. 24–34). Vv. 13–14 set the stage for the examinations. "They brought to the Pharisees the man who had formerly been blind. Now it was a sabbath day when Jesus made the clay and opened his eyes" (5:9b).

The first examination of the man by the Pharisees comes in vv. 15–17. The emphasis is again on how this happened. "The Pharisees again asked him how he had received his sight." The man takes this as a request for the technique. "He put clay on my eyes, and I washed, and I see." The Pharisees are divided. Some say, "This man is not from God, for he does not keep the sabbath" (m. Shabbath 7:2 lists "kneading" as a class of work forbidden on the day of rest. Jesus' mixing a paste out of saliva and earth violated this; also b. Aboda Zarah 28b indicates that some thought anointing the eyes was not legal on the sabbath; cf. Deut 13:1–5). Others say: "How can a man who is a sinner do such signs?" (3:2; 7:31). Being divided, they asked the man whose eyes had been opened: "What do you say about him, since he has opened your eyes?" The man replies: "He is a prophet" (v. 17; cf. 6:14).

Next comes the examination of the man's parents in vv. 18–23. Again, the emphasis is on how. The Pharisees ask the man's parents: "Is this your son, who you say was born blind? How then does he now see?" The parents, fearful lest they should be put out of the synagogue, say: "He is of age, ask him." It was not until their conference with the parents that the Pharisees really believe the man had been healed.

Following the parents' direction, the Pharisees return for a second examination of the man (vv. 24–34). They say to him: "Give God the praise [= "Promise before God that you will tell the truth," so TEV; cf. Josh 7:19]; we know [the authorities have reached a consensus] that this man is a sinner." The man who was formerly blind replies: "Whether he is a sinner, I do not know; one thing I know, that though I was blind, now I see." Whatever interpretation may be put on the facts, the experience cannot be denied. He can see. The Pharisees ask: "What did he do to you? How did he open your eyes?" The man's answer drips with irony. "I have told you already [v. 15b], and you would not listen. Why do you want to hear it again? Do you too want to become his disciples?" In the "you too" is an implied declaration of discipleship by the man who has by now moved from regarding Jesus as a man, to speaking of Jesus as a prophet, to implying that Jesus is his Master. The Pharisees revile him, saying, "You are his disciple, but we are disciples of Moses" (cf. Matt 23:2; b. Yoma 4a, where Pharisees claim to be Moses' disciples over against the Sadducees).

The man's answer indicates that he thinks their stance is incredible. "Why, this is a marvel. You do not know where he comes from, and yet he opened my eyes [cf. 3:2]. We know that God does not listen to sinners, but if anyone is a worshipper of God and does his will [1 John 3:22], God listens to him [b. Berakoth 6b: "The words of any man in whom the fear of God dwells are heard"; *Exodus Rabbah* 21:3: "The man who does the will of God and prays in complete faith is heard both in this world and in the world to come"; b. Sanhedrin 90a: R. Akiba says: "May it never come to pass that God makes the sun stand still for those who transgress his will"). Never since the world began [i.e., there is no record of such in the Scriptures] has it been heard that anyone opened the eyes of a man born blind. If this man were not from God, he could do nothing." The man's christology continues to evolve. Jesus is a man who healed him; he is a prophet; he is his Master; he is from God, does God's will, and has his prayers answered in ways no one else ever has. If conversion here is enlightenment (3:3: "see the kingdom of God"; cf. Heb 6:4; 1 Pet 2:9; Mk 8:22–26, 10:46–52), having one's sight restored (Philo, *Who Is the Heir?* 76–77, regards impiety as an obstruction of perception; *On the Virtues* 179 compares repentance to a blind person recovering sight), christology is the result of progressive reflection on one's experience with Jesus. The result of the man's confession fulfills the fears of his parents (v. 22): "And they cast him out" (v. 34b).

There are three passages in John that refer to exclusion of Christians from the synagogue (9:22, 34; 12:42–43; 16:2). From the third text, which appears in a prediction made by Jesus in a farewell speech, it is clear that the Gospel knows of Christian exclusion from the synagogues after Easter. That the references are only three prevents one's assuming that the problem dominates the community during the composition of the Fourth Gospel. It was likely a problem in the community's past, as was the transfer of allegiance from the Baptist's disciples to Jesus. It is significant that the exclusion from the synagogues is tied to a confession of Jesus as Christ (9:22), to believing in him (12:42), and to becoming his disciple (9:28, 30–33). It is carried out by the Pharisees (9:22, the Jews = the Pharisees, so v. 13; 12:42). At no point, however, is it ever linked, in the Fourth Gospel, with synagogue prayer (as, e.g., the benediction against the heretics mentioned in b. Berakoth 28b: R. Gamaliel said to the Sages: Is there anyone among you who can compose a benediction relating to the Minim? Samuel the Less stood up and composed it; cf. Justin, *Trypho* 137). This prevents one's assuming that the occasion for the exclusion of the Johannine Christians from the synagogue was the benediction against the heretics.

The third expansion of the reaction to the miracle by means of dialogue comes in vv. 35–38. The dialogue is between the healed man and

Jesus. Jesus hears the man has been cast out, finds him, and asks: "Do you believe in the Son of Man?" The man responds: "And who is he, Sir?" Jesus replies: "You have seen him, and it is he who speaks to you." Here Jesus helps the process of the man's faith along. P75, Sinaiticus, and a few others do not have vv. 38–39a. Some scholars think, as a result, that this material is a liturgical interpolation due to the use of the chapter in connection with baptism. The man replies: "Lord, I believe"; and he worships him. With this, his process of conversion is complete. For him, light means salvation/sight.

The fourth piece of dialogue that enlarges the reaction to the miracle in John 9 is found in vv. 39–41. Jesus says: "For judgment I came into this world, that those who do not see may see, and that those who see may become blind." The Pharisees ask: "Are we also blind?" Jesus responds: "If you were blind, you would have no sin/guilt [*hamartian*]; but now that you say, 'We see,' your sin/guilt [*hamartia*] remains." If people can feel the need for light, then help can be forthcoming. But if they absolutize their blindness as sight, then help is impossible. For them, light means judgment/blindness (3:19–20).

In John 9, as in chapters 5 and 6, the miracle functions as a sign. That is, it is used in the interests of instruction. It teaches that Jesus is indeed the light of the world. In antiquity, accounts of miracles served basically three purposes. (a) Legitimation is the first (e.g., Suetonius, "Life of Vespasian," says that immediately after being acclaimed emperor, Vespasian lacked "prestige and a certain divinity." After the healing of blind and lame men in Alexandria on his way back to Rome, he was legitimated as emperor). This is the way miracles often function for Jesus' contemporaries in the Fourth Gospel (e.g., 3:2; 6:14; 7:31). (b) Evangelization is the second function (e.g., Apuleius, *Metamorphoses* 11, tells how Lucius joins the Isis cult after being miraculously changed from donkey to human). In John, certain individuals are evangelized as a result of miracle: e.g., 4:46–54; 9:30–33. (c) Instruction is the third function of miracle stories in antiquity (e.g., Aelian, Fragment, 89, tells how Euphronius went to the temple of Asclepios to be healed of pneumonia. His cure was the occasion for instruction about proper lifestyle; Wisdom of Solomon 16:26 says that the sending of manna occurred to teach the Israelites that God's word preserves those who trust in him). The Fourth Gospel's signs function in this way, to teach in a tangible way about christology. So in John 6 the multiplication of loaves teaches that Jesus is the bread of life; in John 9 the giving of sight to the blind man instructs people that Jesus is the light of the world.

In John 7–9 diverse materials that echo various christological controversies between church and synagogue have been brought together under the umbrella of Tabernacles. Jesus proclaims himself the fulfillment of the Tabernacles' ceremonies of water and light. In so doing he gives the Johannine community a historical warrant for the supersession of this aspect of Jewish worship in the Christian community after his glorification.

THE DOOR/THE GOOD SHEPHERD

John 10:1–11:54

J ohn 10:1–11:54 is a large thought unit set temporally at or near the Feast of Dedication (10:22). Geographically the story moves from Jerusalem (10:22), to the place across the Jordan where John originally baptized (10:40), back to Bethany near Jerusalem (11:18), and then to a town called Ephraim in the country near the wilderness (11:54). The thought unit consists of the usual discourse (chap. 10) and sign (chap. 11). Like chapters 7–9, and unlike chapters 5 and 6, the discourse comes first. The two chapters are tied together in multiple ways: (a) as discourse and sign; (b) by cross-references (e.g., 10:31: "The Jews took up stones again to stone him" // 11:8: "Rabbi, the Jews were but now seeking to stone you, and are you going there again?"; 10:18: "No one takes [my life] from me, but I lay it down of my own accord" // 11:6: "So when he heard that he was ill, he stayed two days longer in the place where he was"; 11:7: "Then he said . . . 'Let us go into Judea again' "; 11:16: "Thomas . . . said . . . , 'Let us also go, that we may die with him' "); and (c) by certain themes that run through both chapters. In chapter 10, a combination of three themes appears: (1) as a good shepherd, I lay down my life for the sheep (10:11, 15); (2) My sheep hear my voice; I give them eternal life; they shall never perish (10:27–28); and (3) I bring my other sheep into the one flock (10:16). In chapter 11, one meets three similar motifs: (1) Jesus goes to Bethany to see about Lazarus even though it will cost him his life (11:7, 16, 50, 53); (2) Jesus calls Lazarus forth from the grave (11:43–44) and promises he will rise at the last day (11:23); (3) Caiaphas prophesies that Jesus must die for the people, to gather into one the children of God scattered abroad (11:50–52).

These three themes that tie chapters 10 and 11 together would evoke in hearers of the Gospel memories of events associated with the origins of the Feast of Dedication (1 Macc 4:59; 2 Macc 10:3–8; Josephus, *Antiquities* 12.7.6–7 §316–26). (1) The high priests of the period prior to and at the time of the Temple's desecration by Antiochus Epiphanes were false shepherds who by their self-serving behavior contributed to the Syrian desecration (Simon, 2 Macc 3:4–4:6; Jason, 2 Macc 4:7–22; Menelaus, 2 Macc 4:23–5:26). (2) The Maccabean martyrs, by contrast, gave their lives for the flock of God (2 Macc 7:37–38), dying in hope of the resurrection/eternal life (2 Macc 7:9). (3) Closely associated with the Feast of Dedication is the theme of the gathering of God's scattered flock together into one (2 Macc 1:27; 2:7; 2:18). 2 Maccabees, a first-century B.C.E. letter from the Jewish brethren in Jerusalem to their brethren in Egypt exhorting them to keep the Feast of Dedication (1:9; 1:18; 2:16), plays up precisely these three themes in connection with Dedication (B. W. Bacon, "The Festival of Lives Given for the Nation in Jewish and Christian Faith," *HibJ* 15 [1916–17]: 258–78; T. C. Smith, *Jesus in the Fourth Gospel* [Nashville: Broadman, 1959], 166–74). 2 Maccabees also focuses on the consecration of the sanctuary (10:3), after its cleansing from the defilement by the Syrians (cf. John 10:36, which says that Jesus, the new tabernacle [1:14] and the new temple [2:21], has been consecrated). It would seem, then, that John 10–11, set at or near the Feast of Dedication, emphasizes precisely the three or four themes that 2 Maccabees associates most closely with the Feast. In linking them to Jesus, the Fourth Gospel portrays Jesus as the fulfillment of the hopes of Dedication and thereby provides a historical warrant for the supersession of yet another aspect of Jewish worship in the Johannine community. John 10–11 thereby becomes the last in a series of seven episodes making the point: the holy man, Jesus, supersedes traditional Jewish worship.

John 10:1–42 constitutes the discourse segment of the large thought unit. It falls into two parts: 10:1–6 (a figure) and 10:7–42 (its explanation). John 10:1–6 is a figure or parable (*paroimia* = a symbolical saying requiring interpretation). Vv. 1–3a focus on access to the sheepfold:

> Truly, truly, I say to you, the one who does not enter the sheepfold by the door but climbs in by another way, that man is a thief and a robber; but the one who enters by the door is the shepherd of the sheep. To him the gatekeeper opens.

Vv. 3b–5 focus on the mutual confidence between sheep and shepherd:

> The sheep hear his [the shepherd's] voice, and he calls his own sheep by name and leads them out. When he has brought out all his own, he goes before them, and the sheep follow him, for they know his voice. A stranger they will not follow, but they will flee from him, for they do not know the voice of strangers.

These two little parables, fused into one figure (v. 6; cf. Lk 6:39; 15:3, for the singular "parable" used to cover multiple examples), furnish the vocabulary, but not the meaning, for what follows.

Part Two (10:7–42) functions as commentary on the figure in three stages: (1) vv. 7–10, (2) vv. 11–18, and (3) vv. 22–42. Stage One (vv. 7–10) is a meditation on the figure of vv. 1–5 by means of a double explanation of "door" (v. 1), with "thief" (v. 1) also present in vv. 8 and 10:

> (a) I am the door of the sheep [v. 7]. All who came before me are thieves and robbers; but the sheep did not heed them [v. 8].
>
> (b) I am the door; if anyone enters by me, he will be saved, and will go in and out and find pasture [v. 9]. The thief comes only to steal and kill and destroy; I came that they may have life, and have it abundantly [v. 10].

Here is yet another instance of an "I am + predicate" saying (remember, "I am the bread of life"; "I am the light of the world"). It also speaks of Jesus' function in salvation. Like a Near Eastern shepherd who slept in the gateway to his sheep pens, Jesus is the means of access — to the flock, to safety, to nourishment, to life (cf. 14:6: "I am the way"; cf. Ignatius of Antioch, *Philadelphians* 9:1, who says: Jesus "is the door of the Father, through which enter Abraham and Isaac and Jacob and the Prophets and the Apostles and the Church"). What he provides is "abundant life," i.e., life to the full. The thief, by contrast, aims not at giving life but at stealing, killing, and destroying. It is difficult at this point to avoid hearing echoes of the problems with the progressives (2 John 9) who believed they could bypass Jesus on their way to God (1 John 2:23; 5:6–8) and who posed a problem of secession for the community, that is, stealing sheep and destroying the flock (1 John 2:19).

Stage Two (vv. 11–18) is a meditation on the figure of vv. 1–5 by means of a double explanation of "shepherd" (v. 2), with "know" and "voice" also appearing in vv. 14 and 16:

> (a) I am the good shepherd. The good shepherd lays down his life for the sheep. The one who is a hireling and not a shepherd, whose own the sheep are not, sees the wolf coming and leaves the sheep and flees; and the wolf snatches them and scatters them. He flees because he is a hireling and cares nothing for the sheep. (vv. 11–13; cf. 1 Sam 17:34–36).
>
> (b) I am the good shepherd. I know my own and my own know me, as the Father knows me and I know the Father; and I lay down my life for the sheep. And I have other sheep, that are not of this fold;

> I must bring them also, and they will heed my voice. So there will
> be one flock, one shepherd. (vv. 14–16).

The language is traditional. "Shepherd" is widely used for leaders (e.g.,
Ezk 34; Jer 10:21; 23:1–2; Philo, *Life of Moses* 1.60–62, tells of a kid that
had run away. Moses followed it. When it had finished drinking, Moses
took it up with great tenderness, put it on his shoulders, and carried it
back to the flock. God is pleased and says to Moses: "How great are your
tender mercies. You took pity on the kid, because you are full of mercy.
Therefore, you shall lead my people Israel and be their shepherd." Also
the common Homeric designation of a ruler = the shepherd of the folk.).
It is no surprise to find early Christians applying the title to Jesus (e.g.,
1 Pet 2:25: the Shepherd and Guardian of your souls; 5:4: when the chief
shepherd is manifested; Heb 13:20: the great Shepherd of the sheep;
Martyrdom of Polycarp 19:2: the shepherd of the catholic church that
is all over the world). The distinction between the good shepherd and
the bad is also conventional (e.g., in 2 Esdras 5:18, Phaltiel says to Ezra:
"Rise therefore and eat some bread, so that you may not forsake us, like
a shepherd who leaves his flock in the power of savage wolves"; cf. Jer
23:1–4, where the shepherds who destroy and scatter are false prophets).
Religious leaders are of two types: responsible and faithless. The designation of false teachers as wolves is, moreover, a common one in Christian
(Acts 20:29: "after my departure fierce wolves will come in among you,
not sparing the flock"; Matt 7:15; Didache 16:3; Ignatius, *Philadelphians* 2:2; 2 Clement 5:2–4; Justin, *1 Apology* 16:13; *Dialogue* 35:3), as in
Jewish (2 Esdras 5:18), and pagan circles (Philostratus, *Life of Apollonius
of Tyana* 8.22, where Apollonius protects his flock from the wolves, i.e.,
representatives of worldly affairs). As the good shepherd, Jesus will lay
down his life for the sheep (disciples) and not allow any false teacher to
snatch them or scatter them. Jesus, the good shepherd, has other sheep
(both Gentiles, cf. 11:51–52, 12:20–24, and 21:11; and members of the
generations after that of the eyewitnesses, those that have not seen and
yet believed; cf. 20:29b; 17:20) not of this flock (Jews who are members
of the generation of the eyewitnesses, those that have seen and believed;
cf. 20:29a; 17:6–8) that he will bring. "So there shall be one flock, one
shepherd" (v. 16; cf. 1 John 1:3: "we [the eyewitnesses] proclaim to you,
so that you may have fellowship with us; and our fellowship is with the
Father and with his Son Jesus Christ"). Jesus' act of self-sacrifice on behalf
of the flock is freely chosen. "No one takes it from me, but I lay it down
of my own accord" (v. 18).

There may be, in the first two stages of explanation (vv. 7–10; vv. 11–18), further ties to the Feast of Dedication. In the modern reconstruction of the ancient Jewish lectionary, certain passages from Scripture are associated with Dedication: e.g., (a) first year: Genesis 46:28–47:31 (shepherds, cf. 46:31–34); Ezekiel 37:16–28 (gathering of scattered people of God so they are one nation under one king, cf. vv. 21–22; (b) second year: Leviticus 24:1–25:13, 34 (blasphemy, cf. 24:16); Ezekiel 34 (critique of shepherds who have allowed God's sheep to become prey for wild beasts; gathering of scattered sheep; God himself will be their shepherd; judgment between sheep; there will be one shepherd over the flock); (c) third year: Deuteronomy 20:10–22:5 (sheep, 22:1); 1 Samuel 17 (David cares for the sheep). Even allowing for (1) the possibility of error in our reconstruction of the details of the ancient Jewish lectionary, and for (2) the possibility that the full lectionary was not in use as early as the late first century, it seems necessary to assume some links between the observance of Dedication and the reading of at least some of these passages in order to account for the remarkable similarities to John 10.

In Ezekiel 34, for example, one finds the dominant threads of John 10's language about sheep and shepherds: (a) unfaithful shepherds (religious leaders in Israel) have not fed the sheep (God's people, v. 3), but have allowed them to be scattered (vv. 5–6) and to become prey for all the wild beasts (v. 8); (b) God will gather them together (vv. 11–13, 16), feed them (vv. 13, 16), and set up over them one shepherd (v. 23). It is difficult not to read stages one and two of the explanation (vv. 7–10; vv. 11–18) as referring, in Jesus' time, to a contrast between Jesus as true shepherd and the established Jewish religious leadership as hirelings (like those in chap. 9?), and, in post-Easter time, to a contrast between Jesus as true shepherd and the leaders of the secessionists as hirelings. In either case, the links of John 10 to Dedication are strong.

The explanation given of the figure (vv. 1–5) so far (vv. 7–18) produces the expected division among the Jews (vv. 19–21; cf. 5:22). Many said, "He has a demon [7:20; 8:48], and he is mad; why listen to him?" Others said, "These are not the sayings of one who has a demon. Can a demon open the eyes of the blind?" (remember 9:30–33).

Stage Three comes in vv. 22–42. This is a controversy section focused on Jesus' works, in the middle of which is an explanation of "sheep," with "voice" (v. 27//vv. 4–5) also involved, followed again by a divided response. The setting is specified in vv. 22–23: "It was the feast of Dedication at Jerusalem; it was winter, and Jesus was walking in the Temple, in the portico of Solomon" (cf. Acts 3:11; 5:12). The local color is accurate. In the winter season when the cold wind sweeps in from the east across the desert, Jesus walks in the east portico of the Temple, the only portico whose closed side would protect it from the east wind. The Jews gathered around him and put their question: "How long will you keep us in suspense? If you are the Christ, tell us plainly" (v. 24).

Vv. 25–30 give Jesus' answer, involving an explanation of "sheep" and "voice." There are two parts to the argument with a provocative climactic statement. (a) Jesus says he has already told them by both word (v. 25a) and deed (v. 25b). Yet they do not believe (v. 26a). This is because they do not belong to his sheep (v. 26b). (b) Jesus' sheep recognize his voice and follow him (v. 27). He gives them eternal life and no one shall pluck them out of his hand (v. 28). The one who both gives the sheep to Jesus and protects them from being snatched away is the Father (v. 29). There is underlying this passage the same emphasis on divine drawing encountered in chapter 6 (cf. v. 37a: "All that the Father gives to me will come to me"; v. 39: "I should lose nothing of all that he has given me"; v. 44: "No one can come to me unless the Father who sent me draws him"; v. 45: "Everyone who has heard and learned from the Father comes to me"; v. 65: "no one can come to me unless it is granted to him by the Father"). There is a divine initiative that lies behind anyone's positive response to Jesus and there is a divine preservation of those who have aligned themselves with Jesus. In John 10:28 both threads are present, but the emphasis is on the divine preservation of Jesus' flock ("My Father, who has given them to me, is greater than all, and no one is able to snatch them out of the Father's hand"; cf. 17:12; 6:64–65). In a context where the good shepherd lays down his life to protect the flock against wolves (in Christian circles, usually false teachers), the emphasis on preserving sheep from being snatched away may echo the problems combatted in the Johannine epistles (2 John 9–10; 1 John 2:19).

The explanation concludes with a provocative statement by Jesus: "I and the Father are one" (v. 30). In context (cf. v. 25, the works done in the Father's name), the claim is to the functional unity of Father and Son very much like that in John 5:17, with very much the same result. "The Jews took up stones again to stone him" (v. 31; cf. 5:18; 8:59). Jesus asks: "I have shown you many good works from the Father; for which of these do you stone me?" (v. 32). The Jews answer: "We stone you for no good work but for blasphemy (cf. Lev 24:16); because you, being a man, make yourself God" (v. 33; cf. 5:18).

The charge of blasphemy is answered by two arguments, vv. 34–36

and vv. 37–38, the first being an argument from Scripture, the second
an argument from Jesus' mighty deeds:

> (a) Jesus answered: "Is it not written in your law, 'I said, you
> are gods'? If he called them gods to whom the word of God
> came (and Scripture cannot be broken), do you say of him
> whom the Father consecrated and sent into the world, 'You are
> blaspheming,' because I said, 'I am the Son of God'?" (vv. 34–36)

The reference is to Psalm 82:6. The train of thought seems to run:
(1) Scripture calls others besides God gods; (2) these others are those
to whom the word of God came (whether Israel at Sinai, angelic messengers, or Israel's judges is not clear), i.e., God made them gods by
giving them his word; (3) Jesus, who has been sent by the Father (v. 36),
speaks as the Father has taught him (8:28b), as an obedient Son (v. 36;
cf. 5:19–20a), i.e., God has made Jesus what he is by giving him the
divine word; (4) if others to whom the word of God has come are called
by Scripture "gods," how much more can the one whom the Father sent
and who, in perfect obedience, speaks only as the Father has taught
him, be so called. The point is that Jesus' claims do not go beyond what
Scripture allows.

> (b) If I am not doing the works of my Father, then do not believe
> me; but if I do them, even though you do not believe me, believe
> the works, that you may know and understand that the Father
> is in me and I am in the Father. (vv. 37–38)

If Jesus speaks only what he has been taught by the Father (8:28b;
12:50), he does only what he sees the Father doing (5:19–20a); he can
do nothing on his own authority (5:30). Since the Jews supposedly have
a relation to the Father, they supposedly know what types of things the
Father does. If so, then they ought to be able to recognize the Father's
activity in the works of Jesus. If they can, then they ought to be able
to understand that the Father and the Son are in intimate union. Both
what Jesus does and what Scripture says testify to Jesus' obedient union
with the Father. For him to say, "I and the Father are one," therefore,
implies not that he is exalting himself alongside God but rather that he
is obediently submissive to God in his words and works.

It is necessary to remember that two other texts allegedly read at Dedication were Leviticus 24:1–25:13, 34, which included 24:16 dealing with
blasphemy, and Numbers 7:10–11, which speaks about the dedication
of the altar. Can it be that the charge of blasphemy in John 10:33 echoes
Leviticus 24:16 and Jesus' words about his being consecrated in 10:36

reflect Numbers 7:10–11? If so, then these two references further link John 10 with the lectionary readings of the feast of Dedication.

What follows is the customary division among Jesus' hearers. On the one hand, "again they tried to arrest him" (v. 39). Jesus escaped and returned to the place beyond Jordan where John the Baptist had at first baptized (vv. 39b–40). Many came to him. They said: "John did no sign [as a prophet would be expected to do to legitimate the truth of what he said; cf. Deut 13:1; Josephus, *Antiquities* 2.12.3 §280], but everything that John said about this man was true" (i.e., Jesus' work and words themselves legitimate John's testimony; cf. 4:39–42). And many believed in him there (vv. 41–42).

If John 10 functions as the thought unit's discourse/dialogue, John 11:1–53 functions as the accompanying sign. John 11:1–53 is an expanded miracle story with the three customary components: (1) the problem (vv. 1–17), expanded by dialogue and action; (2) the miracle (vv. 17–44), expanded in two cycles that loosely correspond to one another (vv. 17–27; vv. 28–44); and (3) the reactions to the miracle (vv. 45–53), expanded by a plot for Jesus' death. The miracle belongs to the category of resuscitation stories, such as are found in Jewish (1 Kings 17:17–24; 2 Kings 4:8–37; 13:20–21; *Midrash Rabbah* on Lev 10:4; b. Abodah Zarah 10b; b. Megillah 7b), pagan (Pliny, *Natural History* 7.37; Philostratus, *Life of Apollonius of Tyana* 4.45; Apuleius, *Florida* 19; Lucian, *Philopseudes* 25), and early Christian sources (Matt 9:18–26// Mk 5:21–43//Lk 8:40–56; Lk 7:11–17; Acts 9:36–43; 20:7–12). Other than possessing the conventional components of miracle stories generally, resuscitation stories have no common pattern. Such stories tell of the resuscitation of a corpse who will eventually die again of some other cause, not of the resurrection of one who, having experienced the ultimate victory over death, will never die again (cf. Rom 6:9).

(1) The problem is stated in vv. 1–2: "Now a certain man was ill, Lazarus." Lazarus (= God helps) is identified by his place (Bethany) and his family (the brother of Mary [the one who anointed the Lord with ointment and wiped his feet with her hair, cf. 12:1–8] and Martha). The statement of the problem is expanded by dialogue. The sisters sent to Jesus, saying: "Lord, he whom you love [*phileis;* also v. 36; but in v. 5, *agapa*] is ill" (v. 3). Two responses by Jesus follow (vv. 4–6; vv. 7–17).

(a) The first response of Jesus (vv. 4–6) consists of a word and an act. Jesus states the ultimate outcome of the illness ("not unto death") and its function ("for the glory of God"). He then waits two days longer in the place where he is. He does this in spite of the fact that he loved Lazarus and his sisters. Here one encounters yet again the Johannine motif that Jesus' behavior is determined wholly by God's leading (5:19) and not by human pressures, especially by those closest to him like his mother (2:3–4) or brothers (7:8–9) or beloved friends (11:5). The first response shows both the illness and Jesus' behavior to be under divine control.

(b) The second response of Jesus (vv. 7–17) consists of a word, a dialogue, and a deed. Once it is clear that Jesus' behavior is divinely determined, he says: "Let us go into Judea again" (v. 7). Dialogue between Jesus and his disciples follows (vv. 8–16). The disciples remind him of the danger of such a course of action: "Rabbi, the Jews were but now seeking to stone you, and are you going there again?" (v. 8; cf. 10:31; 8:59; 7:1, 19). Jesus replies: "Our friend [*philos*] Lazarus has fallen asleep [= death, e.g., 1 Cor 15:6], but I go to awake him out of sleep" (v. 11). The disciples misunderstand: "Lord, if he has fallen asleep, he will recover" (i.e., his fever has broken; the crisis is past, v. 12). Then Jesus tells them plainly: "Lazarus is dead; and for your sake, I am glad that I was not there, so that you may believe" (vv. 14–15). Resigned, but faithful, Thomas says: "Let us also go that we may die with him" (v. 16). Then Jesus acts: "he came" to find Lazarus had already been in the tomb four days (v. 17). Burial was on the day of death. It was followed by a week of mourning. In popular Jewish belief, the human spirit hovered near the body for three days, then departed as the color of the corpse began to change. Normally death would be irrevocable and all hope abandoned for one buried four days (*Ecclesiastes Rabbah* 12:6; *Leviticus Rabbah* 18:1). The problem is acute (cf. 5:5: paralyzed for thirty-eight years; 9:1: blind from birth).

(2) The miracle comes in vv. 17–44. It is expanded into two cycles that loosely correspond to one another: a Martha cycle (vv. 17–27) and a Mary cycle (vv. 28–44).

Martha Cycle	*Mary Cycle*
Occasion: Jesus comes (vv. 17, 20a)	Occasion: Jesus calls (v. 28)
Mourners (vv. 18–19)	Mourners (vv. 30–31)
Martha goes to meet him (v. 20b)	Mary goes to him (vv. 29, 32a)
Martha says: "Lord, if you had been here" (vv. 21–22)	Mary says: "Lord, if you had been here" (v. 32)
Dialogue (vv. 23–27)	Dialogue and action (vv. 34–44)

The Martha Cycle begins with Jesus coming to Bethany (v. 17). Bethany is identified as the one "near Jerusalem, about two miles off" (v. 18; i.e., not the Bethany of 1:28). In accordance with custom, mourners have come to console the sisters (v. 19; m. Ketuboth 4:4: "Even the poorest in Israel should hire not less than two flutes and one wailing woman"). That the mourners were "many" testifies to the families' wealth (cf. 12:1–5). Mary sits (the posture for the mourner, cf. Job 2:13) in the house; Martha goes to meet Jesus (v. 20; cf. Lk 10:38–42, where also Martha is the active one). Martha lays responsibility on Jesus: "Lord, if you had been here, my brother would not have died. And even now I know that whatever you ask from God, God will give you" (vv. 21–22). Dialogue ensues that is distinctive to the Martha Cycle (vv. 23–27).

> (1) Jesus says: "Your brother will rise again."
>
> Martha replies: "I know he will rise again in the resurrection at the last day."
>
> (2) Jesus says: "I am the resurrection and the life; the one who believes in me, though he die, yet shall he live, and whoever lives and believes in me will never die. Do you believe this?"
>
> Martha replies: "Yes, Lord; I believe that you are the Christ, the Son of God, he who is coming into the world."

Martha has said that Jesus can forestall death or bring someone back from the dead (vv. 21–22). Jesus' response is in the form of a promise: "Your brother will [future tense] rise again" (v. 23). In ancient Judaism there was a diversity of belief about life after death. Sadducees denied any resurrection from the dead (Mk 12:18–27; Acts 23:8; Josephus, *War* 2.8.14 §165); Essenes held to the immortality of the soul (Josephus, *War* 2.8.11 §154–55); Pharisees believed in the resurrection of the dead (Acts 23:8; Josephus, *War* 2.8.14 §163; cf. m. Sanhedrin 10:1, a Pharisaic/rabbinic document that says all Israelites have a place in the world to come except those who deny the resurrection of the dead). Jesus' promise is akin to Pharisaic belief. Martha verbalizes the same Pharisaic Jewish belief in the future resurrection (v. 24; cf. 5:28–29; 6:39, 40, 44, 54).

Jesus' response is to link that hope with christology by means of another "I am + predicate" saying ("I am the resurrection and the life"; remember 6:35, 48; 8:12). It means Jesus' role in salvation is to give life, both in the present ("will never die"; cf. 6:54a) and in the future ("yet shall he live"; cf. 6:54b), because he has life in himself (5:26; 1:4). This is the role of the one who is coming into the world. In his response to Martha, Jesus makes the general promise ("Your brother will rise again") based upon his role in salvation ("I am the resurrection and the life"). Such a promise can be understood at two levels: (a) the general promise that Lazarus will share in the expected resurrection of the dead at the last day (so Martha's initial perception); (b) and he will rise (i.e., be resuscitated) very soon (v. 4, "This illness is not unto death," leads the reader to hear this more specific promise whether the character in the story, Martha, did or not).

The Mary Cycle (vv. 28–44) begins with Jesus calling for Mary (v. 28). When Mary goes out, the mourners who were with her in the house follow her, supposing that she is going to the tomb to weep there (vv. 29–31). When she comes to Jesus, Mary falls at his feet and says: "Lord, if you had been here, my brother would not have died" (v. 32). She too lays responsibility on Jesus. What follows is a combination of dialogue and action distinctive to the Mary Cycle (vv. 33–44).

Vv. 33–38 pose serious difficulties for interpretation. When Jesus sees Mary weeping (*klaiousan* = wailing of mourners), and the Jews who came with her also weeping (*klaiontas* = wailing of mourners), he is "deeply moved [*evebrimēsato*] in spirit and troubled [*etaraxsen heauton*]" (v. 33). The Greek term translated "deeply moved" is often used of "anger" (Mk 1:43; 14:5; Matt 9:30; Dan 11:30 LXX), and is so taken by the German interpretive tradition here. The English tradition prefers "deeply troubled," allowing "troubled" (cf. 12:27; 13:21), which follows, to control the connotation of "deeply moved," which precedes. Very early the statement caused discomfort (cf. P45, P66, D, and others have "was troubled *as if* angry / deeply moved"), perhaps because it attributes deep emotion to Jesus. The question of why Jesus is emotionally affected remains to be answered after the entire unit is examined.

When Jesus asks where Lazarus has been laid and they show him, "Jesus wept [*edakrysen* = to shed tears]" (v. 35). The reaction of those who observe his tears is mixed (vv. 36–37). Some say: "See how he loved [*ephilei*] him!" Others are critical: "Could not he who opened the eyes of the blind man have kept this man from dying?" Then Jesus, "deeply moved [*embrimōmenos*] again," came to the tomb (v. 38).

In vv. 33–38 there are three references to Jesus' emotional response to Lazarus' death and its attendant circumstances: (a) he was deeply moved and troubled (v. 33); (b) he wept (v. 35); and (c) he was deeply moved again (v. 38). The attempts at interpretation are legion: e.g., (1) they are reflections of Jesus' humanity (cf. 1:14, 45; 4:6; 12:27; 19:34, 40; 20:17, 27); (2) they reflect Jesus' grief (a) over human sin, which is the cause of suffering and death; (b) over human lack of faith, etc.; (3) they are reflections of Jesus' anger over (a) the too intense emotion arising within himself; (b) the unbelief of the Jews and the half belief of Mary (cf. 1 Thes 4:13); (c) the hypocritical sorrow of the mourners, etc.; (4) they are John's correction of the Stoic doctrine of the Wise Man who displays detachment from the disrupting aspects of human nature.

The issues are two: Jesus' being deeply troubled (vv. 33, 38) and his weeping (v. 35). Assistance in understanding Jesus' being deeply moved in spirit and troubled is given by positions (1) and (4) above. Epictetus, *Encheiridion* 16, states his view of the Stoic approach to grief:

> When you see someone weeping in sorrow … straightway keep before you this thought: "It is not what has happened that distresses this man (for it does not distress another), but his judgment about it." Do not, however, hesitate to sympathize with him so far as words go, and, if occasion offers, even to groan with him; but be careful not to groan also in the center of your being.

By contrast, John portrays Jesus as a human figure who feels grief at the center of his being over the loss of a loved one, just as he does when he contemplates his own death (12:27) and faces his betrayal by a disciple (13:21).

The key to a correct reading of Jesus' weeping (v. 35) seems to be the distinction drawn between Jesus' tears (*dakryō* = to shed tears) and those of Mary and the mourners (*klaiō* = to wail in mourning). Seneca offers help in two of his epistles.

(a) Epistle 99, "On Consolation to the Bereaved," 16, says:

> Tears fall, no matter how we try to check them, and by being shed they ease the soul. What, then, shall we do? Let us allow them to fall, but let us not command them to do so; let us weep according as emotion floods our eyes, but not as much as mere imitation shall demand.

(b) Epistle 63, "On Grief for Lost Friends," 1, says:

> Let not the eyes be dry when we have lost a friend, let not them overflow. We may weep, but we must not wail.

These two texts speak about appropriate expressions of grief: tears, yes, but sincere tears; tears, yes, but not wailing. In John 11:33–38 Jesus is deeply moved by sorrow and weeps appropriately, allowing tears to fall. He does not wail, however, as do Mary and the mourners. "Profound grief at such bereavement is natural enough; grief that degenerates to despair, that pours out its loss as if there were no resurrection, is an implicit denial of that resurrection" (D. A. Carson, *The Gospel according to John* [Grand Rapids: Eerdmans, 1991], 416).

When he comes to the tomb, a cave with a stone lying upon it, he says: "Take away the stone" (v. 39a). Martha replies: "Lord, by this time there will be an odor, for he has been dead four days" (v. 39). The situation is hopeless, but Jesus has promised that they will see the glory of God (v. 40; cf. v. 4). So they take the stone away (v. 41a). Jesus lifts up his eyes (a posture of prayer, Ps 123:1; Lam 3:41; 1 Esdras 4:58) and prays: "Father, I thank thee that thou hast heard me. I knew that thou hearest me always, but I have said this on account of the people standing by, that they may believe that thou didst send me" (vv. 41–42; cf. v. 4). The point is well put by R. H. Fuller:

> Jesus lives in constant prayer and communication with his Father. When he engages in vocal prayer, he is not entering, as we do, from a state of non-praying into prayer. He is only giving overt expression to what is the ground and base of his life all along. He emerges from non-vocal to vocal prayer here in order to show that the power he needs . . . for the raising of Lazarus . . . depends on the gift of God. That is why the prayer is a thanksgiving rather than a petition. (*Interpreting the Miracles* [London: SCM, 1963], 107)

After saying this, he cries with a loud voice: "Lazarus, come out" (v. 43). The dead man comes out, "his hands and feet bound with bandages, and his face wrapped with a cloth" (v. 44a). In Jewish burial, a corpse was normally placed on a length of linen, feet at one end, which was then folded over the head and stretched down to the feet where it was tied. Arms were tied to the body with linen strips. The face was bound with another cloth. A person bound in this way, if resuscitated, would be able to shuffle at best. Jesus says: "Unbind him, and let him go" (v. 44b). With this, the miracle is done.

(3) The reactions to the miracle (vv. 45–53) are divided as usual. On the one side, there is belief: "many of the Jews therefore who had come with Mary and had seen what he did believed in him" (v. 45). On the other side, a plot for his death develops (vv. 46–53). When some report to the Pharisees, the Council is gathered together to consider the implications of Jesus' signs. The problem is stated clearly:

> What are we to do? For this man performs many signs. If we let him go on thus, every one will believe in him, and the Romans will come and destroy both our holy place [cf. Jer 7:14; Acts 6:14] and our nation. (vv. 47–48)

Josephus' statement that Herod had John the Baptist killed because, when crowds flocked to him, Herod feared he would lead a popular insurrection (*Antiquities* 18.5.2 §118–119), lends credibility to Jewish fears. The problem is the success of Jesus and the threat such success poses to the Jewish system of worship and national identity. Caiaphas, who is high priest in that memorable year, utters his opinion:

> You know nothing at all; you do not understand that it is expedient for you that one man should die for the people, and that the whole nation should not perish. (vv. 49–50; cf. 2 Macc 7:37–38)

The Evangelist adds his comment on Caiaphas' words. "He did not say this of his own accord, but being high priest that year he prophesied that Jesus should die for the nation, and not for the nation only, but to gather into one the children of God who are scattered abroad" (vv. 51–52; cf. 1 Pet 1:1). At least some Jewish high priests were believed to have had the gift of prophecy (Josephus, *Antiquities* 11.8.4 §327–28; 13.10.3 §282–83; *War* 1.3.8 §68). One did not need to understand that what he said was prophetic (*Mekilta* on Exod 15.17 says: "All prophets who have prophesied have not known what they prophesied; only Moses and Isaiah knew it"). Caiaphas' prophecy not only states that Jesus is to die but also the purpose and effect of his dying: "to gather into one the scattered children of God" (cf. 10:15–16; 12:32). The idea of the great eschatological gathering together of the people of God has deep roots in both Jewish (Isa 11:12; 27:12–13; 43:5; 56:8; Jer 31:8, 10; 32:37; Ezk 11:17; 28:25; 34:13; 36:24; 39:28; Hos 1:11; Mic 2:12–13; Zeph 3:20; 2 Macc 1:27; 2:7, 18) and early Christian tradition (Mk 13:27; 2 Thes 2:1), but the close connection of this event with the death of Christ is specifically Johannine (C. H. Dodd, "The Prophecy of Caiaphas [John 11:47–53]," *Neotestamentica et Patristica* [Leiden: Brill, 1962], 134–43). Jesus, the good shepherd, will by his death bring together all his sheep (Jewish and Gentile; those who have seen and those who have not seen), so there will be one flock and one shepherd (10:16; cf. Ezk 37:22, 24).

As a result of the plot against him, Jesus leaves Judea and goes to a town called Ephraim in the country near the wilderness. There he stays with his disciples (v. 54).

John 10–11 is a large thought unit, put together out of diverse materials, that aims to depict Jesus, through discourse and sign, as the fulfillment of the Feast of Dedication. In this way the holy man gives a warrant from his earthly career to his community after his glorification for worship that supersedes the variety of forms of Jewish worship: whether Temple sacrifices (2:13–3:21), or purification rituals (3:22–4:3), or Temple worship on Gerazim or in Jerusalem (4:4–54), or the water rituals that promise healing of the body (chap. 5), or Passover (chap. 6), or Tabernacles (chaps. 7–9), or Dedication (chaps. 10–11). The use of seven cycles raises the matter above the level of the particular to the level of the general. Traditional worship, as such, is superseded in Jesus' lifetime by the divine presence that tabernacles in the holy man, and after Jesus' glorification by the divine presence in the Johannine community through the Spirit bestowed by the glorified Jesus. The one who came as revealing, enabling presence, who picked/produced a new community, has now given them warrants in seven episodes from his earthly ministry for a new type of worship.

THE ONE WHOSE HOUR
HAS COME

John 11:55–12:50

The plot/story of the Fourth Gospel is simple. John tells of one who came as revealing, empowering presence (1:1–18); who picked/produced a new community (1:19–2:12); who provided them with warrants from his public ministry for a different kind of worship (2:13–11:54); who privately predicted what their future would be like, offering promise, parenesis, and prayer for that time (13:1–17:26); and who ultimately made provision for their community life, worship, and ministry before he returned to whence he had come (18:1–21:25). In seven episodes surveyed so far (2:13–3:21; 3:22–4:3; 4:4–54; chap. 5; chap. 6.; chaps. 7–9; 10:1–11:54), the hearer of the Gospel has been told that in his public ministry Jesus, the holy man, superseded traditional Jewish worship in its various dimensions. Throughout, this period has been characterized as a time when his hour/time has not yet/fully come (2:4; 7:8). In the next section of the Fourth Gospel (chaps. 13–17), Jesus' hour has come (13:1) and the episodes therein are all conditioned by that fact. In between 2:13–11:54 and 13:1–chapter 21 stands a thought unit (11:55–12:50) that functions as a hinge.

After an introduction (11:55–57) that locates the events near Passover, the unit falls into two parts built around (1) two days (12:1–11 and 12:12–36) and (2) two conclusions (12:37–43 and 12:44–50). The thought unit serves as a conclusion to what has come before (so 12:37–50) and as an introduction to what follows (so 11:55–12:36). The awkwardness that a modern reader feels when reading 11:55–12:50 is due, in no small part, to the fact that the last of the unit goes with what comes before (2:13–11:54), while the first of the segment goes with what comes after (13:1–chap. 17). Although unsettling to a modern reader, it follows the ancient directives for relating one part to another in narrative (Lucian, "How to Write History," 55, says of the historian: "When he has finished the first topic he will introduce the second, fastened to it and linked with it like a chain . . . ; always the first and second topics must not merely be neighbors but have common matter and overlap").

Because John here uses the "chain link principle," it will serve the interests of understanding by the modern reader better if the conclusion to 2:13–11:54 is treated first and the introduction to 13:1–chapter 17 is examined second. John 12:37–50 functions as the conclusion to 2:13–11:54. It actually consists of two conclusions: vv. 37–43, which are a conclusion to the signs material, and vv. 44–50, which are a conclusion to the sayings material.

John 12:37–43 ends the public ministry of the holy man, Jesus, who did many wonderful signs, on the discouraging note of unbelief. "Though he had done so many signs before them, yet they did not believe in him" (v. 37; cf. Deut 29:2–9 for the similar experience of Israel in the wilderness in the days of Moses). Signs may be a catalyst for belief (4:46–54; chap. 9), but they do not compel belief (7:19–23; 10:25–26). What follows are two reasons for the unbelief (vv. 38–41 and vv. 42–43).

(1) The unbelief is a fulfillment of Scripture (vv. 38–41). "It was that the word spoken by the prophet Isaiah might be fulfilled" (v. 38). Two quotations from Isaiah follow. (a) The first quotation is from Isaiah 53:1: "Lord, who has believed our report, and to whom has the arm of the Lord been revealed?" The fact of unbelief as a response to Jesus places him alongside the messenger of Isaiah 53, who had the same experience. (b) The second quote is from Isaiah 6:10: "He has blinded their eyes and hardened their heart, lest they should see with their eyes and perceive with their heart, and turn to me to heal them" (v. 40). Vv. 39 and 41 give two reasons for Isaiah's words. First, v. 41 says Isaiah said this because "he saw his [Jesus'] glory and spoke of him." The Fourth Evangelist believes Isaiah's vision of the heavenly throne room (Isa 6:1–13) included a view of Christ. This is a Christianization of a reading of Isaiah 6 like that in the Targum on Isaiah where in 6:5 Isaiah declares he has seen not the King, the Lord of hosts, but "the glory of the shekinah of the King of the ages" and in 6:1 he says, "I saw the glory of the Lord." For John, Jesus is the tabernacling of the divine glory (1:14; cf. 11:4, 40). So if Isaiah saw God's glory, he must have seen Christ. Isaiah's words, moreover, refer to the events of Jesus' time (cf. 1 Cor 9:9–10). Second, v. 39 says the unbelief is divinely determined: "they could not believe." This is also the gist of v. 40. There is a divine blinding and hardening (remember Deut 29:4: "to this day the Lord has not given you a mind to understand, or eyes to see, or ears to hear"; cf. Mk 4:12//Matt 13:13–15//Lk 8:10; Acts 28:26–27). Such a text functions to offer an explanation for the reality of unbelief: if God

is in control of all that happens, and if some do not believe, then their unbelief cannot be outside the divine sovereignty over history.

Ancient Judaism reflects a lively debate about the limits of free will and divine sovereignty in human affairs. (a) Certain streams of Judaism focus exclusively on human freedom. Sirach 15:12–17, e.g., in a context emphasizing responsibility for human actions, says:

> Do not say, "It was he [God] who led me astray. . . . " It was he who created man in the beginning, and he [God] left him [man] in the power of his own inclination. If you will, you can keep the commandments, and to act faithfully is a matter of your own choice. . . . Before a man are life and death, and whichever he chooses will be given to him.

The same point of view is found in the Psalms of Solomon 9:4: "Our works are in the choosing and power of our souls, to do right and wrong in the works of our hands." Josephus says this is the position of the Sadducees who contend "there is no such thing [as fate], and that the events of human affairs are not at its disposal; but they suppose that all our actions are in our own power, so that we are ourselves the cause of what is good, and receive what is evil from our own folly" (*Antiquities* 13.5.9 §173). (b) The Pharisees' position is verbalized by R. Akiba: "All is foreseen and yet there is freedom of choice" (m. Pirke Aboth 3.15). Josephus says that when the Pharisees "determine that all things are done by fate, they do not take away the freedom from men of acting as they think fit; since their notion is, that it has pleased God to make a temperament, whereby what he wills is done, but so that the will of men can act virtuously or viciously" (*Antiquities* 18.1.3 §13; cf. *War* 2.8.14 §163: "to do what is right, on the contrary, is principally in the power of men, although fate does cooperate in every action"). (c) Josephus (*Antiquities* 13.5.9 §172) says that the Essenes affirm "that fate governs all things, and that nothing befalls men but what is according to its determination." The Damascus Document 2.7–8, 11, 13, even seems to hold to double-edged predestination ("For from the beginning God chose them not; he knew their deeds before ever they were created and he hated their generations, and he hid his face from the land until they were consumed"). Yet the responsibility for human decision by those chosen of God is not removed (cf. 1 QS 1.11; 5:1, 6, 8, 10, 21–22; 6:13–14; 9:17).

The Fourth Gospel is closer to the Essenes' position than to the other options described. On the one hand, divine sovereignty dominates John's story. (a) What happens in salvation history is according to the divine plan (e.g., John's decrease, 3:30; Judas' betrayal, 13:18–21; 17:12; Jesus' death, 3:14; 19:24, 28, 36, 37; Jesus' resurrection, 20:9). (b) The life of faith is due to divine initiative (e.g., Jesus chooses disciples, 6:70; 13:18; 15:16, 19; the Father gives disciples to Jesus, 6:37, 39; 10:29; 17:6, 9, 11, 24; the Father draws people to Jesus, 6:44; the Father grants the possibility of one's coming to Jesus, 6:65). (c) The authority of government is under divine control (19:11). On the other hand, the responsibility of humans for their decisions is asserted (e.g., 5:40; 6:40; 7:17; 19:11). The guilt of those not believing in Jesus is, therefore, assumed; yet their inability to believe after all the signs of Jesus can only be according to the divine plan.

(2) The second reason for failure to believe in Jesus after all his signs is offered in vv. 42–43: "Nevertheless many even of the authorities believed in him but for fear of the Pharisees did not confess it, lest they should be put out of the synagogue: for they loved the praise of men more than the praise of God" (cf. 9:22, 34; 16:2). If the first reason emphasizes divine sovereignty, this one focuses on human culpability. These two reasons (vv. 38–41 and vv. 42–43) are offered for the fact of unbelief in the face of Jesus' signs.

Vv. 44–50 function as the conclusion to the sayings material in 2:13– 11:54. The paragraph falls into an ABB′A′ pattern.

A   The functional oneness of Jesus and the Father (vv. 44b–45)

B   The intent of Jesus' coming: salvation (vv. 46–47)

B′   The consequence of rejection of Jesus: judgment (v. 48)

A′   The functional oneness of Jesus and the Father (vv. 49–50).

A (vv. 44–45) has Jesus cry out: "The one who believes in me, believes not in me but in him who sent me (5:23b). And the one who sees me, sees him who sent me." Jesus is God's agent who declares to the world what he has heard from the Father (8:26; m. Terumoth 4:4 says an agent must act according to the mind of the sender). To see Jesus is to see the Father (14:9).

A′ (vv. 49–50) reinforces the point: "I have not spoken on my own authority; the Father who sent me has himself given me commandment what to say and what to speak. . . . What I say, therefore, I say as the Father has bidden me." The emphasis in a concentric pattern without a center is on the outer members, A and A′. The thrust here, then, is that Jesus' sayings during his public ministry have been the very words of God. The outcome of belief in Jesus' words is eternal life (v. 50a).

B (vv. 46–47) focuses on the intention behind Jesus' coming: "I have come as light into the world, that whoever believes in me may not remain in darkness [8:12; 9:5; 3:19–21]. . . . I did not come to judge the world but to save the world" (3:17).

B′ (v. 48) focuses on the consequence of human rejection of Jesus' words: "The one who rejects me and does not receive my sayings has a judge; the word that I have spoken will be his judge on the last day." Future eschatology functions as a warning against rejection of Jesus' sayings. If vv. 37–43 serve as a conclusion to Jesus' signs in 2:13–11:54, vv. 44–50 serve as a conclusion to Jesus' sayings during his public ministry. At this point, the public ministry when the hour has not yet come is at an end.

John 11:55–12:36 functions as an introduction to what follows in the Gospel (13:1–chap. 17), the period when Jesus' hour has come. This segment of the hinge section (11:55–12:50) is composed of an introduction (11:55–57) followed by two days (12:1–11 and 12:12–36). The introduction defines (a) the time of the remainder of the Gospel's narrative ("Now the Passover of the Jews was at hand"; cf. 2:13; 6:4), (b) the prescribed behavior for pilgrims ("many went up from the country to Jerusalem before the Passover, to purify themselves"; cf. Num 9:6–14; 2 Chron 30:17–19; Josephus, *War* 1.11.6 §229; 6.5.3 §290; m. Pesahim 9, for certain acts of purification required of pilgrims; cf. Acts 21:24), (c) the air of expectancy among the pilgrims ("They were looking for Jesus . . . as they stood in the Temple"), and (d) the designs of the religious authorities (they gave "orders that if anyone knew where he was, he should let them know, so that they might arrest him"; m. Sanhedrin 7:10 says that a person who leads the people astray can be captured by stealth).

The first day (12:1–11) is set "six days before the Passover" (v. 1). In John, Nisan 15 (the Passover) is Saturday; Jesus is crucified on Friday, Nisan 14, the Day of Preparation for Passover (19:14: in the afternoon when the Passover lambs are being slain; cf. Exod 12:6). The exact day referred to by "six days before the Passover" is difficult to decide. Depending on how one reckons, anytime from the 8th (Saturday) to the 10th (Monday) would be possible. Since sabbath travel would be unlikely, arrival on the 8th is improbable; arrival on the 9th (Sunday) is more likely (perhaps on Saturday evening, which technically would be the 9th). A supper on Sunday evening would technically be on Monday the 10th. If so, then it would fit into the Evangelist's Passover lamb symbolism (Exod 12:3 says the Passover lamb is to be consecrated on the 10th).

The scene is suppertime in Bethany with Lazarus, recently raised from the dead, as one of those reclining at table with Jesus and with Martha

serving (vv. 1–2). Mary's act is the center of the story (cf. Matt 26:6–13//
Mk 14:3–9; Lk 7:36–50). She takes "a pound of costly ointment of pure
nard" and anoints Jesus' feet (to have anointed his head would have had
Messianic implications; she can do this because those eating were reclining, with their feet away from the table). Because of the excess used, she
has to wipe his feet, and does so with her hair. The house is filled with
the fragrance of the ointment (v. 3). The reactions to this act are two: one
by Judas (v. 4–6), the other by Jesus (vv. 7–8). (a) Judas, who is to betray
him, is critical: "Why was this ointment not sold for three hundred days
wages and given to the poor?" The Evangelist explains Judas's motives.
"This he said, not because he cared for the poor but because he was a
thief, and as he had the money box he used to take what was put into
it" (v. 6). (b) Jesus defends Mary's action. The Greek is difficult. "Let her
alone," is no problem. The difficulty comes with what follows: "in order
that she might keep it for the day of my burial" (v. 7). This should be
understood as Jesus' answer to the question in v. 5 (Why did she not sell
it?). She did not sell it in order that she might keep it for the day of my
burial. She should be allowed to do what she has done, for unknowingly
she has prepared Jesus for his burial (B. Lindars, *John* [Greenwood, S.C.:
Attic Press, 1972], 418–19). Whether v. 8 belongs in the text is uncertain
(some manuscripts exclude it altogether, and since it is identical to Matt
26:11 it may be the result of scribal harmonization). Either way, the thrust
of the story so far seems to be on a proleptic preparation of Jesus' body
for burial. The incident ends on a distinctively Johannine note (vv. 9–11).
A great crowd comes, not only on account of Jesus, but also to see Lazarus
whom he had raised from the dead (v. 9). This results in Lazarus being
included in the death plot of the chief priests "because on account of him
many of the Jews were going away and believing in Jesus" (vv. 10–11).

The use of the term "the Jews" in a positive sense here is instructive.
(a) In the Fourth Gospel "the Jews" means Judeans in contrast to Samaritans (e.g., 4:9) and Gentiles (e.g., 18:33, 35, 39; 19:3, 19). (b) The
expression sometimes designates the authorities (e.g., 1:19), like the
Pharisees (e.g., 9:13, 15, 16, 18, 22, 40); at other times it refers to the
people (e.g., 11:45–46; 12:11). (c) Salvation is "from the Jews" (4:22);
Jesus is a Jew (4:9). (d) On occasion "the Jews" refers to believers in Jesus
(e.g., 8:31; 10:19–21; 11:45; 12:11); mostly it designates those who reject
Jesus (2:18, 20; 5:10, 15, 16, 18; 6:41, 52; 7:1, 11, 13, 15; 8:22, 48, 52,
57; 9:18, 22; 10:24, 31, 33; 13:33; 18:14, 31, 36; 19:17, 31, 38; 20:19). In
John, then, "the Jews" are neither a static nor a homogeneous character.
Nor are "the Jews" pictured in totally negative terms. Like everything else

in the Fourth Gospel, the estimate of "the Jews" is determined by their response to Jesus. This indicates that the Fourth Gospel is not anti-Semitic; it is pro-Jesus and simply evaluates everything, "the Jews" included, in christological terms. This is matched, in John, by the Jewish authorities' clear-cut evaluation of everything in anti-christological terms (e.g., 9:22; 12:42–43; 15:21; R. A. Culpepper, "The Gospel of John and the Jews," *RevExp* 84 [1987]: 273–88).

The second day (vv. 12–36) is built around two initiatives taken by others to which Jesus must react: one is the initiative of the crowd (12:12–13, 17–18), the other is the initiative of the Greeks (vv. 20–22). The next day (v. 12) a great crowd who had come to the feast heard Jesus was coming to Jerusalem. "They took branches of palm trees and went out to meet him, crying, 'Hosanna! Blessed is he who comes in the name of the Lord, even the King of Israel!'" (v. 13). The crowd's initiative reflects Jewish nationalism. (a) The palms would have this meaning: e.g., when Judas rededicated the Temple (164 B.C.E), the Jews brought palms to the Temple (2 Macc 10:7); when Simon conquered the Jerusalem citadel (142 B.C.E.) the Jews took possession carrying palms (1 Macc 13:51); in the Testament of Naphtali 5:4 palms are given to Levi as a symbol of his power over all Israel; the palm appears on coins of the second revolt of the Jews against Rome (132–35B.C.E.). So the palms signal a welcome to Jesus as a national liberator. (b) The expression they "came out to meet him" reflects the normal Greek practice involved in the joyful reception of Hellenistic sovereigns into a city (Josephus, *War* 7.5.2 §100–103). (c) The exclamation, "Hosanna" (= Save/deliver us now) was used in addressing kings (2 Sam 14:4; 2 Kings 6:26). The crowd's initiative, therefore, is an appeal for Jesus to accept the role of a nationalistic deliverer.

Only after the crowd has expressed its nationalistic conceptions does Jesus react by getting the donkey and sitting on it (v. 14). V. 15's quotation from Scripture tells the hearer the meaning of Jesus' reaction. The first line is probably from Zephaniah 3:16, a passage whose context is universalistic (to Jerusalem will stream people from all over the earth to seek refuge, 3:9–10); the second line is from Zechariah 9:9, a passage emphasizing universalism and peace (a colt was ridden by a monarch when he came on an errand of peace; a horse was used in time of war, 1 Kings 4:26; Isa 31:1–3). Jesus' entering Jerusalem on a donkey, then, is an act of prophetic symbolism designed to counteract the crowd's nationalism (remember 6:15) with a message of universal kingship (12:32) and peace (18:36). The Evangelist notes that the reason the crowd went to meet Jesus was because they had heard about the raising of Lazarus (cf. 2:23; 4:45; 6:14; 10:21). The note of universalism continues with the Pharisees' response: "the world has gone after him" (v. 19).

The second initiative taken in this section that requires a reaction from Jesus comes in vv. 20–22. It illustrates the fact that the world has gone after him (cf. v. 19). There were some Greeks (godfearers?) among those who had come up to worship at the feast. Josephus (*War* 6.9.3 §427) says people of this sort liked to go up to Jerusalem as pilgrims (cf. Acts 8:27–28). These people come to Philip, a Galilean (the region of the Gentiles), and say: "Sir, we wish to see Jesus" (v. 21). Philip tells Andrew and together they tell Jesus. The symbolism is carefully done. Gentiles are to be introduced to Jesus only through (Hellenistic?) Jewish disciples of Jesus.

Jesus' reacts in both word (vv. 23–36a) and deed (v. 36b) to the Greeks' appeal. The reaction in word is threefold: vv. 23–26, vv. 27–30, and vv. 31–36a. (a) Jesus' reaction to the Greeks' request is first of all recognition that it is time for him to die. And Jesus answered them (Philip and Andrew): "The hour has come for the Son of Man to be glorified" (v. 23). Jesus' universal kingship comes only after his glorification. The principle behind this fact is stated in v. 24: "Unless a grain of wheat falls into the earth and dies, it remains alone; but if it dies, it bears much fruit." This principle applies not only to christology but also to discipleship: "Those who hate [= to prefer a higher value than] their life in this world will keep it for eternal life. If people serve me, they must follow me; and where I am, there shall my servants be also" (vv. 25–26).

(b) The Johannine equivalent to the Synoptic Gethsemane narrative (Matt 26:36–46//Mk 14:32–42//Lk 22:39–46) comes in vv. 27–30. "Now is my soul troubled (11:33; 13:21). And what shall I say? 'Father, save me from this hour?' No, for this purpose I have come to this hour. Father, glorify thy name" (vv. 27–28a). V. 27 is what may be called an interior monologue, a form found as early as Homer in Greek literature. In the *Iliad*, many of the interior monologues come when a character experiences fear on the verge of battle or upon facing some other dangerous situation (e.g., Odysseus 11.402; Menelaus 17.97; Agenor 21.562; Hector 22.122).

> The psyche has been divided into two parts which dispute for mastery, often in a manner hinting at a concept of the ego, which cares for its own preservation, and a superego which drives the individual toward acceptable action. (R. Scholes and R. Kellog, *The Nature of Narrative* [London: Oxford University Press, 1966], 180)

Jesus' interior monologue is resolved in prayer: "Father, glorify your name" (v. 28a). Jesus turns toward his death because the universal mission demands it. As a human, he is troubled by the prospect, but will not seek to avoid it because the universal mission is his purpose (4:42; 1:29). Jesus' prayer is answered by a voice from heaven: "I have glorified it [in the signs], and I will glorify it again [in his being lifted up]" (v. 28). Those around mistake it for thunder (Sibylline Oracles, 5.344–45: "it will be possible to hear a heavenly crash of thunder, the voice of God") or an angel's speech (Lk 22:43; Dan 10:9). Jesus answers: "This voice has come for your sake, not for mine" (v. 30; cf. 11:42). Jesus hears from God in the depths of his being and needs no external word.

(c) Vv. 31–36a offer yet another variation on the theme that Jesus must die if the universal mission is to be accomplished: "Now is the judgment of this world, now shall the ruler of this world [14:30; 16:11] be cast out; and I, when I am lifted up [3:14; 8:28; cf. Isa 52:13; for "lifted up" with the meaning of both exaltation and execution, cf. Gen 40:13, 19] from the earth, will draw all people unto myself" (vv. 31–32). Two dimensions of the benefits of Jesus' glorification are given: first, the Christus Victor motif (the ruler of this world is cast out; cf. Col 2:15); second, the releasing of the magnetic power of divine love that pulls people to Jesus ("I will draw all people unto myself"; cf. Rom 5:8). Jesus' divine knowledge is again demonstrated: "this he said to show by what death he was to die": not stoning (cf. 8:59; 10:31) but crucifixion (v. 33).

The crowd, perplexed by Jesus' reference to his departure, speaks: "We have heard from the law that the Christ remains forever. How can you say that the Son of Man must be lifted up?" (v. 34). Jewish eschatological expectation included various notions of the duration of the Messiah's reign. Some thought in terms of a reign of limited duration (he is to die, so 2 Esdras 7:28–30; he is to be taken into heaven, so 2 Baruch 30:1). Others thought in terms of an eternal reign (T. Reuben 6:12; Sibylline Oracles 3:48; 1 Enoch 49:2; Psalms of Solomon 17:4). If the appeal for permanence is to the law (Scripture), perhaps Isaiah 9:7 is the basis ("Of the increase of his government and of peace there will be no end, upon the throne of David, and over his kingdom, to establish it, and to uphold it with justice and with righteousness from this time forth and for evermore"; cf. Ezk 37:25; Ps 72:17; 89:35–37). Of course, the Johannine community not only knows his kingship is eternal but also that it is not of this world (18:36).

Just as the conclusion to the signs material ended with an emphasis on the light (v. 46), so the part of the conclusion to the sayings material that constitutes Jesus' verbal response to the initiative of the Greeks concludes with a warning that employs the motif of light: "The light is with you a little longer. Walk while you have the light, lest the darkness overtake you; the one who walks in darkness does not know where he goes. While you have the light, believe in the light, that you may become children of light" (vv. 35–36; cf. 1 QS 1.9; 2.16; 3.13, etc.). In this little parable of the traveller at sunset, Jesus urges his hearers to avail themselves of the light before darkness falls (9:4). Jesus' reaction in deed to the initiative of the Greeks is to depart and hide himself from the crowd (v. 36b).

The train of thought in this introduction to the time of Jesus' hour runs from an anticipation of Jesus' burial (12:1–11), to an assertion of his universal, peaceful kingship (12:12–19), to the necessity for his glorification if the universal kingship is to become a reality and the Gentiles are to benefit (12:23–36). Jesus approaches his death in John 12 with an emphasis on the universal outreach of his mission, an emphasis that will not be resumed until 21:11. In the meantime, Jesus turns his attention to his own, to whose needs he will now attend (13:1–17:26).

WASHER OF THE DISCIPLES' FEET

John 13:1–35

The Jesus of the Fourth Gospel is one who comes as revealing, empowering presence (1:1–18); who picks/produces a new community (1:19–2:12) and, in his public ministry, provides them with warrants for a new type of worship (2:13–11:54); and who privately predicts what their future will be like, offering promise, parenesis, and prayer for that time (13:31–17:26). At the beginning of the section of the Gospel that focuses on Jesus' provision for his own, now that his hour has come, is John 13:1–35. This large thought unit functions as an introduction to what follows, just as 1:1–18 does for the Gospel as a whole. The unit falls into a concentric pattern.

    A   13:1: (1) The hour of departing to the Father has come.
              (2) Jesus' love for his own

      B   13:2: Inspired by the devil, Judas is to betray Jesus.

        C   13:3: Jesus' knowledge

          D   13:4–5: He rose from supper, laid aside his garments, and began to wash the disciples' feet.

            E   13:6–11: A disciple (Peter) does not understand now; afterward he will understand.
                Peter said (v. 6b) — Jesus answered (v. 7)
                Peter said (v. 8a) — Jesus answered (v. 8b)
                Peter said (v. 9) — Jesus answered (v. 10–11)

            E′ 13:12b–17: Do you all know what I have done? If you know. . . .

              a   v. 12b: Do you know?

                b   v. 13: I am Teacher and Lord.

                  c   v. 14: If I, then you. . . .

                  c′ v. 15: Do as I have done.

                b′ v. 16: A servant is not above his master.

              a′ v. 17: If you know. . . .

D′ 13:12a: When he had washed their feet, and had taken his garments, he resumed his place at the table.

C′ 13:18–26a: Jesus' knowledge

B′ 13:26b–30: Inspired by Satan, Judas goes out to betray Jesus.

A′ 13:31–35: (1) Now is the time of his glorification and of Jesus' going away.
(2) Jesus' love for the disciples is the basis for their love of one another.

Two components of the pattern are out of sequence (E′, 13:12b–17, and D′, 13:12a). There are two reasons: aesthetic requirements and the demands of the story. (a) The practice of having a part of a pattern appear out of order is typical of ancient Mediterranean literature. In Greco-Roman aesthetics perfect symmetry is not considered beautiful. There must be a minor flaw in the midst of overall balance in order to imitate nature. (b) Also, the inversion in the order of D′ and E′ is due to the fact that Jesus must finish the act of washing the disciples' feet (v. 12a) before he can look back on it and speak about it (v. 12bff.). The emphasis falls on the outer components of the pattern. It is Jesus' love for his own that is the focus of the thought unit. Everything else is explanation of that love.

A (v. 1) indicates (a) the time (merely "before the feast of the Passover," nothing more specific about the particular day); (b) Jesus' act ("he loved them [the disciples] to the end" — temporally, to the end of his life? or adverbially, to the uttermost?); and (c) the causes of Jesus' act ("Jesus knew that his hour had come" [2:4; 7:30; 8:20; 12:23, 27]; and "having loved his own who were in the world," i.e., loving his own [disciples] is habitual with Jesus). Two periods of time are distinguished here: before his hour had come and when his hour had come. Since chapter 12, the latter applies. The time has come for Jesus to be glorified. An agent who is sent on a mission must return and report to his sender ("Behold, we send you a great man as our agent, and he is equivalent to us until such time as he returns to us" [j. Hagigah 76d]). The reader must wait to discover from the narrative that follows exactly what Jesus' "loving them [his disciples] to the end" will mean.

B (v. 2) says that the devil (6:70; 8:44; 12:31; 13:27; 14:30) had already put it into the heart of Judas to betray Jesus (i.e., the plot is satanic; cf. Lk 22:3). In John one not only acts like one's father, one also desires his will (8:44). So the devil puts his will into Judas's heart. This is similar to what one finds at Qumran where there are two spirits, the Spirit of Light and the Spirit of Darkness, that struggle for the hearts of people (e.g., 1 QS 4). At Qumran the Evil Spirit is known by the behavior it inspires: e.g., greed (cf. John 12:6), falseness and deceit (cf. John 13:18), and the ways of darkness (cf. John 13:30).

C (v. 3) returns to Jesus' prophetic knowledge of people and future events (1:48; 2:25; 4:17–18, 29; 5:6; 6:61, 64; 11:4, 11; 13:1, 3, 11, 18; 16:32; 18:4; 19:28): "Jesus, knowing that the Father had given all things into his hands [5:22, 26], and that he had come from God and was going to God" (8:14). It is on the basis of this knowledge of whose agent he is and what authority he possesses that Jesus will act.

D (vv. 4–5) tells us about Jesus' action undertaken on the basis of his knowledge (v. 3) and love (v. 1). He "rose from supper, laid aside his garments, and girded himself with a towel. Then he poured water into a basin, and began to wash to disciples' feet, and to wipe them with the towel with which he was girded." This is prophetic symbolism (cf. Isa 8:1–4; Jer 13:1–11; Ezk 12:1–7). Jesus' "laying aside [*tithēsin*] his garments" is suggestive of his "laying aside [*tithēmi*] his life" (echoing the language of 10:17–18). What he is doing, then, symbolizes something done in and through his death. What he does, moreover, is a servant's task (1 Sam 25:41). Indeed, the task of washing feet was so menial that it is placed among work Jewish male slaves should not be required to do; such work is to be reserved for Gentile slaves, for wives, and for children (*Mekilta* on Exodus 21:2 [82a]). The recipients of his benefaction are the disciples, not the world. Just as in this section of the Gospel generally (chaps. 13–17) Jesus is acting for his own, so in this text in particular (v. 5) Jesus washes the disciples' feet. The message of the act of prophetic symbolism is: as a servant, Jesus lays aside/down his life to benefit his disciples (cf. Lk 22:27; Phil 2:7–8).

E (vv. 6–11) offers a first interpretation of the symbolic act. Its form is that of a threefold dialogue between Peter and Jesus (remember 3:1–12 and the threefold dialogue between Nicodemus and Jesus):

(1) Peter said: "Lord, do you wash my feet?" (v. 6b)

Jesus answered: "What I am doing you do not know now, but afterward you will understand." (v. 7; cf. 13:19, 36; 2:22; 12:16; 14:29; 16:12, 22)

(2) Peter said: "You shall never wash my feet." (v. 8a)

Jesus answered: "If I do not wash you, you have no part in me." (v. 8b)

(3) Peter said: "Lord, not my feet only but also my hands and my head." (v. 9)

Jesus said: "The one who has bathed does not need to wash (except for his feet) but he is clean all over; and you are clean, but not all of you." (v. 10)

The Evangelist explains v. 10b: "for he knew who was to betray him; that is why he said, 'You are not all clean" (v. 11).

On a literal, surface level what is happening is this: (a) Peter says he will not allow his Master to do the menial task of a slave, washing his (Peter's) feet. (b) Jesus's response is that only if his feet are washed can Peter sit at table with him. (c) Peter is so desirous of table fellowship with Jesus that he asks for a bath. (d) Jesus, however, says that since he (Peter) took a bath before he came to the supper, all he needs now is to have the dust removed from his feet. This reflects Mediterranean customs. A person invited to a dinner party takes a bath (at home or in the public baths) before coming to supper. Upon arrival, the individual needs only to have his feet washed before the meal. The difficulty is discerning what this symbolizes in John 13.

The crucial thing to note is that there are two different washings mentioned in this text. Vv. 6 and 8 speak of the washing of feet; vv. 9–10 refer to a bath affecting the entire body. The latter (the bath) has already happened; the former (the foot washing) is now being offered. The bath of the whole person is linked with becoming a disciple of Jesus (one who is clean = one who is chosen, cf. 6:70–71 = one who believes in Jesus, cf. 6:64); the washing of the feet is in preparation for eating with Jesus (v. 8b). In John, the disciples have already been made clean (had a bath) by the word that Jesus has spoken to them (15:3). They are clean all over. What is now being offered is something over and beyond that benefit. It is the cleansing from the dust of defilement in their daily walk so as to be prepared to eat with Jesus. What this text says, then, is that Jesus' death takes care of the daily sins of disciples who have already been cleansed from the principle of sin. It is the very problem (post-baptismal sins) already encountered in 1 John 1:7,9 and 2:1–2 that surfaces here again.

Once this is seen, the textual problem of v. 10 can be addressed. The short text reads:

The one who has bathed does not need to wash, but he is clean all over [so Sinaiticus, Old Latin, Origen, etc.; NEB, JB].

The long text reads:

The one who has bathed does not need to wash, except for his feet (only), but he is clean all over [so P66, Vaticanus, D, etc.; RSV, NAB, NIV].

If the short text is adopted, then it says simply: after once being cleansed totally, one does not need another cleansing of the same type. The washing of the feet as a necessary act is still implicit from the context (v. 8), but it is not explicit in v. 10. If one takes the longer text, then it says: The one who has bathed and remains washed does not need to wash again, except for his feet, but is clean all over. This makes explicit in v. 10 that the washing of the feet is a necessary act. Either way the overall meaning of vv. 6–11 is the same. The only difference in the two textual variants is whether or not the necessity of the washing of the feet is implicit or explicit in v. 10. In vv. 6–11 Jesus' washing of the disciples' feet symbolizes not their initial cleansing, but rather the continual cleansing from their sins that disciples receive through Jesus' death in preparation for mealtime with him.

D′ (v. 12a), "When he had washed their feet, and taken (*elaben*) his garments, and resumed his place," suggests Jesus' "taking back [*labō*] his life" (echoing the language of 10:17) and resuming his place in glory (17:5, 24). From that position he teaches his disciples about the significance of his death (16:12–15; 14:25–26).

E′ (vv. 12b–17) offers another interpretation of the meaning of Jesus' washing of the disciples' feet. Here Jesus' act is an example for the disciples. V. 13 and 16 establish Jesus' authority in relation to the disciples. He is Teacher and Lord (v. 13). A servant is not greater than his master (v. 16; cf. Matt 10:24–25; *Genesis Rabbah* 78: "the sender is greater than the sent"). Vv. 14–15 draw out the implication of this master-servant relationship:

> If I then, your Lord and Teacher, have washed your feet, you also ought to wash one another's feet. For I have given you an example, that you also should do as I have done to you.

Tacitus, *Annals* 15.62, says that Seneca, when facing death, bequeathed to his friends the only possession yet remaining to him, "the pattern of his life" (cf. Lk 22:24–27). This saying of Jesus is usually understood as a general lesson to disciples on humility and service (cf. 1 Pet 5:5: "Be clothed with humility as with a slave's apron"; Phil 2:3, 8). It is sometimes regarded as an interpretation of the footwashing that is contradictory to that offered in vv. 6–11. If one assumes that, whatever the source of the material in vv. 6–11 and vv. 12–17, the final form of the Gospel is a coherent whole, then vv. 12–17 need to be read as of one piece with vv. 6–11.

If vv. 6–11 interpret the washing of the disciples' feet as Jesus' cleansing of disciples from their daily sins by his death, then how should vv. 14–15 be read? Two matters deserve attention, one from this text (v. 15), the other from the context. (a) V. 14 says: "You ought also repeatedly to wash [present infinitive] one another's feet." This could be taken as a command analogous to 1 Corinthians 11:24 ("Go on doing this for my remembrance") were it not for v. 15: "You should go on doing *as* I have done to you." Jesus does not say, "Do *what* I have done to you," but rather, "Do *as* I have done to you." A disciple's actions should be of the same character as those of Jesus when he washed the disciples' feet. V. 15 clarifies the meaning of v. 14, preventing v. 14's being taken as a command to go on washing feet in the Christian community. (b) Does "doing *as* Jesus did" mean being a humble servant? It may mean that in 1 Peter 5:5 and Philippians 2:3, 8, but it does not mean that in this context. If the washing in vv. 6–11 symbolizes the forgiveness of disciples' daily sin by Jesus, then for the disciples to wash one another's feet (i.e., act *as* he did toward disciples) means for them to forgive one another those daily trespasses that characterize one human being's infringement upon another. That is, to do as Christ has done to them has a specific (forgive one another), rather than a general (be a humble servant), application. The point is similar to that in Matthew 18:21–22, 23–35, and in Luke 17:3–4. Moreover, if the disciples act *as* Jesus acted, since he did this as part of preparation for supper, this will apply above all to preparations for mealtime with Jesus. "If you know these things, blessed are you if you do them" (v. 17).

To this point, the train of thought in 13:1–35 has led to reflection on preparations for mealtime with Jesus. There have been two matters specified. First, a prerequisite for table fellowship with Jesus is the washing of one's feet by Jesus (= having the stains of daily sin removed by the benefits of Jesus' death). Second, preparation for mealtime with Jesus includes doing to other disciples *as* he has done to us (= forgiving others their trespasses as he has forgiven ours; cf. Matt 5:23–24; 18:23–35).

There is in 13:1–17's references to the two washings no explicitly sacramental or anti-sacramental note. The two washings are rather associated with becoming a disciple of Jesus (cleansing by his word, 15:3) and with disciples' being forgiven their daily transgressions. It is difficult to imagine, however, that an early Christian could have avoided hearing echoes of baptism in the language about the bath that cleanses the whole person (cf. 3:5; 1 Cor 6:11; Eph 5:26; Tit 3:5–6; Heb 10:22), or echoes of the Eucharist in the teaching about preparations for mealtime with Jesus.

C′ (vv. 18–26) focuses again on Jesus' knowledge. There are two subsections (vv. 18–20; vv. 21–26), each containing a prediction of betrayal by Jesus during supper (in Mk 14:17–21//Matt 26:20–25, before supper; in Lk 22:22–23, after supper). This emphasis on Jesus' knowledge is typically Johannine. Jesus anticipates every move of his adversaries and remains in complete control of the situation (13:11, 18–19, 26–27; 16:33; 18:4–6, 33–37; 19:26–27, 30). His life will not be taken from him; he will lay it down freely (10:17–18).

> (a) I know whom I have chosen; it is that the Scripture may be fulfilled, "He who ate my bread has lifted up his heel against me."
> (v. 18; Ps 41:9 in a form closer to the MT than to the LXX)

The purpose of telling the disciples now is that hopefully, when it happens, they will believe that "I am he" / *egō eimi* (v. 19). Here is another use of the absolute form of *egō eimi* (remember 4:26; 6:20; 8:24, 28; 8:58). It, like 4:26 and 8:24, 28, should most likely be translated "I am he," that is, the revealer of all things (in this case, of events before they happen). The consequence of Jesus' being the revealer is that "whoever receives anyone whom I send receives me; and the one who receives me receives him who sent me" (v. 20). The identification of sender and agent is firmly fixed (m. Berakoth 5:5: "a man's agent is like to himself"; cf. Acts 9:4–5; 22:7–8; 26:14–15; Matt 10:40; 25:40). When Jesus says this, he is "troubled in spirit" / *etarachthē tō pneumati* (11:33; 12:27), grieved as any human would be that a trusted intimate will betray him.

> (b) Truly, truly, I say to you, one of you will betray me. (cf. Mk 14:18)

The dialogue and action that follow have to do with the disciples' uncertainty about whom he is speaking (v. 22; cf. Mk 14:19–20). The first exchange is between Peter and the beloved disciple (vv. 23–24). The beloved disciple is lying close to the breast of Jesus, just as the Son is described in 1:18 as in the Father's bosom. It is an expression of intimacy (cf. Lk 16:22). The beloved disciple is as intimate with Jesus as Jesus is with the Father. Such a one would know the mind of the one with whom he was intimate. So Peter beckons to the beloved disciple and says: "Tell us of whom he speaks." The second exchange is between the beloved disciple and Jesus. He asks Jesus: "Lord, who is it?" Jesus replies: "It is he to whom I shall give this morsel when I have dipped it." In the social custom of that day, it was a mark of special favor for the host to dip bread in the sauce and personally serve a guest. This act represented love's last appeal to one on the verge of perdition (W. E. Hull, *BBC* 9:330). The revealing act follows. "So when he had dipped the morsel, he gave it to Judas, the son of Simon Iscariot." Now at least one or two disciples know what Jesus knows — the identity of the betrayer.

The beloved disciple, introduced here without explanation, is met again in 19:26–27; 20:2–10; 21:7, 20, 24; probably in 19:35; and quite possibly in 18:15. His identity has been the subject of much debate. Some regard him as an ideal figure (e.g., a symbol for Gentile Christians or for itinerant prophets); other believe him to be a historical figure (e.g., John, the Son of Zebedee; John Mark; Matthias; or Lazarus).

The various references in John that mention the disciple whom Jesus loved may be classified in four categories. (a) He is an intimate of Jesus. John 13:23–26 and 21:20 say he lies close to the breast of Jesus, just as the Son is in the bosom of the Father in 1:18; so he could know the mind of Jesus and make it known, just as the Son knows the mind of the Father and can make him known. John 19:26–27 notes that at the cross he is entrusted by Jesus with his mother. John 21:7 tells that, after the resurrection, he recognizes Jesus' identity from the boat when Jesus speaks to the disciples. This depiction of one disciple's special intimacy with Jesus is a trait shared with various apocryphal writings that also refer to certain other disciples as special intimates of Jesus (e.g., Gospel of Philip 2.3.63 [NHL 138], designates Mary Magdalene as the disciple whom Jesus loved more than all the rest; Gospel of Thomas 34 [NHL 119], makes James, the brother of the Lord, the ideal disciple; Thomas the Contender 138 [NHL 189] treats Judas Thomas in this way).

(b) The disciple whom Jesus loved is associated with Peter but is treated more favorably than he. In 13:23–26, Peter must ask the beloved disciple for information about the meaning of Jesus' words. In 18:15–16, he is known to the high priest and gains entrance to the high priest's residence when Jesus is arrested. From that privileged position, he assists Peter in gaining admission. In 20:2–10, he outruns Peter to the tomb and, upon entry, sees and believes. Upon learning of his own fate, in 21:20–23 Peter asks Jesus about that of the Beloved disciple in a way that possibly reflects some competitiveness on Peter's part. Does this portrayal of the relation between the two disciples reflect the Johannine community's understanding of itself over against other churches that looked to Peter as their authority?

(c) The beloved disciple's fate was misunderstood in the early church. Jesus' word to Peter, "If it is my will that he remain until I come, what is that to you?," was misunderstood. As a result the saying spread abroad "that this disciple was not to die" (21:22–23). Since apparently he had died, 21:20–23 tries to clarify exactly what Jesus had said.

(d) This disciple is the guarantor of the events of Jesus' passion from chapter 13 (the last supper) to chapter 21 (the resurrection appearances). He is present at the last supper (13:23–26), at Jesus' trial before the high priest (18:15–16), at Jesus' crucifixion both before (19:26–27) and after he died (19:35: "He who saw it has borne witness — his testimony is true, and he knows that he tells the truth — that you also may believe"; cf. 1 John 1:3), and at the resurrection appearance in 21:7, 20–23. He is designated as "the one who is bearing witness to these things, and who has caused these things to be written (cf. 19:19); and we know that his testimony is true" (21:24). If the disciples addressed in the farewell discourse are described by Jesus as his "witnesses because you have been with me from the beginning" (15:27), the beloved disciple is designated the special eyewitness of passion week whose testimony lies behind the Fourth Gospel and who is responsible for its being written by the "we" of the leadership of the Johannine community after his time. There is an analogous concern in Luke-Acts to ground the Jesus tradition in the testimony of the Twelve (Acts 1:21–22; 13:31).

All four categories function to ground the Fourth Gospel in the eyewitness testimony of one who was especially intimate with Jesus. There is little difficulty is seeing that this is the case with categories (a) and (d). What about (b) and (c)? The emphasis on the beloved disciple's competitive edge over Peter in their relation with Jesus, (b), simply serves to grant the guarantor of the Johannine tradition an extra special status. The explanation of the stated misunderstanding about the beloved disciple's death, (c), is a necessary clarification in order to protect his status in the community.

As has been noted from 1 John 1:3, eyewitness testimony is crucial to the Johannine understanding of Christian faith. The Son is in fellowship with the Father; the eyewitnesses are in fellowship with the Son and, thereby, with the Father; those who have not seen and heard are in fellowship with the Father and the Son by means of their fellowship with the eyewitnesses who have seen and heard. The Fourth Gospel enshrines the eyewitness testimony in a written form of a type that allows the story of Jesus' life as a whole to control the way the individual pieces are to be understood. The beloved disciple is the guarantor of the truthfulness of this testimony.

B′ (vv. 27–30), tells how "after the morsel, Satan entered into him [Judas]." Then Jesus says: "What you are going to do, do quickly." Here, as elsewhere, Jesus has the initiative. It is almost as if he must grant Judas permission. No one takes his life from him; he lays it down freely (10:17–18). The Evangelist adds his comment about what others at the table thought Jesus meant by this comment. "Some thought that, because Judas had the money box, Jesus was telling him, 'Buy what we need for the feast'; or, that he should give something to the poor." The concluding words are ominous. "So, after receiving the morsel, he immediately went out; and it was night" (v. 30). The meal had become for Judas not communion with Jesus but with the devil.

There is a warning in these words. Judas has eaten with Jesus (vv. 18, 26–27, 30), yet he is the possession of Satan (vv. 27; note the possession of Judas by Satan is after the meal). This would seem to imply that eating with Jesus does not guarantee one's discipleship, as Judas's example shows. Although the sacramental note is not primary but secondary in 13:1–35, it is difficult to see how an early Christian could have avoided hearing this point. If so, then it is similar to Paul's emphasis in 1 Corinthians 10:1–5 ("our fathers...all ate the same supernatural food and all drank the same supernatural drink....Nevertheless with most of them God was not pleased; for they were overthrown in the wilderness"). Mealtime with Jesus is not to be understood as a mechanical appropriation of the benefits of his death. So far, 13:1–35 has revolved around mealtime with Jesus and has dealt with two matters: (1) instructions about preparation for its benefits ([a] receiving forgiveness through Jesus' death for the sins of one's daily walk; and [b] forgiving one another within the community for transgressions against us); and (2) a warning about appropriation of its benefits (mealtime with Jesus offers no mechanical benefits; it is possible to have eaten with Jesus and still betray him). Doubtless, the Johannine community would know this from bitter experience. Those who "went out from us" (1 John 2:19) had doubtless shared in the sacred meal before their secession.

A′ (vv. 31–35) in its beginning functions similarly to 12:20–23. There the Greeks come, wanting to see Jesus, and Jesus says: "The hour has come for the Son of Man to be glorified." Here Judas goes out to betray Jesus, and Jesus says: "Now is the Son of Man glorified." The aorist passive ("is glorified") speaks of an event that is still future as though it had occurred, so certain is the Johannine Jesus of what is to transpire (cf. 17:22 for the same device, which is analogous to the prophetic perfect in Hebrew). The pieces are in place for Jesus' departure (vv. 1, 3).

Before he goes, he gives his disciples a new commandment grounded in his love of them. "A new commandment I give to you, 'Love one another just as I have loved you,' in order that you also love one another" (v. 33; cf. Epistle of the Apostles 18). The difficult sentence is best understood if punctuated this way. If so, then (a) "Love one another as I have loved you" is the content of the new commandment, and (b) "in order that you also love one another" is the purpose of the new commandment's being given. What follows in v. 34 ("By this all will know that you are my disciples, if you have love for one another") is the consequence of the new commandment's being kept. The commandment is "new" in two ways. First, it is new in the sense that it belongs to the new covenant. Just as the old covenant involved the gift of commandments (Exod 20), so also does the new. The new commandment is grounded in a new act of deliverance that evokes a new sense of gratitude. Second, it is new in that the norm of behavior is Jesus. The commandment of the new covenant is that disciples of Jesus should love one another (fellow members of the covenant community) as Christ loved them (contrast, "Love your neighbor [fellow Israelite] as yourself"). In a Johannine context, this means "to the end" (13:1), "laying aside one's garments for" (13:4) / "laying down one's life for" (10:11, 15). The point has been made already in 1 John 3:16: "By this we know love, that he laid down his life for us; and we ought to lay down our lives for the brethren."

THE WAY, THE TRUTH, AND THE LIFE

John 13:31–14:31

The Jesus of the Fourth Gospel is one who comes as revealing, empowering presence (1:1–18); who picks/produces a new community (1:19–2:12) and provides them during his public ministry with warrants for a different type of worship (2:13–11:54); and who privately predicts what their future will be like, offering promise, parenesis, and prayer for that time (John 13:31–17:26). John 13:31–17:26 is the Last Discourse of Jesus. It is given privately to his disciples, at mealtime, during the last week of Jesus' life. It conforms to what is known as a farewell speech. Judaism utilized this form frequently (e.g., Gen 47:29–49:33: Jacob; Deut: Moses; Josh 22–24: Joshua; 1 Sam 12: Samuel; 1 Chron 28–29: David; Tobit 14:3–11: Tobit; Testaments of the XII Patriarchs: the twelve sons of Jacob; Jubilees 10: Noah; 20–22: Abraham; 35–36: Rebecca and Isaac; Josephus, *Antiquities* 8.45–47 §309–26: Moses; 1 Enoch 91: Enoch; 2 Esdras 14:28–36: Ezra; 2 Baruch 77: Baruch), as did early Christians by the second half of the first century (Acts 20:17–38: Paul; 2 Tim 3:1–4:8: Paul; 2 Peter: Peter; Mk 13: Jesus).

All of these farewell speeches conform loosely to the same basic pattern. (1) A noteworthy figure knows he is about to die, gathers his primary community about him and tells them (e.g., T. Zebulon 10:4: "I am now hastening away to my rest"). This sometimes produces grief and requires reassurance from the hero (1 Enoch 92:2: "Let not your spirit be troubled"; T. Zebulon 10:1–2: "And now, children, do not grieve because I am dying, nor be depressed because I am leaving you. I shall arise again in your midst"; Jubilees 22:23: "Do not fear, my son, . . . and do not be in terror").

(2) The hero gives a farewell speech to his primary community that includes a prediction of the future. It was a widespread belief in Mediterranean antiquity that one who was about to die had prophetic powers (Diodorus Siculus 18.1.1; 37.19.3: so Pythagoras; Cicero, *On Divination*

1.30.63: so the Stoic Quintus; 1.30.64–65 and 1.67.129–30: so Posidonius; Josephus, *War* 7.8.7 §353: so the Indians; Plato, *Apology* 39: so Socrates, who says: "I would fain prophesy to you; for I am about to die, and that is the time when men are gifted with prophetic power"; Philo, *Moses* 2.288; 1 Enoch 91:1: so Enoch, who says: "the Spirit is poured over me so that I may show you everything that shall happen to you forever"). The predictions are diverse; they run the gamut from prophesied slavery to heresy that will arise. Sometimes the prediction sounds the note of persecution to come (e.g., 1 Enoch 95:7 and 98:13 have Enoch predict persecution in terms of woes on the wicked: "Woe unto you, sinners, for your persecute the righteous"; "Woe unto you who rejoice in the suffering of the righteous ones"). At other times, the prediction promises that God will be close to those left behind (e.g., T. Joseph 10:2: "if you pursue self-control and purity with patience and prayer with fasting in humility of heart, the Lord will dwell among you"; 11:1: 'keep the fear of God before your eyes and honor your brothers. For everyone who does the Law of the Lord will be loved by him").

(3) The farewell speech also contains an exhortation about how to behave after the hero has departed. Again the content is varied, from instructions about carrying the patriarch's bones to sacred soil to defending against heretics. Sometimes the exhortations include (a) keep the commandments (e.g., 1 Enoch 94:1–5: Enoch advises his descendants: "Love righteousness and walk therein.... Walk in the way of peace.... Hold fast my words"; Jubilees 21:5: Abraham says to Isaac: "keep his commandments"); (b) love one another (e.g., Jubilees 20:2: Abraham says to his children: "each one might love his neighbor": 36:3–4: Isaac tells Jacob and Esau: "among yourselves, my sons, be loving of your brothers as a man loves himself . . . and loving each other as themselves"; 36:8: "each one will love his brother with compassion"); and (c) maintain unity (e.g., T. Zebulon 8:5–6: Zebulon says to his sons: "Love one another, and do not calculate the wrong done by each to his brothers. This shatters unity"; T. Joseph 17:2–3: Joseph exhorts his community: "love one another and in patient endurance conceal one another's shortcomings. God is delighted in harmony among brothers").

(4) The farewell speech with its predictions and exhortations sometimes closes with a prayer for those the hero is leaving behind (e.g., Deut 33; 2 Baruch 48; Jubilees 1:19–21; 10:3–6; 35:17; 22:28–30, so Abraham's prayer for Jacob that God "might protect him and bless him and sanctify him for a people who belong to your heritage"). John 13:31–17:26 fits this pattern perfectly. Jesus knows that his hour has come to be glorified

(13:1, 3, 31–33); he predicts what will happen after his departure (e.g., persecution, 16:2–3) and exhorts his disciples to proper behavior (e.g., love one another, 13:34; 15:12, 17); he closes his Last Testament with a prayer for his disciples (e.g., that God keep them, 17:11b; that God sanctify them, 17:17).

There are features in chapters 14–16 that raise questions about their unity. (a) It is strange that a long discourse follows the words of 14:30, "hereafter I will not talk much with you." (b) It is perplexing that after 14:31b ("Rise, let us go hence") a discourse and a long prayer follow before Jesus and his disciples go out (18:1). (c) It is surprising that after 13:36 (Simon Peter says: "Lord, where are you going?") and 14:5–6 (Thomas says: "Lord, we do not know where you are going") Jesus should say in 16:5: "I am going... yet none of you asks me, 'Where are you going.'" (d) It is interesting to note the frequent repetitions of subject matter in 13:31–14:31 and 16:4–33 (R. E. Brown, *The Gospel according to John XIII–XXI* [Garden City, N.Y.: Doubleday, 1970], 589–93, has a detailed chart). This has led to the hypothesis that multiple versions of the same basic material have been included in John's farewell speech (analogous to Ezk 38 and 39?). Whatever the source of the materials or the date at which various pieces were incorporated into the Gospel, this commentary's task is to interpret the text in its present form. The repetition, with variation, of similar material in 13:31–14:31 and 15:1–16:33 conforms to the rules of Hellenistic rhetoric:

> We shall not repeat the same thing precisely — for that, to be sure, would weary the hearer and not elaborate the idea — but with changes. (*Rhetorica ad Herrennium* 4.42.54)

The material in 13:31–17:26 falls into several thought units: 13:31–14:31 is obviously the first (as signalled by 14:31b); 15:1–16:33 is the second (which itself consists of three virtually self-contained components: 15:1–17; 15:18–16:15; and 16:16–33); 17:1–26 is the third (as signalled by 17:1a). In this section of the commentary, 13:31–14:31 is the unit under consideration. This subsection, 13:31–14:31, consists of three components: 13:31–14:14; 14:15–24; and 14:25–31.

John 13:31–14:14 is a meditation on Jesus' departure. It deals with where Jesus is going, for what purpose, how disciples get there, why, and what are the results of his departure. This meditation falls into three parts (13:31–38; 14:1–6; 14:7–14), each with a similar pattern of arrangement.

Jesus' assertion	13:31–35	14:1–3, 4	14:7
Disciple's question	13:36a, 37a	14:5	14:8
Jesus' response	13:36b, 38	14:6	14:9–14

The entire meditation is held together by an inclusion (13:33: I am going; 14:12: I go).

Understanding the first part, 13:31–38, depends on (a) grasping the form of the subunit and (b) recognizing its dual function in the narrative. Formally, it begins with Jesus' assertion: Jesus is going away (vv. 31–33).

> Now
> > is the Son of Man glorified
> > > and God is glorified in him;
> > > if God is glorified in him,
> > God will also glorify him in himself
> and he will glorify him at once.

"Little children, yet a little while I am with you. You will seek me; and as I said to the Jews [8:21] so now I say to you, 'Where I am going you cannot come.'"

Peter's twofold question follows (13:36a, 37): (a) "Lord, where are you going?"; (b) "Lord, why cannot I follow you now? I will lay down my life for you."

Jesus' dual response comes in 13:36b, 38: (a) "Where I am going you cannot follow me now; but you shall follow afterward"; (b) "Will you lay down your life for me?... The cock will not crow, till you have denied me three times."

John 13:31–38 functions in a dual role in the narrative. It is both a conclusion to 13:1–35 and an introduction to 13:31–14:31. In doing so it fulfills Lucian's rule ("How to Write History," 55) for relating two adjoining sections: they must link up like a chain (remember chap. 12). Vv. 34–35 function primarily in the conclusion to 13:1–35; v. 33 functions primarily in the introduction to 13:31–14:31.

The point here is that Jesus is going to the Father; he is going before the disciples do; and until he goes they are unable to follow. Christ and Christians are not on the same footing in salvation history. Jesus possesses a soteriological priority that is expressed here in terms of the chronological priority of Jesus' going.

The second part, 14:1–6, focuses on where Jesus is going, for what purpose, and how one gets there. It begins with Jesus' assertion (vv. 1–3, 4):

Let not your hearts be troubled; you believe in God [or, believe in God], believe [or, you believe] also in me. In my Father's house are many dwelling places [*monoi*]; if it were not so, would I have told you [or, I would have told you.] that [or, Because] I go to prepare a place for you? [or, .] And [or, and] if I go and prepare a place for you, I will come again, and I will take you to myself, in order that where I am, you may be also. And you know the way where I am going.

The disciples need reassurance after hearing that Jesus is going away (remember 1 Enoch 92:2; T. Zebulon 10:1–2; Jubilees 22:23). So he tells them where he is going: to his Father's house/heaven (Philo, *On Dreams* 1.256, speaks of heaven as "the paternal house"). He also tells them for what purpose he is going: to prepare a place for them among the many abiding places/rooms (*monai*) in his Father's house (Testament of Abraham 20:14: "Take my friend, Abraham, into Paradise where there are the tents of my righteous ones and the mansions [*monai*] of my holy ones"; 1 Enoch 39:4: "There I saw other dwelling places of the holy ones and their resting places too"; 41:2; 22:4; 2 Enoch 61:2; 2 Esdras 7:80, 101; *Joseph and Aseneth* 8:11; Lk 16:9, 22–26) and then to return, to take them to himself, and to keep them with him (12:26; 17:24). The language is similar to that in 1 Thessalonians 4:16–17 (cf. Mk 13:24–27):

1 Thes 4:16–17	*John 14:3*
The Lord will descend from heaven.	I will come again.
We shall be caught up to meet the Lord.	I will take you to myself.
We shall always be with the Lord.	Where I am you will be.

John 14:3 appears to be a Johannine adaptation of the tradition reflected in 1 Thessalonians 4:16–17 (and Mk 13:24–27). If so, the coming of Jesus mentioned here is a reference to the parousia (cf. 21:22–23 ["If it is my will that he remain until I come, what is that to you?"] where Jesus' coming is clearly the parousia).

Jesus assumes the disciples know the way to the Father's house. After all they heard him say not only, "I am the door" (10:7, 9), but also "My sheep hear my voice . . . and they follow me; and I give them eternal life, and they shall never perish" (10:27–28). Thomas, however, puts the twofold question: "Lord, we do not know where you are going; how can we know the way?" (v. 5).

Jesus' response is in terms of yet another "I am + predicate" saying.

I am the way and the truth and the life;
no one comes to the Father except through me. (v. 6)

This saying has two parts, one positive (the first line), the other negative (the second line). The negative second line clarifies the focus of the positive first line. The issue is how one comes to the Father. The negative second line says that no one comes to the Father except through Jesus. He is the one way (10:9; cf. Acts 4:12; 15:11; 1 Tim 2:5; Mk 8:38; Lk 12:8–9; Heb 9:15). The positive first line says this too. Jesus is the way; he functions as the avenue of access to the Father. The question about line one has to do with the function of "the truth and the life." The "I am + predicate" sayings in John generally speak about Jesus' role in salvation. As bread of life, he nourishes people; as the resurrection and life, he gives life; as the life, he gives life. To be given life is a part of the way to the Father. As the truth, Jesus reveals it (1:17) and bears witness to it (18:37). Knowing the truth is also part of the way to the Father. One might then paraphrase: "I am the way to the Father, that is, the revealer of truth and the giver of life."

The second part of 13:31–14:14, 14:1–6, has like the first part, 13:31–38, shown that Christ and Christians are not on the same footing. Jesus has soteriological priority because he both prepares a place for his disciples with God and is himself the way to the Father (15:5b: "apart from me you can do nothing").

Part three, 14:7–14, focuses on why Jesus is the way and some results of his going to the Father. This subunit follows the pattern of the first two. It begins with an assertion of Jesus. "If you had known me, you would have known my Father also; henceforth you do know him and have seen him (v. 7; cf. 10:30; 5:17). Philip's response follows: "Lord, show us the Father, and we shall be satisfied" (v. 8). Is this to be understood, after the analogy with Exodus 33:18 (LXX, *deikson moi*), as a request for a theophany? Jesus' reaction rules that option out. "Have I been with you so long, and yet you do not know me, Philip? The one who has seen me has seen the Father" (v. 9). This is true because of the union between Jesus and the Father ("I am in the Father and the Father [is] in me"). This union means that when Jesus speaks, it is the Father's words that one hears; when Jesus acts, it is the Father's works that one sees (vv. 10–11; cf. 5:19–20a, acts; 12:50, words). The revelatory role belongs to the incarnate Jesus whose works and words are those of the Father.

Jesus not only reveals the Father; he also empowers the disciples because he goes to the Father (vv. 12–13). V. 12 says: "the one who believes in me will also do the works that I do; and greater works than these will he do, because I go to the Father." This has sometimes been taken to mean miraculous works (cf. Mk 16:17–18), sometimes missionary successes (cf.

4:35–38). Because v. 10b includes Jesus' words as part of his works, v. 12 cannot be reduced to miracles. Because Jesus' works in John include miracles, the greater works cannot be taken to exclude the miraculous. The disciples' total work (of which words and miracles are both parts) will be greater in scope than that of the incarnate Jesus. It will not be independent of or even on the same level as that of Jesus, however. Vv. 13–14 say: "Whatever you ask in my name, I will do it." This is the other side of the coin. The disciples greater works are dependent on Jesus' glorification and his answers to their prayers.

Once again, in subunit three, as well as in the previous two, the qualitative soteriological difference between Jesus and the disciples is emphasized. Here Jesus' superiority is grounded in (a) his revelatory role (vv. 7–11), and in (b) his empowering role (vv. 12–13). It is difficult to avoid hearing this as a defense against problems like those already encountered in the Johannine epistles where progressives passed beyond christology (2 John 9; 1 John 2:23) into allegedly direct contact with the Father, a position already rejected by the Fourth Gospel (1:18; 3:13; 6:46) and here addressed again in detail.

John 14:15–24 is a meditation on the differences between the disciples and the world held together by an inclusion (vv. 15 and 24, love me . . . keep my commandments/words). Unlike the world, the disciples experience the Paraclete, the resurrection appearances, and the abiding presence of the Father and the Son. This meditation falls into three parts (vv. 15–17; vv. 18–21; vv. 22–24), each with a similar pattern of organization (F. F. Segovia, "The Structure, *Tendenz*, and *Sitz im Leben* of John 13:31–14:31," *JBL* 104 [1985]: 471–93).

Love for Jesus	14:15	14:21a	14:23a
Promise by Jesus	14:16–17a	14:18, 21b	14:23b
Difference between disciples and world	14:17b	14:19–20	14:22, 24

The first subunit, 14:15–17, focuses on two major differences between the disciples and the world. (a) The disciples keep Jesus' commandments (plural, not singular, so not the new commandment of 13:34 but rather the complete revelation imparted by Jesus; cf. 1 John 3:23–24a). They keep the commandments because they love (maintain covenant fidelity toward) Jesus. (b) The disciples are the recipients of a promise made by Jesus: "I will pray the Father and he will give you another Paraclete to be with you forever, even the Spirit of truth." (c) The gift of the Paraclete, moreover, sets the disciples off from the world. Whereas the world cannot receive the Spirit, the Paraclete will dwell with and be in the disciples.

There are five Paraclete sayings in John's farewell speech (14:15–17; 14:25–26; 15:26–27; 16:7b–11; and 16:12–15, which actually does not use the term but does speak of the Spirit of truth, which is a synonym for Paraclete in 14:17 and 15:26). The Greek term "Paraclete" (*paraklēton*) is variously translated: e.g., Comforter, Counselor, Consoler, Advocate, Strengthener, Helper, Someone to stand by you, He who is to befriend you. No one term covers all the functions of the Johannine Paraclete. For insiders/disciples, the Paraclete is an abiding presence (14:16–17); a teaching presence, calling to mind Jesus' words (14:26); and a presence that both guides into all truth and declares the things to come (15:11–13). In relation to outsiders, the Paraclete bears witness to Jesus (15:26–27) and exposes the unbelieving world, proving it guilty before God (16:8–11).

The hypothesis that fits the most facts is that the Paraclete is the Spirit of prophecy (M. E. Boring, "The Influence of Christian Prophecy on the Johannine Portrayal of the Paraclete and Jesus," *NTS* 25 [1978]: 113–23). A comparison of the Johannine Paraclete's functions with those of early Christian prophecy as known from elsewhere is persuasive: console and comfort: 1 Cor. 14:3; teach all things, guide into all truth: Acts 13:1; 1 Cor 14:31; witness to Jesus, convict of sin: 1 Cor 14:24–25; declare the things to come: Rev 1:1–3; 22:6, 10; 1 Thes 4:16–17; be with disciples "to the age": 1 Cor 13:8–10. The cognates *parakalein* and *paraklēsis*, moreover, are connected with prophecy in the New Testament (Acts 15:32; 1 Cor 14:3, 31; 1 Thes 4:18). If Paraclete means "the verbal manifestation of the Spirit," then it is clear why the Paraclete is called "another Paraclete." Jesus in his earthly career is the one on whom the Spirit descends and remains (1:33) and, therefore, the one who utters the words of God continuously because it is not by measure that God has given the Spirit to him (3:34). Just as Jesus, in his earthly career, is the prophetic voice of the Spirit, so after Jesus' glorification when the Spirit is given to the disciples, the early Christians are the prophetic voice of the Spirit, the Paraclete. In this, the disciples are manifestly different from the world.

The second subunit in the meditation of 14:15–24 is 14:18–21. Here the disciples' difference from the world has a twofold basis. (a) They show their love (manifest covenant fidelity toward) Jesus by keeping his commandments. (b) They receive Jesus' promise of his presence ("I will not leave you desolate; I will come [*erchomai*] to you"; "The one who loves me will be loved by my Father, and I will love him and manifest [*em-*

phanisō] myself to him"), which sets the disciples off from the world ("Yet a little while, and the world will see me no more, but you will see me; because I live, you will live also"). The presence of Jesus referred to here is that of the resurrection appearances (cf. 20:19, Jesus came [*ēlthen*]; 20:26; 21:13, also Jesus came; 21:1, Jesus manifested himself [*ephanerōsen*]). The second subunit (vv. 18–21), like the first (vv. 15–17), distinguishes the disciples from the world by two means: religious experience and obedient activity. In the first, the religious experience is reception of the gift of the Paraclete; in the second, it is seeing the risen Christ.

The third subunit, 14:22–24, also focuses on the difference between the disciples and the world based on the usual two criteria, religious experience and obedient activity: (a) "If people love me, they will keep my word." (b) Jesus' promise is to those who manifest covenant fidelity: "my Father will love them, and we will come to them and make our abiding place with them." That such an indwelling presence of Father and Son is part of what sets the disciples apart from the world is revealed in Judas' question: "Lord, how is it that you will manifest yourself to us, and not to the world?" The religious experience here is neither the presence of the Paraclete nor the resurrection appearances but rather the indwelling of the Father and the Son in the believers (cf. 1 John 2:23; this is an anticipation of the New Age beyond the resurrection: John 14:2–3; Rev 21:22).

In this thought unit (13:31–14:31) so far there have been two types of sayings about the coming of Jesus (14:3; 14:18), another about the coming of the Father and Jesus (14:23), and yet another about the coming of the Holy Spirit (14:16–17). Although there have been attempts to collapse these various comings into one (resurrection appearances = gift of the Spirit = presence of Father and Son = parousia), the Fourth Gospel in its present form does not permit such reductionism (David Earl Holwerda, *The Holy Spirit and Eschatology in the Gospel of John* [Kampen: J. H. Kok, 1959]). The Gospel clearly distinguishes between resurrection appearances (20:14–18; 20:19–23; 20:26–29; 21:4–14), the gift of the Spirit (20:22; 7:39), and the parousia (21:22–23; cf. 5:28–29; 6:39, 40, 44, 54; 11:24). The schema that makes the most sense of all the Johannine references is one that distinguishes between (1) Jesus' resurrection appearances (referred to in 14:18–20; 14:28; 16:16, 22), (2) the gift of the Spirit generally (7:39; 20:22) and of the Spirit of prophecy in particular (referred to in the five Paraclete sayings of 14:16–17; 14:26; 15:26; 16:7–11; 16:13–14), (3) the indwelling presence of Jesus and the Father in the time after the resurrection (14:23), and (4) the parousia (referred to in 14:3; cf. 17:24; 21:22).

If the first meditation, 13:31–14:14, focuses on the difference between Jesus and his disciples, the second, 14:15–24, concentrates on the difference between the disciples and the world. The third and final subunit, 14:25–31, is a meditation on what Jesus says while he is with his disciples before his departure. Its function is consolation for the disciples. The unit is held together by an inclusion (v. 25: "These things I have spoken to you while I am still with you"; v. 30: "I will no longer talk much with you"). What Jesus says is considered from three angles: (a) in relation to the Holy Spirit's function (vv. 25–26: "the Holy Spirit, whom the Father will send in my name, he will teach you all things, and bring to your remembrance all that I have said to you," that is, the Spirit is Jesus' representative/agent who teaches = brings to your remembrance); (b) in terms of the benefits for the disciples (vv. 27–29: Jesus gives his peace [16:33; cf. Lk 24:36], promises he will come to them in resurrection appearances [14:18], and tells them beforehand so that they may believe when it does take place [16:4; cf. 13:19; 16:4]); and (c) in terms of the limited duration of time remaining (vv. 30–31: There is not much time for talking left because the ruler of this world is coming [cf. 18:3]. He, however, has no power over Jesus [cf. 7:8; 7:30; 8:20]; Jesus acts only in accordance with the Father's directions [cf. 10:18; 12:27; 18:4]). The gist of this meditation is: separation is imminent, but be consoled because what is happening to Jesus is according to the Father's plan (vv. 30–31); because he will come to you after his resurrection (v. 28); and because the Father will send the Paraclete to bring to your remembrance all that Jesus said (v. 26).

The large thought unit, 13:31–14:31, deals with the question: what is the position of Jesus' disciples? The answer has two foci. (1) The position of his disciples is derived from the prior activity of Jesus. As relates to the disciples' existence in this life, Jesus reveals the Father and empowers for ministry. As relates to disciples' hope for the future, Jesus prepares a place with the Father and will take the disciples to himself at the parousia. (2) The position of the disciples derived from the prior activity of Jesus sets them apart as different from the world. As regards their behavior, unlike the world, disciples obey the word/commands of Jesus. As regards their religious experience, unlike the world, disciples are promised resurrection experiences, the gift of the Spirit of prophecy, and the indwelling presence of Jesus and the Father. The thought unit concludes with yet another point. (3) The prediction of Christ's imminent departure is matched by his promises for the disciples' future, a fact that ought to bring consolation to the disciples.

There is no indication that eschatology is the issue in this thought unit (i.e., revising the traditional futurist eschatology of the church into a realized eschatology). There is no evidence that the struggle with the Jews is uppermost in the Evangelist's mind (i.e., exclusion from the synagogue). What is of concern here is the status of disciples after Jesus' departure, i.e., in relation to Jesus and in relation to the world (Bruce Woll, *Johannine Christianity in Conflict: Authority, Rank, and Succession in the First Farewell Discourse* [Atlanta: Scholars Press, 1981]). This is precisely the focal point of the argument against the progressives/secessionists of 2 and 1 John. The Fourth Gospel continues the struggle of the epistles, at least in this thought unit.

THE TRUE VINE

John 15:1–16:33

The Last Discourse of Jesus, 13:31–17:26, consists of three components: a first farewell speech (13:31–14:31), a second farewell
speech (15:1–16:33), and a long prayer (17:1–26). The first version of
the farewell speech contains three parts: (1) the soteriological priority of
Jesus and the derivative nature of the disciples' existence (13:31–14:14);
(2) the difference between the disciples and the world (14:15–24); and
(3) the consolation offered by Jesus in the face of imminent separation
from his disciples (14:25–31). The second version of the farewell speech
is also comprised of three subunits: (1) 15:1–17, a meditation on Jesus as
the source of the community's life (i.e., the derivative nature of Christian
existence); (2) 15:18–16:15, a meditation on the tensions between the
disciples and the world; and (3) a meditation on the sorrow of passion-
separation and the joy of Easter-consolation (16:16–33). Both versions of
the farewell speech are built out of similar materials and are organized
in terms of a similar three-point outline. (Remember the rule verbalized
by *Rhetorica ad Herennium* 4.42.54: "We shall not repeat the same thing
precisely — for that, to be sure, would weary the hearer and not elaborate
the idea — but with changes.")

John 15:1–17 is the first of three components in the second farewell
speech, 15:1–16:33. It is a meditation on Jesus as the source of the
community's life. It falls into two parts: a figure (vv. 1–6) and a reflection on the figure (vv. 7–17; remember the same procedure in John 10;
R. E. Brown, *The Gospel according to John XIII–XXI* [Garden City, N.Y.:
Doubleday, 1970], 667).

The figure of the vine and the branches, 15:1–6, contains two paragraphs that loosely correspond to one another.

15:1–4	15:5–6
I am the true vine (v. 1a)	I am the vine (v. 5a)
Every branch of mine (v. 2a)	You are the branches (v. 5b)
The fate of unfruitful branches (v. 2b)	The fate of unfruitful branches (v. 6)
Necessity of abiding for fruit bearing (v. 4)	Necessity of abiding for fruit bearing (v. 5c)

The first paragraph of the figure begins with the last of the "I am +
predicate" sayings: "I am the true vine" (v. 1; "I am the vine," v. 5). The
vine usually symbolizes Israel in Jewish and early Christian tradition (Hos
10:1–2; Isa 5:1–7; Jer 2:21; Ezk 15:1–5; Ps 80:8–18; *Leviticus Rabbah* 36
[133a]; 1 QH 6.15–16; Mk 12:1–11); occasionally the king (Ezk 17:6–8)
or the Messiah (2 Baruch 36–37; 39:7; Didache 9:2?). Here Jesus speaks
of himself as the true vine (i.e., the faithful Israel, in contrast to faithless
Israel that has become a wild vine, Jer 2:21; the true Messiah, in contrast
to the thieves and robbers, 10:8). Since the "I am + predicate" sayings
in John speak of Jesus' role in salvation, for him to be the true vine is
for him to function as the source of life and fruitfulness for the branches.
The emphasis is on the derivative nature of the disciples' life.

If Jesus as the true vine is in the foreground of the figure, in the background is the second line of v. 1: "and my Father is the vinedresser"
(as is implicit in Isa 5:1–7 as well). The vinedresser does two things
to insure fruitfulness: (a) "Every branch . . . that bears no fruit, he takes
away/*airei*" (i.e., in winter, he cuts off dry and withered branches), and
(b) "every branch that does bear fruit he prunes/*kathairei,* that it may
bear more fruit" (i.e., in spring, he removes the useless growth from the
living branches). Whereas the basic thrust of the both paragraphs has to
do with (a), what happens to branches that bear no fruit (cf. vv. 2a, 6),
v. 3 relates to (b), branches that are alive but need pruning (*kathairein*)
to be fruitful. "You are already made clean/*katharoi* [here, in the sense
of pruned] by the word which I have spoken to you."

If the vine supplies life and if the vinedresser prunes, the branches (disciples) have their role as well. They are to "abide in me, and I in you."
Why? Because "as the branch cannot bear fruit by itself, unless it abides in
the vine, neither can you, unless you abide in me" (v. 4). "Bearing fruit"
here has been understood to mean either winning unbelievers to Jesus
(cf. 4:35–38) or manifesting all the fruits of the Christian life, especially
love of the other members of the community (13:34–35). The immediate
context, the explanation in vv. 7–17, seems to indicate the latter (bearing
fruit = loving one another). Such fruit-bearing is not possible unless disciples abide in Jesus and Jesus in them. At this point, "it will have been
difficult for the Evangelist and his readers not to think of . . . the 'many
Antichrists' who led out members from the church and formed heretical
groups" (cf. 1 John 2:18–19; 4:1–6; G. R. Beasley-Murray, *Word Biblical
Commentary: John* [Waco: Word, 1987], 273).

The second paragraph of the figure begins with repetition for emphasis: "I am the vine, you are the branches. Those who abide in me, and I in

them, they are those who bear much fruit, for apart from me you can do nothing" (v. 5). If the first paragraph dealt with pruning of live branches, the second paragraph attends to dead branches and their fate: "If people do not abide in me [cf. 2 John 9], they are cast forth as branches and wither; and the branches are gathered, thrown into the fire and burned" (v. 6). This separation from Christ is probably the sin unto death mentioned in 1 John 5:16–17.

The commentary on the figure of 15:1–6 that comes in vv. 7–17 is arranged in a concentric pattern (Brown, *John XIII–XXI*, 667):

A   v. 7a: If my words abide in you,

   B   v. 7b: Ask whatever you will and it will be done for you.

      C   v. 8: Bear fruit and so prove to be my disciples.

         D   v. 9: As the Father loved me, so I have loved you.

            E   v. 10: If you keep my commandments, you will abide in my love.

               F   v. 11: The purpose of these words is joy.

            E′   vv. 12–14: You are my beloved if you do what I command you.

         D′   v. 15: What I heard from the Father, I made known to you.

      C′   v. 16a: I chose you to bear fruit.

   B′   v. 16b: Whatever you ask the Father, he may give it to you.

A′   v. 17: This I command you. . . .

The first half of the pattern emphasizes that bearing fruit is dependent on abiding in Christ (vv. 7–10); the second half focuses on bearing fruit understood as loving one another (vv. 12–17). The centerpoint is Jesus' desire for the joy of the disciples (v. 11).

In vv. 7–10 covenant structures of thought dominate. Deuteronomy 7:7–16 assists in understanding such thought forms. Its train of thought runs: (a) the Lord set his love on Israel and chose her, i.e., God's love means election (v. 7); (b) the Lord keeps covenant and steadfast love with those who keep his commandments, i.e., God's love means covenant fidelity toward those who obey (v. 9); (c) the Lord will love you, bless you, multiply you, take away diseases, destroy enemies (vv. 13–17), i.e., God's love means bestowal of all these benefits. John 15:9–10 says the Father loves Jesus (i.e., has chosen him, remains faithful to him, and blesses him); that Jesus loves the disciples in the same way; and that the disciples' role in the covenant is to abide in his love, i.e., keep his commandments. If the disciples do abide in Jesus and his words in them (i.e., they obey them), then there are two benefits for the disciples: answered prayer (v. 7; cf. 1 John 3:22) and fruitbearing (v. 8). To receive such benefits brings joy.

V. 12 ("This is my commandment, that you love one another, as I have loved you") and v. 17 ("This I command you, to love one another") form a frame around the second part of the explanation, indicating its thrust. This love is characterized in two ways. (a) V. 13 spells out the first: "Greater love has no man than this, that a man lay down his life for his friends." The notion of a friend of God has deep Jewish roots (e.g., Isa 41:8: Abraham; Exod 33:11: Moses; Jubilees 30:21: Israelites; m. Pirke Aboth 6.1: those concerned with Torah; Wisdom of Solomon 7:27: holy souls; Philo, *Who Is the Heir?* 21: all wise men), as well as Greco-Roman ones (e.g., Epictetus, *Discourses* 4.3.9: "I am a free man and a friend of God, so as to obey him of my own free will"). The notion of dying for one's friends, however, is Hellenistic (Aristotle, *Ethics* 9.8, 1169a: "To a noble man there applies the true saying that he does all things for the sake of his friends . . . and, if need be, he gives his life for them"; Plato, *Symposium* 179B: "Only those who love wish to die for others"). 1 John 3:16 has already made the point: "By this we know love, that he laid down his life for us; and we ought to lay down our lives for the brethren." (b) Vv. 14–15 offer the second characteristic of Jesus' love that is to characterize the disciples' relating to one another: "No longer do I call you servants, for the servant does not know what his master is doing; but I have called you friends, for all that I have heard from my Father I have made known to you." This is a feature of the relationship between God and his friends in the Old Testament (e.g., Abraham in Gen 18:17; Moses in Exod 33:11). It characterizes the eyewitnesses in the Johannine community (13:25–26; 1 John 1:3). Such a free flow of communication among the brethren is a part of their loving one another (cf. 3 John for the problem of obstructions to such communication). Jesus has chosen the disciples and appointed them (cf. Num 27:18; Acts 13:47 citing Isa 49:6; 1 Tim 1:12; i.e., set aside for a specific task) to bear fruit: not in this instance for missionary activity (as in 4:38; 17:18; 20:21) but for love within community (as in 1 John 3:14–15; 4:16). In the context of loving community life, prayers are answered (v. 16b; cf. Mk 11:23–25 and the discussion of it by Sharyn E. Dowd, *Prayer, Power, and the Problem of Suffering* [Atlanta: Scholars, 1988]).

The basic direction of thought in 15:1–17 is that abiding in Jesus results in fruitfulness, i.e., loving one another within the life of the community.

If this fruitfulness produced by abiding in the vine is a reality, then there are positive benefits (like answered prayer and joy), and the negative consequences (like being taken away and burned) are avoided. The central point of 15:1–17 is the soteriological priority of Jesus and the derivative character of the disciples' existence. In a community where progressives "have gone beyond / are not abiding in" the doctrine of Christ (2 John 9) and have become secessionists (1 John 2:19), refusing to receive fellow Christians who visit (3 John), this twofold message is needed: (a) "Without me you can do nothing" (v. 5); (b) "Love one another, as I have loved you" (v. 12).

The second part of 15:1–16:33 comes in 15:18–16:15. It is a meditation on the tensions between the disciples and the world. This section falls into an ABA' B' pattern.

> A   15:18–25: Persecution of the disciples comes (vv. 18–20) because the persecutors do not know the one who sent Jesus (v. 21) or Jesus (vv. 22–25).
>
> > B   15:26–27: The Holy Spirit, when he comes, will bear witness concerning Jesus, as will the disciples (i.e., there will be a second time of confrontation).
>
> A'   16:1–4a: Persecution of the disciples comes (v. 2) because the persecutors have not known the Father or Jesus (v. 3).
>
> > B'   16:4b–15: The Holy Spirit, when sent, will expose the world and prove it guilty (vv. 8–11), as well as teaching the disciples (vv. 13–15).

A, 15:18–25, makes clear that the community of those who love one another will be confronted by a hostile world. (a) Just as the relation of the Son to the Father is used in 15:10 as a model for the disciples' association with Jesus (keep my commandments just as I have kept my Father's commandments), so in 15:18 the relation of the Son to the world is paradigmatic of the relationship between believers and unbelievers ("If the world hates you, know that it has hated me before it hated you"). This should not surprise the disciples when they remember Jesus' word (13:16; cf. Matt 10:24//Lk 6:40): "A servant is not greater than his master" (v. 20a). So "if they persecuted me, they will persecute you" (v. 20b). This is a theme already addressed by 1 John (3:13: "Do not wonder, brethren, that the world hates you"). (b) The reason the world acts this way is because it does not know (= is not in covenant relation with) "him who sent me" (v. 21; cf. 1 John 4:6: "We are of God. Whoever knows God listens to us, and whoever is not of God does not listen to us"). Since Jesus,

and by derivation his disciples, are God's agents, if people had a relation to God, they would know what to look for in his agents and so be
able to recognize them (m. Berakoth 5:5: "A man's agent is like to himself"). Not to recognize God's agents is to expose one's lack of a relation
to/knowledge of their sender. To reject the agent is to reject the sender:
"The one who hates me hates my Father also" (v. 23). If Jesus had not
worked in the midst of the world as God's agent, the world "would not
have guilt/*hamartian*" (the term can mean either sin or guilt, as in 9:41;
cf. Rom 5:13). As it is, the world stands guilty of hatred/rejection of the
Father and of Jesus, his agent. This hatred is not evidence that things
are out of God's control, however. Rather it fulfills the word written in
their law: "They hated me without a cause" (v. 25; Ps 69:4 or 35:19). To
say Scripture is being fulfilled is to claim that the divine plan is being
accomplished. God is in control.

B, 15:26–27, shifts attention from persecution to the role of the Holy
Spirit:

> But when the Paraclete comes, whom I shall send to you from the
> Father, even the Spirit of truth, who proceeds from the Father, he
> will bear witness to me; and you also are witnesses, because you have
> been with me from the beginning.

(a) The Paraclete here is closely tied to Jesus. Jesus sends the Spirit (cf.
Acts 2:33; Eph 4:8, 11); the Spirit bears witness to Jesus. Pneumatology
is subordinated to christology. (b) The Paraclete's witness is directed toward the world. This means that the synonym, Spirit of truth, used here
for the Paraclete functions differently from its usage elsewhere in the milieu. In T. Judah 20:1, 3, 5 ("So understand, my children, that two spirits
await an opportunity with humanity: the spirit of truth and the spirit of
error.... The things of truth and the things of error are written in the af-
fections of man.... And the spirit of truth testifies to all things and brings
all accusations"); 1 QS 3 ("He has created man to govern the world, and
has appointed for him two spirits in which to walk until the time of his visitation: the spirits of truth and falsehood"); and Hermas, *Command* 3:4
("you ought as God's slave to have lived in truth and a bad conscience
ought not to have dwelt with the spirit of truth, nor to have brought
grief to the revered, true spirit"), the spirit of truth bears witness within
the righteous individual regarding right and wrong. In John 15:26, the
Spirit of truth bears witness about Jesus to the world. Verbal similarity
does not yield functional identity. (c) The disciples are also designated as
witnesses "because you have been with me from the beginning" (cf. Acts

1:21–22). Are they witnesses alongside the Spirit of prophecy or are they the human vehicles of the Spirit of prophecy? Either way, that the disciples have been with Jesus from the beginning means that the tradition about the earthly Jesus controls the content of the prophetic witness. There can be no witness that denies that Jesus Christ has come in the flesh (1 John 4:1–2).

The concept of witness to Jesus occupies a prominent place in the Fourth Gospel. At least ten witnesses to Jesus are referred to in the Gospel (using *marturia* or *marturein*). They include: (a) John the Baptist (1:7, 8, 15, 19, 32, 34; 3:26; 5:33); (b) Jesus himself (5:31; 8:13–14); (c) Jesus' works (5:36; 10:25); (d) the Scriptures (5:39); (e) the Father (5:37; 8:18); (f) the Samaritan woman (4:39); (g) the crowd (12:17); (h) the Paraclete (15:26); (i) the disciples who were with Jesus from the beginning (15:27); and (j) the beloved disciple (19:35; 21:24). As indicated above, in 15:26–27 the witness of the disciples and the Paraclete may be two sides of the one coin, the Spirit of prophecy.

A', 16:1–4, turns attention once again to the reality of persecution in the disciples' lives (cf. Mk 13:9; Matt 10:17; Lk 6:22). The unit is held together by an inclusion: v. 1 ("I have said all this to you to keep you from falling away") and v. 4a ("I have said these things to you, that when their hour comes you may remember that I told you of them"). The inclusion makes explicit the aim of the paragraph. It is to prevent the problems that may arise later from shaking the disciples' faith.

(a) The problem is stated in v. 2: "They will put you out of the synagogues (9:22, 34; 12:42–43); indeed the hour is coming when whoever kills you will think he is offering service [*latreian*] to God." The persecution includes both excommunication and martyrdom. On the one hand, there is no evidence in the text to link this excommunication with the *Birkat ha Minim* (a prayer of the synagogue liturgy that curses certain heretics/*minim* and, in some versions of the prayer, Jewish Christians/*nosrim*, and that, according to b. Berakoth 28b–29a, was formulated at Jamnia under Rabbi Gamaliel at the end of the first century). Luke 6:22 is but one indication that such excommunication because of christological claims of disciples would have gone on in many places at various times before the Jamnia prayer. That excommunication in the Fourth Gospel's three references to it is always because of christology and when implemented by the Pharisees/Jews is never connected to synagogue prayer supports one's skepticism about J. L. Martyn's hypothesis (*History and Theology in the Fourth Gospel*).

On the other hand, there is evidence from antiquity that Jews sometimes sought to kill Christians (Justin, *Dialogue* 133: "you hate and murder us"; 95:4: "them that believe on him [Jesus] . . . when you have the power, put them to death"; cf. Martyrdom of Polycarp 13:1, where the Jews are prominent in bringing brushwood and kindling for the bishop's fiery death "as is the custom with them"). There is also evidence that Jewish zealots would have seen killing Christians as a religious exercise (m. Sanhedrin 9:6 says that those, like Phinehas [Num 25:6–13], who were zealous and set upon certain religious criminals to kill them are granted exemption from punishment; *Numbers Rabbah* 21: "everyone who sheds the blood of the godless is like one who offers a sacrifice" [again, related to Num 25:6–13]). (b) The reason for such persecution is given in v. 3: "And they will do this because they have not known the Father, nor me" (cf. 15:21). The disciples are given the prediction as part of the farewell speech so they will not fall away.

B', 16:4b–15, returns once again to the topic of the Paraclete. An inclusion holds the unit together: vv. 4b–7 ("I did not say these things to you from the beginning. . . . I tell you the truth: it is to your advantage that I go away, for if I do not go away, the Paraclete will not come to you; but if I go, I will send him to you") and vv. 12–15 ("I have yet many things to say to you. . . . When the Spirit of truth comes"). The Paraclete is sent by Jesus after his glorification. His coming will be to the disciples' advantage. Two Paraclete sayings comprise this section (vv. 7–11; vv. 13–15). One deals with the Spirit's relation to the world (vv. 7–11; as 15:26–27), the other with the Spirit's role in the believing community (vv. 13–15). Together they define the benefits of the Spirit's coming.

John 16:7–11 portrays the Paraclete as a prosecuting counsel in a cosmic trial involving Jesus and the unbelieving world:

> When he [the Paraclete] comes, he will convict [*elegksei*; cf. 8:46; 1 Cor 14:24; 2 Tim 4:2] the world of sin and of righteousness and of judgment: of sin because they do not believe in me; of righteousness because I go to the Father and you see me no longer; of judgment because the ruler of this world has been judged.

The prosecuting counsel will convict the world on three counts: sin, righteousness, and judgment. The explanation given of the three counts offers not the content of sin, righteousness, and judgment (e.g., of sin in that they do not believe) but rather the ground of conviction (e.g., of sin because they do not believe). Read in this way, the world is convicted by the Spirit of prophecy: (a) of sin because the world does not believe in Jesus and that is the essence of sin in John; (b) of righteousness because, being glorified, Jesus' righteousness is vindicated by God (cf. 1 John 2:29; 3:7; 1 Tim 3:16); (c) of judgment because the ruler of this world has already been judged, making judgment of his domain, the world, certain (cf. 12:31; 1 John 2:13–14; 5:18). The situation presupposed is very much like that reflected in 1 Corinthians 14:23–25. The whole church has assembled and outsiders and unbelievers enter; the prophesying that is taking place results in conviction of unbelievers, who then fall on their faces and worship God. In this role, the Paraclete confronts the world (as in 15:26–27).

In the final saying about the Spirit of truth in the farewell speech (vv. 13–15), the Spirit of prophecy's role in relation to the community of believers is described (as in 14:26):

> He will lead you into all truth, for he will not speak from himself, but what things he hears he will speak, and the things that are coming he will declare to you. He will glorify me, because he will receive from what is mine and declare it to you. Everything the Father has is mine. Because of this I said he will receive from what is mine and declare it to you.

According to this saying, Jesus has been given all things by the Father (cf. 1:18; 5:22, 26; 13:3; 17:2, 7). The Spirit receives from the Son's bounty and declares it; he is the Son's agent (an agent can appoint an agent, b. Kiddushin 41a). An agent acts according to the mind of his sender (m. Terumoth 4:4). Again, pneumatology is subordinated to christology. The Spirit does not offer a new revelation independent of Christ. This has two facets. On the one hand, he explicates the content of the revelation in Jesus ("what things he hears he will speak") as it applies to a new time and context. On the other hand, "the things that are coming he will declare to you." This has variously been taken to mean (a) the hour that is coming, that is, the time of Jesus' glorification; (b) the significance of Jesus' teaching for the time of the church after Jesus' glorification; or (c) the ultimate future. Isaiah 41:21–29 offers insight about what was expected of prophecy in antiquity. In this passage Yahweh challenges the idol-gods of the nations to present their case by uttering true prophecy. This involves two things. First, tell us the former things that we may know, Second, declare to us the things to come that we may know. Prophecy was understood to include both an interpretation of the past and a prediction of the future. These two functions John 16:13–15 ascribes to the Spirit of prophecy. He will take what belongs to the past, Jesus' revelation on earth, and interpret it for a new situation (Odes of Solomon 3:10: "This is the Spirit of the Lord which is not false, which teaches the sons of men to know his ways"). He will also declare the future as it must be in light of what God has revealed in Jesus Christ (cf. Rev 1:1–3; 22:6–7; 1 Thes 4:15–17; a fragment of the "Preaching of Peter," preserved in Clement of Alexandria's *Miscellanies* 6.6, which says the Lord sent his apostles out to evangelize the world, in part by declaring what would take place). In performing these two functions, the Spirit of prophecy leads the believing community into all truth (i.e., into the whole of the revelation in Jesus Christ in all of its implications). This would include doing the truth (2 John 4; 3 John 4) as well as believing the truth (1 John 2:21). The Johannine community as a prophetic conclave rooted in the Incarnation would have found the ground of its self-understanding in such a saying. The saying would also have provided a criterion to discern among the spirits, separating true from false (1 John 4:1–2).

The third component in the second version of the farewell speech (15:1–16:33) comes in 16:16–33. It is a meditation on the sorrow of passion-separation and the joy of Easter-consolation. The unit falls into a loosely organized concentric pattern (Brown, *John XIII–XXI*, 728).

A   v. 16: Prediction of separation and subsequent consolation

   B   vv. 17–19: Dialogue showing the disciples' lack of understanding

      C   vv. 20–23: Promises of blessings for the disciples (begins, "Truly, truly, I say to you")

      C'   vv. 23b–28: Promises of blessings for the disciples (begins, "Truly, truly, I say to you")

   B'   vv. 29–31: Dialogue showing disciples' lack of understanding

A'   vv. 32–33: Prediction of separation and consolation

A, v. 16, begins with Jesus' words: "A little while and you will see me no more; again a little while and you will see me." The first little while refers to the time up to Jesus' death; the second little while alludes to the time between Jesus' death and his resurrection appearances. There will be both separation and consolation.

B, vv. 17–19, offers a dialogue between disciples and Jesus. The disciples are puzzled: "What is this that he says to us? . . . What does he mean by a little while? We do not know what he means." Jesus, because of his prophetic knowledge (1:47–48; 2:24; 6:61, 64), knew what they wanted to ask him: "Is this what you are asking yourselves, what I meant?"

C, vv. 20–23a, allows Jesus to make two promises to the disciples: (a) that their sorrow will turn to joy, and (b) that they will then understand. (a) Vv. 20–22 give the promise of a reversal of emotion in an aba' pattern.

> a   You will be sorrowful but your sorrow will turn to joy. (v. 20)
>
> > b   Your circumstances will be like that of a woman giving birth. In labor she has sorrow; after the birth she is joyful. (v. 21; cf. Isa 26:16–21; 66:7–14)
>
> a'   So you have sorrow now, but I will see you again and your hearts will rejoice. (v. 22)

The reversal will come when the pain of separation is overcome by the joy of being reunited after the resurrection. The resurrection appearances are described in terms of Jesus' seeing the disciples again. They are not understood by the Evangelist as only in the subjectivity of the disciples (i.e., not that they will see Jesus, but that Jesus will see them).

(b) The second promise given by Jesus to the disciples is that "in that day (the time of the resurrection appearances) you will ask nothing of me" (v. 23a). The Fourth Gospel reflects the belief throughout that after Easter the disciples have new insight (e.g., 2:22; 12:16; 14:26; 16:13–15). When this new discernment is achieved the disciples will not be forced to ask Jesus questions out of their bewilderment (as, e.g., in v. 18; cf. also 13:36a, 37a; 14:5, 22).

C', vv. 23b–27, offers yet two more promises to the disciples in an aba' pattern.

> a   vv. 23b–24: Prayer in Jesus' name will be answered (14:13–14; 15:7, 16b).
>
> > b   v. 25: Jesus' communication to the disciples will be plain (16:14).
>
> a'   vv. 26–27: Prayer in Jesus' name by those who love Jesus and believe that he came from the Father will be answered.

(a) The post-resurrection period (in that day, v. 26) will be a time when the disciples' prayers in Jesus' name will be answered. They will have access to the Father because they love Jesus and believe in him (cf. 1 John 3:22; James 4:3; Matt 7:7). (b) Jesus' communication with his disciples in the post-resurrection period will be clear. He will tell them plainly of the Father. This may very well refer to his communication through the Paraclete (cf. 16:13–15).

B', vv. 28–31, presents another dialogue between Jesus and his disciples that reveals their failure to understand to this point. Jesus speaks: "I came from the Father and have come into the world; again, I am leaving the world and going to the Father" (v. 28). He is the descending-ascending redeemer (see Appendix). The disciples respond: "Ah, now you are speaking plainly, not in any figure" (v. 30). They wrongly assume the time of clarity has already arrived. They do not yet see the necessity of Jesus' glorification if they are to understand clearly. Remember John 3. Only those born of the Spirit can see the realm of God. Jesus' answer is an ironic question: "Do you now believe?" (v. 31).

A', vv. 32–33, points to (a) the disciples' impotence prior to Jesus' glorification ("The hour is coming . . . when you will be scattered, every man to his home"; regrettably the prophecy of Zech 13:7 will be fulfilled; the disciples will forsake him); (b) the Father's presence even in Jesus' darkest hour ("yet I am not alone, for the Father is with me"); (c) Jesus' promise that the disciples can have peace and good cheer because, in spite of their tribulation in the world, the world has been defeated ("I have overcome the world") and they can, therefore, overcome the world as well (1 John 2:13–14; 4:4; 5:4–5).

The second version of Jesus' farewell speech (15:1–16:33) has incorporated the same three emphases as the first (13:31–14:31): (1) Jesus' soteriological priority and the derivative nature of the disciples' existence (15:1–17); (2) the difference/tensions between the disciples and the world (15:18–16:15); and (3) consolation for the disciples in view of imminent separation (16:16–33). The second emphasis could conceivably, though not necessarily, relate to the Johannine community's exclusion from the synagogue; the first is best understood against the background of the tensions encountered already in the Johannine epistles. Indeed, the farewell speech in both its versions treated so far seems to continue the fight of the epistles against the tenets of the progressives/secessionists.

THE INTERCESSOR

John 17:1–26

The one who came as revealing, empowering presence (1:1–18), who picked/produced a new community (1:19–2:12) and gave them warrants during his public ministry for a different type of worship (2:13–11:54), has privately predicted what their future will be like, offering promise and parenesis for that time (13:31–16:33). Now before he turns his attention to issues that are more inclusive, even if they also involve the disciples (chaps. 18–21), Jesus prays specifically for himself and for his own (17:1–26).

Farewell speeches in antiquity sometimes close with a prayer. A Jewish example is Jubilees 22:28–30, where Abraham's farewell discourse ends with a prayer for Jacob that God "might protect him and bless him and sanctify him for a people who belong to your heritage." An example from Christian circles is Luke 22:14–38, a farewell speech of Jesus at the last supper, which has Jesus not only predict what will come and exhort the disciples how to behave, but also pray for Peter "that your faith may not fail" in vv. 31–32. The Fourth Gospel merely follows conventional usage in ending its farewell discourse with Jesus' prayer of petition and intercession.

The Johannine Jesus is depicted throughout the Gospel as a person of prayer (as he is also in the Synoptics: Matt 14:23; 19:13; 26:36–44; 27:46; Mk 1:35; 6:46; 14:32–39; 15:34; Lk 3:21; 5:16; 6:12; 9:18, 28–29; 11:1; 22:41–45; 23:46). Some references to Jesus' prayer come in the farewell speech and predict his future intercession for disciples after Easter (14:16: "I will pray the Father and he will give you another Paraclete"; 16:26; cf. 1 John 2:1–2; Rom 8:34; Heb 7:25; 9:14). Other references treat his prayer life during his pre-Easter career (6:11; 11:41–42, a verbalized thanksgiving for being heard by the Father at the non-vocal level; 12:27–28, an interior monologue about what Jesus should pray for that ends in petition: "What shall I say? Father, save me from this hour? . . . No. . . . Father, glorify your name"). The two instances of prayer during Jesus' earthly career (11:41–42; 12:27–28) are closely connected with immediate, clear-cut answers from God (Lazarus is raised in chap. 11; a voice comes from heaven in response to the prayer in chap. 12). When these two instances are linked in the Gospel's plot with the post-Easter intercession of 14:16 (that the Father will give the Paraclete to the disciples), which the readers know has been answered in their own community's experience, the effect is to give assurance that the petitions and intercessions of 17:1–26 will be answered as well (as will doubtless also the promises of answers to disciples' prayers in 16:23b, 26). The hearer's of the Fourth Gospel can say with Martha: "I know that whatever you ask from God, God will give you" (11:22). It is the earthly Jesus who prays in John 17, but his intercession for disciples in vv. 9–24 prefigures his heavenly intercession.

John 17 consists of three separate parts: (1) a petition by Jesus for himself (vv. 1–8); (2) an intercession by Jesus for his disciples (vv. 9–24), itself in three parts (vv. 9–19; vv. 20–23; v. 24); and (3) a recapitulation by Jesus of his ministry and a recommitment by him to his mission (vv. 25–26). (1) In vv. 1–8 Jesus prays for himself. The material falls into an ABCB′A′ C′ pattern.

> A   v. 1: Jesus' prayer
>> B   v. 2: The basis for the prayer that precedes
>>> C   v. 3: A comment on "eternal life" in v. 2
>> B′   v. 4: The basis for the prayer that follows
> A′   v. 5: Jesus' prayer
>>> C′   vv. 6–8: A comment on "Jesus' work" in v. 4

A, v. 1, gives Jesus' petition for himself: "Father, the hour has come (12:23, 27–28; 13:1, 31); glorify your Son that the Son may glorify you." This is for what Jesus prays: to be glorified so that he may glorify the Father. The notion of glory is a complex one. Glory is what makes one impressive to others. It may mean: reputation (e.g., Lk 14:10; 1 Thes 2:6); honor (i.e., status/prestige, e.g., Gen 45:13; Isa 16:14; m. Pirke Aboth 4:12; riches, e.g., Gen 31:1; Ps 49:16); splendor (e.g., Matt 4:8; 6:29; Rev 21:24, 26); power (e.g., 2 Baruch 21:23; Ps 57:5 [56:5 LXX]; Ps 108:5: "Be exalted, O God, above the heavens. Let your glory be over all the earth" [107:5 LXX]); the divine presence or radiance (e.g., Exod 16:10; 24:16; Philo, *Special Laws* 1.45). To give glory to God is not to add something not present in God to God but to acknowledge something already present in God (e.g., Acts 12:23; Rev 4:9; 16:9). To glorify someone other than

God is to acknowledge that person's honor or power. If God glorifies someone, he grants that person to participate in his honor or power or divine radiance (TDNT 2:232–54).

In the Fourth Gospel this construct makes sense of most references: e.g., 1:14: glory as of an only Son from the Father (honor, status, power that normally accompany an only son); 2:11: the miracle manifested his glory (power); 11:4: Lazarus' death will be a means by which the Son of God may be glorified (if glorified by humans, then honored; if glorified by God, then granted his power); 11:40: if you believe, you will see the glory of God (the power of God); 12:43: for they loved the glory of men more than the glory of God (honor of men, honor of God); 12:23: the hour has come for the Son to be glorified (to be exalted, to be granted certain status and power). So in 17:1, "glorify your Son" means "God, exalt me, vindicate me"; "that the Son may glorify you" means "that the Son may exalt, honor you, vindicate you" (cf. "hallowed be your name," Matt 6:9). That Jesus prays for his glorification assumes that it can come no other way (cf. Matt 4:8–10).

B, v. 2, presents the basis for the petition in v. 1. "Give me honor/status . . . just as [*kathōs,* cf. 17:18] you have given me power over all flesh, for the purpose of giving eternal life to all whom you have given me" (cf. 5:26: "For as the Father has life in himself, so he has granted the Son also to have life in himself"; 11:25–26: "I am the resurrection and the life; . . . whoever lives and believes in me shall never die"). Jesus asks for public status to match his divinely given authority (cf. Rev 5).

C, v. 3, offers a commentary on the "eternal life" mentioned in v. 2. "This is eternal life, that they know [= be in covenant relation with] you the only true God, and the one whom you sent, Jesus Christ" (cf. 1 John 5:20–21, where the difficult text speaks about the true one [God] and the true one, Jesus Christ, in connection with eternal life and with an exhortation to avoid idols). This is similar to confessions like 1 Corinthians 8:6 and the preaching of 1 Thessalonians 1:9–10 that defend against polytheism. Eternal life means being in covenant relation with the only true God and the one he has sent (1 John 1:3: "and our fellowship is with the Father and with his Son Jesus Christ"; 2:24: "abide in the Son and in the Father").

B', v. 4, gives the basis for the petition to follow: "I glorified you [acknowledged your power, honored you; cf. 5:30] on earth [13:31], having accomplished the work [4:34; 19:30; 5:36] which you gave me to do." Jesus has been faithful to his mission of salvation. What he has seen the Father doing, he has done (5:19–20a); what he has heard the Father speaking, he has said (12:50). On this basis, he makes his petition.

A', v. 5, gives a second form of Jesus' prayer of petition for himself: "and now, Father, glorify me in your own presence with the glory I had with you before the world was made" (cf. 1:1–4; Heb 1:2–3). To "glorify me with the glory" means to "honor me with the status." This honoring takes place in the Father's presence (1:1, 18). It is not a development beyond his previous status (as, e.g., in Rom 1:3–4; Phil 2:6–11; Lk 24:26; Acts 2:36), but a restoration of a former status that he had before creation (1:1, 18; 6:62; 3:13). The one who possessed heavenly glory has come and faithfully done the Father's work; now he asks to be restored to his former status.

C', vv. 6–8, functions as commentary on Jesus' work mentioned in v. 4. Of what does it consist? "I have manifested your name to the men whom you gave me [10:29; 6:36, 44; 17:2] out of the world." Jesus is the revealer of God's name (remember 8:58, *egō eimi* / I am; cf. Isa 52:6: "Therefore my people shall know my name . . . they shall know that it is I [*egō eimi*] who speak"; Ezk 39:7) and God's words to the disciples. As a result, the disciples know and believe that everything God gave Jesus is from the Father (v. 7–8; cf. 16:30b?). Jesus' work has been effective. Having made his petition for himself (cf. Acts of Thomas 144–48 for a similar petition by an apostle facing martyrdom, who prays that, since he has faithfully accomplished the work God gave him, he may inherit his heavenly reward), Jesus now turns his attention to his disciples: to those present with him in his earthly ministry (vv. 9–19) and to those who will believe because of them (vv. 20–23), as well as both together (v. 24).

John 17:9–19 comprises Jesus' intercession for his disciples who accompany him during his earthly ministry. It falls into four subunits (vv. 9–11a; vv. 11b–13; vv. 14–16; vv. 17–19), each one dealing with two matters: (a) either for whom or for what Jesus prays, and (b) why he prays this way. (1) Vv. 9–11a constitute the first unit. (a) It tells first for whom Jesus prays: "I am praying for them [the disciples who have believed during his earthly ministry, so vv. 6–8]; I am not praying for the world but for those whom thou hast given me." If his verbal prayer in 11:41–42 was for the sake of those standing by (the world), this prayer is verbalized for the sake of his own (the disciples). (b) Why does he pray for the disciples? It is because "they are thine . . . and now I am no more in the world, but they are in the world." Since Jesus is going to the Father, the Father needs to look after his own, the disciples, who remain in the world.

(2) Vv. 11b–13 comprise the second unit. (a) It speaks first of all about

what Jesus prays for: "Holy Father [cf. Didache 10:2], keep them in your name [i.e., in loyalty to you]... that they may be one, even as we are one." This is a prayer for the unity of the disciples that is grounded in their being kept by the Father in his name. (b) The reason for this intercession is: "While I was with them, I kept them in thy name...; I have guarded them, and none of them is lost [6:39; 10:28–29] but the son of perdition [6:70–71; 13:11], that the Scripture might be fulfilled [Ps 41:9; cf. John 13:18]. But now I am coming to you." Why Jesus prays for the Father to keep/guard the disciples is that this has been his job during his earthly ministry but now he is going to the Father. He has done a good job too; only one has been lost, the son of perdition (Judas Iscariot). Son of perdition can denote either the person's character (e.g., Ps 57:4 LXX) or the individual's destiny (e.g., Isa 34:5 LXX) or both (they are combined in 2 Thessalonians 2:3 [cf. 2:8]). In the case of Judas, it is likely both (cf. 12:6, character; 3:36, destiny). That one of the disciples is lost does not undermine God's sovereignty in human affairs (cf. 10:28–29) because it is a fulfillment of Scripture (Ps 41:9), i.e., it happened according to the divine plan.

(3) Vv. 14–16 make up unit three. (a) For what Jesus prays comes in v. 15: "I do not pray that you should take them out of the world, but that you should keep them from the evil one" (cf. 1 John 5:19: "the whole world is in the power of the evil one"; but 5:18: God keeps those born of God "and the evil one does not touch them"; 4:4: "for he who is in you is greater than he who is in the world"; and so 2:13, 14: "you have overcome the evil one"). This request is not that the disciples be in the world but not of it, but rather that while they are in the world they be protected from the evil one (cf. Matt 6:13). (b) Why this prayer is made is given in vv. 14, 16: they are not of the world, as Jesus is not of the world, and therefore the world has hated them (cf. 15:18–20). Protection is necessary, given their hostile circumstances due to their difference from the world.

(4) Vv. 17–19 form the fourth unit in Jesus' intercession for his earthly disciples. (a) What Jesus is praying for is given in v. 17: "Sanctify [*hagiason*] them in the truth; thy word is truth." In the LXX, *hagiazeiv* means, in general, to set apart and dedicate a person or thing for the service of God (e.g., a priest, Exod 28:41; a prophet, Jer 1:5; cf. Sirach 45:4; 49:7; 2 Macc. 1:25–26, where "sanctify" and "choose" are used interchangeably) and, in particular, to dedicate a sacrifice (e.g., Exod 13:2; 28:41; 29:1; 40:9; Lev 16:4; Deut 15:19). Here the prayer is that the disciples be set apart for God's service, namely, the service of the truth or God's word (cf. 18:37). (b) Why this request is made is indicated in vv. 18–19: "As you

sent me into the world, so I have sent them into the world [cf. 20:21]. And for their sake I consecrate [*hagiazō*] myself, that they may also be consecrated [*hegiasmenoi*] in truth." Jesus, who was consecrated (*hegiasen*) by the Father and sent into the world (10:36), consecrates (*hagiazō*) himself (i.e., concurs with the Father's decision about him) in order that his disciples may be set apart in a similar way for the service of the truth/ word.

The train of thought has run from the disciples' general need of God's care because Jesus is going to the Father (vv. 9–11a), to their need to be guarded because Jesus, their keeper in the past, is going away (vv. 11b–13), to their need to be protected from the evil one because of the world's hatred of them (vv. 14–16), to their need to be set apart for the service of the truth/word, even as Jesus is (vv. 17–19). Once the intercession for the disciples chosen during Jesus' earthly career is over, Jesus turns his attention to those who will believe because of these first disciples.

John 17:20–23 comprises Jesus' intercession for "those who believe in me through their [the first disciples'] word." It falls into two subunits (vv. 20–21 and vv. 22–23), each with three components. (1) The first subunit consists of these three components: (a) for whom Jesus prays (v. 20); (b) for what he prays (v. 21a); and (c) why he asks for this (v. 21b). (a) Jesus' prays for those who will become his followers through the word of the first disciples (cf. 20:29 for the distinction between those who have seen and believed and those who have believed even though they have not seen). (b) What he is praying for is: "that they may all be one; even as you, Father, are in me and I in you, that they may also be in us." The aim is for a unity made possible by disciples participating in the fellowship of the Father and the Son (1 John 1:3; Eph 4:3–6). (c) Why Jesus prays for this unity is: "so that the world may believe that you have sent me." The unity of believers is aimed at leading the world to faith in Jesus. It has evangelistic goals. This unity is spiritual in that it has a spiritual root (participation in the fellowship of the Father and the Son, v. 21); it is visible insofar as it can be witnessed by the world and lead the world to faith in Jesus. Biblical faith regards human disunity as having a spiritual root (Gen 11, the story of the tower of Babel, implies that human pride lies behind human inability to communicate; Eph 6:12 says that it is the principalities and powers that resist God's saving actions designed to bring unity to the human community). If it has a spiritual root, then it has a spiritual cure (participation in the fellowship of the Father and the Son after having believed in Jesus; cf. Acts 2, where it is the gift of the Holy

Spirit that enables Babel to be reversed; Eph 6:10–20, where it is spiritual warfare that enables the church to resist division).

How can the unity of the disciples function evangelistically? How does the Johannine community confront the world with decision?

> It does so, in part, by being what it is...the community of love is itself a part of the Gospel (147)....
>
> The Johannine community confronted the world not merely with a doctrine or a creed but, as all sectarian groups do, with an alternative society, a counterculture, in which its message of the messiahship of Jesus was realized. It sought to draw people out of the world and into the messianic community, and it did this not only by its words but by *being* that community. (David Rensberger, *Johannine Faith and Liberating Community* [Philadelphia: Westminster, 1988], 147, 150)

(2) The second subunit (vv. 22–23) also consists of three components. (a) V. 22a speaks about the means that enable unity. "The glory which you have given me I have given them." Here glory does not mean honor but rather the divine presence (cf. Exod 24:16). Just as the Father had given Jesus the Holy Spirit without measure (3:34; 1:33), so the glorified Jesus gives his post-Easter disciples the Spirit (7:39; 20:22) to enable them to realize in their life together the fellowship of Father and Son. The perfect tense of "I have given them" (*dedōka*) in v. 22 does not mean that the Jesus who prays is already ascended (cf. v. 13: "these things I speak in the world"). The perfect tense functions here much as a prophetic perfect does in Hebrew, a future event is spoken of as past because of the certainty of its fulfillment (cf. Rom 8:30, where an aorist is used for "glorified" for the same reason, and 2 Cor 5:1, where a present tense for "we have" is used for the same purpose). (b) For what Jesus prays comes in vv. 22b–23a: "that they may be one even as we are one...that they may become perfectly one." It is once again the prayer for unity of believers. Since the Johannine epistles reveal the existence of deep divisions in the Johannine communities, "it is scarcely conceivable that the Evangelist did not have them in mind as he penned the prayer" (G. R. Beasley-Murray, *Word Biblical Commentary: John* [Waco: Word, 1987], 307). (c) Why the intercession for unity is made comes in v. 23b: "so that the world may know that you have sent me and have loved them [the disciples] even as you have loved me." The evangelistic purpose crops up again, this time along with another aim: that the world recognize the disciples as beloved of God just as Jesus is.

John 17:24 is the third part of Jesus' intercession for his disciples, this time both for disciples made during his earthly career and for disciples enlisted by the original witnesses. Whereas the two previous sections of the intercession for disciples have concentrated on the disciples' existence in the world, this part of the prayer focuses on the future, life beyond this world:

> Father, what you have given me, I desire that where I am they also may be with me, in order to behold my glory which you have given me, because you have loved me before the foundation of the world.

What the Father has given Jesus is the whole company of his disciples (10:29). This is for whom he prays (v. 24a). Jesus' intercession for them is that they may be where he is, that is, in the Father's house (14:1–3). This is for what he prays. Why he asks for this thing is so that his disciples may behold his glory (status, i.e., as an only Son) given by the Father who has loved him from before the creation (v. 24c; 1:1–4, 18; 1 John 3:2: "when he appears ... we shall see him as he is").

The prayer's conclusion comes in vv. 25–26, signaled by the address, "O righteous Father." It consists of two components: (a) a recapitulation of Jesus' ministry (vv. 25–26a), and (b) a recommitment by Jesus to this mission and its goal (v. 26b, c). (a) Vv. 25–26a summarize Jesus' mission so far: "The world has not known you [cf. 16:3], but I have known you [cf. 1:18]; and these [disciples] know that you have sent me [v. 8]. I made known to them your name [v. 6]." Jesus is the revealer of God. Unlike the world, the disciples believe in the revealer. He is for them the locus of the divine presence in the world. (b) V. 26b, c verbalizes Jesus' continuing commitment to his mission: "and I will make it [God's name] known, that the love with which you have loved me may be in them, and I in them." Jesus' continued commitment to the task of revealer will be worked out both in his glorification (cf. 18:6, 8; 19:30; chaps. 20–21) and in his sending the Paraclete (14:25–26; 16:13–14).

Because the Fourth Gospel and 1, 2 John do not use the term *"ekklēsia/ church"* (3 John 6, 9, 10 does; as does Rev 1:4, 11, 20; 2:1, 7, 8, 11, 12, 17, 18, 23, 29; 3:1, 6, 7, 13, 14, 22; 22:16), the question is sometimes raised: what is the concept of the church in the Johannine writings? (1) It is spoken of, not in terms of the Greek assembly, but in terms of a flock (10:1–30) or a vine (15:1–6). As such, it is viewed as the community attached to Jesus. Viewed from the divine side, this community is composed of those whom the Father has given Jesus out of the world (6:37, 65; 10:29; 17:6), whom Jesus has chosen (15:16) or drawn to himself (12:32), and who have been preserved by Jesus and the Father (6:39; 10:28–29; 17:12). From the human side, it is comprised of those who believe in Jesus (3:16, 36; 4:39; 9:38; 11:48; 20:30–31; cf. 1 John 5:13), abide in Jesus (15:4), and know that Jesus came from the Father (17:8).

(2) This community has a worship, a creed, a ministry, and a mission. (a) Its worship, which supersedes traditional Jewish worship, is in the Spirit (4:24) and involves the Spirit of prophecy, the Paraclete (14:16–17; 14:26; 15:26–27; 16:7–11; 16:13–15). The Eucharist is central (6:51–58); baptism is practiced (3:5; 4:1–2; 13:10). (b) Its creed is "Jesus is the Christ, the Son of God" (20:31; cf. 1 John 4:15: "Jesus is the Son of God"; 2 John 7: "Jesus Christ has come in the flesh"). (c) Its ministry is not entirely clear. It does, however, include prophets (1 John 4:1–2), elders understood in the sense of mediators of the eyewitness tradition (2, 3 John; 1 John 1:1–5; cf. Acts 20:17ff), and an eyewitness guarantor of the Jesus tradition, the beloved disciple (21:24). (d) Its mission is grounded in that of Jesus (4:31–38; 17:18; 20:21). As such, it is directed toward the world (1:29; 12:46; 3:16–17; 12:47; 6:33; 12:20–23; 7:35).

(3) The marks of the Johannine community are unity, universality, holiness, and apostolicity. (a) The unity of the community is central (17:11, 20, 23). (b) Universality is assumed (4:39–42; 10:16; 11:52; 12:20–24; 12:32; 21:11). (c) Holiness is understood in terms of love of one another (13:33–34; 1 John 3:11, 14, 16). (d) Apostolicity is involved because the normative tradition comes from the eyewitnesses (1 John 1:1–5) and the foundation document of the community is rooted in the tradition of an eyewitness (21:24). To progress beyond the christological core of the eyewitness tradition is to remove oneself from fellowship with the Father and the Son (2 John 9) and from fellowship with the community in fellowship with the eyewitnesses (2 John 10–11; 1 John 2:19).

THE ENTHRONED KING

John 18–19

The one who came as revealing, empowering presence (1:1–18), who picked/produced a new community (1:19–2:12) and provided them during his public ministry with warrants for a different kind of worship (2:13–11:54), and who privately predicted what their future would be like, offering promise, parenesis, and prayer for that time (13:31–17:26), now proceeds to make provision for their community life, worship, and ministry before he returns finally to whence he has come (chaps. 18–21).

The Passion Narrative in the Fourth Gospel consists of two large thought units: (1) chapters 18–19, and (2) chapters 20–21. The first focuses on Jesus' arrest, trials, crucifixion, and burial; the second on his resurrection. John 18–19, the first, is a large thought unit held together by an inclusion: Jesus in a garden (18:1, *hopou en kēpos;* 19:41, *en...hopou...kēpos*). It falls into three carefully constructed parts: (a) the arrest (18:1–12); (b) the trials (18:13–19:16); and (c) the death of Jesus (19:17–42). Each must be examined in order.

The arrest of Jesus (18:1–12) is told in a distinctively Johannine way that concentrates on a cluster of christological emphases encountered already in the Gospel. The unit falls into a concentric pattern.

A   vv. 1–3: A band of soldiers and officers come for Jesus.

   B   vv. 4–8a: Jesus' willingness to be taken

      C   vv. 8b–9: Jesus' concern for his disciples

   B′   vv. 10–11: Jesus' willingness to be taken

A′   v. 12: A band of soldiers and officers seize Jesus.

A, vv. 1–3, sets the stage. After the prayer of chapter 17, Jesus crosses the Kidron valley and goes to a garden where he often met with his disciples (Lk 22:39, "as was his custom"), a place known therefore to Judas. Judas secures a troop to arrest Jesus made up of two groups: (1) a band of soldiers (Romans; cf. 18:12, their captain, *chiliarchos*), and (2) the servants of the chief priests and Pharisees (cf. 7:32, 45). Jesus will be confronted

232

in the garden by representatives of the entire unbelieving world, Gentile and Jew (1:10–11; cf. Acts 4:25–28). This troop comes to the garden with "lanterns and torches and weapons." Such a military column would have been visible from a great distance, allowing anyone sought by them to flee. That Jesus does not flee points to his free choice in the matter (cf. 10:17–18; 12:27).

B, vv. 4–8a, focuses on three characteristics of the Johannine Jesus. There is first of all his prophetic knowledge: "Then Jesus, knowing all that was to befall him" (cf. knowledge of others, 1:47–48; 2:24; 4:17–19; 6:15; knowledge of the mind of God, 1:18; 5:20; 6:46; 11:41–42; knowledge of the future, 6:64; 7:8; 12:27; 13:1, 11, 21, 38; 16:2–4). Second, there is Jesus' initiative in the events of his passion: "Then Jesus . . . came forward and said to them, 'Whom do you seek?' They answered him, 'Jesus of Nazareth.' Jesus said to them, 'I am he.'" Judas, who in Mark 14:43–46 takes the initiative in Jesus' arrest, in John simply stands by with the troop as Jesus takes the initiative. As Jesus in 10:17–18 has said: "I lay down my life. . . . No one takes it from me, but I lay it down of my own accord. I have power to lay it down."

Third, there is the numinous quality of Jesus' presence: "When he said to them, 'I am he' [*egō eimi*], they drew back and fell to the ground." The *egō eimi* in 18:5 is, at the first level of meaning, properly translated "I am he," but the reaction of the troop indicates that more is involved. The falling down is a normal accompaniment of a theophany (e.g., Dan 10:9; Acts 9:4; 22:7; 26:14; Rev 1:17). This would argue that *egō eimi* here functions also as it does in 8:58, as the name of God (remember 17:6). Several parallels cast light on the matter: (a) The pre-Christian Jewish apologist Artapanus (Eusebius, *Preparation for the Gospel* 9.27) tells how the Egyptian Pharaoh fell as if dead when Moses uttered the name of God in his ear. (b) Rabbinic sources say that in the special ritual on the Day of Atonement when the High Priest spoke the name of God, the priests standing near him fell on their faces (b. Kiddushin 71a; j. Yoma 3.40d; *Ecclesiastes Rabbah* 3.11.3). (c) *Genesis Rabbah* 91:6 tells how when seventy Egyptians are sent to arrest Simeon, they fall on their faces and gnash their teeth as soon as they hear his voice. (d) The Pseudo-Clementine *Homilies*, 2.24, give an account of the rivalry between Dositheus and Simon for the leadership of the Baptist sect. When Dositheus hears the words "I am (he)" from Simon, he falls down and worships. If the Johannine Jesus knows what is to happen and takes the initiative to set events in motion, he speaks as the one who reveals God's name. So awesome is his presence that he must again take the initiative and ask, "Whom do you seek?" When they answer, "Jesus of Nazareth," he says again, "I told you that I am he." It is as though he must give permission before they can take him.

C, vv. 8b–9, concentrates on Jesus' concern for his disciples: " 'If you seek me, let these men go.' (This was to fulfill the word which he had spoken, 'Of those whom you gave me I lost not one' [17:12])." Here the word of 13:1 is being worked out: "having loved his own who were in the world, he loved them to the end." In John, instead of the disciples forsaking him and fleeing (Mk 14:50), Jesus dismisses them out of concern for their safety.

B', vv. 10–11, returns to the theme of Jesus' willingness to be taken. Peter draws his sword and cuts off the right ear (Lk 22:50) of Malchus, the high priest's slave. Jesus responds: "Put your sword into its sheath [18:36; cf. Matt 26:52]; shall I not drink the cup [cf. Mk 10:38–39; 14:36] which the Father has given me?" His willingness to be taken is due to his obedience to the Father (cf. 12:27–28a; 5:19, 30; 8:28; 12:50).

A', v. 12, concludes the scene of the arrest: "The band of soldiers and their captain and the officers of the Jews seized Jesus and bound him." From the preceding paragraph, however, the reader knows that Jesus has not been seized against his will; he has surrendered himself in accordance with his Father's will.

The trials of Jesus (18:13–19:16) are likewise told in a distinctively Johannine way. In Mark the Jewish trial is twofold (first, at night before the high priest [14:53] with all the chief priests, elders, and scribes assembled; second, in the morning before the whole council [15:1]). In John the Jewish examination is also twofold but does not include any appearance before the council (first, at night before Annas, the father-in-law of Caiaphas [18:13]; second, at night [18:28] before Caiaphas [18:24]). In Mark the issues center on the Temple (14:56), christology (14:61–62), and blasphemy (14:64), all at the first trial. In Luke the appearance before the council is concerned with the question of christology (22:67–71). In John the questions in the appearance before Annas focus on Jesus' disciples and his teaching (18:19). The Jewish interrogation in John falls into two parts: before Annas (18:13–23) and before Caiaphas (18:24–28a).

Only the examination before Annas (vv. 13–23) contains any details. The arresting troop bring Jesus to Annas, the father-in-law of Caiaphas, who was high priest that memorable year (v. 13) and who had made the prophecy that it was expedient that one man should die for the people (11:49–52). Annas had been installed as high priest in 6 C.E. by Quirinus; he was deposed in 15 C.E. by Valerius Gratus (so Josephus, *Antiquities*

18.2.1, 2 §26, 34). Since all five of his sons eventually succeeded him as high priest (so Josephus, *Antiquities* 20.9.1 §198), as did his son-in-law, Caiaphas (Lk 3:2), who was high priest from 18 to 36 C.E., Annas must have remained the power behind the throne. This may explain the troop's action.

Although Jewish court procedure normally consisted in hearing witnesses (cf. Susanna; m. Sanhedrin 5), the high priest (Annas; cf. Acts 4:6, where Annas is called high priest even though he was not officially) questions Jesus (cf. 7:51; m. Sanhedrin 5:4). The questions concern Jesus' disciples (cf. 11:48, which would indicate the concern is about their number because of the danger that a sizeable group would provoke Rome [cf. 11:48]) and his teaching (since a false prophet secretly entices the people to lead them astray [cf. 7:12: "he leads the people astray"; b. Sanhedrin 43a: "he beguiled and led Israel astray"; Justin, *Trypho* 69: "they dared to call him a magician and a deceiver of the people"]).

Jesus' response does not deal with his disciples because, out of his concern, he has already dismissed them (18:8–9). Rather it focuses first on the public character of his teaching: "I have always taught in synagogues [e.g., 6:59] and in the Temple [e.g., 2:16; 7:14; 10:22], where all Jews come together; I have said nothing secretly." He then calls for witnesses who heard him to be produced: "Why do you ask me? Ask those who have heard me what I said to them; they know what I said." In effect, he asks for a just hearing to determine whether or not he is a false prophet. His demand is met with violence. "One of the officers standing by struck Jesus with his hand, saying, 'Is this how you answer the high priest?'" (v. 22). Jesus' answer pronounces judgment upon the judges: "If I have spoken wrongly, bear witness to the wrong; but if I have spoken rightly, why do you strike me?" (cf. Acts 23:3). The issues dealt with by Annas are two that have surfaced earlier in the Gospel's narrative: (a) Are Jesus' disciples a large enough body to provoke Roman intervention (11:48)? and (b) Is Jesus a false prophet who is secretly leading Israel astray (chaps. 7–8)? Annas then sends him bound to Caiaphas the high priest (v. 24). Nothing is recorded in John about the content of this examination.

While the questioning of Jesus proceeds in John's narrative, yet another examination takes place, that of Peter (vv. 15–18, 25–27). Two disciples follow Jesus to Annas's quarters, Peter and "another" (so P66, Vaticanus, Sinaiticus, etc.; "the other," so the Byzantine family and many others) disciple (v. 15). The textual variant shows that from an early date "another disciple" was identified with the beloved disciple (cf. also the Gospel of the Hebrews, which says John — who is taken to be the beloved disciple — used to supply fish to the High Priest's court, when he worked for Zebedee). While the identification with the beloved disciple is not certain, it is probable.

This other disciple, who is known to the high priest, gets Peter admitted to the courtyard. There Peter faces questions from three quarters: (a) The maid who admitted him asks: "Are not you also one of this man's disciples?" (v. 17). (b) The servants and officers standing with Peter before the charcoal fire ask him: "Are not you also one of his disciples?" (v. 25). (c) A kinsman of Malchus, whose ear Peter had cut off, asks: "Did I not see you in the garden with him?" (v. 26). Three questions meet with three denials. And then the cock crowed (v. 27), fulfilling Jesus' prophecy in 13:38: "Will you lay down your life for me? Truly, truly, I say to you, the cock will not crow, till you have denied me three times." Peter has tried to follow Jesus now (13:37; 18:15); he has attempted to lay down his life for Jesus (13:37; 18:10); but in the pressure of the moment, he denies Jesus. He will not be able to do otherwise until Jesus has been glorified and the Holy Spirit has been given to him (7:39; 20:22). Jesus has soteriological priority (remember 13:36–14:14; 15:1–17).

The trial before Pilate (18:28–19:16) follows. It takes place at the praetorium (18:28), either Herod's old palace near the Jaffa gate or the fortress of Antonia (the remains of which lie under the convent of the Sisters of Zion on the Via Dolorosa). There are indications that on occasion the procurators were in residence in the Antonia (e.g., Josephus, *War* 5.5.8 §244; 2.12.1 §224–27; *Antiquities* 20.5.3 §106–12). The major drawback of the Antonia location is that the pavement at the Zion convent dates from the time of Hadrian. In support of Herod's palace is the fact that this palace was used by the procurators (e.g., Josephus, *War* 2.14.8 §301, tells how the procurator Florus [64–66 C.E.] came from Caesarea, lodged at the palace, and set up his judgment seat [*bēma*] in front of the building. In 2.16.5 §403–404, Antonia is clearly distinguished from the palace. Philo, *Embassy to Gaius* 38:299 and 39:306, tell how Pilate set up golden shields in the palace of Herod. In this connection, he calls Herod's palace the residence of the procurators. Mk 15:16 uses *aulē*, not *praitorion*. Josephus uses *aulē* for the palace that Herod built in 23 B.C.E. but never for the fortress Antonia.). The evidence seems to favor Herod's palace, although due to lack of excavation the pavement (19:13) has never been discovered (cf. *RevBib* 59 [1952]: 513–50, for arguments by Vincent for Antonia and Benoit for Herod's palace).

When the Jews bring Jesus to the praetorium it is early (the time when Roman civil servants took up their office duties, e.g., Seneca, *De tra* 2.7.3). They did not enter the praetorium so that they might not be defiled ("The dwelling places of Gentiles are unclean," m. Oholoth 18:7), but might eat the Passover on the morrow (v. 28). This fact sets the stage for the manner in which the trial before Pilate is carried out in 18:29–19:15. The section is arranged in a concentric pattern, alternating between outside and inside the praetorium (A. Janssens de Varebeke, "La structure des scenes du récit de la passion en Joh., 18–19," *ETL* 38 [1962]: 504–22):

> A 18:29–32: Outside — Jews demand Jesus' death.
>
> > B 8:33–38a: Inside — Pilate questions Jesus about kingship.
> >
> > > C 8:38b–40: Outside — Pilate finds Jesus not guilty.
> > >
> > > > D 9:1–3: Inside — Soldiers scourge and mock Jesus.
> > >
> > > C′ 19:4–8: Outside — Pilate finds Jesus not guilty.
> >
> > B′ 9:9–11: Inside — Pilate talks with Jesus about power.
>
> A′ 9:12–15: Outside — Pilate attempts to release Jesus, but the Jews demand Jesus' death.

A, vv. 29–32, has Pilate (Philo, *Embassy to Gaius* 38; Josephus, *Antiquities* 18.3.1–2 §55–62; 18.4.2 §88–89; Tacitus, *Annals* 15:44; an inscription discovered in the Herodian theater in Caesarea calls Pilate "prefect of Judea") go outside to the Jews and ask: "What accusation do you bring against this man?" For them, to bring a specific charge is not necessary: "If this man were not an evildoer, we would not have handed him over." Pilate is satisfied that they can handle the matter: "Take him yourselves and judge him by your own law." All this is prelude to what is revealed in the Jews' response: "It is not lawful for us to put any man to death." The ones who had long been seeking Jesus' death (7:20; 8:40, 44, 59; 10:31; 11:8, 16, 50) now ask Pilate to do the deed. Since this would be by crucifixion instead of stoning, it fulfills the word Jesus had spoken about what death he was to die (12:33: "when I am lifted up from the earth"). Except for certain specified cases (e.g., if Gentiles entered the Temple's inner courts, they could be executed; cf. Josephus, *War* 6.2.4 §124–26; 5.5.2 §193–94), the power of execution seems to have resided with Rome. The stoning of Stephen (Acts 7) was a mob action; the martyrdom of James, the brother of Jesus, was due to a high priest exceeding his authority, for which he was deposed (Josephus, *Antiquities* 20.9.1 §200–203). Neither was a lawful execution.

B, 18:33–38a, moves inside for Pilate's questioning of Jesus. Roman court procedures called for a detailed examination of the accused. So Pilate asks Jesus: "Are you the King of the Jews?" (v. 33). Since Herod the Great had held the title (Josephus, *Antiquities* 14.14.4 §385), Pilate's question focuses on Jesus' political claims and aspirations. After a verbal skirmish (Jesus: "Did others say this to you about me?"; Pilate: "Your own nation and the chief priests have handed you over to me"), Pilate asks again: "What have you done?" (v. 35). Jesus' answer in v. 36 indicates that he poses no military threat to Rome:

> My kingship is not of [*ek*] this world; if my kingship were of this world, my servants would fight, that I might not be handed over to the Jews; but my kingship is not from here [*enteuthen*].

The origins of Jesus' kingship are not of this world (3:31; 8:23; 16:28); therefore, his is not a rebellion to be fought with weapons or worldly means (cf. 18:10–11).

A similar encounter is known from the end of the first century (Eusebius, *Church History* 3.20). The emperor Domitian examined two descendants of Jesus' family. He asked them about the Christ and his kingdom, its nature, origin, and time of appearance. They explained that "it was neither of the world nor earthly, but heavenly and angelic, and it would be at the end of the world, when he would come in glory to judge the living and the dead and to reward every man according to his deeds." Domitian then despised them as simple folk and dismissed them. The procurator, Pilate, will have a similar reaction (v. 38), but first he needs clarification.

Pilate says: "So you are a king?" (v. 37). Jesus responds: "You say that I am a king" (i.e., you are the one who has chosen the categories of kingship). Jesus then explains himself in his own categories: "For this I was born, and for this I have come into the world, to bear witness to the truth" (i.e., the category I am comfortable with is witness to the truth). Truth here, as elsewhere in the Fourth Gospel, means something like "the divine plan of salvation" (Ignace de la Potterie, "The Truth in Saint John," in *The Interpretation of John*, ed. John Ashton [Philadelphia: Fortress, 1986], 53–66). Jesus' self-interpretation is that of witness to God's plan of salvation (truth). There is also an invitation to Pilate: "Every one who is of the truth hears my voice" (v. 37b; cf. 10:4, 14, 27). Pilate brushes it off as irrelevant: "What is truth?" (v. 38a; cf. Acts 26:28).

C, vv. 38b–40, has Pilate come outside after examining Jesus to tell them his findings: "I find no crime in him" (Lk 23:4). Like Domitian at a later time, Pilate does not find matters of eternal salvation politically threatening. Therefore, he offers the Jews a way to secure Jesus' release: "You have a custom that I should release one man for you at the Passover; will you have me release for you the King of the Jews?" (v. 39)?.That on occasion prisoners were released by the Romans in Jerusalem at Passover is not open to doubt (Josephus, *Antiquities* 20.9.3 §209); that it was a custom is at least a possibility (if one accepts the interpretation of m. Pesahim 8:6 and b. Pesahim 91a offered by C. B. Chavel, "The Releasing of a Prisoner on the Eve of Passover in Ancient Jerusalem," *JBL* 60 [1941]: 273–78, whose argument is endorsed by Rudolf Schnackenburg, *The Gospel according to St. John* [New York: Seabury, 1980], 3:252). The point is that there is a procedural way to release an innocent man. The Jewish reply is: "Not this man, but Barabbas" (v. 40). The Evangelist adds: "Now Barabbas was a robber" (*lēstēs*; Josephus uses the term for the Zealots; Mk 15:7 says Barabbas had committed murder in the insurrection). Confronted with a choice between the witness to the truth and a criminal, the Jews prefer Barabbas (= Son of the Father). Irony reigns.

D, 19:1–3, moves back inside the praetorium. Frustrated by Jewish rejection of his attempt to release Jesus by means of the Passover custom (18:39), Pilate tries another tack. He will scourge him (19:1) and ridicule him (19:2–3). The scourging could be either a further attempt to obtain a confession (as in Acts 22:24; cf. John 19:4b) or a lesser punishment than crucifixion and a substitute for it (as in Lk 23:16, 22; note that in John 19:1–3 there are no questions put to Jesus). In John's plot, it is probably the latter. The ridicule takes the form of treating Jesus as a mock-king. He is arrayed in a purple robe, crowned with a crown of thorns, which is an imitation of the radiate crown of divine rulers, acclaimed "King of the Jews," and struck with the soldiers hands (cf. Isa 50:6). It all adds up to Roman ridicule of a Jewish claimant to royalty.

C', 19:4–8, shifts the scene back outside. Jesus comes out, wearing the crown of thorns and the purple robe and probably covered with blood from his scourging, a pitiful sight held up to ridicule for all to see. "Here is the man," Pilate proclaims. His kingship is a farce; he is no threat. Pilate can let him go. But no. The chief priests and officers cry out: "Crucify him, crucify him." Put out, Pilate attempts to transfer responsibility to the Jews: "Take him yourselves and crucify him, for I find no crime in him" (remember 18:38b). The Jews respond to Pilate's proclamation of Jesus' innocence: "We have a law, and by that law he ought to die, because he made himself the Son of God" (v. 7; cf. 5:18; 8:59; 10:33, 36; Lev 24:16: "the one who blasphemes the name of the Lord shall be put to death").

The Jewish claim that Jesus made himself the Son of God is the key to what follows in the story. Vv. 8–12a are shaped in the form of Mediterranean stories that deal with a numinous figure's encounter with a representative of state power (e.g., in Philostratus, *Life of Apollonius of Tyana* 4.44, the Roman official, Tigellinus, examines Apollonius after his arrest, concludes from the conversation that the philosopher is supernatural, and, to avoid fighting with the gods, frees him). Vv. 7–8 begin the incident. Upon hearing that the one arrested may be a Son of God, Pilate is afraid.

B', vv. 9–11, returns to inside the praetorium and allows Pilate a chance to probe Jesus' identity further. He asks Jesus: "Where are you from?" Jesus is silent. Exasperated, Pilate says: "Will you not speak to me? Do you not know that I have power to release you, and power to crucify you?" Jesus replies: "You would have no power over me unless it had been given you from above; therefore he who delivered me to you has the greater sin" (v. 11). Two things stand out: (a) If Jesus has been brought to Pilate, it is because God wills it. Only when Jesus' hour has come can he be taken (7:8, 30, 44; 8:20, 59; 10:39; 13:1; 18:4–11). Although this is the primary meaning of v. 11a, it is not improper to infer also that what applies to Jesus in particular at this moment would be heard by the Fourth Gospel's readers as generally true about the relation of Christians and the State. The State and its rulers have power only because God has given it (cf. Rom 13:1; Prov 8:15–16; Dan 2:37; 4:17, 32; 5:18; Jer 27:5; Wisdom of Solomon 6:1–3). (b) There are degrees of guilt. The one who delivered Jesus to Pilate (Caiaphas, 18:28; 11:49–50) has the greater sin (cf. 9:41).

A', vv. 12–15, moves back outside the praetorium. V. 12 completes the conventional form of "numinous man encounters ruler" that began in v. 7b. "Upon this [i.e., because of Jesus' words] Pilate sought to release him." The tradition limited the Johannine use of the conventional form. Jesus was not released as Apollonius was, but the procurator wanted to and tried to release him because of his words (cf. 7:46). The Jews, however, hold the trump card to all Pilate's maneuvering. "If you release this man, you are not Caesar's friend; everyone who makes himself a king sets himself against Caesar." Since Pilate's position rests precariously upon the emperor's goodwill, the question of the procurator's loyalty does the trick. He will pronounce sentence.

Several acts are involved in preparation for pronouncing judgment: (a) Pilate brings Jesus out (v. 13). (b) Pilate either sits down himself or sets Jesus upon the judgment seat at a place called The Pavement (v. 13). The verb in Greek (*kathisen*) can be either transitive (Pilate made Jesus sit on the judgment seat) or intransitive (Pilate himself sits on the judgment seat). Two early Christian sources take it as transitive (The Gospel of Peter 7 reads: "And they clothed him with purple, and set him on the seat of judgment, saying, 'Judge righteously, King of Israel' "; Justin, *1 Apology* 35: "They tormented him, and set him on the judgment seat, and said, 'Judge us' "). If one reads this way, Jesus is portrayed here as judge, as he has been depicted as king. Although in John Jesus does function as judge (5:22), in the context of the Roman trial he is exclusively king (18:33, 36, 37, 39; 19:3, 5, 12, 15, 19). Moreover, in 12:14 where the verb is also used, it is intransitive (Jesus sits upon the animal). Probably v. 13 should be understood to refer to Pilate's sitting upon the judgment seat, in preparation for pronouncing judgment upon Jesus.

(c) A final questioning of the accusers to determine their precise position takes place. Pilate says to the Jews: "Here is your King" (v. 14). The question is implicit in the proclamation. What shall I do with him? They cry: "Away with him, crucify him." Such a response is incredible, so Pilate asks: "Shall I crucify your King?" The chief priests answer: "We have no king but Caesar" (v. 15). The official representatives of Judaism, the chief priests, not only disavow Jesus but also proclaim their loyalty to Caesar who is otherwise offensive to them on religious grounds. Their words drip with irony. Instead of "May you be our King, you alone" (= eleventh benediction, Eighteen Benedictions), or "From everlasting to everlasting you are God; beside you we have no king, redeemer, or savior, no liberator, deliverer, provider, none who takes pity in every time of distress and trouble; we have no king but you" (= the hymn sung at the conclusion of the Greater Hallel by the high priests as part of the Passover Haggadah), Judaism's priestly leadership confesses, "We have no king but Caesar."
(d) Preliminaries completed, sentence is pronounced: "He handed him over to them to be crucified" (v. 16). Who is "them"? From the context, it must be the chief priests who are mentioned in v. 15b (cf. 19:6: "Take him yourselves and crucify him").

The Evangelist notes the time in v. 14: "now it was the day of Preparation of the Passover [cf. b. Sanhedrin 43a: Jesus was hanged on the eve of Passover; the Quartodeciman practice of the church in Asia apparently was associated with the belief that Jesus suffered on Nisan 14, and was based not on an appeal to the Fourth Gospel but on the uninterrupted tradition derived from the fathers of their church (so Eusebius, *Church History* 5.24.1–7, 16)]; it was about the sixth hour." At the very time that the sacrifice of the Passover lambs begins (Exod 12:5–6), the Lamb of God (1:29, 36; 12:1–11 [cf. Exod 12:3]) is sentenced to die.

Jesus' crucifixion, death, and burial are narrated in 19:17–42. The material falls into two blocks, each with five components, according to the pattern ABCDE:A' B' C' D' E'.

A vv. 17–22: The Jews' act and request of Pilate

  B vv. 23–25a: The soldiers' act

    C vv. 25b–27: The presence of the beloved disciple and others

      D vv. 28–29: The act of Jesus' loved ones

        E v. 30: Jesus' death

  A' v. 31: The Jews' request of Pilate so they could act

    B' vv. 32–34: The soldiers' acts

      C' vv. 35–37: The presence of the beloved disciple

        D' vv. 38–40: The acts of his friends for Jesus

          E' vv. 41–42: Jesus' burial

A, vv. 17–22, has the chief priests take Jesus ("them" in v. 17 is the same as in v. 16). Responsibility from 11:49–50 on is placed on the chief priests (cf. 18:3, 10, 13–14, 15, 19, 24, 35; 19:6, 15); 11 Q Temple 64:6–13, moreover, indicates that in early Judaism the death penalty by crucifixion could be found in Deuteronomy 21:22–23, implying that this death penalty was not used only by Romans (O. Betz, "The Temple Scroll and the Trial of Jesus," *SwJournTheol* 30 [1988]: 5–8). Just as Jesus' disciples will experience persecution and death at Jewish hands (16:2), so the Master himself is already the object of such hate (15:18; cf. 1 Thes 2:15). Jesus, however, still has the initiative: "he went out, bearing his own cross" (v. 17; Plutarch, *Divine Vengeance*, 554 A/B, says: "Each criminal as part of his punishment carries his cross on his back"). Mark 15:21 says Simon of Cyrene was compelled to carry his cross for him; Luke 23:26 says Simon carried the cross behind Jesus. Certain Gnostic groups, desirous of having the Savior avoid any suffering, contended that Simon of Cyrene was crucified in Jesus' place (Basilides, so Irenaeus, *Against Heresies* 1.24.3–6: Simon of Cyrene was crucified; Jesus, assuming the form of Simon stood by and laughed at them; *Second Treatise of the Great Seth* 7.56: Simon was crucified instead of Jesus). In addition to the emphasis on Jesus' initiative, it is possible that the Fourth Gospel's omission of any reference to Simon of Cyrene would have been heard by early Christians as an attempt to avoid any hint that Jesus himself possibly did not suffer (remember 1 John 5:6–8).

They (the same "they" as in vv. 16–17? Cf. v. 23, the soldiers crucified Jesus, but on whose authority? Remember 18:3; cf. Acts 2:23: "you [Jews] crucified and killed by the hands of lawless men [Romans]") crucify Jesus with two others, one on either side (v. 18), near the city (v. 20) at Golgotha. Tradition that goes back at least to the time of Constantine locates the spot at the site of the current Church of the Holy Sepulchre (Eusebius, *Life of Constantine* 3.26, and *Onomasticon*; the Bordeaux Pilgrim [333 C.E.]; Cyril of Alexandria, *Catechetical Lectures* 4:10, 14; 10:19; 13:23; the pilgrim Aetheria [385 C.E.]).

Pilate writes a title (*titlos*) and puts it on the cross. The Romans are involved in more than the sentencing. According to Roman custom, such a sign was carried in front of the condemned one or put around his neck (Suetonius, *Caligula* 32, and *Domitian* 10); at the crucifixion, it could be attached to the cross as a warning to others to avoid his crime. Pilate's sign reads: "Jesus of Nazareth, the King of the Jews." It is written in Hebrew, Latin, and Greek, a universal message for all to see (cf. 11:52; 12:19, 20–23; Josephus, *War* 5.5.2 §194, says the warnings against Gentile encroachment in the Temple were in Greek and Latin; Julius Capitolinus, a fourth-century biographer, says that when the emperor Gordianus Pius was murdered in Persia, the soldiers erected a sepulcher for him and added a *titulus* in Greek, Latin, Persian, Aramaic, and Egyptian to be read by all). The chief priests object: "Do not write, 'The King of the Jews,' but 'This man said, I am King of the Jews.'" Pilate's response is his first firm stance of the day: "What I have written, I have written" (i.e., there will be no changes). Jesus' cross becomes his throne, his crucifixion his enthronement as king, his being lifted up the occasion for a universal proclamation of his kingship.

B, vv. 23–25a, focuses on actions taken by the soldiers who had crucified Jesus (cf. 18:3, 12, where they may be Romans but are under Jewish direction). It was customary for the soldiers to take the clothing of the one crucified, as spoils. (a) Jesus' garments, except for his tunic (undergarment), are divided into four parts, one for each soldier. (b) Since the tunic was without seam, woven from top to bottom, rather than divide it, the soldiers cast lots to see whose it will be. This act, the Evangelist says, is to fulfill Scripture (cf. 13:18; 17:12; 19:36): "They parted my garments among them, and for my clothing they cast lots." Ps 22:18's parallelism is taken by the Fourth Evangelist to refer to two acts: first, dividing the garments and, second, casting lots for the clothing (cf. Matt 21:4–7 for a similar procedure). If an act fulfills Scripture, it happens within the overall plan of God.

C, vv. 25b–27, turns its attention to the presence of loved ones at the cross. (a) There are certain women present. How many is uncertain. There could be two, three, or four. Probably there are two groups of two each: Jesus' mother and her sister; Mary the wife of Clopas and Mary Magdalene (v. 25b). (b) The beloved disciple is also there (v. 26). Jesus first of all acts on their behalf. When the crucified Jesus sees his mother and the beloved disciple, he says to his mother: "Woman, behold your son." Then he says to the beloved disciple: "Behold your mother." The Evangelist adds: "And from that hour the disciple took her to his home" (v. 27). The story is told from the point of view that the beloved disciple takes responsibility for Jesus' mother, not vice versa. The language is that of binding agreements (cf. Tobit 7:11–12). (a) The motif of Jesus having the initiative continues. Even from the cross he takes responsibility for his own (cf. 1 Tim 5:8, 4b). He loves them to the end (13:1). (b) That he speaks to both his mother and the beloved disciple from the cross guarantees that the Jesus who is crucified is the same one who has already been encountered in 2:1–11 and 13:23–25. The anti-docetic implications are real. The Incarnation continues through the crucifixion (remember 1 John 4:1–2; 5:6–8; 1:1–2).

D, vv. 28–29, allows those present at the cross to do something for Jesus. "Knowing that all was finished [*tetelestai;* cf. 13:1, *eis telos*]," Jesus says, "I thirst" (in order that the Scripture might be fulfilled [*teleiōthē*], i.e., Ps 69:21). Three Johannine emphases appear in a cluster. (a) Jesus' knowledge again comes to the fore (cf.18:4; 16:4; 13:1; 12:23). He knows the place of what happens to him within God's plan. (b) He thirsts as a truly human being would (cf. 4:6–7; 11:33–38; 12:27; 13:21). Again, an anti-docetic note is heard. (c) What happens fulfills Scripture (19:24; 18:9; 17:12; 13:18), indicating that it is according to the divine plan. "A bowl full of vinegar stood there [probably the soldier's]; so they [the loved ones of vv. 25b–26] put a sponge full of vinegar [because the soldier would not want to use his bowl for such a purpose] on hyssop [a small bushy plant used in connection with the Passover; cf. Exod 12:22] and held it to his mouth [because the cross need not have been that much higher than those who stood on ground level]." In this way his loved ones sought to quench his thirst (cf. Prov 31:6).

E, v. 30, records his death. "When Jesus had received the vinegar, he said: 'It is finished' [*tetelestai*]; and he bowed his head and gave up his [human] spirit." Two Johannine themes recur. (a) Jesus finishes the Father's work (cf. 4:34: "My food is to do the will of my Father, and to accomplish [*teleiōsō*] his work"; 17:4: "I glorified you on earth, having accomplished [*teleiōsas*] the work which you gave me to do"). (b) Jesus has the initiative; he gives up his life (cf. 10:18: "I lay down my life. . . . No one takes it from me, but I lay it down of my own accord").

A′, v. 31, gives yet another Jewish request of Pilate (remember v. 21). They ask Pilate to have the legs of those crucified broken (so they would suffocate and die), so that they might be taken away. Although the usual Roman practice was to leave a corpse on a cross (with exceptions, so Philo, *Flaccus* 83), it was contrary to Deuteronomic law that dead bodies of criminals should remain on the cross after sunset (Deut 21:23; Josh 8:29; 10:27). Accordingly, "Jews used to take so much care of the burial of men, that they took down those that were condemned and crucified, and buried them before the going down of the sun" (Josephus, *War* 4.5.2 §317). Since it is the Day of Preparation for Passover, and since on the morrow Passover and the sabbath will coincide, it is perceived by the Jews as especially important that the bodies not be left on the crosses.

B′, vv. 32–34, narrates the soldiers' actions: (a) They broke the legs of the two crucified with Jesus, but seeing he was already dead, they did not break the legs of Jesus (vv. 32–33). The Evangelist sees the events as a fulfillment of Scripture: "Not a bone of him shall be broken" (v. 36; cf. Exod 12:46; Num 9:12, of the Passover lamb [cf. 1:29, 36; 18:28; 19:14]; Ps 34:20, of the righteous man [cf. 19:24, from Ps 22:18; 19:28, from Ps 69:21; 1 John 2:1]). The plan of God is being carried out. In this identification of Jesus, in his death, with the Passover lamb, John is one with Paul (1 Cor 5:7). In the Fourth Gospel, to say that Jesus dies as the true Passover lamb is to continue the theme from the public ministry: Jesus supersedes the Jewish Passover (remember chap. 6; Rudolf Bultmann, *The Gospel of John* [Philadelphia: Westminster, 1971], 697, n. 1).

(b) One of the soldiers pierced Jesus' side with a spear, a thrust doubtless aimed at Jesus' heart to be sure of his death (Quintilian, *Declamationes maiores* 6.9): "and at once there came out blood and water" (v. 34b). The reference to the discharge of blood and water would be heard by Mediterranean readers as a testimony to the real humanity of the crucified one. Several parallels confirm the point. First, the *Iliad* 5.340–41 says that from a goddess, wounded with a lance, "blood-water" alone issued forth instead of blood and water, because gods who neither eat bread nor drink wine have no blood. Second, Plutarch, *Moralia* 180e, has Alexander the Great tell those who regarded him a god, "This is blood, as you can see, and not blood-water, such as flows in the holy gods." Third, 4 Maccabees 9:20 tells how, at the martyrdom of the eldest of the seven brothers, not only blood but also blood-water flowed from his body onto the instrument of torture. His was a truly human death. Moreover, it is significant that Irenaeus (*Against Heresies* 3.22.2) interprets the flow of blood and water from Jesus' side, along with his hunger and thirst and physical fatigue, as a sign of his humanity.

Vv. 35 and 37 are interpretive comments by the Evangelist. V. 35 offers a witness of the event: "He who saw it has borne witness [almost certainly the beloved disciple] — his testimony is true [here the leaders of the Johannine community speak, as in 21:24], and he knows [i.e., the eyewitness; cf. 8:14] that he tells the truth — that you may go on believing [present subjunctive]." In a community in which some have progressed beyond the doctrine of Christ (2 John 9), involving in part a denial that his coming in the flesh continued through the passion (1 John 4:1–2; 5:6–8), a guarantee of the continuing Incarnation becomes a function of eyewitnesses (1 John 1:1–2), one of whom is appealed to here in 19:35. V. 37 claims the event fulfills Scripture: "They shall look on him whom they have pierced" (Zech 12:10). Once again, the reader is told that events happen according the God's purpose.

D', vv. 38–40, tells of the actions of two of Jesus' friends on his behalf. Joseph of Arimathea, a secret disciple of Jesus (12:42–43), secures permission from Pilate to take Jesus' body away (v. 38). Nicodemus (3:1; 7:50) brings a hundred pounds of myrrh and aloes (v. 39). Together they bind the body of Jesus in linen cloths with the spices, "as is the burial custom of the Jews" (v. 40; cf. 2 Chron 16:14; Josephus, *Antiquities* 17.8.3 §199). His death is a catalyst for these two hesitant men to move to a more public expression of their devotion to Jesus.

E', vv. 41–42, recounts Jesus' burial. The two men, Joseph and Nicodemus, lay Jesus' body in a new tomb where no one has ever been laid, in a garden near the spot of his crucifixion (v. 41–42; almost certainly that marked in the Church of the Holy Selpulcher: Eusebius, *Life of Constantine* 3.26; Bordeaux Pilgrim; Cyril of Alexandria, *Catechetical Lectures* 13:39; 14:5, 22; 18). This act keeps Jesus from being buried in the place away from the city provided by the Jews for criminals (Josephus, *Antiquities* 5.1.14 §44). His burial in this manner displays the honor shown to the crucified king of the Jews.

There have been two main lines of interpretation of Jesus' death in the Fourth Gospel. One reads it in light of Paul and concludes that Jesus dies as an atoning sacrifice. The other interprets it in light of the Gospel's emphasis on revelation and concludes that Jesus' death is but the completion of his entire life work, that is, the crowning part of the revelation imparted in the Incarnation. A survey of the Gospel's varying emphases is clarifying. (1) What does Jesus' death mean for him in John? (a) It is a real death of a truly human being (19:26–27; 19:28; 19:34–37; 19:40). (b) It is the completion of Jesus' obedience to the Father, the accomplishment of the Father's work (12:27–28; 17:4; 19:30). (c) It is an integral part of his glorification (7:39; 12:16, 23; 17:1, 5). (2) What does Jesus' death mean for God? It is a part of the carrying out of the divine plan (19:24; 19:28; 19:36; 19:37) (3) What does Jesus' death mean for humans? (a) It is the defeat of the ruler of this world (12:31; 16:11; 16:33b). (b) It functions as a magnet that draws all people to himself (12:32), gathering together the scattered people of God (10:16b; 11:52). (c) It is *for* us (6:51: the bread which I shall give for the life of the world is my flesh; 10:11: the good shepherd lays down his life for the sheep; 11:50: it is expedient that one man should die for the people; 12:24: it is the means by which more people are reached; 13:8–10: it is a means of cleansing post-baptismal sin; 13:14–15: it is an example for disciples to relate to one another as he has related to us; 12:1–11; 19:14, 31, 36: as Paschal lamb he dies that we not suffer death but have life). Such a survey yields two conclusions. First, the dominant depiction of Jesus' death in the Fourth Gospel has nothing to do with an atoning sacrifice. It is rather part of his return to the Father, his glorification (16:28). Second, there is implicit in John 13:8–10 the same notion of Jesus' death as propitiation/expiation/atoning sacrifice for sin that one encounters in 1 John 2:2 and 4:10. On either reading, the one who dies is understood by the Fourth Gospel as making provision *for* us.

THE LIVING LORD

John 20–21

The second large thought unit making up the Johannine Passion Narrative is comprised of chapters 20–21, focusing on the resurrection traditions of the community. This unit is held together by an inclusion (Peter and the beloved disciple, 20:2–10 and 21:20–23). It falls into two parts, 20:1–31 and 21:1–25, each organized in similar ways (chap. 20 = resurrection narratives in two cycles, concluding with a statement of the Gospel's purpose; chap. 21 = a resurrection narrative in two parts, ending with a statement of the subject's grandeur). Each part must be examined in order.

John 20:1–31 contains two sections: (1) resurrection narratives in two cycles (vv. 1–29) and (2) a statement of the Gospel's purpose (vv. 30–31).

(1) The resurrection narratives are held together by an inclusion (believing without having seen Jesus, vv. 8 and 29b). Within the frame are two cycles: vv. 1–18 and vv. 18–29.

The first cycle, vv. 1–18, is a synthesis of at least three originally separate resurrection narratives: (a) some women find the tomb empty (vv. 1–2, 11–13; cf. Mark 16:1–8); (b) some men discover an empty tomb (vv. 3–10; cf. Lk 24:24, 12?); (c) Mary Magdalene experiences a resurrection appearance (vv. 14–18; cf. Matt 28:9–10, 1). It is held together by a threefold repetition of Mary's lament (they have taken him away, vv. 2, 13, 15). It is organized in a concentric pattern:

A vv. 1–2: Mary carries a message to the disciples based on what she saw.

> B vv. 3–10: The two disciples come to the tomb; one looks in and sees; the other goes in, sees, and believes.

> B' vv. 11–16: Mary at the tomb, looks in; later sees Jesus and believes.

A' vv. 17–18: Mary carries a message to the disciples based on what she has seen and heard.

In A, vv. 1–2, the story begins with Mary Magdalene coming to the tomb early, while it is still dark, and finding the stone taken away (v. 1). She then

248

runs to Simon Peter and to the disciple whom Jesus loved and confronts them with her fears: "They have taken the Lord out of the tomb, and we [an echo of the tradition of more than one woman finding the tomb empty, as in Mk 16:1//Matt 28:1//Lk 24:10?] do not know where they have laid him" (v. 2).

In B, vv. 3–10, the two male disciples go to the tomb. The beloved disciple outruns Peter and, reaching the tomb first (v. 4), looks in, sees the linen cloths lying there, but does not yet go in (v. 5). When Peter arrives, he goes in and sees the linen cloths lying, and the napkin that had been on Jesus' head not lying with the linen cloths but rolled up in a place by itself (vv. 6–7). Only then does the beloved disciple go in. When he does, he sees and believes (v. 8). Peter's lack of faith at this point is explained by the Evangelist: "for as yet they [an echo of the tradition that others besides Peter found the tomb empty, as in Lk 24:24?] did not know the Scripture, that he must rise from the dead" (v. 9).

Vv. 3–10 function apologetically in several ways in the Johannine plot. First, they confirm the testimony of vv. 1–2. According to Jewish law, two witnesses are needed to authenticate the fact of the empty tomb (Deut 19:15; John 5:31–32). In the ancient Jewish world, moreover, the testimony of a woman is less highly regarded than that of a man (Lk 24:11). So, as in Luke 24:24, 12, John 20:1–10 places the discovery of the empty tomb by men alongside its discovery by a woman or women. The one confirms the testimony of the other.

Second, the position of the grave cloths refutes the possibility, verbalized three times in the context by Mary Magdalene (vv. 2, 13, 15), that Jesus' body has been stolen. The charge that Jesus' body was stolen from the tomb, either by his disciples or by a gardener, is echoed in other early Christian sources (e.g., Matt 27:64; 28:13–15; Gospel of Peter 5:30; Justin, *Trypho* 108:2; Tertullian, *Shows* 30; *Apology* 23). Such a claim is not surprising, since robbing tombs was common enough to be part of an ancient novel's plot (in Chariton's novel, Callirhoe, presumed dead, awakes in the tomb and is carried off by grave robbers, beginning a painful separation for her and her lover, Chaereas) and for official action to be taken against it. For example, a decree of the emperor Claudius (41–54 C.E.), a copy of which was found at Nazareth, orders capital punishment for those destroying tombs, removing bodies, or displacing the sealing stones (a translation of the text may be found in C. K. Barrett, *The New Testament Background: Selected Documents* [New York: Harper Torchbooks, 1961], 15). If anyone had removed the body of Jesus, would he have stripped it first? Would he have left the cloths lying in an orderly fashion on the floor? Would he have taken the time to roll up the napkin and put it in a place by itself? Would he have left the costly cloths (so John Chrysostom, *Sermons on John* 85:4)? Jesus' body is absent from the tomb, but not because it has been stolen.

Third, the difference between the grave cloths in the case of Lazarus (11:44: "the dead man came out, his hands and feet bound with bandages, and his face wrapped in a cloth. Jesus said to them, 'Unbind him, and let him go' ") and those of Jesus (20:6-7: the body is gone and the linen cloths are lying there and the napkin is rolled up in a place by itself) speak about the nature of Jesus' resurrection. His situation is not that of a resuscitated corpse, as is the case of Lazarus. It is something else entirely:

> The explanation that best fits the Johannine view of the mode of resurrection is that the body had been swiftly dematerialized, leaving the swathing clothes as they were, with the cloth that had been wrapped around the head still lying on the slightly raised ledge where the head had been laid, and keeping its annular shape. (W. F. Howard, "John," *IB* 8:790)

The risen Jesus' body passes through his grave clothes just as it does through walls or doors (20:19, 26). His corpse has not been resuscitated; he has been transformed from mortal into immortal (cf. 1 Cor 15:53-55).

In addition to the apologetic points made by vv. 3-10, there is another. The beloved disciple sees the empty tomb and believes. He comes to faith without seeing Jesus himself. He, thereby, becomes not only a witness to the authenticity of the tradition of the empty tomb (21:24) but also a prototype of faith for those of subsequent generations who will believe without themselves seeing the risen Jesus (20:29b).

B', vv. 11-16, functions in two ways. First, it removes the certainty of Jesus' resurrection from angelic announcement (as in Mk 16:6: "He has risen, he is not here; see the place where they laid him") to personal experience (Mary sees and recognizes the risen Jesus). This echoes the perspective of the earliest oral tradition (1 Cor 15:3-5). Second, it offers another proof that Jesus' body has not been stolen. The lament of Mary about the possibility of Jesus' body being stolen is heard twice in this paragraph (vv. 13, 15). That she encounters the risen Jesus proves that the body has not been stolen; Jesus has been raised.

A', vv. 17-18, begins just as Mary recognizes the risen Jesus. He says to her: "Stop holding on to me, for I have not yet ascended to the Father; but go to my brethren and say to them, I am ascending to my Father and your Father, to my God and to your God" (v. 17). The present imperative with a negative (*mē*) in a prohibition normally signifies the breaking off of an action already in progress, or sometimes of the attempt to perform an action (C. K. Barrett, *The Gospel according to St. John* [London: SPCK, 1958], 470). Hence, one may suppose that Mary has either seized Jesus' feet or is on the point of doing so when Jesus stops her. Since John 20:14–18 seems to be a variant form of the tradition found in Matthew 28:9 (Jesus met Mary and her companion and said, " 'Hail.' And they came and took hold of his feet and worshipped him"), the former is likely. Mary grasps Jesus' feet and Jesus tells her to stop because he has not yet ascended to the Father.

Several things must be noted about this text. First, the one whom Mary encounters is the same one she saw crucified (19:25). Second, the risen one whose body can pass through grave clothes (20:5–7) and doors (20:19, 26) is still corporeal. He can be seen (v. 14; 1 John 1:1) and touched (v. 17; 1 John 1:1). This means the Incarnation continues even after the resurrection, even if in a new type of body (cf. 1 Cor 15:44). That Mary has grasped him and is told to desist means the risen Jesus is no purely spiritual being (cf. Lk 24:37–43). Third, the ascension takes place after the resurrection, not before the crucifixion as Cerinthus and his kind asserted (Irenaeus, *Against Heresies* 1.26.1). Taken together, these three points stand in the way of the progressives' christology, as it is known from 1 and 2 John. The Savior ascends after the cross and remains a corporeal being even after the resurrection. "The incarnation did not cease with the cross and the tomb; it continues even now in transcendental glory" (Philip Edgcumbe Hughes, *The True Image* [Grand Rapids: Eerdmans, 1989], 382).

The ascension is variously understood in early Christianity. (a) Some Gnostic Christians, like Cerinthus, understand it to be purely spiritual and to occur before Jesus' death. This position the Johannine community rejected, as did mainstream Christians generally. (b) For other Christians, the resurrection equals the ascension (so T. Benjamin 9:5, in what is perhaps the most explicit Christian interpolation in the Testaments, says: "he shall ascend from Hades and shall pass on from earth to heaven"; Gospel of Peter, where Jesus comes out of the tomb supported between two angels who take him into heaven). (c) For still other Christians, the resurrection and ascension are different events but they occur on the same day (Lk 24:50–53; Epistle of Barnabas 15:9: "Wherefore we also celebrate with gladness the eighth day in which Jesus also rose from the dead, and was made manifest, and ascended into Heaven"; Aristides, *Apology* 15 [Greek]: "after three days he came to life again and ascended into heaven"). (d) For yet other Christians, resurrection and ascension are different events occurring on different days, so there is an interval of some duration between them (e.g., Acts 1:3: 40 days; Ascension of Isaiah 9:16: 545 days; Irenaeus, *Against Heresies* 1.1.5; 1.28.7; 1.30: eighteen months; Apocryphon Jacobi: 550 days; Kerygma Petrou: 12 years; Pistis Sophia 1; Book of Jeu 44: 11 to 12 years). The Fourth Gospel belongs to category (c). The resurrection and the ascension are different events but they occur on the same day. If the ascension has not yet taken place in 20:17 ("I have not yet ascended"), it has already taken place by 20:22 ("Receive the Holy Spirit") because, according to 7:39, the Spirit is not given until Jesus is glorified (17:5, 24 indicate that ascension and glorification are synonymous) (so Jay Morris).

Such differences of opinion about the ascension affect the way resurrection appearances are understood. If ascension is identical with resurrection or occurs on the same day, then some of the resurrection appearances happen after the ascension. Paul assumes this view because he regards the christophany he experienced (1 Cor 9:1) as the equivalent of the resurrection appearances to Cephas and the Twelve, even though it happened probably several years after Easter (1 Cor 15:1–11). When Acts limits the appearances to forty days, it places Paul's experience of the risen Christ in a different category from that of the Twelve. It is his conversion, but it is not a resurrection appearance. Acts' limitation of the duration of the resurrection appearances is probably a defensive act against heretics' claims that their teaching came from a post-resurrection appearance of the risen Christ (as, e.g., in the Apocryphon of John, the Letter of Peter to Philip, the Sophia of Jesus Christ, the Pistis Sophia, the Book of Thomas the Contender, the Dialogue of the Savior, the Second Treatise of the Great Seth, and the Gospel of Mary). Logically, if not chronologically, Acts reflects a more advanced position than the Fourth Gospel at this point.

The second cycle of the resurrection appearances of 20:1–29 comes in vv. 18–29 (v. 18 serves as a hinge, being both a conclusion to vv. 1–18 and an introduction to vv. 18–29). This unit is held together by a threefold repetition of language about the disciples being shown Jesus' hands and side (vv. 20, 25, 27). It is arranged in an ABA′B′ pattern.

A   v. 18: Mary's testimony, "I have seen the Lord."

  B   vv. 19–23: Appearance to the disciples
        time reference, v. 19a
        disciples gathered with the door shut, v. 19b
        Jesus same and stood among them, v. 19c
        and said, "Peace be with you," v. 19d

he shows his hands and side, v. 20a
disciples respond, v. 20b
Jesus said, vv. 21–23

A' vv. 24–25: Disciples' testimony, "We have seen the Lord."

B' vv. 26–29: Appearance to Thomas
time reference, v. 26a
disciples gathered with door shut, v. 26b
Jesus came and stood among them, v. 26c
and said, "Peace be with you," v. 26d
Invitation to touch hands and side, v. 27
Thomas's response, v. 28
Jesus said, v. 29.

Early Christian narratives of resurrection appearances are of two types: (a) some function simply to show Jesus is alive (e.g., Matt 28:9; Lk 24:13–32); (b) others function not only to show Jesus is alive but also to allow him to give further instruction to his disciples (e.g., Matt 28:18–20; Lk 24:36–49). The appearance stories in vv. 19–23 and vv. 26–29 belong to category (b). Each has the same seven components, the last of which is: Jesus said.

B, vv. 19–23, is set on the evening of resurrection day, the first day of the week, behind closed doors because of the disciples' fear of the Jews. Jesus comes and stands among them and greets them: "Peace be with you." He shows them his hands and his side. "Then the disciples were glad when they saw the Lord" (v. 20). Here there is the same combination of ingredients seen earlier. The risen Jesus can come through closed doors, yet he is corporeal, still carrying the wounds from his experience of crucifixion. It is thereby that his identity can be established. It is in this sense that Ignatius can rightly say: "He was in the flesh even after the resurrection" (*Smyrneans* 3:1–2). Having established that Jesus is alive in vv. 19–20, the story turns in vv. 21–23 to the further equipping and instructing of the disciples. There are four components: (a) Again Jesus says, "Peace be with you" (v. 21a; cf. 14:27; 16:33). (b) "As the Father has sent me, even so I send you" (v. 21b; cf. 17:18). (c) He breathed on them, and said: "Receive the Holy Spirit" (v. 22; 7:39; 17:22). (d) "If you forgive the sins of any, they are forgiven; if you retain the sins of any, they are retained" (v. 23).

Taking the appearance story as a whole, its function seems to be to show how its events fulfill various promises of Jesus made in chapters 14–17 (A. M. Hunter, *According to John* [Philadelphia: Westminster, 1968], 187–88).

I am coming back to you (14:18; 16:22)	1. Jesus came (20:19)
Peace I leave with you (14:27)	2. Peace be with you (20:21)
Then your hearts will rejoice (16:23)	3. Then the disciples were glad (20:20b)
As you have sent me, I have sent them (17:18)	4. As the Father has sent me, even so I send you (20:21)
If I go, I will send the Spirit to you (16:7b)	5. Receive the Holy Spirit (20:22)

The promise-fulfillment schema shows it is the same Jesus before and after Easter with whom the disciples deal. Since it is the same person, he is addressed by the same name: Jesus (20:19, 26; 21:4, 13, 15, 23). From the Johannine perspective, no language can be used of Jesus either before or after Easter that negates his name and its gender implications: e.g., one cannot appropriately speak of the earthly Jesus as "she"; one cannot legitimately speak of "Jesus Christ" before Easter and "Christa" after Easter; one cannot correctly pray in the name of the Daughter instead of the Son (likewise Luke-Acts: the one who was raised = Jesus [Acts 4:33; 5:30; 13:31–32; 17:3, 18]; the one who appeared = Jesus [Lk 24:15, 36]; the one who ascended = Jesus [Acts 1:11]; the one exalted = Jesus [Acts 2:22, 23, 32, 36]; the one seen by Stephen the martyr standing at God's right hand = Jesus [Acts 7:55, 59]; the one who encountered Saul on the road to Damascus = Jesus [Acts 9:5; 22:8; 26:15]; the one whom Christians await = Jesus [Acts 1:11]).

This scheme may assist the reader in understanding the most difficult component, v. 23. How does "If you forgive [aorist subjunctive] the sins of any, they are forgiven [perfect tense]; if you continue to retain [present subjunctive] the sins of any, they are retained [perfect tense]" fit into this pattern? Consider the context since chapter 13. (a) In 17:22 Jesus prays: "The glory [the Holy Spirit] which you have given me [1:33; 3:34], I have given them [20:22; the equivalent of a prophetic perfect in Hebrew, a future event spoken of as already past because of the certainty that it will transpire] that they may be one." The Spirit is to be given so the disciples may be one. In 20:22–23 the Spirit is given so they may forgive sins [= a means of being one?]. (b) In 13:14–15 Jesus tells the disciples that they should wash one another's feet as he has washed theirs. He is an example and they should do to one another as he has done to them. His washing of feet symbolizes forgiveness of daily post-baptismal sins. So if the disciples do as he has done, they will forgive one another as he forgives them. (c) In 13:34 the new commandment concludes the thought unit, 13:1–35. Within its context, to love one another as Jesus has loved them means, at least, to forgive one another as they have been forgiven.

(d) In 15:1–17 the disciples are to bear fruit, that is, to love one another. In the larger context, this must mean, in part at least, to forgive one another. The train of thought from chapter 13 on has been focused on the disciples loving one another, forgiving one another, being one. This is possible because the glory (Spirit) given to Jesus will be given to them. It is in this context that 20:22–23 should be read. If disciples forgive other disciples' sins against them, the sins are removed as an obstacle to community oneness; if they continue to hold on to the sins against them (remember the present tense), the sins remain as obstacles to community harmony (cf. Eph 4:26). To enable correct behavior (v. 23), as well as to empower their mission (v. 21), the Holy Spirit is given to the disciples. Read in this way, v. 23 fits into the overall pattern as a fulfillment of Jesus' promise (implicit in his prayer) of 17:22. He will give the Spirit in order that they may be one (which is accomplished by their forgiving one another their transgressions). The ones whose sins are forgiven are fellow Christians; the sins forgiven are the post-baptismal transgressions of disciples against other Christians; the problem addressed is that of Christians holding on to the sins done against them instead of releasing them and others who did them.

The forgiveness of fellow disciples' sins against oneself is made possible by the gift of the Holy Spirit (v. 23; 17:22). Three passages in the New Testament speak about the gift of the Spirit after Easter: (a) John 20:22, (b) Acts 2, and (c) Ephesians 4:8. Ephesians locates the risen Christ's giving gifts to humans after his ascension, but with no specification of exactly when. Acts 2 locates the gift of the Spirit on Pentecost (fifty days after Passover), after the period of resurrection appearances is past. John 20:22 locates the gift of the Holy Spirit on Easter day, as part of a resurrection appearance. It is possible that another New Testament writing, Mark, treats the rending of the veil of the Temple in 15:38 as the Markan equivalent to Pentecost (S. Moyter, "The Rending of the Veil: A Markan Pentecost," *NTS* 33 [1987: 155–56). It is likely that these are independent traditions dealing with the same event, each Gospel interpreting it from its own theological angle of vision. In John, the foundation document for a community troubled by progressives who want to avoid an incarnation that continues through Jesus' death, it is important to guarantee the identity of the one known before Golgotha and the one encountered after Easter. One way of doing this is to depict post-resurrection events as fulfillments of the promises of the pre-crucifixion Jesus. This is artistically focused in the story of a resurrection appearance in 20:19–23.

A', vv. 24–25, allows the disciples present at the resurrection appear-

ance of vv. 19–23 to proclaim: "We have seen the Lord" (cf. v. 18: Mary
Magdalene). The one they tell is Thomas (11:16; 14:5; 21:2), who was
not with them "when Jesus came" (14:18). Thomas's response sets up
the resurrection appearance to follow in vv. 26–29. He says: "Unless I see
in his hands the print of nails, and place my finger in the mark of the
nails, and place my hand in his side [19:34], I will not believe" (v. 25b).
The account of the crucifixion does not specifically say Jesus' hands were
nailed to the cross, only that he was crucified (19:18). It was, however,
part of Christian tradition (Col 2:14) and would normally have occurred
(as ossuary remains from Giv at ha-Mivtar, discovered in 1968, indicate.
Cf. J. A. Fitzmyer, "Crucifixion in Ancient Palestine, Qumran Literature,
and the New Testament," *CBQ* 40 [1978]: 493–513). Thomas's demand
has to do with the question of whether or not the one whom they have
seen is really Jesus. The only way he will believe that it is the same Jesus
is by empirical verification of the wounds in his body.

B', vv. 26–29, provides a resurrection appearance to satisfy Thomas's
demands. Again the mysterious appearance of Jesus (Jesus came and
stood among them) is experienced in spite of closed doors (v. 26). This
time Thomas is present. The risen Jesus says to him: "Put you finger here,
and see my hands; and put out your hand, and place it in my side; do not
be faithless, but believing" (v. 27). That is, "It is I, Jesus, the same one who
was crucified, as my wounds show." To a disciple who doubted the identity of the one who appeared with the one who died, effective empirical
proof is offered.

Thomas responds: "My Lord [cf. v. 18] and my God" (v. 28). In the New
Testament there are, outside the Fourth Gospel, several places where
Jesus may be spoken of as God (Rom 9:5; 2 Pet 1:1; Tit 2:13; Heb 1:8–9;
1 John 5:20). In John there are three (1:1; 1:18, assuming the best textual reading; 20:28; cf. also 10:33–36, by implication?). The combination
"Lord and God" is used for the Father in Revelation 4:11. The Roman
emperor Domitian wished to be addressed in similar terms (Suetonius,
"Domitian," 13:2; Dio Cassius, *Roman History* 67.13.4; Philostratus, *Life
of Apollonius* 8.4; Dio Chrysostom 45.1). Whether or not the Evangelist intended the ascription to be a counterblast to the emperor cult (as
B. A. Mastin, "The Imperial Cult and the Ascription of the Title *Theos*
to Jesus [John 20:28]," *Studia Evangelica* 6 [Berlin: Akademie Verlag,
1973], 352–65; and *NTS* 22 [1975], 32–51), it would have had the potential to be heard by the community as a counterbalance to political
religion.

Jesus responds to Thomas's confession: "Because you have seen me in the past and continue to see me [perfect tense], you have believed and continue to believe [perfect tense]" (v. 29a). The verb tenses are appropriate to Thomas's situation. He had seen Jesus (i.e., prior to Easter) and now he continues to have the experience (i.e., in a resurrection appearance); he, therefore, believed (prior to Easter) and continues to believe (after Easter). Because of his empirical experience, he believes in Jesus who is the same person prior to and after Easter (remember 1 John 4:2: "Every Spirit which confesses Jesus Christ having come and remaining [perfect tense] in flesh is of God"). Continuing to believe in Jesus is the desired aim. Thomas has done so because of his empirical experience, but there are others who will not have such experience and yet need to believe (remember 17:20: "those who believe in me through their word"; 1 John 1:3: "that which we have seen and heard we proclaim to you, so that you may have fellowship with us [the eyewitnesses]; and our fellowship is with the Father and with his Son Jesus Christ"). The situation is analogous to that described by Rabbi Simeon b. Laqish:

> The proselyte is dearer to God than all the Israelites who stood by Mount Sinai. For if all the Israelites had not seen the thunder and the flames and the lightnings and the quaking mountain and the sound of the trumpet they would not have accepted the law and taken upon themselves the kingdom of God. Yet this man has seen none of all these things yet comes and gives himself to God and takes on himself the yoke of the kingdom of God. Is there any who is dearer than this man? (*Tanhuma* §6 [32a]; C. K. Barrett, *The Gospel according to Saint John* [London: SPCK, 1958], 478)

"Blessed [cf. 13:17; Rev 14:13; 19:9; 20:6; 22:14; Lk 10:23] are those who do not see and yet believe" (v. 29b). Congratulation to those disciples who believe in Jesus whether or not they have experienced him during his earthly career.

The first part of John 20–21 ends with a statement of the Gospel's purpose (20:30–32):

> Many other signs Jesus did in the presence of his disciples which are not written in this book; but these are written in order that you may go on believing [present subjunctive, so P66, Vaticanus, Sinaiticus; an inferior textual variant has an aorist subjunctive] that the Christ, the Son of God, is Jesus, and that going on believing [present participle], you may go on having [present subjunctive] life in his name.

(a) The rhetoric of the conclusion is conventional (cf. 1 Macc 9:22: "Now the rest of the acts of Judas, and his wars and the brave deeds that he did, and his greatness, have not been recorded, for they were very many";

Lucian, *Demonax* 67). (b) The statement of purpose takes on new meaning if read in light of the problems of the epistles (2 John 9: progressives have moved beyond the doctrine of Christ; 1 John 2:19: secessionists have withdrawn from the community, largely over christology [so 1 John 2:22–23]). The need is for Christians to remain in the christological faith of the community that they may continue to have life (1 John 5:12: "the one who goes on having the Son goes on having life) in the name of the one who alone gives life (17:2; 11:25–26; 10:28; 6:54; 5:26, 28–29; 4:14; 3:36; 3:15–16). Contrary to the claims of progressives for whom the Christ did not come in the flesh in any permanent way, they need to continue to believe that the Christ is Jesus. That the Gospel is addressed to Christians is demanded by chapters 13–17, D. A. Carson's special pleading not withstanding (*The Gospel according to John* [Grand Rapids: Eerdmans, 1991]). (c) In placing the statement of purpose in a location prior to the actual ending of the Gospel, the Evangelist employs a technique used elsewhere in the Gospel (cf. 12:36b–37, which reads like a conclusion to what has come before, but which is followed by vv. 38–50), by the author of 1 John (cf. 5:13 = the statement of purpose, which is followed by vv. 14–21), and the writer of Revelation (cf. 22:5 = the end of the visions, but vv. 6–21 follow). Given this technique employed in the Johannine writings, the location of the Gospel's statement of purpose before the actual end says nothing against chapter 21's place in the Fourth Gospel.

The second half of John 20–21 is 21:1–25. This subunit contains: (1) a resurrection narrative (vv. 1–24), and (2) a statement of the subject's grandeur (v. 25).

(1) The resurrection narrative in vv. 1–24 belongs to that type of appearance story that not only shows Jesus is alive, but also allows him to give further instruction to disciples (as, e.g., in Lk 24:36–49; Matt 28:16–20). This appearance story falls into two parts: vv. 1–14 and vv. 15–24.

The first part (vv. 1–14) is held together by an inclusion (Jesus revealed himself, v. 1; Jesus was revealed, v. 14). V. 1 introduces the story: "After this Jesus revealed himself again to the disciples by the Sea of Tiberias; and he revealed himself in this way." (a) As in Matthew 28, the location of Jesus' appearances moves from Jerusalem to Galilee. (b) As in John 20:19–23 and 20:26–29, this resurrection appearance occurs after Jesus' ascension. (c) As in Luke 24:15, 30, Jesus revealed himself by coming, taking, giving (v. 13), that is, in the context of a meal (remember 6:11). The narrative of the appearance, given in vv. 2–12, is composed of two sections (vv. 2–6b; vv. 6c–12b), each with eight corresponding components, though not always in the same order.

Peter's initiative (vv. 2–3a)	Peter's initiative (v. 7b)
Others follow (v. 3b)	Others follow (v. 8)
Caught nothing (v. 3c)	Caught many (v. 6c)
Jesus not recognized (v. 4)	Jesus recognized (v. 7a)
Jesus said (v. 5a)	Jesus said (v. 10)
They replied (v. 5b)	Peter responded (v. 11)
Jesus said (v. 6a)	Jesus said (v. 12a)
They responded (v. 6b)	They responded (v. 12b).

Seven disciples are together (v. 2), one of whom is Peter. When he says he is going fishing, the others go with him (v. 3a). This behavior on the part of the seven disciples (= disciples generally) is entirely appropriate within the Johannine context. They are together. They act together. This unity is what the Johannine Jesus has prayed for (17:11) and has given the Holy Spirit to enable (20:22; 17:22). So far, their commission has been "to be" the community (chaps. 13–17); it has not been to leave their occupations and "to go" make disciples. Only in 21:3–14 will they learn of their task to be Jesus' fishermen.

They fish all night (a common occurrence since then they could sell a fresh catch the next morning) but catch nothing (v. 3b). At daybreak, Jesus stands (v. 4; cf. 20:19, 26) on the beach, unrecognized, and asks: "Children, do you have anything to eat?" (J. H. Moulton and W. Milligan, *Vocabulary of the Greek New Testament* [Grand Rapids: Eerdmans, 1952], 551–52). "No," they reply. "Cast the net on the right side of the boat, and you will find some." When they do as Jesus has directed, they are "not able to haul it in, for the quantity of fish" (v. 6; Lk 5:4–7). The beloved disciple recognizes Jesus: "It is the Lord" (cf. 20:18, 25). He has the discernment. Peter has the devotion: "he put on his clothes... and sprang into the sea." The other disciples come in the boat, "dragging the net full of fish." They do their duty. When they reach land, there is a charcoal fire with fish on it and bread for breakfast (v. 9). Jesus asks them to bring some of their catch, which numbers 153 fish. In spite of the great number of fish, the net is not torn (v. 11). Jesus invites them to eat (v. 12a). They know it is he (v. 12b). "Jesus came, and took the bread and gave it to them, and so with the fish" (v. 13). "This was now the third time Jesus was revealed to the disciples after he was raised from the dead" (v. 14; remember 20:19–23, 26–29). Just as Jesus was recognized in 20:20, 27 by his wounds, so here he is recognized by his role as nourisher of his people (remember 6:4–14;

cf. Lk 24:13–30: Acts 10:41). It is the same Jesus, only now risen from the dead.

In this first part of the resurrection appearance narrative the focus seems to be not only on who Jesus is (nourisher of the people) but also on what the disciples are to do (follow Jesus' directions in their fishing). The presence of symbolism is obvious: the 153 three fish and the untorn net. About the meaning of the symbolism there is widespread agreement: (a) The 153 fish symbolize the universal outreach of the church's fishing expedition in obedience to Jesus' command. There is little agreement among interpreter's about why this is so. For example, Jerome, in his commentary on Ezekiel 47:9–12, says:

> Writers on the nature and properties of animals, who have learned *Halieutica* in Latin as well as in Greek, among whom is the learned poet Oppianus Cilix, say that there are one hundred fifty three kinds of fishes. (cited in Hoskyns, *Fourth Gospel* [London: Faber and Faber, 1947], 554)

Although there is no such statement in the extant writings of Oppian, and although different ancient writers speak otherwise (R. M. Grant, *HTR* 42 [1949]: 273–75), some such ancient belief must lie behind John 21:11. (b) The untorn net symbolizes the unity of the church. In spite of the number and variety of persons included within the community, its basic unity is not destroyed. Now, at last, the disciples as a group have spelled out for them what it means to be sent by Jesus (20:21b; 17:18). It means fishing, at Jesus' command, for all kinds of people and including them in his community (10:16; 11:52; 12:32; 17:20; cf. Rom 11:25) that is characterized by oneness (17:20–23). The first part of the resurrection appearance story revolves around the symbolism of fish and fishing. This symbolism points to the responsibility of disciples for those outside the Christian community.

The second part of the resurrection appearance (vv. 15–23) is held together by a dialogue between Jesus and Peter. It falls into an ABB′ A′ pattern.

A vv. 15–17: Peter's task

  B vv. 18–19: Peter's death

  B′ vv. 20–23: beloved disciple's death

A′ v. 24: beloved disciple's task

A, vv. 15–17, employs the symbolism of sheep and focuses on one disciple's (Peter's) responsibility for those within the Christian fellowship.

Vv. 15–17 function to rehabilitate Peter after his denials. Just as Peter's denial took place in three stages (18:17, 25, 27), so his rehabilitation occurs in three steps (vv. 15, 16, 17). (a) After breakfast Jesus asks Peter, "Simon, son of John, do you love [*agapas*] me more than these?" (i.e., more than this fishing gear). Peter says, "Yes, Lord, you know that I love [*philō*] you." Jesus says, "Feed my lambs." (b) A second time Jesus asks, "Simon, son of John, do you love [*agapas*] me?" Peter replies, "Yes, Lord, you know that I love [*philō*] you." Jesus says, "Tend my sheep." (c) A third time Jesus asks, "Simon, son of John, do you love [*phileis*] me?" Peter is grieved and says, "Lord, you know everything [e.g., 1:47–48; 2:25; 4:17–19; 6:64–65; 11:4; 13:1, 11, 38; 16:32]; you know that I love [*philō*] you." Jesus says, "Feed my sheep." Two things may be said about this exchange.

First, the alternation between two forms of the word "love" is merely stylistic and has no theological import. In Johannine literature, both verbs are used for God's love for humans (*agapan*, 3:16; 14:23; 17:23; 1 John 4:10, 19; *philein*, 16:27; Rev 3:19); both are used of the Father's love for the Son (*agapan*, 3:35; 10:17; 15:9; 17:23, 24, 26; *philein*, 5:20); both are used of Jesus' love for humans (*agapan*, 11:5; 13:1, 23, 24; 14:21; 15:9; 19:26; 21:7; *philein*, 11:3, 36; 20:2); both are used of love of humans for other humans (*agapan*, 13:34; 15:12, 17; 1 John 2:10; 3:10, 14, 23; 4:7, 20; *philein*, 15:19); both are used of humans' love for Jesus (*agapan*, 8:42; 14:15, 21, 23, 24, 28; *philein*, 16:27). As a matter of practice, the Fourth Gospel varies Greek words where the same meaning is intended (e.g., three different words are used for "to go away" in 16:5–10; three for "grieve" in 16:20–22; two for "ear" in 18:10, 26; two for "keep" in 17:12).

Second, the religious point is highlighted by a parallel from *The Fathers according to Rabbi Nathan* 17. In this text, Moses, when about to leave the world, appoints Joshua as shepherd of the people Israel. He says:

> Joshua, this people which I am handing over to you, . . . not sheep but lambs I hand over to you, for they have not yet had much practice in the commandments and they are not yet become . . . sheep. (As it is said: "If you know not, O you fairest among women, go your way forth by the footsteps of the flock and feed your kids beside the shepherds' tents." (Canticles 1:8)

In like manner, the one who is the Good Shepherd now says to a rehabilitated Peter, "Feed/tend my lambs/sheep." If the disciples in general are given the task of fishing (the evangelistic ministry), Peter is assigned the care of the flock (the pastoral ministry; for church leaders as shepherds, cf. Eph 4:11; Acts 20:28; 1 Pet 5:2–4).

Rehabilitation completed, Jesus now prophesies Peter's death (vv. 18–

19a; after all, a good shepherd lays down his life for the flock, 10:11) and asks for his assent to it (v. 19b). These verses pick up the theme of 13:36–38 (Peter cannot follow Jesus now, but afterward he will). After Jesus' glorification and the gift of the Spirit, it will be time for Peter to follow. (a) Jesus predicts: "When you were young, you girded yourself and walked where you would; but when you are old, you will stretch out your hands, and another will gird you and carry you where you do not wish to go." The expression "stretch out the hands" is used in antiquity for crucifixion (e.g., Epictetus 3:26:22; cf. Epistle of Barnabas 12:4, Justin, *1 Apology* 35, and Irenaeus, *Demonstration of the Apostolic Preaching* 79, all of whom take the expression in Isa 65:2 as a foreshadowing of crucifixion; Barnabas 12:2 and Justin, *Trypho* 90–91, take Moses' outstretched hands in Exod 17:12 as a type of crucifixion). This is, then, as v. 19a indicates, a prophecy of Peter's death by crucifixion (a tradition known to Tertullian, *Scorpiace* 15, and linked with this passage; also to Eusebius, *Church History* 2.25; Origen [so Eusebius, *Church History* 3.1] and the Acts of Peter claim that Peter was crucified upside down [victims were sometimes crucified upside down; Seneca, *Consolation to Marcia* 20]; the earliest reference to Peter's martyrdom outside John does not specify how he died, 1 Clement 5:4). (b) Jesus then says to Peter: "Follow me" (v. 19b). This command also echoes 13:36–38. In this context, to follow Jesus means to follow him in death. Jesus calls Peter to assent to the content of the prophecy. The pastor/shepherd of the church will die a martyr's death, a vocation to which he is asked to commit himself. The readers (after 64 C.E.) would know that both Jesus' prophecy and Peter's assent to it have been fulfilled.

B', vv. 20–23, turns to the matter of the beloved disciple's death. The reference to this disciple employs an allusion to 13:25, where he has a preferential position as intimate of Jesus. Peter, for whom martyrdom has been prophesied, asks about this other disciple's destiny: "Lord, what about this man?" Jesus replies: "If I wish him to remain until I come (i.e., the Parousia; cf. 14:1–3; 1 John 2:28; 3:2), what is that to you? Follow me." Whatever is assigned to the beloved disciple does not affect Peter's destiny. Peter is to follow Jesus in a death by crucifixion. Mark 9:1 ("Truly, I say to you, there are some standing here who will not taste death before they see the kingdom of God come with power") may be a variant form of the saying in John 21:22. In John it is applied specifically to the beloved disciple. The community interpreted the saying to mean that the beloved disciple would not die (v. 23a). Most likely, he has died in the meantime. This requires clarification on the part of the author(s): "Jesus did *not* say to him that he was not to die, but, *if* it is my will that he remain until I come, what is that to you?" (v. 23b). If Peter's death as crucified martyr is appropriate for him in his role as good shepherd, the beloved disciple's death in old age is appropriate for one who functioned in his lifetime as witness and interpreter of Jesus' life.

A', v. 24, focuses on the beloved disciple's task: "This is the disciple who is bearing witness [guaranteeing and interpreting, by means of the written Gospel] to these things [the things in the whole of the Fourth Gospel], and who has caused these things to be written" (cf. 19:19, 22 where *grapsas* is also causal; cf. Rom 15:15 together with 16:22; 1 Pet 5:12; Judg 8:14). The beloved disciple is here (a) a particular, historical individual who is the authoritative teacher of the Johannine community (like the Teacher of Righteousness at Qumran), (b) who is anonymous (also like the Teacher of Righteousness at Qumran). "And we know that his testimony is true" (v. 24b). The "we" confessing confidence in the beloved disciple's witness refers either to the community at large (as in 1 John 3:2, 14; 5:16, 19) as their views are expressed by their representatives, the editors, or to other eyewitnesses (as in 1:14; 1 John 1:1–5; 4:14) who have editorial responsibility for the Gospel.

Peter and the beloved disciple stand side by side in John 21 (as in 13:23–25; 18:15–16; 20:2–10), each with his own specific ministry and destiny. If evangelistic outreach belongs to the disciples as a whole, pastoral care of the flock is given to Peter and the role of prophetic witness to the beloved disciple (cf. Eph 4:7, 11; 1 Cor 12:5; 1 Pet 4:10–11). The general commission of 20:21b ("As the Father has sent me, even so I send you") now takes on specific shapes for different individuals. Some things in mission everyone shares; other expressions of mission vary, depending on the particular role assigned to an individual by the risen Jesus (Rom 12:3–8; Eph 4:11–12).

The one who came as revealing, empowering presence; who picked/produced a new community and provided them during his public ministry with warrants for a different type of worship; who privately predicted what their future would be like, offering promise, parenesis, and prayer for that time; has now made provision for their community life, worship, and ministry before he finally returns to whence he has come.

(2) The Fourth Gospel concludes with a statement of the subject's grandeur: "But there are also many other things which Jesus did; were every one of them to be written, I suppose that the world itself could

not contain the books that would be written." The rhetorical flourish is conventional (Philo, *Posterity of Cain* 43 §144: "Were He to choose to display His riches, even the entire earth, with the sea turned into dry land, would not contain them"; Iamblichus, *Life of Pythagoras* 35); the distinctive subject is wonderful.

APPENDIX:
DESCENDING-ASCENDING
REDEEMER FIGURES IN
MEDITERRANEAN ANTIQUITY

I n spite of past popularity, the contention that the Christian conception of Jesus as a descending-ascending savior figure was derived from
the Gnostic redeemer myth faces serious problems. Three are widely
noted; another needs attention.

(1) The sources from which our knowledge of the Gnostic myth comes
are late: e.g., the Naassene hymn, the hymn of the Pearl, the Mandean
materials, the Manichean evidence, the accounts in the church fathers,
and the Nag Hammadi documents. Sources from Chenoboskion like the
Paraphrase of Shem, the Apocalypse of Adam, and the Second Logos of
the Great Seth do contain a myth of a redeemer that is only superficially
Christianized. Hence the Gnostics may not have derived their myth from
Christians. It does not follow, however, either that Christians got it from
Gnostics or that it is pre-Christian.

(2) A redeemer myth is not essential to Gnosticism. Though Gnosticism may contain a redeemer myth (e.g., the Naassene hymn), it may
exist without one. In Carpocrates' system, for example, Jesus' soul re-
membered what it had seen in its circuit with the unbegotten God
(Irenaeus, *Against Heresies* 1.25.1–6). The Ophites in Origen's *Against
Celsus* 6.28, know of no descending-ascending redeemer. They look
to an earthly being who fetches gnosis from heaven. In *Poimandres,*
the writer is the recipient of a vision in rapture. He then teaches
the way of salvation. Indeed, the proto-Gnosticism of Paul's opponents in 1 Corinthians apparently did not contain a redeemer myth.
Such evidence demands that a distinction be drawn between two issues: (a) whether or not there was a pre-Christian Gnosticism, and
(b) whether or not there was a pre-Christian Gnostic redeemer myth.

Since a redeemer myth is not constitutive for Gnosticism, the existence of a pre-Christian gnosis is no guarantee for the presence of a Gnostic redeemer myth.

(3) In the Christian sources where the Gnostic myth has been assumed to be influential (e.g., the Fourth Gospel), there is no ontological identity between Christ and the believers as in Gnosticism. There is, in the Christian writings, no pre-existence of the soul or redeemed redeemer. Given these difficulties, why the attractiveness of the Gnostic hypothesis?

(4) The pattern of descent-ascent in the Gnostic redeemer myth "has been and remains the strongest support for the hypothesis" that early Christian christology is connected with Gnostic mythology (Wayne Meeks, *The Prophet King* [Leiden: Brill, 1967], 297). Generally overlooked is the fact that myths of descending-ascending redeemers are found elsewhere in the Mediterranean world prior to and parallel with the origins of Christianity. If so, then the strongest support for the Gnostic hypothesis collapses and the question deserves reexamination.

The existence of the Greco-Roman mythology is not as well known to New Testament scholars as that of Gnosticism but is instructive nonetheless. (a) In his *Metamorphoses* (7 C.E.), Ovid tells of the visit of Jupiter and Mercury in the guise of mortals, seeking a place for rest, but finding it only in the humble home of old Baucis and Philemon. The gods save the couple from the destruction of the neighborhood by water and grant them not only their prayer that they would not be separated by death but also a type of immortality by changing them into intertwining trees near the gods' temple (8.626–721). Acts 14:8–18 shows that this myth of descending-ascending gods was know to Christians in the first century. (b) Tacitus, in his *Histories* (98–117 C.E.), tells of the origin of the Serapis cult in Ptolemaic times. A young man of more than human size appeared to Soter and instructed him to send to Pontus and fetch his statue. The god told Ptolemy that if he did as he was directed, it "would bring prosperity to the realm" and the city would be "great and illustrious." Serapis then ascended to heaven in a blaze of fire (4.83–84).

The descent-ascent mythology could be used by Greco-Roman authors to interpret the lives of historical figures just as Gnostics employed their myth for Simon, Menander, and Christ. (a) Vergil's *Fourth Eclogue* runs:

> The last age of the Sibyl's poem is now come. . . . Now a new offspring is *sent down from high heaven*. Do thou, chaste Lucina, favor the birth of the child under whom the iron breed will first cease and a golden race arise throughout the world. Now shall *thine own Apollo bear sway*.

Augustus' birth is here viewed in terms of the myth of Apollo's descent for redemptive purposes: the cessation of war and the establishment of peace. (b) Horace's *Odes* 1.2 (23 B.C.E.) reflects a similar tendency. The odist asks: "Whom of the gods shall the folk call to the needs of the falling empire?" (25–26). "To whom shall Jupiter assign the task of atoning for our guilt?" (29–30). Then various gods are addressed: Apollo, Mars, and finally Mercury. It is the last of these deities whose descent is described as changing his form, assuming on earth the guise of man (41–44). It is the epiphany of Mercury that is used to interpret the career of Augustus. The petition closes: "Late mayest thou return to the skies and long mayest thou be pleased to dwell amid Quirinus' folk" (45–46). From these selected examples, one sees that a Greco-Roman mythology of descending-ascending gods who appear on earth for redemptive purposes both existed early enough to be available for Christian appropriation and had, by the beginning of our era, already been used to interpret the lives of historical figures.

The Hellenistic-Jewish mythology of a descending-ascending redeemer is usually overlooked or denied. Since the Jewish mythology has received inadequate attention, it will be the focus of attention here. The first part of this appendix will attempt to establish the existence of a descent-ascent pattern used for redemption figures in ancient Judaism; the second will argue that this Jewish myth, in its various forms, served as the source for certain early Christians' speech about Jesus.

The Descent-Ascent Pattern
Used for Redemption Figures in Judaism

The descent-ascent pattern is found connected with redemption figures in at least two streams of ancient Judaism. On the one hand, the wisdom tradition reflects such a myth. In contrast to Proverbs 8:22–36 where heavenly wisdom is accessible to the person who earnestly seeks it, certain writings near the beginning of our era speak of the *descent* of wisdom from the heavens with saving intent. (a) In Sirach 24 pre-existent wisdom comes down from heaven, appears on earth among humans, tabernacling in Jacob as the law. (b) In Baruch 3:27–4:4 heavenly wisdom is given by God to Israel. She appears on earth and lives among men as the law. In these two sources, the wisdom myth is used to interpret the meaning of a historical entity, the law. (c) The Wisdom of Solomon refers to pre-existent wisdom's being sent from the heavens (9:10) as a savior figure both in this world (7:27; 8:10) and for the next (6:18–20; 8:13, 17). The author can actually talk about being "saved by wisdom" (9:18; cf. 10:1, 4, 6, 13, 15, etc.). (d) Both 2 Esdras 5:9–10 and 2 Baruch 48:36 refer to the *ascent* of wisdom, departing the earth during the crisis preceding the End. (e) 1 Enoch 42:1–2 contains a reference both to the *descent* and the *ascent* of wisdom. She comes down from heaven but, finding no dwelling place, returns to heaven and takes her seat among the angels.

How does one explain these sources' difference from Proverbs 8 and their similarity with one another? The usual explanation has been the hypothesis of a common myth used by all (whether from Gnosticism or from the Isis cult). It may just as easily be explained by the changed theological climate for understanding wisdom in Judaism, a change paralleled by Greek developments described in the latter parts of Gilbert Murray's *Five Stages of Greek Religion* (Garden City, N.Y.: Doubleday Anchor, 1951). However one explains the phenomena, the hypostatized wisdom of post-biblical Jewish literature is an anonymous savior figure. Its pattern (descent-ascent), function (soteriological), and use to interpret a historical entity (the law) show that the wisdom myth near the beginning of our era to be analogous to the Gnostic, Greco-Roman, and Christian ones.

On the other hand, Jewish angelology also employs the descent-ascent pattern for redemption figures. This is true both for the *mal'ach* Yahweh and for the archangels. Consider first the angel of the Lord. (1) The Jewish Scriptures in both the Hebrew and Greek forms speak of the *mal'ach* Yahweh who is sometimes indistinguishable from God. So one finds the paradoxical juxtaposition of two conceptions: (a) the angel is sent by God (e.g., Gen 19:1, 13) and (b) the angel is God in action (e.g., Gen 22:11–18). Hence the angel is closely identified with God's name (e.g., Gen 16:13a; Exod 23:20–21). (2) The *mal'ach* appears sometimes as a man or men (e.g., in Gen 18:2, 22, three men eat with Abraham, v. 8). Philo (*Abraham* 22, 113) says "though they neither ate nor drank, they gave the appearance of both eating and drinking." Philo confirms what the text (vv. 10, 13, 17, 20) affirms: the men represent the *mal'ach* (cf. Josephus, *Antiquities* 1.11.2 §197). Genesis 32:24–25 speaks of a man, though Hosea 12:5 says it was the *mal'ach*. Judges 13:6, 8 calls the angel a man of God, but v. 16 makes it clear that he will not eat food. (3) The angel's coming and going are sometimes explicitly spoken of as a descent and an ascent (e.g., Exod 3:8 has the Lord or the *mal'ach* say, "I have come down," and Judg 13:20 states that the "angel ascended"). (4) Among the functions of the angel are redemptive activities (in Gen 19:12ff he saves Lot; in Gen 22:11ff he saves Isaac; in Gen 48:15–16 he is the angel "who redeemed me from all evil"; in Exod 3:2ff he comes down to deliver the people from the hand of the Egyptians; in Judg 6:11ff he came down to send Gideon to deliver the people; if the "angel of his presence" in Isa 63:9 is the *mal'ach*, then he is the one who "saved them, in his love and pity he redeemed them").

It is now time to turn to the archangels. (1) In Tobit (second century B.C.E.), Raphael is sent to heal both Tobit and Sarah, the daughter of Raguel (3:16–17). He accompanies Tobias on his journey and keeps him safe and sound (5:21). He gives Tobias the remedy for his father's eye ailment and a means of ridding his bride of the demon. As a result Tobias drives the demon away (8:3) and cures his father's blindness (11:8, 12–14, 16). Reciting Raphael's benefits, Tobias says to his father:

> he has led me back to you safely,
> he cured my wife,
> he obtained the money for me,
> and he also healed you. (12:3)

The angel then says to father and son:

> God *sent me* to heal you and your daughter-in-law, Sarah. I am Raphael, one of the seven holy angels . . . [12:14–15a]. All these days I merely appeared to you and did not eat or drink, for you were seeing a vision. And now give thanks to God, for *I am ascending to him who sent me*. (12:19–20a)

Here in a this-worldly context we meet an angelic redemption figure who descends and ascends and who, while on earth, appears to be a man.

(2) In the Hellenistic-Jewish *Joseph and Aseneth* (first century B.C.E.), Aseneth is held up as the model proselyte. Her passage from idolatry is facilitated by an angel, the Prince of the heavenly hosts. Following Aseneth's prayer there was a cleft in the heavens and a man, flashing with light, stood over her (14). The archangel says:

> God has heard your prayer. He has looked upon your sorrow and tears, and has forgiven your sin. Be of good cheer, for your name is written in the Book of Life. . . . From this day forth you shall eat the bread of life and drink the cup of immortality, and be appointed with the oil of joy . . . many shall in like manner come to Him through your example by repentance. (15)

Aseneth then wants to feed the angel. He sends her for a honeycomb that is miraculously there, eats of it himself, and gives some to the maiden, saying: "Now you have received the food of life and your youth shall know no old age and your beauty shall never fade." In this context he also says: "You are blessed, Aseneth, for you have seen some of the secret things of God; it is of this honeycomb that the angels eat in Paradise . . . and whoever tastes it shall not die forever" (16). Then, after blessing her seven maidens (17), he goes back to heaven, with Aseneth then recognizing his true identity. Here one finds the descent and ascent of an archangel, who appears to Aseneth as a man, connected with her redemption from pagan idolatry and her gaining of immortality.

(3) The Testament of Job (early first century C.E.), which probably comes from Egyptian Judaism, depicts a descending-ascending angelic redeemer. Chapters 2–5 tell the story of Job's conversion. Job is at a loss to know whether the god worshipped in the nearby temple is the one who made the heaven and the earth. His conversion results from a night vision in which the angel comes to him as a voice in a great light for the purpose of the salvation of his soul (3:5b). He tells Job all that the Lord commanded (4:2), including the promise of the restoration of goods lost in this life because of Satan and ultimately resurrection from the dead if Job endures (4:6–8). After sealing Job, the angel departs (5:2). By the revelation the hero is set apart from the rest of deceived human-kind. Chapters 2–27 depict him as overcoming Satan by his endurance, which is based on the knowledge of the future hope, the heavenly city, imparted to him by the angel. Once again, this time in an early first-century Hellenistic-Jewish source, one meets a descending-ascending angelic redeemer figure.

(4) The Hellenistic-Jewish Apocalypse of Moses (early first century C.E.) describes the account of Adam's death in terms of angelic descent and as-cent. When Adam dies, the angels descend and take his soul into heaven, interceding for him before God (33:1–5). Adam is pardoned by God and washed in the lake of heaven by one of the seraphim (37:2–3). Then the archangel Michael takes Adam's soul into Paradise in the third heaven to await the last day (37:4–6). There is no doubt that in this document the descent and ascent of the angelic hosts is for the purpose of the redemption of Adam.

(5) The Testament of Abraham (first century C.E.) describes the descents and ascents of the archangel Michael, the purpose of whose coming to Abraham is twofold. On the one hand, the archangel "told him every-thing which he had heard from the Most High" (9:17–18), which included the announcement of his death. On the other hand, he gave Abraham the assurance that he would go to his Master among the good (1:5–10). Hence he tries to get the patriarch "to follow him" into heaven (7:4; 8:11;

15:28–29; 19:8; 20:21). Isaac describes his dream about the deaths of his father and mother in this way:

> I saw the heaven opened and I saw a luminous man *descending* from heaven, shining more than seven suns. And this man of the sunlike form came and took the sun from my head and *went back up into the heavens* from whence he had *descended*. . . . And after a little time . . . I saw this man coming forth from heaven a second time, and he took the moon from me, from my head. I wept greatly and entreated the luminous man and said, "My lord, take not my glory from me. . . . " He said, "Allow them to be taken up to the king on high, for he wants them there" (7:3–17).

In this source there is an archangel described as a man who descends and ascends. The purpose of his coming and going is to take Abraham and Sarah to God, an activity that is certainly redemptive.

(6)   Origen uses the Prayer of Joseph (first or second century C.E.) to add weight to his argument that John the Baptist was an angel who assumed a body for the sake of bearing witness to Christ. This apocryphal work, current among the Hebrews, he says, spoke of Jacob-Israel as the archangel of God, the chief captain among the sons of God, a ruling spirit, the firstborn of every creature, who descended to earth and tabernacled among humans. He fought with the angel Uriel when the latter tried to exalt himself beyond his rightful position. Once again, here is the typical pattern of angelic descent (with ascent implied), involving the taking of bodily form and the struggling with evil successfully. The conclusion seems irresistible: in certain circles of ancient Jewish angelology, both B.C.E. and in the first and second centuries C.E., there existed a mythology with a descent-ascent pattern, in which the redeemer figure descends, takes human form, and then ascends back to heaven either after or in connection with his saving activity.

Though the *mal'ach* Yahweh and the archangel traditions were originally distinct, by the beginning of our era they had, in certain circles at least, merged into one. Either one of the archangels could absorb the functions of the others so that he was almost the equivalent of the ancient *mal'ach* or the scriptural references to the angel of the Lord could be referred to an archangel (e.g., Philo, *On Dreams* 1.157). Whether separately or in synthetic form, the two Jewish traditions of angelology provided a myth of a descending-ascending redemption figure alongside a similar mythology of such a figure in Jewish wisdom literature.

In certain Jewish circles the angel and wisdom traditions merged not only with one another but also with the concepts of the logos and the firstborn son, among others. (1) The identification of wisdom and angel is made already in 1 Enoch 42:1–2 where it is said that when heavenly wisdom came down, found no dwelling place, and returned to heaven, she took her seat among the angels. The same identification is found in the Wisdom of Solomon 10:6 where wisdom is identified with the *mal'ach* who delivered Lot, and in the parallelism between 10:15–16, where wisdom delivers Israel from Egypt amid wonders and signs and 18:15 where the *mal'ach* Yahweh performs the same task.

(2) The merger of concepts and traditions in the Wisdom of Solomon goes further than the mere equation of wisdom and angel. In 9:1–2 wisdom and logos/word are equated (cf. Sirach 24:3); in 9:17 the parallelism links wisdom and Holy Spirit; in 18:15 logos and angel are identified. The resulting configuration yields a divine redeemer figure who is variously identified as Wisdom-Logos-Angel-Holy Spirit.

(3) Philo offers further evidence for the merger of traditions and concepts. (a) Though on occasion he represents either the logos as derived from wisdom (*On Dreams* 1.108–9) or Sophia as derivative from the word (*On Flight and Finding* 97), in *Allegorical Interpretation* 1:65, he makes the two completely identical: "Now wisdom is the word of God." (b) He can identify pneuma/spirit with wisdom (*On the Creation* 135; *On the Giants* 22, 27). (c) He can equate the logos and angel, either archangel (*Who Is the Heir?* 42, 205) or *mal'ach* (*On the Cherubim* 35; *Questions and Answers on Exodus* 2:13). (d) He sometimes links the word, the firstborn Son, and the angel of Yahweh (*On Husbandry* 51). At other times the Son, the logos, and the archangel are meshed. For example, in *Confusion of Tongues* 146–47 Philo says:

> But if there be any as yet unfit to be called a son of God, let him press to take his place under God's firstborn, the Word, who holds the eldership among the angels, their archangel as it were. And many other names are his, for he is called "the Beginning," and the Name of God, and His Word, and the Man after His image, and "He that sees," that is Israel.... For if we have not yet become fit to be thought sons of God yet we may be sons of His invisible image, the most holy Word. For the Word is the eldest-born image of God.

(e) Yet another designation for the many-named logos, or wisdom, is high priest (*On Dreams* 1.215; *On Flight and Finding* 108). In Philo, therefore, one meets a heavenly, divine figure (in *On Dreams* 1.230, the logos is *theos*), Son-Word-Angel-Wisdom-High Priest-Man, the many-named one. The merger of traditions is evident.

(4) Still further evidence comes from a collection of fragments con-

tained in the *Apostolic Constitutions* and widely believed to reflect Jewish liturgy of a type of syncretistic Judaism similar to that found in Philo. Though they cannot be dated with any certainty prior to the second century C.E., they confirm the existence of an ongoing Jewish tradition in which the wisdom and angel traditions merged with one another and with others such as Son, Word, and High Priest. Fragment 7 (= *Constitutions* 8.12.6–27) is especially clear about the many-named heavenly, divine figure. In 7.7 one hears that God has begotten his only Son before all ages, that is, God the Logos/Word, the living Sophia/wisdom, the firstborn of every creature, the angel of Great Counsel, God's High Priest. Fragment 14 (= *Constitutions* 7.26.1–3) says the Son who created the world is also the one through whom humans gain knowledge and immortality, that is, the many-named one is a redeemer.

This syncretistic practice of Hellenistic Judaism is a part of the tendency of the larger culture of the time to think in terms of one heavenly reality that could be addressed or described by many names. (a) Cleanthes's *Hymn to Zeus* begins: "Thou, O Zeus, are praised above all gods: Many are thy names and thine is all power for ever." (b) A third-century B.C.E. inscription by Artemidorus of Perga, who settled on the island of Thera, speaks of "this Hecate, of many names." (c) Plutarch makes the same point in his *On Isis and Osiris*, especially 67, 70, 78. The one logos that orders all things is given different modes of address among different peoples. (d) Tacitus, *Histories* 4.84, says the god Serapis was identified by some as Asclepios, by others as Osiris, by still others as Jupiter, but by most as Pluto. (e) Diogenes Laertius (*Lives of Eminent Philosophers* 7.135) says that Stoics hold: "God is one and the same with Reason, Fate, and Zeus; he is also called by many other names." (f) No passage is clearer than that in Apuleius's *Metamorphoses* (11), where Lucius cries out to Isis:

> O blessed queen of heaven, whether thou be the Dame Ceres...
> or the celestial Venus... or... the sister of the god Phoebus... or...
> Proserpine... by whatever name or fashion or shape it is lawful to
> call upon thee, I pray thee....

Lucius's cry to the goddess is heard. Isis replies:

> For the Phrygians... call me the Mother of the gods at Pessinus;
> the Athenians... Cecropian Minerva; the Cyprians... Papian Venus;
> the Cretans... Dietynnian Diana; the Sicilians... infernal Proserpine;
> the Elusinians... Ceres; some Juno, others Bellona, others Hecate,
> others Rhamnusia... and the Egyptians... do call me by my true
> name, Queen Isis.

It is inevitable that certain Jewish circles, living in this type of world, would conceive of one heavenly redeemer figure who descended and ascended with a redemptive function and who could be addressed or spoken of with many names: e.g., Word, Wisdom, Angel, Son, Man, High Priest. At the same time, it is also true that other circles of Jewish life continued to maintain the traditions separately (e.g., either wisdom or angel) or in varying stages of merger (e.g., wisdom-word merged, but separate from angel, as in Sirach; or angel-son-spirit merged, as in the Prayer of Joseph, but separate from logos and wisdom). The conclusion seems irresistible. A myth of a heavenly redeemer who descended and ascended in the course of his/her saving work existed in pre-Christian Judaism and alongside first- and second-century Christianity. It existed in a multiplicity of forms, with the different varieties depending upon the degree of syncretism existing at a given time and place. In its extreme form, the diverse traditions ran together so that the communities conceived of one redeemer who was many-named. Hellenistic Judaism, just as Greco-Roman paganism, Gnosticism, and early Christianity, employed mythologies of descending-ascending redeemers near the beginning of our era. Having established this fact, it is now necessary to ask about the relationship between the Jewish myths and that of the Christians.

Early Christian Use of the Jewish Descending-Ascending Redeemer Pattern

In this section of the appendix, we will examine six selected non-canonical Christian authors and three New Testament writers to check their possible use of Jewish redeemer mythology. Since Jewish and pagan mythology employed, from pre-Christian times, a *pattern* (descent-ascent) and a *function* (soteriological) analogous to that of the Christian myth, either could conceivably have been the source of the Christian usage. In order to determine which of these, if either, constituted the source of the Christian descent-ascent pattern, *terminology* must be decisive. What we will be looking for are signs of a descent-ascent pattern used for the church's savior figure in connection with a cluster of names/titles or other language characteristic of the Jewish myths in their various forms. We begin with an examination of the six selected non-canonical writings.

(1) Justin Martyr presents us with as full a Christian adaptation of the Jewish synthesis as I can find in the second century. Though Justin's christology has usually been regarded as an appropriation of the Stoic logos thought (e.g., *1 Apology* 46; *2 Apology* 10), sometimes, especially in his

Dialogue with Trypho, we find Christ spoken of in terms of the Son-Wisdom-Word-Angel vocabulary of Hellenistic Judaism. This terminology is used for the descent-ascent christology of Justin (*Trypho* 38, 48, 56, 59, 61, 126, 128). This descending-ascending many-named one in Justin functions as a savior or revealer of God (e.g., 56, 128). When one finds the pattern, function, and terminology of Justin's christology in the *Dialogue* corresponding to the mythology of Hellenistic Judaism, it is difficult to resist the conclusion that this Christian is using the Jewish categories.

In *Dialogue* 61, for example, Justin says:

> God has begotten of Himself a certain, rational Power as a Beginning before all other creatures. The Holy Spirit indicates this Power by varying titles, sometimes . . . *Son,* or *Wisdom,* or *Angel,* or . . . *Word.* He even called Himself Commander-in-Chief when He appeared in human guise to Joshua, the son of Nun. Indeed, He can justly lay claim to all these titles from the fact both that He performs the Father's will and that He was begotten by an act of the Father's will.

The same cluster of Son-Angel-Word-Wisdom titles occurs again in *Dialogue* 128–29. Elsewhere one finds combinations of Son-Wisdom-Angel (*Dialogue* 62; 126); Son-Word-Angel (*1 Apology* 63); or Son-Angel-Priest-Man (*Dialogue* 34). When Justin refers to Christ as Angel, sometimes it is to (a) the *mal'ach* (*Dialogue* 56, 59, 60, 61–62, 128); sometimes to (b) the *mal'ach* bearing the name Israel (*Dialogue* 75, 114, 125, 130, 134, 135); sometimes to (c) Isaiah's Angel of Great Counsel (*Dialogue* 126); and sometimes to (d) an archangel (*Dialogue* 34). He is careful to specify why Christ can be spoken of as an angel. He can be called Angel because "He delivers the messages of God, the Creator of all, to whomsoever God desires" (*Dialogue* 56), "in order that by (this) expression you may recognize him as the minister of the Father" (*Dialogue* 58), "because he came to men (since by that power the Father's messages are communicated to men)" (*Dialogue* 128). Justin is also careful to specify that although as the *mal'ach* Christ appeared under the guise of incorporeal beings, in the Incarnation he has become human (*1 Apology* 63).

In his *Dialogue* the need to argue from Scripture for the Son as distinct from the Father doubtless prompted Justin to make use of the Angel-Wisdom-Word-Son category to an extent not found in his more Gentile-oriented apologies. When he needed to talk to a Hellenistic Jew, Justin employed the Hellenistic Jewish mythology of a divine redemption figure called by such names as Word-Wisdom-Son-Angel to speak of Jesus. When he spoke to Gentiles, he used primarily the Word-Son categories, with the Logos understood in terms of the immanent logos of the Stoics.

(2) The Shepherd of Hermas offers another example of a second-century Christian's appropriation of one variety of the Hellenistic Jewish mythology. Hermas is primarily concerned about the period after Christ's ascension and before the parousia. Very little is said about activities of the savior before the ascension. Whenever he does refer to such a time (e.g., Parable 5.6.3–8), the pattern is pre-existence–incarnation (connected with the cleansing of the sins of the people)–ascent or exaltation. After his ascent the redemptive activity of the Savior continues. (a) In this connection one meets a most reverend or glorious angel who is identified with Christ. This angel justifies those doing penance (Command 5.7), judges souls, rewards the just, bestows grace, incorporates people into the church (Parable 8.1.1–2; 8.2.1–4), and tests Christians like Hermas (Parable 7.1, 2, 5). His functions make it difficult to distinguish between God and his angel. This makes it seem that we are nearer to the Old Testament understanding of the *mal'ach* than to any specific figure in later angelology. Yet in Parable 8.3.2–3, a glorious angel is identified with Michael. Here is a notorious crux. Is Christ identified with Michael or is the archangel a separate figure still? Even if Michael here is to be distinguished from Christ, as seems necessary, the church's savior is elsewhere identified with the chief of the archangels. For example, Christ is the Son of God in the midst of the six glorious angels (archangels) of which he is chief (Parable 9.12.8; cf. Parable 5.6.4, 7). It would seem, then, that in Hermas the *mal'ach* and the archangel traditions of Judaism have merged, with the archangel component the dominant one. (b) Most instructive is Hermas's identification of the glorious angel with the Son of God and with the Holy Spirit (Parable 9.1.1–3; cf. Parable 5.6.5–7). The redeemer can, in the same context, be spoken of as "the splendid man" (Parable 9.12.8). In Hermas, then, the savior is described basically in terms of an angelology that has coalesced with the categories of Son and Spirit. This is virtually identical with the thought forms of the prayer of Joseph. It is also similar to the position of Justin and doubtless from the same ultimate root, Hellenistic Judaism. Nevertheless, the differences between Justin and Hermas make it probable that each is using a different version of the Jewish mythology.

(3) Sibylline Oracle 8, which probably comes from the period before 180 C.E., confronts one with the pre-existent Word (446). In describing the Word's relation to creation (447–55), though the term "Wisdom" is not used, there are echoes of Proverbs 8:22ff. The Incarnation is then described (456–74):

From heaven he came....
First ... the holy, mighty form of Gabriel was displayed.
And second the archangel addressed the maiden in speech....
Thus speaking, God breathed grace into the sweet maiden....
The Word flew into her body,
Made flesh in time ... this, a great wonder to mortals,
Is no great wonder to God the Father and to God the Son.
Bethlehem was chosen the homeland ... of the Logos.

Here we have a synthesis of Angel-Word-Son with possible echoes of Wisdom. If 462 uses God synonymously with archangel, then we also have a blending of archangel and *mal'ach* traditions. Significantly, the point at which the angelology is used is at the descent from heaven. Once again, the Jewish roots of the thought and language seem obvious. Nevertheless, the differences between the form of the myth here and its form both in Justin and Hermas point to the varieties in which the Jewish mythology circulated.

In Justin, Hermas, and Sibylline Oracle 8, the angel component is central in the forms of the myth appropriated by the Christians. Other Christian authors of the second or early third centuries reflect the same Jewish world of thought but are reluctant to accept a form of it which includes an angel ingredient. Three examples illustrate the matter.

(1) The Epistle of the Apostles knows the Hellenistic Jewish synthesis of Son-Word-Wisdom-Angel but uses it in a significantly different way from that of Justin, Hermas, and Sibylline Oracle 8. In chapter 3 we are told that Jesus *is* the Son sent by God and the Word become flesh. In 13, however, Jesus is not identified with but rather *puts on* the Wisdom of the Father. In 14, Christ *takes the form* of the angel Gabriel and appears to Mary "in the appearance of the shape of an angel." This does not identify Christ and Gabriel. It rather reflects reluctance on the part of this author to regard Jesus as an angel. Rather Christ takes the form of Gabriel in his function as messenger of God, that is, in his descent.

(2) In the works of Tertullian we find an excellent example of the tendency to separate the Wisdom-Logos-Son-Spirit part of the myth from the angel component due to the controversy context in which the North African worked. On the one hand, Tertullian employed the familiar cluster Wisdom-Word-Son-Spirit to speak of Christ (*Against Hermogenes* 18; *Against Praxeas* 7, 19). He also was not adverse to identifying Christ with the *mal'ach* Yahweh who met Abraham under the tree at Mamre (*Against Marcion* 9; *Against Praxeas* 16; *On the Flesh of Christ* 6). On the other hand, he resisted any attempt to understand the Incarnation, as some heretics like Apelles did, by analogy with the flesh of angels when

they appear among humans. Unlike the corporeality of angels, the flesh of the incarnate Word was that which could suffer and die, that is, the flesh preceded by birth (*On the Flesh of Christ* 6; *Against Marcion* 9). The heretics, obviously drawing on an existing strand of christology, argued: Christ bore the nature of an angel. To that Tertullian responded: It is true that Christ has been called the Angel of Great Counsel, "but that expresses his *official function as messenger rather than his nature*. He is not on this account to be regarded as an angel like Gabriel or Michael. Knowing, however, that angel terminology was indigenous to some christology, "if such an expression is to be hazarded," Tertullian preferred to say, "that the Son is actually an angel, that is a messenger from the Father, than that there was an angel in the Son" (*On the Flesh of Christ* 14).

It is obvious that Tertullian's distaste for angel christology derives in large measure from its docetic implications. It leads to a denial of the real human nature of the incarnate one. His particular situation may very well be indicative of the larger scene in which angel christology was eventually eliminated, in part, due to its potential for heretical abuse. Jewish angelology was certainly docetic (Tobit 12:19; Philo, *Abraham* 22:18; 2 Enoch 56:2; Josephus, *Antiquities* 1.11.2 §197; Targum on Genesis 19:3; Pesikta 57a; Justin, *Dialogue* 57). In any case, in Tertullian we can see the full scale synthesis breaking up under the pressure of false belief with the Son-Word-Wisdom-Spirit cluster separating from the angel component.

(3) In the Odes of Solomon the break with the angel component is complete. This early Christian hymnbook speaks of a savior figure (Odes 12, 29, 37, 41, 42), Christ, whose activity in redemption is described in terms of a descent-ascent pattern (Odes 12, 22, 23). The dominant name for the Christian's redeemer is "the Word" (Odes 12, 16, 29, 37, 41). At points the divine Word is spoken of in language that echoes heavenly Wisdom of Proverbs 8. He can also be described as the Son of God (Odes 36, 41, 42) and as the Man or Son of Man (Odes 36, 41). In Ode 41 we hear:

> His Word is with us. . . . The Savior who gives life. . . . (11)
>
> The Man who humbled himself. . . . (12)
>
> The Son of the Most High appeared. . . . (13)
>
> And light dawned from the Word. . . . (14)

The clustering of the names Word-Son-Man for the descending-ascending redeemer is significant in two ways. On the one hand, it argues for the Jewish roots of the mythology here employed for Christ. On the other hand, it reveals a form of the myth apparently devoid of an angel ingredient.

It cannot be fortuitous that these Christian authors, when speaking of the church's savior who was pre-existent, descended among humankind, and then ascended into the heaven, used clusters of titles such as Word-Wisdom-Son-Angel-Spirit. Such a cluster existed from pre-Christian times in certain circles of Hellenistic Judaism and was used for a heavenly redemption figure. The conclusion must certainly be that these Christian writers of the second and third centuries derived their categories from the mythology of Hellenistic Judaism. At the very least, therefore, one must say that *a* source for the early Christian pattern of a descending-ascending redeemer is Hellenistic Judaism.

Having seen that certain second- and early third-century Christian authors used the Hellenistic Jewish mythology of a many-named descending-ascending redeemer in their speech about Jesus, we may now turn to the New Testament, especially Paul, Hebrews, and the Fourth Gospel, to see whether there exists any demonstrable link between their christologies and the Jewish mythologies appropriated by the non-canonical writers surveyed. It will be necessary to show that these New Testament authors employ not only the same *pattern* but also some of the same *terminology* for their savior figure that is found in the Jewish redeemer myths.

(1) In the seven indisputably genuine Pauline letters one finds implicit a pattern of pre-existence–descent (redemptive activity)–ascent (redemptive activity)–parousia. The combination of all of these movements within one thought unit in the letters is, to my knowledge, not to be found. Moreover, though the ascent is implied in statements about Christ's being at the right hand of God (e.g., Rom 8:34; 1 Cor 15:24–27) or about his future coming (e.g., 1 Thes 1:10; 4:16–17; Phil 3:20–21), the actual movement itself is rarely spoken of, unless one wrongly takes all resurrection statements to be such. Only at Romans 1:3–4, where pre-existence is not assumed in the pre-Pauline fragment but is implied in the Pauline redaction, and at Philippians 2:9–11, where pre-existence is sometimes assumed to be present in vv. 6–8, is the exaltation or ascent mentioned explicitly. In only two passages, then, is an ascent (more properly, an exaltation) possibly joined with an implicit or explicit descent (becoming human). Furthermore, in both of these texts the descent is not explicitly for a redemptive purpose. The soteriological effects are the result of the exaltation or ascent. In these two passages, therefore, the pattern is closer to the mythology of the immortals than to any other in antiquity (cf. the

Romulus tradition in Plutarch's *Lives* where the pattern is: [a] came from the gods; [b] life of virtue; [c] taken up to heaven; [d] given a new name or status with benefits resulting for the Romans, his people).

Rather than focus on the ascent, Paul normally uses a pattern that combines pre-existence–descent (redemptive acts). In doing so he frequently uses formulaic material. (a) In Galatians 4:4–5 we find reference to the sending of the Son (*exapostellein*) followed by a purpose clause (*hina*) that explains the saving significance of the "sending" (cf. John 3:17; 1 John 4:9). Here one finds pre-existence assumed in a formula that speaks of the sending (descent) of the Son into the world for a redemptive purpose. Nothing is said about what happened afterward to the one who was sent. (b) Romans 8:3 also uses a formula about the "sending" of the Son, using the verb *pempein*/to send (cf. John where the phrase "the Father who sent me" occurs twenty-six times in stereotyped fashion). Here again pre-existence is assumed and the sending is for a redemptive purpose. (c) Romans 8:32's "gave himself up [*paredōken*] for us all" (cf. John 3:16: *didonai*) may belong with the "sending" formulae that refer to the descent of the pre-existent one rather than to the passion formulae that use *paradidonai*.

Many scholars argue for the roots of the "sending" formulae in Jewish Wisdom speculation. They note (a) in the passages where pre-existence alone is spoken of (1 Cor 8:6; 10:4; Rom 10:6–7), the parallels are to wisdom; the "sending" verbs (*exapostelleiv* and *pempeiv*) are found in Wisdom of Solomon 9:10 in connection with the sending of Sophia/wisdom. (b) The purpose of the sending in 9:10 is given in a final *hina* (purpose) clause; in the same context, 9:17, like Galatians 4:6, speaks of sending (*pempein*) of the Holy Spirit; (c) "Sending by God" and the title "Son of God" are combined only in the realm of logos and wisdom speculation of Egyptian Judaism. (d) The "gave" formula may find its background there also (cf. Wisdom of Solomon 9:17a: *edōkas sophian*/ he gave wisdom). The argument, though very persuasive, needs modification on (c). Just as the wisdom tradition could speak of a sending of wisdom by God for a redemptive purpose, so also could the various streams of Jewish angelology. For example, the *mal'ach* is sent by God in Genesis 19:13, Exodus 23:20–21, etc., and the archangel in Tobit 12:19–20. In certain places (e.g., Prayer of Joseph), the angel is the firstborn Son of God. It is possible, therefore, that both major streams of Jewish thought that spoke of a descending-ascending redeemer could speak of God's sending a Son for redemptive purposes. When Paul used such language of Christ, its background was apparently the wisdom tradition, doubtless merged with others, certainly the Son and quite possibly angel. In this connection, it is interesting to note that Galatians 4:4ff. precedes a remarkable statement in v. 14 where Christ is spoken of as an angel with no hostile overtones.

2 Corinthians 8:9's descent pattern most likely also derives from some form of wisdom speculation in Hellenistic Judaism since Philo can speak of the riches of wisdom (*On the Posterity and Exile of Cain* 151; cf. *Who Is the Heir?* 126ff; 182ff; 230ff). Paul, therefore, knew the myth of wisdom, and possibly that of the descending angel.

This survey of Paul makes it appear unlikely that the second- and early third-century non-canonical Christians' use of the Hellenistic Jewish descent-ascent myth was mediated to them through Paul. There are enough differences to force the conclusion that the apostle and later Christian writers reflect independent appropriations of different variations of the Jewish synthesis.

The christology of the Epistle to the Hebrews follows a pattern of pre-existence–descent (redemptive activity)–ascent (redemptive activity)–parousia. Pre-existence is implied in the prologue's statement that Christ is the agent of creation (1:2). He is said to have appeared (9:11, 26) or to have come into the world (10:5). Of his life in the world, it is said that he was made like his brethren (2:17), was tempted as we are (4:15), learned obedience through suffering (2:10; 5:8), suffered death (2:9), offered his body as a sacrifice (10:10), through his death destroying the devil (2:14–15). He was exalted above the heavens (7:26), entering into heaven (9:24) or the Holy Place (9:12). He took his own blood and secured an eternal redemption (9:12, 24), making a purification for sins (1:3; 2:17; 7:27). He now lives to make intercession for us (7:25). He will appear a second time (9:28), a coming that is imminent (10:37).

Among the key titles used for this descending-ascending redeemer are certain of those associated with the mythology of Hellenistic Judaism: Son of God (1:2; 3:6; 4:14; 5:5, 8; 6:6; 7:3; 11:28, etc.), high priest (2:17; 3:1; 4:14; 5:6, 10; 6:20; 7:17; 9:11; 11:21) and word of God (4:12–13). Further, in 1:3 Hebrews uses *hapaugasma* (reflection) of the Son. Though the term is found only here in the Bible, it is used of sophia/wisdom in Wisdom of Solomon 7:26 and Philo (*On the Sacrifices of Abel and Cain* 146). Also in 1:3 Hebrews employs "*charakter* [stamp] of his nature" for the Son, a term used by Philo of the logos/word (*On Noah's Work as a Planter* 18). Further, 1:3 speaks of the Son as "upholding the universe by the word of his power," a concept and language found in Philo's discussion of the logos (*On Noah's Work as a Planter* 8; *On the Change of*

Names 256). Considering pattern and terminology, it is difficult to resist the conclusion that the Hellenistic Jewish mythology of a descending-ascending redeemer who was many-named has been appropriated by the author of Hebrews for his speech about Jesus.

At the same time, there is a very definite polemic against angels in Hebrews. From 1:4–2:16 the author struggles to assert the superiority of the Son over angels. (Worship of angels was a problem for early Christianity: e.g., Col 2:18; Kerygma Petrou; Ascension of Isaiah 7:21; cf. Rev 19:10; 22:8–9). It appears, then, that in this epistle the attempt to separate the angel component from the Son-Word-High Priest-Wisdom synthesis is sharper than in the second- and third-century non-canonical writers we have examined. It is, therefore, unlikely that these later Christian authors derived their use of the Jewish mythology from the Epistle to the Hebrews. Again, though both the canonical document and the non-canonical writings have their roots, at least in part, in the Hellenistic Jewish myth of a descending-ascending redeemer variously called by such names as Wisdom-Word-Son-Angel-High Priest–Man–Holy Spirit, they seem to be independent adaptations of the common background. Further, in spite of their use of a similar Jewish pattern, Paul and the author of Hebrews obviously are drawing on forms of the myth with different configurations of components. Given the various combinations possible in the mythology, this diversity should come as no surprise.

In the Fourth Gospel we find again the familiar christological pattern of pre-existence–descent (redemptive activity)–ascent (redemptive activity)–parousia. Pre-existence is found not only in the prologue (1:1–3, 10) but also in the body of the Gospel (e.g., 1:30; 3:31; 6:51; 8:58; 17:5, 24). The descent is spoken of in a number of ways. Two formulae found in Paul are also used by John: "God sent his Son, that" (3:17) and "God gave his Son, that" (3:16). Distinctively Johannine descriptions include: "I proceeded and came forth from God" (8:42); "I came from God" (17:8); "I came down from heaven" (6:38); "I am from above" (8:23). By virtue of his coming into the world Christ makes the unseen Father known (1:18), baptizes with the Holy Spirit (1:33; 20:22), takes away the sin of the world (1:29), gives eternal life to those who believe on him (3:16; 5:21, 25–26; 6:51; 11:26; 17:3), defeats the ruler of the world (12:31). The ascent is also referred to in various ways: Christ is going to God (13:3, 33, 36), will be lifted up (double meaning, 12:32), will be glorified (12:23; 13:31; 17:5), is going away (16:7). As a result of his ascent, the Gentiles can be included (12:20–26, 32), the Spirit is given (14:16–17; 14:25–26; 15:26–27; 16:7–11; 16:13–15), Christ prepares a place for his disciples (14:3). The traditional parousia concept is found, for certain, in 21:22 and in 5:28–29. It may also be seen in the farewell speech (e.g., 14:2–3).

A number of lines of evidence point to the roots of the Fourth Gospel's christology in the Hellenistic Jewish *katabasis-anabasis* mythology. The names or titles employed for Christ in John are those of the Jewish synthesis: e.g., Word-Son of God-Son of Man (Man?). (a) The background for the logos/word in 1:1–18 is almost certainly the Wisdom myth assimilated with logos thought such as one finds in Hellenistic Judaism. (b) The clue to the Son of God language in the Gospel seems to be two formulae already discussed in the section on Paul ("God sent the Son, that"; "God gave the Son, that") which have their background in Wisdom-Logos speculation. (c) The background for the Johannine Son of Man sayings constitutes a major problem. The cause of the difficulty is that in John's Son of Man sayings one finds two circles of thought, a Synoptic type Son of Man (1:51; 3:14–15; 5:27; 8:28; 12:34) overlapped with a non-Synoptic Son of Man (3:13; 6:27, 53, 62; 12:23; 13:31–32) who descends and ascends. Since "Son of Man" and "Man" were linguistically interchangeable, the explanation for the distinctiveness of the Johannine Son of Man sayings may very well be that the apocalyptic tradition has been assimilated to the "Man" of Hellenistic Judaism, that is, to the many-named descending-ascending redeemer. If so, then the use of the *katabasis-anabasis* pattern for the one savior who is variously called Word-Son of God-Son of Man is intelligible.

It is, moreover, possible that John reflects an anti-angel tendency. Certain passages have been so interpreted: 1:51; 5:1–9; the Paraclete sayings that employ the expression "Spirit of truth": 14:16; 15:26; 16:13. If so, then there is in the Fourth Gospel an attempt to separate the Wisdom-Logos-Son-Man synthesis from the angel component. If not, then it is still true that the Evangelist chose not to employ the total synthesis but only a part of it. In this, he is the precursor of later Christian developments. Nevertheless, there is not enough similarity between John and most of the second-century Christians we have examined to posit their dependence on the Fourth Gospel. Rather we must suppose that John and the non-canonical authors represent independent appropriations of the Hellenistic Jewish mythology. There are also enough differences with Hebrews and Paul in terminology and in emphasis to disallow any assertion of interdependence among them. Again, we seem to be dealing with independent appropriations of various forms of the Jewish mythology.

As a result of this survey of selected non-canonical and canonical Christian writers, we are forced to conclude that the linguistic links between the Christian and Jewish mythologies point to the latter as the source for the former. Certain early Christians took over Hellenistic Judaism's myth of a descending-ascending redeemer who was many-named and used it as one way of understanding Jesus' identity. Among those early Christians who did so was the Johannine community from whom the Fourth Gospel came.